THE FATE OF SUDAN

ABOUT THE AUTHOR

JOHN YOUNG has been involved in research around peace, security, governance, federalism conflict, elections, and political parties in the Horn of Africa since 1986, but in recent years has had a particular interest in peace and security issues in Sudan. These research interests have been pursued in various capacities as an independent and UN journalist, academic researcher, Canadian government consultant, peace monitor in the north–south Sudan conflict, evaluator of various peace support programs, and, most recently, political adviser to the Carter Center for the April 2010 national elections and southern Sudan referendum.

THE FATE OF SUDAN

THE ORIGINS AND CONSEQUENCES OF A FLAWED PEACE PROCESS

JOHN YOUNG

Zed Books

LONDON | NEW YORK

The Fate of Sudan: The Origins and Consequences of a Flawed Peace Process
was first published in 2012 by
Zed Books Ltd, 7 Cynthia Street, London N1 9JF, UK
and Room 400, 175 Fifth Avenue, New York, NY 10010, USA

www.zedbooks.co.uk

Cover image © Sven Torfinn/Panos.
Cover design by www.roguefour.co.uk

FSC
www.fsc.org
MIX
Paper from
responsible sources
FSC® C013604

Designed and typeset in Monotype Bulmer
by illuminati, Grosmont
Index by Rohan Bolton
Printed and bound in the UK by CPI Anthony Rowe,
Chippenham and Eastbourne

Distributed in the USA exclusively by Palgrave Macmillan, a division of
St Martin's Press, LLC, 175 Fifth Avenue, New York, NY 10010, USA

A catalogue record for this book is available from the British Library
Library of Congress Cataloging in Publication Data available

ISBN 978 1 78032 326 8 hb
ISBN 978 1 78032 325 1 pb

CONTENTS

ACKNOWLEDGMENTS

For a book of this nature there are far too many people to thank. In addition, some cannot be thanked or quoted because given their positions it would cause them embarrassment. There are also many other ordinary but anonymous people who have informed my views. In Sudan a *sitt al-chai* (tea lady) or a soldier sharing a place in the back of a truck are often more informative than a cabinet minister or general. But, with those caveats, a few people and organizations deserve a particular note of thanks. The first must go to Mahgoub Mohamed Salih, the dean of Sudanese journalism, and the South Sudanese statesman Bona Malwal, who employed me as a neo-phyte journalist for the *Sudan Times* between 1986 and 1989 and to whom I still regularly go for advice and wisdom. The second note of appreciation is to the Carter Center, which employed me as a political adviser through the final heady days of the Sudan peace process and demonstrated remarkable tolerance for someone whose views were sometimes very different from their own. Lastly, two individuals must be noted. The first is my friend and frequent translator/fixer Riak 'Franco' Pouk Nyab for his advice and good humor during our many travels in South Sudan. The second is my wife, Thea Geddert, who shared some of my Sudan adventures, read and corrected drafts of this book, and has been very patient about my passion for Sudan.

ABBREVIATIONS

ABC	Abyei Boundary Commission
AEC	Assessment and Evaluation Commission
AJOC	Abyei Joint Oversight Committee
ANC	African National Congress
AU	African Union
AUHIP	African Union High Level Implementation Panel
AL	Arab League
BEG	Bahr el Ghazal
CANS	Civil Administration of New Sudan
CCSS	Coordinating Council of Southern Sudan
CPA	Comprehensive Peace Agreement
DoP	Declaration of Principles
DPA	Darfur Peace Agreement
DUP	Democratic Unionist Party
EDF	Equatoria Defense Force
EPLF	Eritrean People's Liberation Front
EPRDF	Ethiopian People's Revolutionary Democratic Front
GNU	Government of National Unity
GoS	Government of Sudan
GoSS	Government of South Sudan
HAC	Humanitarian Affairs Commission
ICC	International Criminal Court
ICF	Islamic Charter Front

ICG	International Crisis Group
ICSS	Interim Constitution for Southern Sudan
IDP	Internally displaced person
IGAD	Inter-Governmental Authority on Development
IGADD	Inter-Governmental Authority on Drought and Development
IMF	International Monetary Fund
IPF	IGAD Partners' Forum
JEM	Justice and Equality Movement
JIU	Joint Integrated Units
JLEI	Joint Libyan Egyptian Initiative
LLMPC	Legitimate League of Muslim Preachers and Clerics
LRA	Lord's Resistance Army
MNR	National Resistance Movement
NASC	National Alliance for the Salvation of the Country
NBI	Nile River Basin Initiative
NCP	National Congress Party
NDA	National Democratic Alliance
NDI	National Democratic Institute
NEC	National Election Commission
NIF	National Islamic Front
NISS	National Intelligence and Security Service
NLC	National Liberation Council
NRM/A	National Resistance Movement/Army
NSCC	New Sudan Council of Churches
NUP	National Umma Party
OAG	Other armed groups
OCV	Out of country voting
OLF	Oromo Liberation Front
OLS	Operation Lifeline Sudan
PAIC	Popular Arab and Islamic Conference
PCP	Popular Congress Party
PDF	Popular Defense Force
PNC	Popular National Congress
PPLF	Political Parties Leadership Forum
RCC	Revolutionary Command Council
RoSS	Republic of South Sudan
SAF	Sudan Armed Forces

SANU	Sudan African National Union
SCP	Sudan Communist Party
SLM/A	Sudan Liberation Movement/Army
SPDF	Sudan People's Democratic Front
SPLM/A	Sudan Peoples Liberation Movement/Army
SPLM–DC	SPLM–Democratic Change
SSDF	South Sudan Defense Force
SSIM	South Sudan Independence Movement
SSLA	South Sudan Legislative Assembly
SSLA	South Sudan Liberation Army
SSRB	South Sudan Referendum Bureau
SSRC	South Sudan Referendum Commission
SSRC	South Sudan Rehabilitation Commission
TMC	Transitional Military Council
TPLF	Tigray People's Liberation Front
UDF	United Democratic Front
UDSF	United Democratic Salvation Front
UNMIS	United Nations Mission in Sudan
UNMISS	United Nations Mission in South Sudan
UPDF	Ugandan People's Defense Force
USAP	Union of Sudan African Parties
WUN	Western Upper Nile

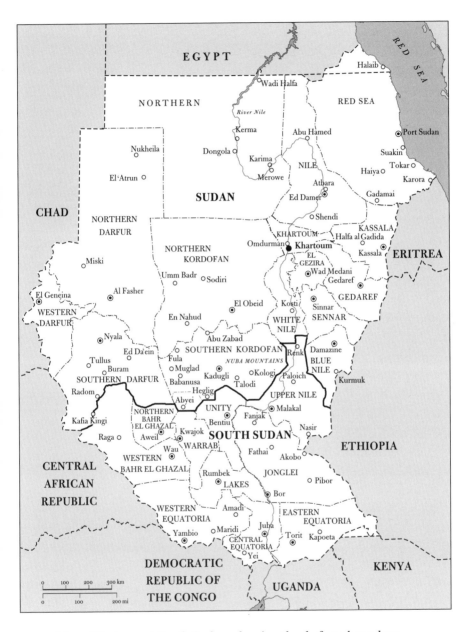

Map of Sudan and South Sudan, showing the de facto boundary
put into effect on 9 July 2011. As this book went to print,
the final boundary was yet to be determined.

PREFACE

On 9 July 2011 South Sudan became an independent state. For many this represented the successful culmination of a decade-long peace process. But long before 9 July it was clear that the secession of South Sudan was not going to bring sustainable peace with its northern neighbor, the governments in Khartoum and Juba had no intention of living up to their commitments to democratic transformation, and, despite the platitudes of the diplomats, the Comprehensive Peace Agreement (CPA) was little more than an extended ceasefire. Indeed, before 9 July war had broken out in the northern states of Southern Kordofan and Blue Nile, rebellions were spreading in the Nuer lands of South Sudan, lawlessness gripped much of South Sudan, the war continued apace in Darfur, there were fears that the recently resolved conflict in eastern Sudan might be resurrected, and there were periodic clashes between the armies of Sudan and South Sudan and numerous aerial bombings of the south. And, just as during the years of north–south war, refugees from Sudan and South Sudan were fleeing to Ethiopia for security.

Former South African president Thabo Mbeki, who served as the lead mediator for the African Union trying to resolve the post-southern referendum issues, repeatedly said that in the event of a vote for secession his objective was to see the emergence of 'two viable states'. To date that objective has not been realized. In spring 2012 when this book was going to press none of the twelve post-secession issues listed in the Referendum Law had been resolved. Not only had the international peacemakers badly failed in Sudan, but so had their chosen model of liberal peacemaking and -building.

This is not an insider's story in the sense that I have sat at a Sudanese negotiating table and served as a diplomat; I haven't. Nor can I offer up the insights of an anthropologist, historian, or constitutional lawyer. This is a study by someone who has worked in Sudan for many years as a teacher, journalist, researcher, peace monitor, political and security analyst, and most recently as a political adviser to the Carter Center's election, referendum, and popular consultation missions. It is written by a jack of many trades and thus able to consider the peace process from different perspectives, though I would not claim to be an expert in any of them. I have, however, closely followed developments in Sudan since 1986, lived in the country for about eight years, travelled extensively, met most of the leading political actors, and include many Sudanese and South Sudanese among my closest friends. I have also published many articles on political and security issues.

Sudanese friends have urged me to move away from writing on political subjects, which, however unintended, contribute to the one-dimensional international perception of Sudan and now South Sudan as countries populated by mad Islamists and constantly fighting tribals. Indeed, works are needed that portray the other Sudan that has always been integral to my experience in the country: a hard land with a terrible climate, but compensated by a generous, warm, good-humored people of enormous dignity who have always made me feel welcome even when I wrote and said things they might heartily disagree with. Unfortunately this book does not meet that need and instead paints a dismal picture of failure by the international community and the country's leaders, who have badly served the interests of the good people of Sudan and South Sudan. As such it is a call for these people to end their misguided faith in the international community and undeserving leaders and take control of their collective destinies.

A book of this nature falls somewhere between history and journalism, and as a result largely relies on interviews and not secondary sources. And the large majority of the interviewees are Sudanese and South Sudanese because this is their story. Where possible I have named my informants, but often the quotations are without attribution to protect them. This is particularly necessary in the analysis of the peacemaking process, where those interviewed were assured of their anonymity.

The Introduction briefly assesses the theory underlying international approaches to peacemaking and peace-building such as that in Sudan, contending that the theorization is based on discarded notions drawn from modernization theory, invariably trading off democracy in favor of peace (a false dichotomy it will be argued here), and does not address the root causes of conflict. Invariably it favors managerial and technical approaches rather than supporting the structural changes that alone offered Sudan the prospect of realizing the CPA-stipulated goals of unity and democratic transformation. As such this chapter frames and informs what follows.

Chapter 1 provides a bare-bones history of post-colonial Sudan with a focus on the National Congress Party (NCP) and the Sudan Peoples Liberation Movement (SPLM), which alone were permitted to negotiate the fate of Sudan. Appreciating that it could not come to power through democratic elections, the NCP operated through and with military regimes to reconstruct the state to force an Arab-Islamic identity on the country and maintain hegemony over a polyglot of tribes inhabiting an increasingly restive periphery. Not content with waging war on the south and other peripheries, under Hassan al-Turabi the NCP attempted to export its Islamist ideology to the region and beyond. As a result of the ensuing threat to the regime he was jettisoned, after which Marshall Omar al-Bashir led a more conventional authoritarian regime that still used Islamist rhetoric and institutions.[1]

Meanwhile, Dr John Garang established the Sudan Peoples Liberation Movement/Army in 1983 with the support of the Ethiopian military regime, which also dictated its objective of a united reformed New Sudan, an aim that had little support in the south but gained the liberation movement international assistance and adherents among the rebellious peripheries of the north. Authoritarianism, lack of a practical reform program, and militarism, however, seriously undermined the SPLA's potential and produced so much opposition as to preclude the possibility of it achieving power on its own. Thus, after being dismissed from Ethiopia with the overthrow of the Derg, Garang increasingly turned to the US and eventually agreed to a regionally based, but American-led, peace process that eventually produced the CPA.

Chapter 2 takes up the story after the NCP coup of 1989 put an end to internal peacemaking efforts, wherupon the regional-based Inter-Governmental Authority on Development (IGAD) took up the peace process. But it was only when the US threw its weight behind the IGAD process that it took off with the 2002 Machakos Protocol, which committed the NCP and SPLM to unity, but granted the south self-determination. The CPA also included protocols on power and wealth-sharing, security arrangements, and means to resolve the conflicts in the northern border territories of Abyei, Southern Kordofan, and Blue Nile, otherwise known as the Three Areas. In addition, the CPA provided for the formation of a Government of National Unity dominated by the NCP and SPLM and the Government of South Sudan dominated by the SPLM, as well as general elections and a referendum on secession for southern Sudan. The weaknesses of the peace process began with the bilateral character of the process, which excluded other political parties, civil society, and representatives of other armed groups and ensured that the neither the process nor the agreement was comprehensive. Crucially the peacemakers failed to tackle the structural problems that fueled the north–south and other conflicts in the country.

As Chapter 3 details, although the SPLM and NCP did not want elections before the end of the peace process, the international backers of the process insisted. In the event the international community largely ignored the widespread electoral abuses of the ruling parties so that what they felt was the core of the peace process – the secession of southern Sudan – could be kept on track. This was accomplished at the cost of dispensing with the CPA commitment to democratic transformation; that in turn caused the embitterment of large numbers of politicians and their supporters in both the north and the south, a legacy that continued beyond the duration of the peace process. The division of spoils resulted in the NCP taking almost all the seats in the north, while the SPLM took almost all the seats in the south, thus creating de facto separate northern and southern states and laying the basis for southern Sudan's eventual secession.

Chapter 4 shows how increasingly the southern referendum and the inevitable vote for secession became the focus of the peace process. This brought to the fore the contradictions in the positions of the peace partners. Thus, whereas the long-standing SPLM program called for unity, during the campaign the southern government claimed to be neutral while in practice it devoted all its human and financial resources to ensure an overwhelming vote for secession. Meanwhile, the NCP conducted

a low-key campaign for unity that made clear it was resigned
to southern secession, but wanted a price to be paid in terms
of the outcome of outstanding issues like shared oil revenues,
Abyei, border demarcation, assurance of a stable post-referendum
relationship with the south, and acquiring various benefits from
the international community such as debt relief. Not being given
the option of confederalism and not understanding that a vote
for unity would not return the south to central rule, but instead
confirm present autonomous arrangements, southerners voted
98.3 percent in favor of secession.

Chapter 5 begins by discusssing the Abyei Protocol, which
provided for a referendum to determine whether the inhabitants of this border territory wished to be linked to the south or
north. But the vote was not held and likewise no agreement was
reached on the status of the Misseirya nomads, who transited
and sometimes lived in Abyei for extended periods of the year.
The process came to an end on 20 May 2011 when SAF expelled
SPLA forces from the territory, dissolved the SPLM-dominated
territorial administration, and caused a massive displacement of
the population to southern Sudan. Although an agreement was
reached in Addis Ababa that SAF and SPLA forces would be
replaced by an Ethiopian army brigade under Security Council
auspices, at the beginning of 2012 SAF was still in Abyei, most
of the displaced were still in South Sudan, and there was little
prospect of a referendum.

The CPA called for popular consultations in Blue Nile and
Southern Kordofan to determine if the inhabitants were satisfied
with the implementation of the CPA, and if not to negotiate with
the national government over desired changes. But the NCP
and SPLM undermined the popular consultation in Blue Nile,
while the Southern Kordofan popular consultation was postponed
until after state elections could be held. In the event the SPLM
refused to accept the outcome of the elections and the NCP

demanded that SPLA forces in the state and Blue Nile disarm. This precipitated a war, which continued into 2012.

Chapter 6 details that, following completion of the referendum, the SPLM and NCP turned their attention to preparing constitutions for the successor states and dealing with the legacy of the peace process. Although the SPLM had long called for federalism, it pressed a largely unitary modeled constitution on the new state, while the powers it granted President Salva Kiir Mayardit brought to the fore the authoritarianism that was always a central feature of the party. But the flawed elections and efforts at constitution-building, together with maladministration and endemic corruption, stimulated a series of rebellions in Unity, Jonglei, and Upper Nile states, which were supported by the NCP.

Meanwhile, the NCP faced a crisis of legitimacy in the wake of the loss of South Sudan and endeavored to use constitution-making to divide the opposition over the role of Islam in the state and to form what it claimed would be a broad-based government. In the event, it was not until the end of 2011 that President Omar Al-Bashir was able to form an NCP-dominated government, but which included the Democratic Unionist Party (DUP) and other factions. Most of the other parties called for a popular insurrection. While the loss of the south and the growing economic crisis deepened anger, the NCP was able to contain dissent and looked hopefully to the rise of Islamist parties as a result of the Arab Spring to ensure its continuing rule.

The flawed April 2010 elections and the completion of the referendum served as a stimulus for Khartoum-assisted rebels to launch armed struggles against the SPLM in Greater Upper Nile. Compounding the problems was the inability of the SPLA and UN forces to contain endemic cattle rustling and tribal conflicts, which reached levels never witnessed before in the territory and cast into doubt the capacity of the SPLM to maintain the integrity of the fledgling state.

Although the peace process ended and the south seceded on 9 July, none of the post-referendum issues – including borders, treaties, citizenship, oil revenues, and the fate of Blue Nile and Southern Kordofan – was resolved, and tensions between the peace partners steadily grew and threatened a return to war.

The Conclusion asserts that it is not too early to concede that, with wars, crime waves, and insecurity the common condition in South Sudan, major regional wars in Sudan, the failure to achieve democratic transformation or establish viable post-secession states, and the prospect of north–south war, the peace process must be judged a failure. This study also makes clear that the flawed international efforts at peacemaking exacerbated the country's conflicts. Some principles are identified that should inform any subsequent peace processes; and it is argued that if the interveners and combatants are not prepared to accept intervention on the basis of these principles, then it is probably better to let them resolve their conflict on the battlefield.

INTRODUCTION

THE FAILURES OF LIBERAL
PEACEMAKING IN SUDAN

Peace is more than cessation of military hostilities, more than simple political stability. Peace is the presence of justice and peace-building entails addressing all factors and forces that stand as impediments to the realization of all human rights for all human beings. (Bendana 2002)

The focus of Sudan's conflicts since pre-colonial times has been the state, and this did not change with the advent of the peace process that led to the signing of the CPA. This chapter thus makes clear the centrality of the state and attributes the failure of the peace process to liberal theorizing on peacemaking, which ultimately denied the need for structural changes to the state, a process that alone could achieve the stated ends of sustainable peace and democracy.

The Sudanese State Historically

Sudan had its origins in an amalgam of existing states – Nubia, Kush, Funj, Fur – and an overlay of the Ottoman Empire, which in turn gave rise to the Mahdiya, the immediate forerunner of the colonial state. And, like European states of an earlier period which were the creatures of war (Tilly 1985: 183), the Sudan of the Mahdiya was largely a creation of war against the Turks. While historians were quick to embrace Tilly's thesis with respect to Europe, African wars were not given the same understanding, despite the fact that in the Horn a Sudanese army expelled a Turkish occupying army while an indigenous Ethiopian army defeated an Italian invasion. It was this Sudanese state that the British overwhelmed in 1898.

Far from being the haphazard acquisition of territory often attributed to the British in Africa, or a result of the attempt to free and later avenge the death of General Charles Gordon by the Mahdists, the penetration of the upper reaches of the Nile followed logically from Britain's imperial interests. These interests centred on Egypt and the Suez Canal, which was the gateway to India. In what was no fly-by-night operation, General Kitchener spent years building a railway from Egypt to transport his army to the battlefield at Omdurman and confront the Khalifa's army, and after its defeat he quickly headed upstream to put a stop to French pretensions at Fashoda. The capture of Sudan in turn was soon followed by the British construction of a railway line from Mombasa to Lake Victoria, one of the sources of the Nile, from which they were able to exert control over the entire White Nile basin. The final piece of modern Sudan – Darfur – was captured by the British in 1916 after the Fur Sultan aligned with the Turks, allies of Germany in the First World War.

While smashing the Mahdi's quasi-feudal patronage-based state, the British-constructed state – like its predecessor – was designed in the first instance to maintain security, an emphasis that did not change with independence. To administer this vast territory the British co-opted the Egyptians, who paid for much of the project, as well as local leaders through a system of indirect rule. With improved security the British constructed a series of dams and waterworks on the Nile, including the Gezira Scheme ('the largest cotton farm in the world'), which served to meet the needs of the Lancashire textile factories. As a result, the tribes of central Sudan, and in particular the Jalien, Shaggiya, and Dangala, who lived along the river north of Khartoum, received the most benefits from British colonialism, the best opportunities for education, and held the most positions in the colonial state. Indeed, state support for favored political parties, which was going to be controversial during the 2010 elections and 2011 southern referendum on independence, was first employed during the colonial period. Development in turn produced a class of tenant farmers, industrial and transport workers, and urban professionals that made for an increasingly sophisticated and politically active community that began to assume the attributes of a nation.

This was in stark contrast to other parts of Sudan, where British policy until the eve of independence was one of benign neglect and a singular focus on security. The south was administered as virtually a separate state after the British introduced 'closed districts' which precluded northern merchants and others from going to the south, restricted Arabic and Islam, and prepared for the south to join the British colonies in east Africa. This decision and the limited attention given to education and development in the territory were only changed on the eve of independence. The focus of development in a relatively small area of central Sudan and the turning over of state power to its leaders in 1956 caused resentment throughout Sudan, but particularly in the south where the tiny indigenous elite viewed the handover as exchanging one colonial authority for another.

Sudan at independence was characterized by the wealth of a few and the poverty of the majority, by fierce competition for resources in conditions of scarcity, and a state which controlled the production and distribution of material and social resources, and thus it became the enduring focus for conflict. Access to state power in such conditions was essential for the welfare of its subjects, but such access has never been equally available to all the people of Sudan, and to many it has not been available at all. This led to ethnic-based political struggles and, when these failed to make headway, to armed struggles. But the ethnic character of the opposition to state rulers did not follow from any innate tribalism, but as a response to the domination of the Sudanese state by a largely riverain core that used it for their personal enrichment and that of their ethnic cohorts. This situation continued irrespective of the ideological character of successive governments, and, with the partial exception of the early Nimeiri regime, all of them attempted to legitimize their control through fostering an Islamic-Arab identity for the country. This identity had little place for southerners and as a result they were the first, but not the last, to rebel. No post-colonial Sudanese government, however, devoted as much energy as the Islamists to turning the state into an instrument to affirm the Arab-Islamic identity of Sudan, introduce its version of sharia, and develop the means of coercion to ensure their continued control and the dominance of the riverain core.[1]

Theoretical Context

Sudan's experience with peacemaking and -building was not unique and in many respects was a prepackaged process served up by the international community and based on extremely weak theoretical formulations. The starting point for contemporary peacemaking is the UN definition: 'action to bring hostile parties to agreement, essentially through such peaceful means as those foreseen in Chapter VI of the Charter of the United Nations' (Boutros-Ghali 1992). It is thus a diplomatic effort to move a violent conflict into nonviolent dialogue where differences are settled through representative political institutions (School of Advanced International Studies 2006). Peace-building in turn is defined as 'a post-conflict activity to identify and support structures which will tend to strengthen and solidify peace in order to avoid a relapse into conflict' (Boutros-Ghali 1992).

Peace-building has gone through various phases, reflective of changes in international political economy and politics. With the end of the Cold War peace-building assumed a triumphalist approach, as befitted an intellectual climate in the West that produced Francis Fukuyama's *The End of History* (1989), effectively an ode to liberal democracy. Like earlier theories of modernization, peace-building also assumed the First World as its starting point and attempted to replicate Western economic and political processes and outcomes.

The end of the Cold War in turn corresponded with an increase in internal state conflicts and this provided the background to the publication in 1992 of the UN's *An Agenda for Peace: Preventive Diplomacy, Peace-Making and Peace-Keeping.* This declaration and the interventions it served to justify were based on a decline in the status accorded to state sovereignty, Duffield argues, because of a false dichotomy between Western politically motivated, restrained, legitimate wars between states and non-Western internal, unrestrained, identity-based wars (Duffield 2002). But the frequent failures of this approach led the UN to issue a *Supplement* in 1995 which called for consideration of the 'root causes' of conflict, and in response there was more nuanced theorization, proposals for longer periods of implementation of peace agreements, and a wider frame of reference for internationally sponsored missions. In 2001 the Security Council went even further and called for a 'focus on fostering sustainable development, the eradication of poverty and inequalities, transparent and accountable governance, the promotion of democracy, respect for human rights and the rule of law and the promotion of a culture of peace and non-violence' (UN 2001).

But these and other attempts to broaden the scope of peace-building in the face of the practical problems confronted in a

growing number of states did not overcome the political character
of the field, or the fact that it was still directed at reproducing
Western liberal states and societies in environments where such
values and institutions frequently had little resonance. A leading
exponent of liberal peace-building acknowledged it to be 'in
effect an enormous experiment in social engineering' (Paris 1997:
54–89) and a 'modern rendering of the mission civilisatrice' (Paris
2002: 637). Indeed, even in the most radical version of directing
peace-builders to overcome the root causes of conflicts, it was
understood they were to be found and confronted in a national
context and not emanating from inequities in the global economy
or international state system.

These new understandings meant that, rather than holding an
election and concluding within two or three years, missions embraced a broader set of goals, including more extensive efforts at
disarmament, demobilization, and reintegration of factional forces,
establishing functioning judicial and administrative structures
within the host state (structures held to be necessary for the
functioning of democratic governance and a market economy)
and promoting the growth of civil society groups within the state,
including human rights NGOs and political party organizations.
The six-and-a-half-year-long CPA was both longer than earlier
peace processes and included all of these components, together
with a commitment to reconcile the people of north and south
Sudan.

But tension remained between what are considered the separate
objectives of peace and democracy, and when this is the case it
is the latter that typically falls by the wayside. Thus Call and
Cousens define peace-building as

> those actions undertaken by international or national actors to
> institutionalize peace, understood as the absence of armed conflict
> ('negative peace') and a modicum of participatory politics (as a
> component of 'positive peace') that can be sustained in the absence

of an international peace operation. If there is a trade-off between these goals, the immediate absence of conflict, in our view, should take priority over participatory politics. (2007: 7)

This is a false dichotomy, and in the case of Sudan democratic transformation was never treated as a major objective in practice by the international community or the peace partners.

Even the efforts to achieve negative peace were never fully realized, and the CPA 'was closer to a suspended war during which local conflicts erupted frequently' (Netherlands Ministry of Foreign Affairs 2010: 8). Since root causes of the conflict were not addressed, in practice peace-building involved managing, rather than resolving, the manifold conflicts that afflicted Sudan, and it did not even prove very effective in meeting those objectives. Indeed, favoring negative peace over the CPA's commitment to democratic transformation will likely ensure that the people of north and south Sudan do not realize either.

Peace-building developed a concern with state failure or 'failed states,' because they were held to pose a threat to security and this figured prominently in the literature after the US misadventure in Somalia in the 1990s, thus again making clear the ideological character of the field. This body of literature was used both to justify and to explain US engagement in Afghanistan and also triggered US peace-making efforts in Sudan. Having defined the problem as a dysfunctional state, the solution was held to lie in its reform, and this provided the rationale and framework for introducing Western norms of liberal market-oriented governance.

State-building assumed a major focus of peace-making literature and practice, and became a central concern of the international community in southern Sudan, but was entirely absent in the north because the NCP was strong enough to resist it. In the south enormous financial and human resources were devoted to creating institutions, delivering services, and equipping and training the southern security services, but by the end of the CPA government structures were weak, corruption was rampant, insecurity was rife, and many considered the SPLA weaker than before the international input. As a result, the peace process bequeathed a largely dysfunctional southern state under an authoritarian ruling party that will be dependent upon the international community for the foreseeable future. Meanwhile, the northern state remained what it was at the outset: a weak state which had lost the south and, unable to achieve hegemony in many parts of the north, completely under the control of the NCP and geared to meeting its interests. Abdelwahab El-Affendi reached a similar conclusion: 'whatever state-building took place in Sudan has been masterminded and controlled by the local actors, who managed to successfully tame and manipulate external input to serve their overall objectives' (El-Affendi 2010).

And, despite a formal concern with institutions, all too often international support has the result of reinforcing the power of favored individuals, who in turn serve to undermine the institutionalization that state-building efforts are directed to achieving. Rarely was that more the case than in southern Sudan, where SPLM leader Dr John Garang was a towering figure, around whom the entire peace process was largely built, and indeed upon which US policy in Sudan was also largely based. When he died seven months after the signing of the CPA, the fallacy of the approach of the international community, which shaped the peace agreement, was clear.

The peacemakers were able to reach agreements between the NCP and SPLM by fudging and postponing the resolution of basic issues of power, supporting the efforts of the peace partners to keep civil society and other political parties out of the process, and trying to make an eminently political process a technical exercise. Meanwhile, the interim period was designed for the NCP and SPLM to carry out a daunting series of tasks and for the establishment of various bodies. But the reality was that few of the requirements laid out in the CPA were fully met, some were dismal failures, and others were never even attempted. This included any attempt to reconcile the peoples of north and south Sudan, which would have been crucial if the CPA's objective of a united Sudan had any hope of being realized.

The critique of the Sudan peace process that will be developed in these pages does not attribute all its failings to the international backers or blame the peace-builders and agencies for usurping local powers and reducing the prospects of the NCP and SPLM to find solutions to their problems, which is often the charge of critics of liberal peace-building. The NCP, SPLM, mediators, and the US and its allies were collectively complicit in the failings of the agreement. The US was crucial in bringing the parties to the negotiating table, and it also had a significant role in shaping the resulting agreement. But it would not be true to say that the warring parties were entirely subject to the demands of Washington. The peace process was able to move forward, albeit haltingly, because the NCP and SPLM leaderships shared with the Americans the same desire to restrict participation, narrow the focus of the negotiations, give short shrift to democratic transformation and reconciliation, and ensure that other conflicts were not taken up, and thus to ensure that the Comprehensive Peace Agreement was not comprehensive and avoided structural transformation.

Paris contends that failed peace processes do not represent a failure of liberal peace-building and can be explained as being due to inadequate implementation (2010). But this misses the point in the case of Sudan. It is not just a matter of failing to implement democratic provisions properly, but of a complete lack of collective will to oversee a democratic transformation, which begs the question of whether there ever was any genuine commitment. Indeed, having pressed elections on the reluctant parties, the international community subsequently demonstrated a marked lack of enthusiasm for them, and when they took place was anxious to downplay the rigging and harassment of the opposition parties, and the resulting de facto division of the country between the SPLM and NCP that the elections produced, all to ensure the continuation of the peace process. Instead of seeing democratic transformation as an integral and necessary condition for sustainable peace, the international sponsors of the peace process, the ruling parties, and the election observation missions viewed democracy as a threat, and passed over the election rigging as easily as they also largely ignored the consistent pattern of human rights abuses carried out by the SPLM and NCP governments over the six-year course of the peace process.

Having made enormous political, financial, and logistical commitments and with the prestige of many countries, institutions, and powerful political figures at stake, it was not realistic to expect the international community to pull the plug on the peace process because of the lack of commitment of the NCP and SPLM to democracy and respect for human rights. As Bendana has noted, public administration and managerial concerns become the focus and principal means to achieve objectives while democracy and participation fall by the wayside (2002). The placing of narrow political concerns above democratic transformation is symptomatic of a process which refused to permit the people of Sudan a role, failed to address the grievances which caused and fuelled the war, ignored election rigging, and will almost certainly ensure that peace will not be sustainable in the north, in the south, and between the north and the south. Bendana concludes that, in its present manifestations, peace-building

> tends to be top-down, externally and supply-driven, elitist and interventionist [and] becomes an inherently conservative undertaking seeking managerial solutions to fundamental conflicts over resources and power, seeking to modernize and re-legitimize a

fundamental status quo respectful, reinforcing and reflective of a national and international and national market-oriented political economy. (Bendana 2002: 5)

Indeed, liberal notions of peace-building go hand in hand with an emphasis on the establishment of a market economy because it is only an economy arranged on such principles that can provide for development and overcome poverty, which is held to be a threat to security. Nonetheless, one of the most striking aspects of the peacemaking process is that while the CPA attempted to respond to regional inequities between north and south Sudan and the three areas of Abyei, Southern Kordofan, and Blue Nile, there was no recognition of the link between economic well-being and democracy-building, or – and this speaks to the limitations of the scope of the peace process – to economic inequities experienced by other peripheral areas. Indeed, consistent with liberal democracy, liberal peacemaking largely ignores the economic dimension of people empowerment and concentrates almost exclusively on the political realm, and in the case of Sudan growing economic inequities went hand in hand with the unfolding peace process.

In southern Sudan there is virtually no formal economy worthy of the name, apart from the international oil industry. With 98 percent of government revenue based on oil rents, and its political survival held to be dependent on the good will of the US, the SPLM was not about to challenge current Western notions of market economy. In any case the SPLM never demonstrated any concerns about neocolonialism, as long as it was not northern Arab neocolonialism, and on the eve of independence the government was selling off large chunks of land to international agro-industrial corporations, announced its intentions of selling government assets, and was looking to the US-based money markets for loans for its ambitious development plans. However, the weakness of the southern state and affiliated agencies, endemic corruption, pervasive crime, lack of an effective judiciary and acceptance of the rule of law means that, despite the endorsement of the market by the ruling SPLM, there has been little investment in the south, the economy of which is dominated by international oil companies and petty traders from Uganda and Kenya.

The NCP, meanwhile, hoped that its good behaviour in accepting southern secession, together with its endorsement of the market and ideological opposition to statist economic policies, would open the door to investment, end US trade sanctions, and relieve its debt, which began with $9 billion accumulated during a building spree of the 1990s under President Jafaar Nimeiri and with accumulated interest payments reaching $39 billion at the end of the peace process. This debt became a powerful form of leverage for the peace sponsors. A ruling party that condemned the Western-dominated international order made clear its deepest desire to be an integral part of that order. With the NCP ideological exponents of the worst excesses of so-called free-market capitalism and the SPLM keen to win American favor, economic orthodoxy as defined by the West was never challenged.

What is most striking is the extent to which peacemakers and peace-builders ignored the centrality of the Sudanese state to sustainable peace and endeavored to resolve the various conflicts afflicting the country as if they were all separate and with no central origins. Thus the primary focus of the international community (and the NCP and SPLM) was on the north–south conflict, and even then the northern territories of southern Blue Nile and the Nuba Mountains were dealt with as an appendage to that process. A separate peace process was carried out under the auspices of Eritrea to deal with the conflict in eastern Sudan, which produced the Eastern Sudan Peace Agreement of 2006. Yet another peace process under the auspices of the African Union (AU) was designed for Darfur and produced the Darfur

Peace Agreement (DPA), also in 2006, which collapsed before the ink was dry. Still another peace agreement was negotiated in Cairo between the NCP and elements of the northern opposition grouped under the National Democratic Alliance (NDA).

It is simply not credible to view all of Sudan's conflicts as separate events, not linked, and not the result of countless marginalized peoples of the periphery rebelling against an oppressive central state. Even less credible was the assumption that these conflicts could be resolved in a sustainable manner without structural reforms to the state. But this is indeed what IGAD, the AU and, more importantly, the US and its allies did, and the failures are there for all to see despite retrospective efforts to claim victories in the secession of the south and the absence of a major north–south war.

The north–south peace process did not bring peace and did not meet its central objective of a unified Sudan. The eastern Sudan peace process met the unstated objective of reconciling Eritrea, the backer of the regional rebels, and the NCP, but has done almost nothing to confront the problems that produced the revolt in the first place. The DPA brought one component of the rebels, the Mini Minawi faction of the Sudan Liberation Movement (SLM), into the government, while the war itself intensified, and Mini subsequently disavowed the agreement and again took up arms. The NDA peace process is even less worthy of the name: it gave its members a tiny proportion of seats in the National Assembly, thus both integrating them and marginalizing them at the same time. The Umma Party stayed outside the entire process, but did not lose much for that.

Even the Navaisha process leading to the CPA was a scaled-down affair that precluded from the outset participation by others involved in conflicts elsewhere in the country, as well as civil society and political parties from both the north and the south. Crucially it denied participation to the South Sudan Defense

Force (SSDF), an armed group of comparable size to the SPLA, and as a result it was widely believed that the signing of the CPA would set the stage for a south–south war. In the event, Dr John Garang, who had opposed constructive negotiations with the SSDF, died in a helicopter crash on 31 July 2005. His successor, Salva Kiir, had long supported reconciliation with the SSDF. With virtually no international support, he signed the Juba Declaration with SSDF leader Paulino Matieb, which provided for the integration of SSDF soldiers into the SPLA on 9 January 2006. And that agreement was of equal or greater importance than the CPA in reducing conflict in southern Sudan. The fact that it did not gain the support of all the components of the SSDF and was not vigorously implemented was the principal cause of subsequent insecurity.

The NCP fought long, hard, and successfully to avoid an all-encompassing peace process, where they would probably have been overwhelmed by the multitude of enemies that their policies had produced. And in this they had the support of the international community, which shared the NCP's contention that Sudan's conflicts were too complicated to be taken up under one roof and instead must be dealt with separately. Western diplomats at the time maintained that the CPA was the first element in a step-by-step process to end all of Sudan's conflicts. But the NCP never saw the north–south peace as part of a comprehensive agreement, and their view carried the day.

Given the extent of the failure of peace-building in Sudan despite the enormous international engagement and commitment to the process, the experience of the country gives support to the path-breaking thesis by Luttwak, who contends that international interventions complicate and often extend wars (1999). Other analysts have provided evidence that shows that military victories are strongly correlated with stable peace. In recent years the wars in the broader Horn – Eritrea, Ethiopia, and Uganda – all ended, and ended conclusively, in the absence of international efforts at peacemaking, through outright military victories. Drawing on this experience in the Horn, Jeremy Weinstein argued the case for 'autonomous development' without international intervention on the grounds that 'war generates stable, self-sustaining, and representative institutions of government' (2005), again drawing on Tilly. He attributes Uganda's economic advancement to the establishment by the National Resistance Movement (MNR) of Resistance Councils which mobilized human and material resources at the local level during the war and which served as critical elements in development and local government in the post-war period. He notes a similar pattern in Eritrea where the Eritrean People's Liberation Front (EPLF) established a wide variety of local-level institutions and provided elementary services during the war.

Weinstein draws a link between the capacity of the MNR and the EPLF and groups in Puntland and Somaliland to carry out autonomous development and the absence of liberal international peacemaking and -building. It is not clear, however, that he appreciates that the key to what he calls autonomous development derives in the first instance from the ability of all these groups to defeat their enemies militarily, and, second, from their philosophy that held that victory would come through the mobilization and institutionalization of their people. In contrast to these groups the SPLM did not militarily defeat its opponents, was not guided by a comparable liberation philosophy, did not effectively mobilize its people, and did not significantly develop institutions or provide services. It was precisely these weaknesses that made it possible for the international community to play such an important role in peacemaking and peace-building in Sudan, particularly in the south. It also helps explain why the SPLM leadership was not particularly concerned at the loss of autonomy in the face of the pervasive engagement of the international community in southern

Sudan. And lastly, in the absence of a SPLM liberationist philosophy, autonomous development was never a concern and instead the movement was guided by a narrow militarism that left little room for governance, democracy, and serving the people.

ONE

PROTAGONISTS AND PEACE PARTNERS: THE NCP AND THE SPLM

Two related themes have played a major role in Sudan's post-colonial development and provide the background to the peace-making efforts that are the focus of this chapter. The first theme was the effort to unite the disparate peoples and regions of Sudan around Islamism and Arabism as ideological identifiers under the domination of a riverain core. Policies with this aim were pursued by all national governments, but the NIF/NCP stood out for being more ruthless in its devotion to these aims, endeavoring to crush other Islamist parties, and exporting its vision. The second theme was the resistance of Sudan's peripheries to this onslaught, which reached its height under the NIF/NCP. Non-Muslim African southerners were by no means the only or even the biggest victims of Khartoum, but they were the first to respond violently in a sustained fashion.

This encouraged the international community to focus its peacemaking efforts on the north–south dimension of the multifaceted conflict and to reduce the protagonists and peace partners to only two parties, the NIF/NCP and the SPLM/A. The various protocols of the Comprehensive Peace Agreement only recognized these two parties; despite rhetoric by the international community about broadening peace-building – but not peacemaking – opposition parties in the north and the south were entirely excluded from the process. Indeed, the international community subscribed to the logic of the NCP and SPLM that only parties with the capacity to wage war deserved a place at the negotiating table.

NCP and Political Islam

The experience of the Mahdiya as 'an Islamic state which attempted to revive the concept and practice of the early Islamic community of Muhammed and his companions' (Flueh-Lobban 1991: 75) served to inspire successive post-colonial parties in northern Sudan led by the heirs to the Mahdi in the Umma Party and by the DUP. Of the major northern political parties, only the Sudan Communist Party stood apart in not basing its legitimacy on Islam.

Sudanese working and studying in Egypt and influenced by Hassan al-Banna and the Muslim Brothers established the Islamic Charter Front (ICF), the forerunner of the Sudanese Muslim Brothers, in the late 1940s. Almost from the outset Hassan al-Turabi, the son of a Sufi leader and holder of graduate degrees in law in London and Paris and dean of the Faculty of Law at the University of Khartoum, became its leader. Turabi endeavored to place his programs in an Islamic context that had historical resonance with Sudanese Muslims. Those programs were also designed to undermine the leading sectarian parties, the Umma and Democratic Unionist Parties.

Turabi had a clear objective, the patience to pursue it, and the agility to take advantage of circumstances when they arose and make self-serving alliances, and this set him and his party apart from the complacent leaders of the sectarian parties, who inherited their support and had little vision. At the top of the

Islamist program was the demand for a sharia-based constitution, with the only consistent challenger being the SCP because the southern parties had no political weight in the country. Turabi wrote, 'The whole of the movement's early history (over a quarter century) was occupied with this competition with the communists' (Turabi 2008: 160). But even the SCP was constrained in its handling of sharia given the religious sensitivities of the northern population.

In the wake of the British decision to link the south with the north and prepare for independence, development and education in the south finally became priorities, but it was too late to narrow the enormous gap between them. Indeed, the Anglo-Egyptian Condominium pursued a 'growth pole' strategy which concentrated investment and development in the favored riverain core at the expense of the south and other peripheries (Warburg 1992: 130). In addition, the British attempted to curb Egyptian influence in Sudan by the imposition in 1922 of 'Closed Districts' in southern Sudan and adjacent areas. Called the 'Southern Policy' it 'excluded northern merchants from operating in the region, restricted the rights of southerners to travel to the north, banned Moslem missionaries, and encouraged southerners not to adopt Arab names or traditions while Christian missionaries were given the main responsibility of education and English was introduced as the language of instruction in southern schools' (Vambheim 2007: 10). Not only were students required to assume Christian names to attend these mission schools, but the government subsidy provided came out of the pockets of Muslims in the north. The policy also had the effect of undermining the development of any common north–south national identity.

Out of concern for the susceptibility of the Sudanese to Islamic extremism and to reduce the influence of Egypt, the British decided in the 1940s to reunite the north and south components of the country and encourage links with its territories in East

Africa. With the decision made to leave Sudan, the British held a conference in Juba in 1947 to allay the fear of southerners that their underdevelopment put them at a disadvantage with the northerners. The southerners attending the conference reluctantly agreed to accept unity and independence pending consideration of a federal system.

The depth of the sensitivities were made clear when in August 1955 southern soldiers in Torit Equatoria ordered to decamp for the north rebelled against their officers; in the following two weeks more than 300 men were killed. The fighting only stopped after the British promised that the rebels would be treated fairly and the causes of the revolt would be investigated. In the event, those rebels who did not flee were either summarily executed or put through unfair trials. The Anyanya rebellion that broke out in the 1960s had its origins among those who fled to the bush in the wake of the August 1955 events at Torit (Johnson 1998).

Although northern politicians won the approval of southerners at the Juba Conference and appeared sympathetic to southern concerns, their hypocrisy – in the subsequent view of southerners – was revealed by their failure to consider federalism seriously and to grant southerners only 6 of 800 civil servant positions when the colonial regime ended (Collins 2008: 65). Fearing political exclusion, some southerners launched a low-level insurgency even before independence, but, with no clear direction and no unified leadership, it had little impact. The south, however, was not alone in its sense of marginalization, as was evident in the establishment in 1958 of the Beja National Congress and the Nuba National Party of Reverend Philip Gaboush.

Ismael al-Azhari and the Khatimiyya-based National Unionist Party led the first post-colonial government. It included only two southerners, both of whom were subsequently dismissed because of their opposition to al-Azhari's unwillingness to give federation due consideration. Meanwhile, the main concern of the northern parties was the implementation of an Islamic constitution and the Islamization and Arabization of the south. Only the SCP consistently proposed regional autonomy to resolve the conflict in the south. With the collapse of the al-Azhari government, the Umma Party and the People's Democratic Party won the 1958 election, but, unable to function as a coalition, the Umma Party leadership effectively turned over the rule of the country to General Ibrahim Abboud. Abboud soon alienated the political parties and deepened resentment in the south by pressing Arabic and Islam on the region. This helped to galvanize the disparate southern rebels under the leadership of the Equatorian Major-General Joseph Lagu and the formation of the South Sudan Liberation Army (SSLA), commonly called Anyanya. Combined with deepening economic problems, this provided the grounds for a student movement of opposition to the regime that spread to the trade unions and professional societies and produced the 'October Revolution' of 1964.

The upshot was that Sirr al-Khatim al-Khalifa was appointed prime minister. He made resolving the southern war a central priority. Lagu thus agreed in November 1964 to a ceasefire, but, with the rebels entering the towns and encouraging revolt, tensions rose and even Khartoum experienced riots, in which fourteen people were killed (O'Ballance 1977: 68). At this time the number of Anyanya fighters was estimated to be 5,000, but only about 10 percent had weapons (79). Anyanya's star rose, however, after Sudan was pressured to accept the transit through southern Sudan of arms from Egypt and Algeria to the Simba guerrillas in the Congo in 1965 and many of the weapons fell into the hands of the southern rebels. Anyanya also received considerable military support from Israel, although Lagu said that 'Israel did not support South Sudan becoming independent, but [the support] was simply a means to keep the Sudanese from going to Egypt and fighting us' (interview, 8 June 2011). Lagu also complained that Israel provided only second-rate weapons, which were not comparable to the superior supplies Russia provided the Sudanese army.[1]

Southerners were, however, divided between those who favored outright southern independence and those who preferred some form of federalism, a battle that was largely fought out within the leading southern party of the day, the Sudan African National Union (SANU). With the acceptance by William Deng of federation, he and his followers returned to Khartoum in February 1965 to negotiate with the al-Khalifa government. Meanwhile, his SANU detractors contended that the ethnic divisions between the north and the south were intractable, and in view of the failings of the Juba Conference northern politicians could not be trusted, and the only realistic option was southern independence. The detractors, however, were divided between those who looked to achieve independence through diplomatic means and those who wanted to align with Anyanya. The in-country mouthpiece of SANU was the Southern Front led by such luminaries as Clement Mboro, Gordon Muortat, and Hilary Logali, and they were subsequently joined by Abel Alier and Bona Malwal. Its support base was mainly southern civil servants and students living in northern Sudan.

Sirr al-Khatim al-Khalifa and his allies supported a Round Table Conference of all the major parties together with international observers to reach 'an agreement which shall satisfy the regional interest of the South, as well as the national interest of the Sudan.' The first meeting was held on 16 March 1965 and abruptly ended on 30 March, but agreed on the appointment of a Twelve Man Committee with six representatives from the north and six from the south, which met for the next six months.

But before the Twelve Man Committee could hold its first meeting, an election was held, on 21 April 1965, which brought to power a new government formed by NUP and the Umma Party under Muhammad Ahmed Mahgoub, a government of a more right-wing character than that of al-Khalifa and less responsive to the interests of southerners. Another development of the October Revolution was the formation of the Islamic Charter Front, which largely served as an umbrella organization for a number of Islamist parties, the key one being al-Ikhwan or the Sudanese Muslim Brotherhood. Largely drawing its support from students (Turabi refers to students as 'the cradle of the Islamic movement'; 2008: 145) and intellectuals, it took five seats in the 1964 election and provided a basis for its leader, Hassan al-Turabi, to assume a critical role on the Twelve Man Committee. The ICF attributed the political problems in the south to the military regime, and when it was overthrown demanded a centralized administration and rapid moves towards Islamization and Arabization of all the country, including the south. At one point Turabi said he would rather the south leave than accept its demand for devolution of power (Collins 2008: 84). The SCP in turn argued for devolution of power, but its southern leader, Joseph Garang, contended that 'there is no real national entity in the south, and for this reason alone the principle of self-determination cannot apply' (Ahmad Alawad Sikainga in Daly and Sikainga 1993: 90).

Philip Abbass Gaboush and Mohammed Abdel-Gadir Osheik were equally adamant in calling for separate regions for, respectively, the Nuba Mountains and the Beja, making clear that even though their people had not taken up arms like the southerners, they too wanted decentralization. The final report of the Twelve Man Committee was presented to Prime Minister Mahgoub on 26 June 1966, but, like the recommendations of the Round Table Conference, they were not implemented and instead were overtaken by the rapidly changing political conditions in the country.

In 1966 Turabi's Muslim Brothers succeeded with the help of then prime minister Sadig al-Mahdi in having the SCP outlawed as

an atheist organization, and as a result its twelve elected members
to the National Assembly were dismissed. The Communists appealed the decision to the courts, which supported them, but
Sadig claimed the decision was unconstitutional and would not
accept it. Turabi said the development 'was achieved in a perfectly
democratic set-up and in accordance with the popular will' (2008:
161). The battle between the Communists and Islamists took
another turn on 25 May 1969 when the Free Officers' Movement seized power and Jafaar Nimeiri emerged as the strongman.
Nimeiri justified the coup on the grounds that civilian politicians
had paralyzed the decision-making process, failed to deal with
the country's economic and regional problems, and – what would
prove the opening for the Islamists – had left Sudan without a permanent constitution. Organized as the Revolutionary Command
Council (RCC), the regime espoused an independent 'Sudanese
socialism.' Leftists played a major role in shaping government
policies and programs, but, according to the future chairman
of the party, Ibrahim Nugud, the SCP made clear it would not
support Nimeiri unless he legalized all political parties.[2]

At this stage the Umma Party and its leader, Imam al-Hadi
al-Mahdi, posed the biggest threat to the regime, and, after
he retreated to his Aba Island stronghold south of Khartoum,
Nimeiri unleashed the air force and army. In the ensuing battle,
in March 1970, an estimated 3,000 were killed, mostly Ansari.
Sadig al-Mahdi in turn was exiled to Egypt, where President
Nasser prevented him from succeeding his uncle as head of the
Ansar. But the Umma Party was not the only group intent on
ridding Sudan of Nimeiri: the Muslim Brothers also attempted
a coup. After its failure, they fled to Libya, where they established military camps and prepared for the next opportunity to
overthrow Nimeiri.

After crushing these two rebellions, Nimeiri turned on the
Communists. In March 1971 he placed the largely communist trade

unions under government control, banned the party's affiliated organizations, and announced the formation of a national political movement, the Sudan Socialist Union (SSU). He then arrested the SCP's Central Committee. However, utilizing covert party elements, Major Hisham al-Ata launched a coup against Nimeiri on 19 July 1971. Within three days loyal army units stormed the palace, rescued Nimeiri, and arrested Ata and his supporters. Nimeiri then ordered the arrest of hundreds of communists and dissident military officers and had some of them executed, including Abd al-Khaliq Mahjub and Joseph Garang.

Having concluded that the southern insurgency of Anyanya could not be militarily defeated, and having isolated the sectarian parties and Islamists who were opposed to any devolution of power, Nimeiri turned to peacemaking. And, with the support of the World Council of Churches and Emperor Haile Selassie, the parties reached the Addis Ababa Agreement, which was signed on 27 March 1972 by Major General Joseph Lagu on behalf of the SSLA and Dr Mansur Khalid on behalf of the government (Collins 2008: 160). The Addis Ababa Agreement rejected the secession demanded by the SSLA in favor of regional autonomy and provided for the integration of Anyanya soldiers into the Sudan Armed Forces (SAF), a climb-down from its position that the south would have a separate army. A number of Anyanya members opposed the Agreement on the grounds that it did not provide outright separation, and others had reservations about integration, including a recently joined junior officer, Captain John Garang. Lagu said that Garang was the author of a number of critical pamphlets and that he ordered him to stop publishing these out of concern that such actions could 'drag the south into a premature conflict.'[3]

The Addis Ababa Agreement, however, faced many challenges. At the top of the list were the problems of unemployed Anyanya fighters, the transfer of Anyanya fighters within the south and from the south to the north, failure to keep the promised one-to-one ratio of northern to southern soldiers in the south, problems related to the retirement of Anyanya soldiers, and failure to recruit southerners into cadet training programs (Shinn 2004: 239–59). And while the police services were under the southern government, the state security organs of the south reported directly to Khartoum. This led to situations where southern Sudanese politicians were sometimes arrested on orders from Khartoum (Malwal 2005). But probably the biggest challenge to the Addis Ababa Agreement was the opposition of the Islamists and sectarian parties to decentralization and recognition of Anyanya.

In 1973 Nimeiri gave Sudan its first permanent constitution, which stated that 'Islamic law and custom' should be the main sources of legislation, and that personal matters of non-Muslims shall be governed by their personal laws (Article 9); it went on to provide protection for Christianity and 'heavenly religions' of the south (Article 16), a marked advance, given the generally negative northern view of the 'pagan' south, and thus not at all in keeping with the views of the Islamic parties.

In the wake of these changes Nimeiri began to align Sudan with the West, but this raised tensions with neighboring anti-West Libya, ironically benefiting the right-wing Islamists and Umma Party activists who had fled to Libya and gained the support of Colonel Gaddafi. After surreptitiously crossing the desert and entering Omdurman on 2 July 1976 the National Islamic Front, made up of the Umma Party, the National Unionist Party, the Democratic Party, and the Islamic Charter Front, attempted to overthrow the regime, but were defeated. Realizing his weakness, however, a year later Nimeiri announced national reconciliation, which brought the opposition leaders back to Sudan. Turabi was quick to rebuild his party while also actively participating in Nimeiri's Sudan Socialist Union, in which he became a senior official. Nimeiri responded positively by appointing him attorney general. Turabi was never a Khomeini figure and instead stressed the liberal progressive nature of Islam, as exemplified by his support for women's rights, which often roused the ire of conservatives. Crucially, however, the incentive to engage women in the Islamist cause was 'the near total control of the women's movement on the campuses by communists' (Turabi 2008: 152). When not preoccupied with writing an Islamic constitution, Turabi drafted a bill for President Jafar Nimeiri in 1980 to redraw the Upper Nile border so as to place the recently discovered oil in the northern state of Kordofan, something he was forced to abandon in the face of strong opposition from southerners. Subsequent plans to build a refinery in the north were eventually carried out, and contributed to the war that would shortly break out.

In February 1981 Nimeiri announced a plan to divide the south. This caused widespread dismay, which intensified when Nimeiri revealed that the proposal had come from Equatorians angry at perceived Dinka domination. Thus on 5 June 1983 the southern regional assembly was dissolved and the region divided into three administratively weak regions: Equatoria, Upper Nile, and Bahr el Ghazal. Also, governors were to be appointed by Khartoum and Arabic made the official language in the south. Collectively these measures amounted to a refutation of the Addis Ababa Agreement and this quickly lost Nimeiri support in the region. Meanwhile, Nimeiri's reversion to pious Islam took a public form when in September 1983 he introduced legislation to implement sharia throughout Sudan; this was followed by the introduction of *hudud* punishments, delivered by 'courts of decisive justice' which ordered executions and amputations.

Now the Islamists were in the political mainstream, they could fund their activities through their involvement in Islamic banking. Turabi was personally affiliated with the Faisal and Tadamon Islamic banks, which, among other interests, provided the funding for the Islamic University. While playing a critical role in weakening the SCP, the Islamists were quick to copy the party's Leninist-type organization structures and methods of working. Operating through small underground cells and fronts, infiltrating popular associations, raising popular slogans, and focusing on student organizations and religious instruction in schools, as well as the military and professional organizations, became the order of the day. As always the objective was the implementation of sharia law. The sectarian parties also voiced support for sharia, but Sadig al-Mahdi concluded that man needed to use reason in the application of Islamic principles and that Islam should only be the guide to a constitution and not the entire basis of it, as was contended by the Islamists.

In both 1958 and 1968 the Islamic constitutions made sharia the basis for all legislation and judicial practice, but on both occasions these efforts were stopped by coups and nothing more was done until prodding by the Muslim Brothers led Nimeiri to establish a committee to bring Sudanese laws into conformity with sharia. Despite this initiative the committee labored for the next five years, proposing seven laws, of which Nimeiri implemented only one, the establishment of a system of Islamic banking. But in August 1983 Nimeiri announced his intention to transform Sudan into an Islamic republic.

For the rest of 1983 and into 1984 various Islamic laws were decreed by Nimeiri and put before a largely captive National Assembly where they were quickly passed. When Nimeiri had trouble reconciling these laws with the constitution, he focused on their implementation; and when not satisfied that they were being implemented with due rigor, he declared a state of emergency and set up emergency courts, which produced a rapid increase in convictions with resulting public floggings and amputations. This evolved into a system of special courts, which in retrospect almost seem designed for the conviction and execution of Mahmoud Taha, leader of the Republican Brothers, a small religious sect of liberal persuasion, but a powerful critic of Nimeiri and his 'September laws,' a term that would stick. Having already been jailed repeatedly, Taha was arrested on 5 January 1985, charged with apostasy, sentenced to death three days later, and hanged on 18 January. The Sudanese collectively were appalled.

Nimeiri then entered a downward spiral: weakened by his loss of support in the south he turned to the Islamists, but they had many enemies and this further reduced his popularity. He then turned on the Muslim Brothers and arrested Turabi and another thousand Islamists over the coming weeks, which the Islamists held was due to pressure from President Bush.[4] On 3 April demonstrations led by professional associations broke out: four days later Nimeiri was living in exile in Egypt. The Muslim Brothers had spent eight years opposing the Nimeiri regime, then became virtually its only supporter before breaking with it only days before it collapsed. They were thus able to go to the street and present themselves as liberators. Indeed, the Muslim Brothers quickly entered into alliance with the sectarian parties and, more discreetly, with Major General Siwar al-Dhahab, a Muslim Brothers sympathizer, who took power on behalf of the army and formed the Transitional Military Council (TMC).

Negotiations ensued between the TMC and the National Alliance for the Salvation of the Country (NASC), representing the demonstrators. When negotiations broke down the TMC assumed state power and announced that elections would be held within a year. Dr John Garang summed up the government as 'Nimeirism without Nimeiri' (Collins 2008: 160) and made the distinction between a genuine popular uprising, which he supported, and the subsequent power grab by Nimeiri's military, and refused its offer of a post. Meanwhile the TMC set about organizing the election, which began on 6 April 1986. The Umma Party won 99 seats with 38.2 percent of the vote, the DUP 66 seats with 29.5 percent of the vote, the National Islamic Front (NIF), which assumed this

name in 1985, 52 seats with 18.5 percent of the votes, and the
SCP only 3 seats. The surprisingly strong performance of the
NIF was largely due to it its skill in manipulating the 'graduate
constituencies,' which permitted high-school graduates to vote
both in a regular constituency and in a separate constituency of
graduates, where it won 23 of 28 seats, some of them in the south.
The NIF pretended to oppose reserving constituencies for the
graduates, but, after conducting a survey of migrant workers in
Arab countries, it asked its members in the diaspora to register
under the names of different regions and vote accordingly (Abdel
Ghaffer 2008: 13). Hence the anomaly of Islamists being elected
in areas of the south with Christian majorities.

Thus began a period of muddle and decline as Sadig al-Mahdi
led a succession of unstable coalition governments that failed to
end the war in the south or revive the economy; instead they preoccupied themselves with removing the 'September Laws' (something all the parties supported but could not agree on what should
replace them). In the north there were real freedoms, but state
services, administration, and the economy all but collapsed.

The decline of the Umma Party and the DUP went hand in
hand with the rise of the NIF, which pressed its demand for a full
Islamic constitution, all the while increasing its strength among
students, merchants, and soldiers, and gaining the necessary
financial resources through a deepening engagement in banking.
Indeed, this period witnessed university student unions shifting
from the Communists to the NIF, and the domination of religious
instruction in the schools by NIF cadres. Crucially the NIF relied
on the adherence of the general public in northern Sudan to
Sufi Islam, whereby no individual, civil society organization or
political party could publicly oppose sharia laws (Abdel Ghaffer
2008: 13).

It was the southern war, however, that played into the hands
of the Islamists. Faced with a growing insurgency the government

was unable to contain, the generals audaciously gave Sadig a memorandum in February 1989 in which they demanded that he either provide them with the necessary weapons to defeat the SPLA or sue for peace. The NIF understood this to mean that a coup was a real possibility, a threat to sharia, and renewed its efforts within the military. In 1988, with the NIF in the government and the DUP in the opposition, the latter reached a framework for peace with the SPLM in Addis Ababa. (This is considered in the next chapter.) Anxious to maintain his alliance with the NIF and not acknowledge the achievement of his arch rival, Osman al-Mirghani, Sadig initially opposed the agreement. But, in the face of rising support from the streets, he was forced to endorse it, and that led to the NIF being replaced in the government by the DUP.

The NIF understood that if the framework agreement was accepted, the NIF's objective of reform would be scuttled and it would face an extended period in the political wilderness. The party leadership also realized that it had reached the limits of what could be achieved through participating in ballot-box democracy, and increased preparations in the military for a coup. The key organizer of the coup was the future first vice president, Ali Osman Taha, of whom it was said that his 'low key style, his child like features and his apparent quiet demeanor allow many people to overlook his manipulative opportunistic, ruthless character' (Gallab 2008). Thus General Omar al-Bashir was given the green light to stage a coup in one week, after another officer, Omar Ahmed Hassan, refused.[5] Born in the Jalli village of Hosh Bonnaga, 60 kilometers north of Khartoum, in 1944, Bashir worked in the local auto garage as a boy, rose in the army to fight in the 1973 war with Israel, and later claimed that he had been an Islamist since his youth. In the early period of the regime he was painfully awkward and kept a low profile, but increasingly he came to the fore, learned English, and became a very effective public speaker and developed a genuine following in the country.

From the outset the coup was made to appear as an action by nationalist military officers to save the country from incompetent politicians. Thus, not only were senior government officials arrested, but also NIF leaders, including Turabi himself, who was held for four months in the notorious Kobar Prison (which, Turabi explained to the author, was a mistake; he should have arranged to have himself transferred to a less harsh prison). Six months later he was placed under house arrest. All this was designed to delude the US, which the NIF was convinced would never accept an Islamist movement coming to power. Indeed, the Egyptian government announced its support for the military takeover and thereby ensured regional recognition for the new government, while the US government cautiously welcomed it. In time neighboring states and the Americans would understand they had been duped, but the NIF gained sufficient time to organize its assets, arrange a suitable leadership, and develop an initial program.

The Salvation Front's first communiqué regretted the political recklessness of the Sadig government, which 'led to the failure of the democratic experiment, lost the national unity by instigating ethnic and tribal feuds until the sons of the homeland carried arms against their brothers in Darfur and Southern Kordofan, not to mention the national and humanitarian tragedy of the South.'[6] The communiqué also referred to the failure of the government to provide 'political stability,' the 'terrible deterioration of the economic situation,' and 'the social class of scroungers getting richer and richer by the day.' At the culmination of the peace process on 9 July 2011 the same problems afflicted the now divided country, including a NCP-created class of nouveau riche scroungers.

In the initial heady days, however, the Islamists saw the coup as constituting a major break with Sudan's past, placing it in the forefront of change in the Islamic world. Making clear the international perspective, Turabi wrote that 'once a single fully-fledged Islamic state is established, the model would radiate throughout the Muslim world' (1992). Their principal vehicle for the revolution was the state. Indeed, in no other period since the Mahdiya has a ruling party reconstructed the state in its own image in as thoroughgoing a way as the transformation carried out by the NIF in the early years after it took power. Mussolini's description of totalitarianism as 'all within the state, nothing outside the state, nothing against the state' (Arendt 1979) described the state the NIF aspired to create and, indeed, went far toward creating.

Very soon upon the NIP coming to power large numbers of army officers and civil servants were arrested, and in some cases killed, and replaced by party functionaries, and even the lowest levels of the civil service were subjected to purges, investigations, and loyalty pledges. Ibrahim put it thus: 'If the Baathists and Communists had come to power they would have slaughtered us so we slaughtered them.'[7] The intelligence services were revamped and expanded, and arbitrary arrests, ghost houses and torture became the order of the day as the NIF attempted to eliminate any elements in the state that might challenge its Islamist program. Trade unions, popular associations, and political parties were banned. Schools and the growing number of universities and technical institutes were used as instruments of control and critical means to implant Islamist ideas and values. While some Sufi and sectarian leaders were jailed, the NIF's approach to them combined ruthless suppression with more subtle means. Thus within a few years it had managed to split the NUP and the DUP into ten groups by offering bribes, providing positions, and astutely playing off internal divisions and pushing the right tribal buttons.

The Popular Defense Force (PDF) was established as both a check on a politically unreliable army and a means to implement the NIF's Islamic Civilization Project and ensure that its version of an Islamic way of life and Islamic values replaced the eclectic Sufi notions of Islam favored by most Muslim Sudanese. The glorification of war and martyrdom in the cause of Islam led to a militarization of Sudanese society (an example being the young children who still wear military camouflage clothing as school uniform), and the war in the south was intensified and became a jihad.

The right-wing Islamists did not have to be prodded by the international community to carry out economic reform. Very soon after coming to power the NIF set out to undermine public services, gut government agencies, reduce financial and banking regulations, privatize government corporations, undermine the quasi-state Gezira Agricultural Scheme, destroy the Islamic tithe-based zakat system, court international oil companies, and compete with other countries in the region in providing long-term and massive land leases. The result was a rapid decline in living standards for most Sudanese and a massive transfer of public wealth as the NIF attempted to enrich themselves, undermine the business interests associated with the sectarian parties, and build new business alliances (El-Battahini, 2011). Per capita consumption grew (at rates ranging between 1.6 to 2.8 percent), while inequality worsened at a much higher rate (4.5 percent). Due to the much higher influence of inequality than consumption growth, poverty has risen during the 1990s, despite the relatively high growth during the second half of the decade (Elbadawi and El-Battahini, 2011). The NIF 'embraced this approach ... because the priorities of the state resource allocation are captured by the arms race and the need to maintain the allegiance of the military-security power base' (Elbadawi and El-Battahini, 2011). Turabi told the author more than once that one of the greatest achievements of the regime was its dismantling of the previous 'socialist' state in favor of a market-driven state.

But, as one observer noted, government policies were not based on 'mere economic rationale but were mainly engineered to weaken political opponents and enhance the NIF's economic and political power base' (El-Amin 2003). Likewise, the NIF's dramatic reduction of service delivery and pursuit of policies that increased inequality are not consistent with the objective of reducing the risk of post-conflict war relapse through more equitable growth and social service delivery. One observer noted the similarity between the NIF's use of violence to maintain its grip on power and impose its Islamist vision on society and the equally ruthless Mahdist regime under the Khalifa) (Ghaffer 2008: 7).

Within a few years the NIF was able to destroy institutions that mediated between the individual and the state. Turabi viewed the northern Sudanese as lazy and shy, and even held their well-known generosity as indicative of a supposed inferiority. The state was to be used to change the character of the people. The government did, however, meet sustained resistance in two crucial areas: first, the south and other peripheral areas, where it faced armed combatants; and second, the family in northern Sudan, an institution with the capacity to resist the party's attempt to change traditional values. The use of the Public Order Police, the neighborhood People's Committees, and a multitude of agencies and bodies to spy and report on people with the objective of changing traditional Sudanese values and behavior ultimately failed. When the Public Order Police invaded households in response to accusations that some women were dancing and wearing immoral clothes, there was outrage and they were forced to back down. Likewise, when security agencies tried to conduct house-to-house searches for young men avoiding conscription, they were again forced to withdraw. In the public sphere, workplaces, the civil service, hospitals, schools, universities, and other state agencies, the NIF state ruled supreme, but the northern household remained a stronghold of freedom and resistance.

Within months of coming to power the NIF freed a group of Abu Nidal terrorists who had killed a British family in Khartoum's Acropole Hotel in 1988. But the early regime was eclectic in its support of terrorists. For instance, in 1993 Ilich Ramirez Sánchez ('Carlos the Jackal') arrived in Khartoum, where he was supported until he became an embarrassment, at which point he was traded off to French intelligence, in 1994. Turabi founded the Popular Arab and Islamic Conference (PAIC) in Khartoum, which brought together Islamist leaders from around the world at its first General Assembly on 25–28 April 1991. Turabi was elected secretary general. In attendance were Yasser Arafat, representatives of Hamas, Osama bin Laden, members of the Filipino Abu Sayyaf movement, Imad Mughniyya of Hizballah, Tunisian leader Rashid al-Ghannushi, Anwar Haddam of the Algerian rebel group FIS, and Ayatollah Mahdi Karrubi, head of the Iranian Society of Combatant Clergy (Glickman and Rodman 2008). At the time the PAIC seemed the vanguard of Islamist struggle, but within a few years it had collapsed.

Researching allegations of Sudanese involvement in international terrorism, the US 9/11 Commission found that

> By the fall of 1989, Bin Ladin had sufficient stature among Islamic extremists that a Sudanese political leader, Hassan al Turabi, urged him to transplant his whole organization to Sudan… Bin Ladin agreed to help Turabi in an ongoing war against African Christian separatists in southern Sudan and also to do some road building. Turabi in return let Bin Ladin use Sudan as a base for worldwide business operations and for preparations for jihad. (9–11 Commission 2004)

It is not clear that bin Laden was much value in fighting southern rebels, although his construction company did build roads and some of them had military value. In any case, when bin Laden became a liability the regime offered to turn him over to the US; when the US refused, in May 1996 the regime forced him out of the county, whereupon he went to Afghanistan. Meanwhile, the NIF confiscated the approximately $200 million in construction equipment he left behind. But before bin Laden left, Turabi arranged a training alliance between him and the Lebanese Hezbollah. In September 1991, an Iranian delegation prepared a military cooperation pact between the two countries, which was followed three months later by a visit by President Rafsanjani to Khartoum, where he proclaimed the north–south civil war a 'jihad' that should be pursued with all vigor (Glickman and Rodman 2008).

All these international endeavors and a ramped-up war in the south were costly at a time Sudan was financially isolated and increasingly dependent on an international network of Islamic charities. In 1993, Sudan received a large payment from the Iranian Foundation for the Oppressed and from Saudi charities and humanitarian charities in the United States and Western Europe (Glickman and Rodman 2008: 78). But this was not enough, and by 1994 Sudan had adopted liberal economic reforms and austerity measures prescribed by the IMF and the World Bank in a desperate bid to return to eligibility for the international donor pool.

Much as Turabi liked to play the international Islamist stage, the primary focus of the regime was the Horn. Appreciating that the Ethiopian Derg was near collapse when the NIF took power, it began supporting the Marxist rebel Eritrean People's Liberation Front and the Tigrayan People's Liberation Front (TPLF), and by 1991 they were leading the governments in Eritrea and Ethiopia. With all three countries committed to good neighborly relations and non-interference in one another's affairs, a new era seemed to be dawning in the Horn. The Ethiopians clearly believed this and promptly ejected the SPLA from its territory. But the Islamists led by Turabi believed that Ethiopia and Eritrea were Christian-dominated states ripe for Islamic revolutions and began supporting a number of Islamic groups in the two countries. Assistance to the Eritrean jihad from bases in eastern Sudan and the NIF's facilitation of 'Afghan' guerrillas entering Eritrea in December 1993 led the government to support a range of rebels against the Sudanese government and to turn over the Sudanese embassy in Asmara to opposition groups operating under the umbrella of the National Democratic Alliance (NDA).

Ethiopia also suffered from NIF support for dissidents in its Muslim-populated western lowlands. Tensions reached breaking point after Khartoum supported efforts to assassinate Egyptian president Hosni Mubarak in Addis Ababa in June 1995; a Jamaat al-Islamiyya assassination squad under Ayman al-Zawahiri entered Ethiopia on a Sudan Air flight with Sudanese passports, probably supported by the Islamist Shura and the External Security Bureau (Rotberg 2005: 126). After the attempt's failure, those who were not killed by the Ethiopians fled to Sudan, where the authorities refused or were unable to turn them over to the Ethiopians. The apparent complicity of elements of the Sudanese government in the failed assassination attempt led Ethiopia and Egypt to call for UN action and the imposition of limited sanctions, travel bans on leading figures in the government, and the downgrading of some Sudanese diplomatic missions.

While not completely breaking relations with Sudan, the Ethiopian government moved to support armed groups along its western border, as well as sending its army into Sudan to capture territory and turn it over to the rebels. A regional war was taking shape that for Eritrea, Ethiopia, and Uganda had the aim of overthrowing the NIF regime in conjunction with the SPLA and the NDA. However, a border war broke out between Eritrea and Ethiopia on 6 May 1998, and very quickly support for Sudanese opposition groups declined or ended out of fear that an alliance between Khartoum and either Addis Ababa or Asmara would give its enemy an undue military advantage.

The regime survived, but the debacle of the assassination attempt against Mubarak, the war with Eritrea and Ethiopia, and the forced departure of bin Laden, all of which could be traced to Turabi, severely tarnished his cult-like image in the NIF leadership. For his part Turabi was frustrated with what he considered the narrow approach of the military and their lack of doctrinal vigor. Reasoning that the regime had failed during a decade of power to gain the support of most Sudanese, he called for democratization. That was seen as a threat to Omar al-Bashir. Turabi effectively acknowledged that the remaking of the state as an instrument of coercion by the NIF to change Sudanese society fundamentally had failed under the present leaders and he wanted to replace them. However, while he was planning the displacement of the leadership, they responded by replacing him.

Turabi badly misunderstood the power realities in the party he had created. For months it was rumored that Turabi and Bashir were involved in a power struggle, and this became apparent in parliament after Turabi sought to amend the constitution to reduce presidential power and move to a parliamentary system. Parliament was expected to support Turabi and vote on the measures on 14 December 1999, but two days before the vote Bashir declared a three-month national emergency, dissolved parliament, and said he was taking 'a disciplinary measure to restore order.' Turabi denounced the move as a *coup d'état* and under his influence the NIF expelled Bashir.

The battle between the two giants of the party came soon after Bashir had negotiated a peace agreement with former prime minister Sadig al-Mahdi and other measures aimed at normalizing relations with Ethiopia, Eritrea, and Uganda. Egypt moved quickly to endorse Bashir's actions against Turabi and the United States issued a statement welcoming any development leading to a change of policy by Sudan.

While the party initially supported Turabi, most of the leaders quickly aligned with Bashir. Only Mustafa Ismael, initially, and Ibrahim Sanoussi, Kamal Omar, and Ali al-Haj remained loyal to their aging guru; all (with the exception of Ali al-Haj, known as the money man in the party) were jailed with Turabi on 12 December 1999 as Bashir launched his sweep of Turabi's closest followers. In addition to the three-month state of emergency, Bashir disbanded the National Assembly, and on 6 May 2000 expelled Turabi from the NIF. How many more in the government, security services, PDF, and army remained loyal to Turabi has never been determined, and they continued to be viewed as a potential threat to the regime. The regime had been constructed around Turabi and loyalty to Islam expressed through him, and that had now ended. However, to the surprise of many, the regime survived. Years of onslaught against popular institutions, the systematic attack on parties and potential rebels, together with the coming of age of a generation more religiously inclined than its predecessor, meant that the regime did not collapse.

And, to further help it over the crisis, by the late 1990s enormous investment by Chinese, Canadian, and Malaysian companies was going into the oil industry of Western Upper Nile (WUN). Development of the oil industry in the early 1980s had been shut down by guerrilla attacks; its resurrection depended upon the government making common cause with the Nuer-dominated SSDF. Considered in greater detail later, this organization, led by Paulino Matieb, a native of WUN, provided security in the area in the crucial early years of the oil industry. The construction of a pipeline, refinery, and a tanker terminal in Port Sudan followed in quick order and by 1999 Sudan was self-sufficient in oil and thereafter rapidly increased production and became a minor exporter. Not only did this new wealth ease fiscal constraints; it also served to broaden the NIF's base of support, further enrich the Islamist leaders, and unleash a construction boom in Khartoum. Indeed, Sudan's nominal GDP grew fivefold from $10 billion in 1999 to $55 billion in 2008 and real per capita GDP increased from less than $1,500 to more than $2,500. But this development exacerbated regional inequities as wealth became even more concentrated in the central core, and the contrast between the center and the peripheries became ever greater. As Collins put it, 'The gleaming towers soaring skyward and luxury hotels of the new Khartoum were more an ominous symbol of the deep divisions between the "haves" at the center and the "have-nots" on the margins than the rising phoenix of a new nation' (2008: 145).

The oil production fields soon became the principal target of the SPLA and at the same time the means by which the regime could purchase ever more sophisticated military equipment to conduct the war. By 2002 southern Blue Nile's SPLM governor Malik Agar Eyre said that if the SPLA could not soon defeat SAF, the government's increased military resources and skill in using them would soon make it unbeatable (Young 2004). The development of the oil industry also went on simultaneously with the massive displacement of people in the production areas, environmental damage to grazing lands and water holes of the pastoralists who inhabited the area, and the imposition of a tight security regime.

The regime had moved even before Turabi's dismissal to open slightly the political space by returning some of the property of the traditional parties and giving them more opportunity to function publicly. Another reflection of the changing character of the regime was the widely circulated joke that after the NIF had led the Sudanese people to the mosque, its cadres had moved on to the souk (market). With Turabi gone, the grey figure of Omar al-Bashir, who had been coming out of the shadows for the two years prior to his master's dismissal, increasingly became a genuine leader and his pictures graced the streets of northern Sudan. But he could never fill Turabi's intellectual or religious shoes. The regime in its middle age was looking more like other African dictatorships, dedicated to its enrichment and maintaining power, albeit by continuing to base its legitimacy on Islam. But, unlike them, it confronted an opponent in the SPLA that professed an ideology of 'New Sudan,' whose crucial components of secularism and acceptance of social and cultural diversity continued to be viewed as a threat to the survival of the regime. And having left the embrace of the Derg, Garang's SPLA tempered its ideological convictions, and improved relations with neighboring states and the broader international community; this made better relations with the US possible.

The other side of closer SPLA relations with the US was increasingly tense relations between the NCP and the Americans. Despite successful US pressure to expel bin Laden, Sudan continued to host a number of Islamist groups that the Americans considered terrorist; and they were still aggrieved at Sudanese support for Saddam Hussein in the First Gulf War. President Clinton had responded by issuing an executive order on 4 November 1997 prohibiting the importing of Sudanese goods, freezing Sudanese assets in the US, and disallowing financial transactions with the regime. Subsequently Clinton had to make a special exemption for Sudanese gum arabic when it was determined to be an essential ingredient in Coca-Cola.

At 8.00 p.m. on 7 August 1998 missiles from a US Navy ship in the Red Sea rained down on the El-Shifa pharmaceuticals plant in Khartoum North on the basis of almost certainly faulty intelligence that identified it as producing a virulent nerve gas. People I met in Khartoum were aggrieved and perplexed that the US would attack a plant devoted to producing malaria prophylactics. One person on the street said he would not have any objection if the US had bombed the Republican Palace, home to President Bashir, but was stunned that they would destroy a medicine plant.

In the event, the NIF moved quickly to invite foreign journalists to view the destroyed plant and organized demonstrations, which I witnessed in Khartoum, that suggested the attack was designed to distract the American public from Clinton's embarrassment over the Monica Lewinsky affair, a view widely held in the US at the time. However, the attack and the earlier dispatch of 20,000 US soldiers to nearby Somalia led to fears that the regime could soon find itself at war with the US.

In the event, the NIF was able to use the 9/11 attack on New York and Washington to its political advantage. With the US in need of intelligence about al-Qaeda and other Islamist groups, the NIF astutely made clear its willingness to be of service by appointing Salah Abdullah Gosh (the last name picked up while he was at university in India) as head of the National Intelligence and Security Service (NISS) with the specific task of expanding and coordinating anti-terrorist intelligence with the CIA. So desperate were the Americans that no one seemed to see the irony in cooperating on terrorism with a regime they deemed to be terrorist. Indeed, the US subsequently flew Gosh to the US on a CIA plane to thank him personally for his efforts in the 'war on terror.' This link was only the most visible of an increasing web that tied the NIF to a number of Western intelligence agencies. However, while Gosh has always been proud and very public about his role in developing these links, and stated pointedly that this saved the NIF from destruction, it was also a source of embarrassment among the party's hard-core supporters, who had been brought up on a hatred of all things associated with the US.

In the 1990s the NIF aspired to defeat the SPLA conclusively, implement its civilization project, export its Islamist vision to the region and the world, and serve as a leader in an international Islamic renaissance, but by the late 1990s all of these endeavors had failed. However, despite a litany of failures the NIF had

learned crucial skills of political survival, including the ability
to make the best of rapidly changing circumstances, and those
circumstances suggested to its leaders that the best means both
to ease international pressure and to maintain its Islamist project,
indeed to survive, was to move from war to peacemaking with
the SPLA.

The National Congress Party – the NIF changed its name after
the expulsion of Turabi – represented both continuity and change
for Khartoum government. Its efforts to impose an Arab-Islamic
identity on the country and preoccupation with implementing
an Islamic constitution and domination of government by the
riverain-core Shaggiya and Jalien tribes were consistent with
the pattern of all post-colonial Sudanese governments. Where
the NCP differed from other ruling parties was in its refusal to
recognize other interests and perspectives, the extent to which
it was prepared to use violence to realize its objectives, foremost
of which was the creation of an Islamic state, and its efforts to
export its ideology, which had almost brought about the NCP's
destruction. Although the NCP suffered grievously from some
of its ill-fated projects, it managed to develop the oil industry
where previous governments had failed. However, while the
benefits of the industry initially were captured almost solely by
the peoples of the core at the expense of the periphery, with
southern independence the party's biggest accomplishment has
become the most important asset of its enemy, the SPLM/A.
Indeed, the oil industry made the independence of southern
Sudan possible.

SPLM/A

In the beginning was John Garang de Mabior. From the Twic
Dinka village of Wangulei, 80 kilometers north of Bor in Jonglei
state, Garang gained a degree in economics in the US before

heading to Dar es Salaam in the 1960s for further study. He returned to Sudan and joined the Anyanya in 1971 as a captain. A year later, as a result of the Addis Ababa Agreement, Garang was absorbed into the Sudanese army. He then went on to acquire an M.Sc. and finally a Ph.D. in agricultural economics in 1981 at the University of Iowa, writing his dissertation on the Jonglei Canal, which was then being constructed.

In 1981 Garang returned to Sudan. Fearing his presence in the south, Nimeiri posted him to the Army General Headquarters in Khartoum with the rank of colonel. But this proved an ideal location for plotting and Garang became head of the Anyanya Absorbed Forces Revolutionary Movement, the foremost covert rebel organization. Meanwhile, upon receiving orders to deploy north, the 105th Battalion of the SAF garrison in Bor, led by Kerubino Kuanyin Bol, revolted on 16 May 1983 and began heading to the Ethiopian border. Nimeiri sent Garang to resolve the problem, but instead he joined the rebels. Days before, Samuel Gai Tut, Akuot Atem de Mayen, and Gordon Kong, all from Anyanya II, had already moved their forces to the Ethiopian borderlands. The uprising in Bor was quickly followed by similar revolts in Ayod, Waat, Pibor, Fosalla, and Akobo. Another thread to this revolt was provided by the Abyei Liberation Front, led by Deng Alor Kuol and Chol Deng Alaak, who went to Ethiopia. The third element was the Student Revolutionary Group, headed by Pagan Amum Okiech, Oyai Deng Ajak and others. Finally, the army mutineers were led by Kerubino Kuanyin Bol and William Nyuon Bany, both of whom converged at Adura Camp in the Gambella region of Ethiopia. They in turn were followed by many refugees.

With the various elements of the revolt in one place, the question of leadership was raised, but it soon became apparent that Garang had already been conducting secret negotiations with the Derg. Fearing an Ethiopian takeover, Akuot Atem assumed command, appointed a cabinet that included Garang, and attempted to negotiate with the Ethiopian army. In response to a request by Ethiopian chief of staff General Mesfin he produced a manifesto that committed to socialism and the total liberation of southern Sudan. Mesfin promptly rejected it and made clear that Ethiopia supported the unity of Sudan and was bound by the African Unity Charter. Garang then wrote an alternative proposal, which would become the SPLA Manifesto, and resolved to fight for the creation of a socialist united secular Sudan and that all the scattered rebel forces, including the Anyanya II, would be grouped together to liberate the whole country. This arrangement was accepted by the Ethiopians and Garang met with Haile Mengistu Mariam to confirm it.

The SPLM's Manifesto concluded that the 1972 Addis Ababa Agreement was 'a deal between the Southern and Northern bourgeoisified bureaucratic elites ... which compromised the interests of the masses in return for jobs' (SPLM 1983: 8–9). It attributed the dismantling of the Agreement to, among other factors: construction of the Jonglei Canal and plans to resettle 2.5 million Egyptian peasants along the Canal; dissolution of the Southern People's Regional Assemblies; attempts to redraw the north–south border to include oil areas; the decision to build the oil refinery in Kosti instead of Bentui, where the oil was discovered; the neglect of southern development; integration of Sudan with Egypt; and the division of the south in order to weaken it (10–12).

The Manifesto accused the military regime of Nimeiri of absorbing 6,000 Anyanya guerrillas into the army, but leaving 32,000 to be absorbed into unproductive civil jobs, to be paid for out of a special fund; this was exhausted two years later, leading to their dismissal. It also concluded that the 6,000 Anyanya soldiers were resisting absorption into the Sudanese army, which led to mutinies; those who mutinied joined with some of the dismissed 32,000 to form what became Anyanya II. Thus Anyanya II was 'jobbist' like its predecessor. The transfer of the 6,000 absorbed Anyanya soldiers and 'their planned eventual liquidation in Northern Sudan' led to a series of revolts that culminated in the founding of the SPLA.

The Manifesto defined the primary objective of the SPLA as 'fighting to establish a United Socialist Sudan, not a separate Southern Sudan' (SPLM 1983: 16). In a prediction that would duly prove to be correct, the Manifesto concluded:

> If left unchecked, these separatist movements in the South, East and the West, coupled with the stubborn determination of a repressive minority clique regime in Khartoum to hang on to power in the Sudan at all costs, will lead to the total disintegration of the Sudan ... the SPLA/SPLM aims to stop this by developing and implementing a consistent democratic solution to both the nationality and religious questions within the context of a United Socialist Sudan. (17)

This sums up the tragedy of Sudan and the SPLM: without democracy Sudan would inevitably disintegrate, and instead of being the vehicle bringing democracy to Sudan the SPLM brought about its destruction.

The Manifesto and the accompanying Penal Code, which described the SPLM as a 'Marxist–Leninist Movement,' was disseminated by the government to embarrass the fledgling movement and accuse it before the US as being part of the communist onslaught on Africa (Akol 2009: 22). According to the Penal Code, 'The Sudan People's Liberation Movement shall have an armed component to be known as "The Sudan People's Liberation Army" which shall at the initial stage ... exercise executive and judicial authority with assistance from the SPLM Provisional Executive Committee' (271). As Lam Akol has pointed out, there are many strange things about this formulation. First, the definition of the SPLM and SPLA is not contained in the constitution, but in a penal code. Second, the army and not the party is to exercise executive and judicial authority. Third, there was no Provisional Executive Committee and many of the other bodies Garang would refer to either did not exist or, like the High Command, never met.

The need to gain the support of Ethiopia and the Eastern Bloc explains the emphasis on Sudan's unity and the Marxist analysis in the Manifesto, but it is not clear why separatists and those on the political right would still join such a movement. And the answer appears to be that prospective joiners of the SPLA simply discounted the Manifesto and believed it to be for 'foreign consumption' (as one SPLM official put it) and was necessary so as to not run afoul of the AU Charter. When some later found out that under Garang the SPLM/A was actually committed to unity and socialism, they defected.

Fearing that Garang was to be imposed on the movement, Akuot Atem struck out with his followers, after which fighting broke out between the various rebel components. Those loyal to Garang met in Itang Gambella in August 1983 and elected him chairman of the SPLM and commander in chief of the SPLA. This was followed by the appointment of the Politico-Military High Command, which was made up of Major Kerubino Kuanyin Bol, deputy chairman and deputy commander in chief; Major William Nyuon Bany, chief of general staff of the SPLM; Captain Salva Kiir Mayardit, deputy chief of staff for security and military operations; and Nyachigag Nyachiluk, alternate member of the Politico-Military High Command.[8]

With the encouragement of the Derg, Garang turned on Anyanya II and killed its leader Gai Tut in May 1984. Assuming command of the remaining forces, Paulino Matieb retreated to Western Upper Nile where he reached an agreement with the government of Jaffar Nimeiri and continued to pose a threat to the

SPLA. As Garang's successor, Salva Kiir often liked to say that the first bullets of the SPLA were directed at killing separatists. What can reasonably be assumed is that with the revolt coming in the wake of a failed experiment in autonomy, most southerners would have preferred a clear commitment to separation from the north (Adwok 2000) and as a result were almost certainly closer in sentiments to Anyanya II. While Lam Akol's claim that more southerners were killed between 1984 and 1989 as a result of rivalry between the various rebel groups than between southerners and SAF (Akol 2009: 260) may be an exaggeration, there is no doubting the bloody character of this period or the internal divisions in the southern movement. There is also no doubt as to the bitterness of the Anyanya II veterans who were militarily defeated in their quest for southern secession by the SPLA, which fought for unity and then abandoned this goal with the death of Garang. One of those veterans was Gordon Kong, who said 'We were in Bilpam [the Anyanya base in Ethiopia] for nine years before Salva arrived as a lieutenant with the SPLA' (interview, 19 October 2011).

As well as arms, the SPLA received military training, passports, intelligence information, a radio station, logistical assistance, and political backing from the Eastern Bloc and Libya, and also sometimes the direct combat help of the Ethiopian army. This apparent advantage ultimately proved to be a weakness since it led the SPLM/A leadership to assume it could quickly defeat the SAF and take power in Khartoum, and as a result it assumed a militarist perspective from its founding.

Although a southern-based movement, it held attractions for northerners. First, it opened the door to the support of northern Sudanese long opposed to a succession of right-wing sectarian and military governments. Second, it undermined Khartoum's contention that the SPLM/A was led by separatists who posed a threat to the unity of the Arab and Islamic world. And lastly, it was hoped that a program of a united reformed Sudan would appeal to the country's African majority, most of whom were Muslims, and in particular those from Darfur and the Nuba Mountains, who served as the backbone of the national army that fought the south during the first civil war.

Since support for a united Sudan never had much resonance among politically engaged southerners, Garang and the other SPLM/A leaders tended to espouse southern nationalism and condemn Arabs in the south, and support unity in the north or outside the country. The tribal and parochial focus of the SPLM/A in practice led to the populist denigration of northerners, which courted racism. Typical was an official publication of the SPLM/A which reported that 'The old Southern Sudan adage that the only good Arab (Sudanese Arab) is a dead one is true' (SPLM/A: 2002). Anti-Arabism was so common in southern and SPLM/A circles that it gave rise to the belief that behind the commitment to bring the marginalized people of Sudan to power was a program to replace Arab hegemony with African hegemony, and that undermined the attraction of the SPLM in the north. Garang was prepared to accept mobilization on an ethnic basis and to press the African card subtly, but was careful to keep religion apart, fearing the power of Khartoum governments to use Islam against the movement.

Armed Struggle, 1983–91

In November 1983 the SPLA launched its first major military operations in Nasir and Malwal Gahoth and by mid-1984 government troops were on the defensive (Akol 2009: 21, 33). However, to bring the SPLA to the attention of the country Garang helped organize an attack carried out by Anyanya II on Chevron's base camp in Rub Kona in Western Upper Nile on 3 February 1984. Three employees were killed and Chevron closed down within days. In the same month Garang organized another attack to stop construction of the Jonglei Diversion Canal, a massive project designed and implemented by the French company Compagnie de Constructions Internationales, to supply water from the southern swamps into the mainstream of the Nile to Egypt. Although the projected 300-kilometer-long canal was almost completed, after the SPLA abducted six hostages the company quickly agreed to withdraw and the project has never been restarted. By these two attacks the SPLM/A and Garang became known throughout Sudan.

In January 1985 two SPLA columns were sent into Equatoria, where they were quickly defeated by the SAF, assisted by the Mundari tribal militia, in part because of the widespread view that the SPLA was a Dinka army coming to dominate them (Collins 2008: 143). Indeed, the war began when Equatorian politicians encouraged Nimeiri to divide the south into its three component parts and the SPLA was held to be fighting to return to a status quo ante that many Equatorians did not want, and from the beginning they assumed a minor role in the struggle in marked contrast to their predominance in Anyanya I (Branch and Mampilly 2005: 5).

In rejecting the Transitional Military Council offer to join its government, Garang said 'unless the Nationality Question is solved correctly, the Religious bigotry is destroyed, and a balanced development for all the regions of Sudan is struck, war is the only inevitable option in the Sudan' (quoted in Johnson 2003: 71). The National Alliance for Salvation of the Country tried its hand at peacemaking, and as a result of meetings with the SPLM/A during the first three months of 1986 in Ethiopia the *Koka Dam Declaration: A Proposed Programme for National Action*, which called for a 'New Sudan that would be free from racism, tribalism, sectarianism, and all causes of discrimination and disparity,' was agreed upon (cited in Collins 2008: 161).

It was also agreed to form an interim government of national unity representing all the parties, including the SPLM/A. In the end nothing came from this initiative. When in August 1986 the SPLA shot down a Sudan Airways flight outside Malakal, killing sixty passengers, Prime Minister Sadig al-Mahdi labeled the SPLM/A a terrorist organization and refused to engage in any peace negotiations.

On 11 November 1987, with the support of the Ethiopian army, the SPLA captured Kurmuk in the northern state of Blue Nile, not far from Damazine and the crucial Rosseires Dam. This unleashed war hysteria in the north bordering on racism, which the Sadig al-Mahdi government capitalized on, and six weeks later the SAF recaptured the town. For Garang the attack represented a first effort to carry the war to the marginalized people of the north. The Derg continued to provide support for the SPLM/A and it steadily captured more territory, and Sadig responded with the creation of the Baggara militia, known as the Murahiliin, to contain the SPLA in northern Bahr el Ghazal and Upper Nile. Made up of the Rizaygat, Missiriya, and Humr, these cattle herders from Western Kordofan and Southern Darfur took their cattle into the pasture lands of the Dinka of Bahr el Ghazal and the Nuer of Unity state on a yearly cycle. The war, the great famine of 1984, and Sadig's decision to use the Baggara to fight the SPLA unleashed havoc in this part of Sudan. Many of the Dinka fled north to be among their kin, who took menial laboring jobs with the Baggara, but the NIF convinced the Rizaygat nomads to attack the Dinka in a church on 27 March 1987 and again, later, in a train as they they tried to escape; an estimated 1,500 were killed (Collins 2008: 174).

The same year saw a new campaign opened up in the Talodi area of the Nuba Mountains of northern Sudan under Yusif Kuwa. While the notion of a united New Sudan was attractive to many, the conflict was rooted in resistance to the suppression of in-digenous cultures and land alienation by agrobusiness interests from central Sudan. The war, drought, and a rinderpest epidemic that killed a million cattle in Bahr el Ghazal and Upper Nile produced famine and the movement of some 2 million people to the northern towns, while others went to Ethiopia; an estimated 250,000 died in 1988, most of whom were civilians. But SAF successes were short-lived, and, fearing a coup or peace agreement being reached as a result of the DUP–SPLM agreement in Addis Ababa, the NIF carried out a coup.

Once in power the NIF set about ramping up the war and enlarging the army and air force, but these efforts could not contain the SPLA, and the Popular Defense Force was organized to secure the regime and deepen the religious character of the war. Forced recruitment brought tens of thousands into the PDF, where the inductees were given a little military training and a lot of religious instruction before being sent to the battlefields of the south, where they were usually slaughtered by the better Derg-trained and -equipped SPLA soldiers

But the SPLA fought not only the SAF; but as an ally of the Derg, it fought their enemies as well. Thus the SPLA fought the Gaajak Nuer militia, the Anuak Gambella People's Liberation Front and, further afield, the Oromo Liberation Front (OLF), each of which received some support from Khartoum. For these efforts the SPLA was duly rewarded by the Derg. Ethiopian and Eritrean armed groups received very little support from Khartoum governments until the coming to power of the NIF, which saw advantage in providing these Ethiopian rebels with the supplies needed for a final push that overthrew the regime in Addis Ababa. But the collapse of the regime came as a great surprise to the SPLA, which fought the victorious EPRDF army in Gambella in a fruitless effort. The SPLA was chased out of Ethiopia and its extensive facilities, training camps, and supplies were captured, its radio station closed down, its political headquarters in Addis Ababa evacuated, and the files kept by the Derg on the SPLM/A were handed over to the Sudanese government. Worst of all, the 400,000 plus population of southerners living in Ethiopia were forced out of their homes into a hostile Sudan, where many died, and others were forced to trek hundreds of kilometers to safety.

Garang was subsequently able to gain some supplies from friends he had made during his extensive travels in Africa, but nothing could replace the level of support provided by the Derg. Garang had kept his disparate army in line by the steady provision of weapons. When the Derg was overthrown, the supplies dried up, and all the bottled-up contradictions in the SPLM/A came to the fore.

Revolt of the Doctors

The biggest schism ever experienced by the SPLM/A, and one whose impact is still being felt today, opened up on 18 August 1991, provoked by Dr Riek Machar Teny, a Nuer; Dr Lam Akol Ajawin, a Shilluk; and Gordon Kong Cuol, a Nuer and Anyanya veteran. Formally, the early leadership of the SPLM/A was provided by the Political Military High Command, but, according to Lam Akol, who was an alternative member of this body, it was not until September 1991 that a first meeting was held, which may well have been ordered because Garang had information about the brewing revolt. As a consequence Lam and Riek refused to attend for fear of being arrested (Akol 2009: 203). Instead they stayed in Nasir and produced a pamphlet, *Why John Garang Must Go Now*, in which the three justified their revolt on account of Garang's 'dictatorial leadership' and the failure of the SPLA to struggle for an independent southern Sudan. They also noted the human rights abuses of the movement, the senior leaders killed on Garang's orders, and the fact that the PMHC had met only once in its eight years' existence. As a result, decision-making was solely a prerogative of Garang. They called their fledgling organization the

Nasir Faction, or SPLA–Nasir, because they first set up in Nasir on the Ethiopian border. Ambition clearly figured in the revolt, and Riek and Lam still aspire to the top leadership in southern Sudan. From the outset they received support from Khartoum and over the years in the face of failures turned ever more to the NIF. But there is no doubt that their condemnation of Garang's dictatorship and appeal for a struggle based on self-determination meshed closely with the sentiments of southerners. Moreover, the split in the SPLM/A had a clear tribal division as many Nuers rallied to Riek while the SPLA took on an even stronger Dinka character.

In late September 1991 the opposing forces began fighting in central Jonglei, and after a ruthless SPLA campaign Riek led his largely Lou Nuer soldiers and civilians south into the Dinka lands where they killed thousands and stole their animal stock and property. When they got to Bor, the home of Garang, they systematically killed civilians and denuded the land of anything movable before Garang could arrive with his army and chase the invaders back to their homeland. Riek's actions gained him support as a great warrior among the Nuer, but damaged his reputation and probably solidified Garang's control over the SPLA. Garang responded to these losses with a lightening attack on Juba in July 1992. After the southern capital was almost captured and SPLA forces entered the center, they were ordered out amid heavy losses. In the ensuing chaos Kerubino Kuanyin Bol and Arok Thon Arok, whom Garang had jailed, escaped from a harsh SPLA prison and joined SPLA–Nasir. On 26 March 1993 the various anti-Garang groups came together and formed SPLM/A–United.

As well as the Nuer-led opposition, in 1994 the NIF began supporting the Ugandan Lord's Resistance Army (LRA) in response to President Museveni's support for the SPLM/A and John Garang. Garang and Museveni had been fellow students at Dar es Salaam University in the 1960s. The LRA, a bizarre and ruthless group dedicated to the Ten Commandments, was led by Joseph Kony, who initially operated from his Acholi heartland in northern Uganda before killing, abducting, and robbing civilians in Equatoria and beyond. The Ugandan People's Defense Force (UPDF) has been singularly unsuccessful in controlling, much less eliminating, the LRA. The SPLA has not been any more successful, but since the LRA posed more of a threat to the civilian population than to the SPLM/A its elimination was never a priority.

Responding to inter-Nuer clan fighting and the increasingly close association of some of his senior commanders and Lam Akol with the NIF, Riek formed the South Sudan Independence Movement (SSIM) in October 1994, which was dedicated to achieving independence, while Lam kept the old name of SPLA–United. Meanwhile, Equatorians joined the Equatoria Defense Force (EDF), which was also opposed to the SPLA of John Garang. On 4 April 1996 all these groups moved to Khartoum and signed a Political Charter which called for a federal state and a referendum for southerners 'to determine their political aspirations' at an unspecified time (Collins 2008: 209). In 1997 SSIM, the EDF, the SPLM Bahr el Ghazal Group, the South Sudan Independence Group (SSIG), and the Bor Group signed the Khartoum Peace Agreement, while Lam's SPLM/A–United signed the Fashoda Agreement (Young 2006: 9).

The Khartoum Peace Agreement also brought together the various military groups under the umbrella of the South Sudan Defense Force and provided for the establishment of a political wing, the United Democratic Salvation Front (UDSF). In addition, it created the South Sudan Coordinating Council (SSCC), subsequently led by Riek, to administer the areas controlled by the government in the south. For SSDF members the Khartoum Peace Agreement was an important step toward the realization of southern self-determination. The NIF in turn viewed it as a means to weaken the SPLM/A and permit the development of the oil industry, since many of Riek's soldiers came from oil-rich Western Upper Nile.

Military Intelligence assumed responsibility for directing the SSDF and ensuring that it never developed an overall command structure or political clout. And without strong leadership the SSDF and the UDSF were unable to provide the pressure to ensure implementation of many of the provisions of the Agreement, particularly the commitment to hold a referendum on southern self-determination. This led Riek to end his alliance with the NIF in December 1999, move to Kenya, and briefly form another armed group, the Sudan People's Democratic Front (SPDF), before rejoining the SPLM/A in early 2002. The Turabi and Bashir factions subsequently argued over which of them had sunk the Khartoum Peace Agreement, critical to the failure of which was SPLM/A pressure on the international community, which shunned the process and agreement. Nevertheless, the soldiers left behind after Riek's departure remained committed to the Khartoum Peace Agreement because of the financial benefits, fear of Dinka domination of the SPLM/A, hatred of John Garang, and the conviction that they alone were committed to southern self-determination. After Riek's departure Gatlauk Deng became chairman of the Southern Sudan Coordinating Council. In April 2001 he brought together the parties to the peace agreement and the various militias at a conference in Juba, at which they joined the SSDF and appointed Paulino Matieb chief of staff (Young 2006b: 10).

From War to Peace

Since the regime made clear that it would only negotiate with the opposition northern political parties if they posed an armed threat, they formed the National Democratic Alliance in Asmara with the

cooperation of Eritrea on 21 October 1989. Eleven political parties
and more than eighty professional associations and trade unions
– most of whom were SPLM/A allies – signed a political charter
that committed them to overthrowing the Islamist regime. From
its inception the NDA leaders appealed to Garang to join, but,
although welcoming the formation of the body, he initially showed
little interest. The main obstacle to reaching an agreement was
resistance by key members of the NDA to accept self-determination for the south. But eventually the Asmara Declaration was
signed, on 17 June 1995, by the SPLM, the DUP, Umma, the
Union of Sudan African Parties, the SCP, the Sudan Alliance
Forces, the Beja Congress, trade unions, and a number of other
essentially paper organizations.[9] It provided for self-determination
as a 'democratic right of all peoples' and referendums for Abyei,
the Nuba Mountains, and southern Blue Nile to decide whether
or not to join the south. But its position on sharia was simply to
call for the 'non-use of religion in politics.'

The chairmanship of the NDA was offered to Garang, but
he astutely proposed DUP leader Osman al-Mirghani, while he
became leader of the crucial armed wing. The northern parties
proved to be poor guerrillas and the SPLM/A leadership always
suspected that the intent of the northern parties was to ride to
power on its back. However, Garang was anxious to use the NDA
and the formal leadership of Mirghani, to send out a number of
signals: first, that a Sudanese Muslim leader was fighting the
regime in alliance with the SPLM/A and it could not be considered a kaffir organization; second, unity of Christians and
Muslims in Sudan was possible; third, both southerners and
northerners were fighting for freedom; fourth, the SPLM/A revolt
was not cooperating with Israel against the Arabs, and lastly it
represented progress on the march to New Sudan.

Indeed, that is what he set out to do with the capture of
Kurmuk and parts of southern Blue Nile in January 1997. Widely

hailed as a major victory for the SPLA it was only made possible because of massive support provided by Ethiopia after the
June 1995 attempted assassination of Hosni Mubarak. Indeed,
Ethiopian Major-General Gebre Tesai Tsadkan told the author
that he ordered the artillery attack on Kurmuk, Sudan, from a
hill in adjacent Kurmuk, Ethiopia, in the company of Garang and
Malik Agar Eyre and his army, then swept through much of the
African populated areas of southern Blue Nile before leaving the
territory to the SPLA.[10] And this time the SPLA was able to hold
the town and southern Blue Nile. Indeed, Tsadkan also said that
the Egyptians closely monitored his forces as they approached
the crucial Rosseires Dam on the Nile.

Nor did the Ethiopians stop at Blue Nile. They captured
Menza, another part of Blue Nile state and handed it over to the
Sudan Alliance Forces of the NDA, which subsequently lost it to
the Sudanese army, and then captured it again for the Alliance
Forces. Ethiopia and Eritrea then joined Uganda in a major assault
against government positions in southern Sudan. This involved
the movement of tanks, artillery, and the like from Eritrea and
Ethiopia through Kenya to Uganda and then north to Equatoria
and southern Bahr el Ghazal. Commanded by their senior officers
soldiers from these three countries, together with the SPLA,
captured wide swaths of territory, thus dramatically changing
the course of the war.

Victories were being racked up in eastern Sudan, nominally by
the Beja Congress and the Rashida Free Lions, joined together
as uneasy bedfellows in the Eastern Front, but in practice with
considerable support from Eritrea and the SPLA. The Beja
Congress had long struggled for the rights of this large and
impoverished Muslim African tribe, and after joining the NDA
it tried to transform itself – never very successfully – into a
guerrilla movement. The Rashida are Arab traders and camel
breeders who moved to Sudan in the 1840s from the Gulf; they

were brought into the struggle through the NDA under the auspices of Mabrouk Mubarak, tribal elder, former DUP MP, and rich businessman with close relations to the Eritreans and an infinite capacity for intrigue. The Eastern Front was a creation of the Eritreans, who largely directed and supplied its military forces from bases along the border. More support came from the SPLA's New Sudan Brigade, which ostensibly was struggling for the liberation of all of Sudan, but in practice served as a valuable means to divide the SAF and reap the benefits of regional support. This low-level insurgency focused on hit-and-run attacks on the oil pipeline and installations and on the crucial Khartoum–Port Sudan road. It led to the displacement of large numbers of people, but the Eastern Front was only able to hold small pockets of territory.

The problem of dependency by the Eastern Front and the SPLM/A on the countries of the region was made clear when the 1998–2000 Ethio-Eritrean War broke out; by 2000 both countries had re-established diplomatic relations with Khartoum. The war led Ethiopia to end all support for the SPLA and the various rebel factions, while the Eritreans reduced support for the rebels and tried to parlay their almost complete control of the Eastern Front into bargaining leverage with Khartoum. Ethiopia, however, did nothing to facilitate Khartoum's repeated and failed attempts to recapture southern Blue Nile, and Eritrea continued to host the various NDA factions and the SPLM/A in Asmara. Nonetheless, Khartoum used the improved political circumstances and the resources it could draw upon from its emergence in mid-2000 as an oil exporter to expand, better equip, and modernize its army. Morale in the SAF, however, remained poor, the officer corps had been decimated by ideologically driven purges, and Sudan's international isolation meant that its officers could not easily take advanced training abroad. The SAF's biggest problem, though, was the unreliability of its army, since it was largely drawn from southerners, Nuba, and Darfuris, who could not be counted upon to fight their own people.

And so the war continued, with one side gaining advantage and then the other, but with no conclusive battles. What can be said is that at the start of the IGAD peace process the government held most of the towns and, through the auspices of the SSDF and other militia allies, controlled most of Greater Upper Nile and the territory around the garrison towns, crucially the oil fields, which were never seriously threatened during the course of the war; important parts of Equatoria courtesy of the Equatoria Defense Forces and the Murle lands of south-east Jonglei through Sultan Ismael Koney; and parts of Western Bahr el Ghazal through SSDF Major General Atom al-Nour. The SPLM controlled more territory in Equatoria, the Bor Dinka heartland in southern Jonglei, and much of the Dinka-populated Warrap, Northern Bahr el Ghazal, and Lakes states, as well as the crucial town of Rumbek. In the late stages of the war the SPLA captured Raga in Western Bahr el Ghazal, but much of the underpopulated south-west was never controlled by either party. While the courage and commitment of its soldiers are not to be doubted, the fact remains that the most significant military accomplishments of the SPLA were the result of Ethiopian and Eastern Bloc support in the early years, and later due to the support provided by Eritrea, Ethiopia, and Uganda.

SPLM/A: Organization, Orientation, and Leadership

Although not strictly speaking an anti-colonial struggle, the SPLM/A's twenty-two-year war can be compared to liberation movements of an earlier generation in Africa. Unlike most of them, however, from its inception the SPLM/A was dominated by soldiers. To the extent that the SPLM/A was struggling for the respect of Africans and their cultures, it could be compared to the African National Congress (ANC), but it focused solely on war to realize its objectives. More appropriate comparisons can be drawn with the Movement for the Popular Liberation of Angola (MPLA), Mozambique's FRELIMO, and in the Horn with the National Resistance Movement (NRM) of Uganda, the EPLF, and TPLF, all of whom carried out armed struggles. As was the case with these latter groups, the SPLM/A faced an indigenous regime which was not going to leave, and this no doubt made the war longer and more vicious. But, unlike them, the SPLM/A did not militarily defeat its opponent and instead needed the international community to end the war.

Another commonality of these groups is that all were guided by Marxist–Leninist conceptions of party organization, strategy, conduct of their wars, and even objectives. In retrospect it is clear that the Marxism–Leninism of Garang and the SPLM/A was very shallow, no serious attempt was made to adapt it to the realities of southern Sudan, and it was largely an opportunistic means to gain the military support of the Derg and the Eastern Bloc. Marxism has proved remarkably amenable to creative adaptation to a range of circumstances and has often proven successful in the Third World, but the statist Marxism and militarism of the Derg that was fully taken on board by Garang showed none of that originality. Gibson noted that,

> While many have learned that 'political power grows out of the barrel of a gun' far too many would-be revolutionaries anywhere have failed to heed Mao's corollary injunction: 'The revolutionary war is a war of the masses; it can be waged only by mobilizing the masses and relying on them.' (Gibson 1972: 12, quoted in Akol 2009: 255)

Garang's New Sudan successfully identified the main contradiction in Sudan between an ethnically exclusive state core and a disenfranchised majority in the periphery, but neither he nor his party was able to translate that singular insight into practical programs. The problem was not just that Garang built the core of the SPLM/A around his Bor Dinka community; it also arose because, while the neighboring liberation movements developed programs that embraced ever wider groups, serving to dilute their ethnic character, the SPLM/A never did.

It must be acknowledged that the SPLM/A faced problems of mobilization not experienced by their counterparts in the region, and in particular the ability of Khartoum governments to frame the war in religious terms in which the Islamic *umma* was threatened by a Christian- and pagan-dominated SPLM/A. Religion never had this kind of significance in Eritrea, Ethiopia, and Uganda, where the revolutionary movements essentially subscribed to the dominant religion. Khartoum governments also subtly used race against the SPLM/A, something which could not be done to any significant extent in Eritrea and Ethiopia, where the movements emerged from sections of the dominant communities. The majority of people in southern Sudan are Nilotic pastoralists who value martial skills highly and are fiercely independent. The EPLF, TPLF, and NRM were largely made up of peasants who proved easier to discipline and organize. Pastoralists can be worthy soldiers if properly motivated and led, but for the most part they were not. And the mistreatment of the largely settled Equatorians by the Dinka-dominated SPLA meant that while they were among the strongest supporters of secession, they did not join the SPLA in significant numbers. In the absence of an ideology meaningful for the southern Sudanese the party/army relied extensively on violence against civilians.

Another reason for disunity and the dependence on violence is that factionalism is a major characteristic of the political culture of the SPLM/A. It begins with the highly decentralized and tribal character of southern Sudanese society, the prevalence of martial values, a culture of cattle raiding among the pastoralists, the limited impact of modernization, and conflict between pastoralists and peasants. Moreover, in the absence of a strong ideology and institutions, tribalism became the mainstay of the SPLM/A. Garang consistently opposed institutionalization of the SPLM/A because it threatened his personalized rule. As a result, opposition focused on Garang and took place outside the formal institutions of the SPLM/A, was based on tribe and clan, and often assumed violent forms. The SPLM/A's failure to significantly weaken primordial identities and martial values, together with continuing insecurity, provided a strong basis for factionalism. The people who led the movement and later the southern government were themselves products of the society with all its contradictions, and their authority was based as much on tribe, clan, region, and local factions as it was on the official positions they held. And when challenged or threatened with a loss of power, they typically looked to their communities for support.

Southern Sudanese society is among the most decentralized in the world. While some tribes, such as the Zande, Anuak, and Shilluk, are relatively centralized under kings with real power, they are the exception, and the dominant pattern is typified by most of the Nilotics, who live in decentralized groups where the chiefs are accountable to the tribes and have little power. Indeed, some anthropologists view the Dinka (who account for about 40 percent of the population of southern Sudan) as a people and its many (and often) warring clans as tribes. The Nuer (the south's second tribe) is known for its capture of much of its neighbors' territories over the centuries, but, when not focused on the land or cattle of others, the Nuer frequently fight among themselves.

Further encouraging factionalism is the conflict between the semi-nomadic cattle-herding Dinka, Nuer, Murle, Taposa, and others and the settled farming people, and this played a major role in dividing southerners. In the wake of the Addis Ababa Agreement of 1972 the peasants of Equatoria, with their better access to schools than the pastoralists, assumed a leading role in the civil service. But the pastoralist Dinkas held political power, and this produced conflict between the two groups, a pattern that was repeated in the post-CPA period.

While tribes carry enormous weight in South Sudan, they cannot be mechanically equated with political factions. The decentralized Nilotic tribes are highly diverse, but even the more hierarchically structured tribes like the Shilluk, Anuak, and Zande are often divided in their support for regional leaders. Although tribal anger can be quickly mobilized, there is widespread intermarriage in the south, tribal identities are invariably in flux, and small tribes are being subsumed, usually peacefully, by more powerful tribes all the time. The two tribes that are sometimes held to be the most antagonistic, the Dinka and the Nuer, will often come together as Nilotics should one of them be threatened. As a result, achieving leadership necessarily means building tribal, clan, and cross-cutting regional alliances, and this is always subject to instability. The critical point, however, is that the SPLM/A failed during twenty-two years of war to establish an ethnically united political leadership and army to challenge the north, and successive northern governments utilized this weakness to exacerbate divisions and turn southerner against southerner.

Despite these limitations, the SPLM/A did acquire a following; this was due to the support given by southerners to any kind of movement that successfully challenged the north, and with its ready supply of weapons and logistics from Mengistu it had the capacity to fight. The result, however, was a kind of tribal war writ large that involved expelling the Arabs from the southern Sudanese homeland. This was at complete variance with the rhetoric of Garang, but this and not the heady notions of New Sudan moved southerners and members of his own organization. Indeed, it was common to be told by senior SPLM/A officials in the liberated territories that, despite party and Garang commitments to New Sudan, they were separatists.

While the ideology and political programs developed by the TPLF, EPLF, and NRM broadened their struggles, served to undermine tribalism, and provided a global vision of liberation, the early SPLM/A's Marxism concocted by Garang and Mengistu provided little insight into either the problems of southern Sudan or how to conduct a popular war. Instead, following his benefactor, Garang used authoritarian measures to solidify his power in the organization. This was made easier because most of the early SPLM/A leaders and virtually all of its followers were drawn from military backgrounds, accepted hierarchical structures, followed orders without question, and accepted his emphasis on discipline. The partial exception was the cultivation of 'Garang boys,' who did not have strong tribal bases or senior military ranks, but were identified early as intelligent and loyal and were brought into Garang's orbit and bestowed with special privileges. This included people like Pagan Amum, Deng Alor, and Nhial Deng. They were the exception in an organization where non-military people were suspect, and Garang built his army on youth who were more likely to blindly follow orders even if it meant going to their deaths, which was the fate of many of them.

The SPLA strategy was

> not to mobilize the people in pursuit of a political aim, so much as to capture state power, and then use that power to effect a radical transformation. This reflected 'the state socialist' (or, less kindly, 'Afro-Stalinist') approach of Mengistu. While Mengistu ruled Ethiopia, the SPLA used Ethiopian state power as part of its structures of control and transformation. (African Rights 1997: 63)

The military doctrine in turn was derived from that of the Derg, including its brutality and forced conscription (63). According to Lieutenant General Alfred Ladu Gore (rtd), 'The liberated territories should have been the nucleus for a new state, but instead was dominated by commanders who used these areas for their personal enrichment' (interview, 19 April 2011). The result was a short-term militarist perspective completely at odds with notions of protracted struggle based on a long-term perspective. The army, not the people, were at the centre of Garang's project. According to Peter Nyaba, a former commander, 'differing views were completely suppressed and a campaign of vilification, marginalization and alienation of the politicians and intellectuals began in earnest' (Nyaba 1997: 34). Along with this went the imprisoning of leading figures in the liberation struggle – Joseph Oduho, Martin Majur, Kawac Makuei, Kerubino Kuanyin, and Arok Thon Arok – and the killing of many more. Indeed, Garang created an archipelago of prisons where thousands were held under inhumane conditions and tortured, a practice that continued into the post-conflict period.

Garang exerted his authority by maintaining complete control over weapons and supplies, dividing military and political authority at the local level, placing his supporters in key positions, and going over the heads of his army high command to deal directly with selected commanders, all of which had the effect of seriously weakening the military capacity of the organization (Young 2005b). Salva told the author that while operating as chief of defense staff, he had no authority over key commanders in the field, who reported directly to Garang. Senior security officials in both Ethiopia and Eritrea told the author in almost identical terms how their efforts to train and create a professional fighting force of SPLA units were repeatedly undermined by Garang.[11] The result was an army dependent upon personal control – and, as has been made clear in the years following the 9 January 2005 peace agreement, only too quick to resort to settling scores, stealing cattle, and pursuing tribalist concerns.

While the EPLF and TPLF operated in largely feudal environments, they nevertheless implemented transformative projects, such as carrying out land reforms, establishing local adminis-trations and community-controlled militias, advancing women's rights, and so on; the SPLM/A, however, never emphasized revo-lutionary goals. Indeed, after the Derg was overthrown SPLM/A leaders revealed themselves as socially conservative and frequently devout Christians with little vision beyond the official position in support of New Sudan, which few of them beyond Garang in any case accepted. What motivated these people was not grand visions, not even in most cases a pan-southern Sudanese national-ism, but merely a desire to carve out a piece of territory where Africans could live their lives free of the demands imposed by an Arab-Islamic riverain elite in Khartoum.

Had Garang and the SPLM/A wanted to carry out transforma-tive changes they would have faced serious obstacles in southern Sudan, where – given the lack of development – most peasants had direct access to the principal means of production, land, and labor, and where there was only limited extraction of surpluses by landlords, feudal classes, or capitalist farmers (Hyden 1980; Mkandawire 2002). Although some from the SPLM/A spent years in Cuba, there is little evidence that they were influenced by the vast array of revolutionary writings from Mao to Cabral. Again, the SPLM/A was in marked contrast to other revolu-tionary parties in the Horn where revolutionary theory figured prominently in party programs and debates. Indeed, after the Derg was overthrown Garang's SPLM/A developed close ties with international Christian organizations like Britain's Christian Solidarity International and the US Samaritan's Purse, whose high-profile evangelical leaders – Billy and son Franklin Graham – were close to the Republican Party and on intimate terms with President Bush. As an autocrat it apparently never occurred to Garang that the movement's weakness was due to its tenuous links with southerners, and they and not the foreigners were the surest road to strengthening the SPLM/A.

SPLM/A, Administration, and Relations with the People

Typically liberation movements in the Horn of Africa had distinct but united political and military spheres throughout the period of armed struggle, and the SPLM/A also adapted this pattern as a means to ensure unity of purpose and leadership. However, Garang ensured that the party was underfunded, secondary to the army, and never achieved the status of a viable body. This can readily be seen in the limited attention given by the SPLM/A to governance in the liberated territories and the negative legacy that had on the post-CPA government. Garang also monopolized the foreign relations of the SPLM/A, beginning with his Ethiopian allies and continuing through to his close relations with the US.

The loss of a base area and the support of the Derg after 1991, the challenges to the ideology of the SPLM/A caused by the end of the Cold War, together with the splits in the movement of Riek, Lam, Gordon, and others encouraged many otherwise passive followers to demand that Garang become more accountable to the membership. The result was the holding of the movement's first convention in Chukudum, eastern Equatoria, 2–11 April 1994. The convention was attended by 516 delegates, most of whom were appointed by Garang and the rest by local SPLM/A authorities (Collins 2008: 209). Only 40 percent of the attendees were civilians and Garang wanted to pre-empt any input from them, but nonetheless a major theme of the conference was the need to establish effective, accountable local government. The conference further demonstrated the support of the majority of the delegates for southern self-determination.

The convention laid down the responsibilities and powers of the chairman of the SPLM/A and his deputy, Salva Kiir. Reformers drew inspiration from this conference because they believed a new era in SPLM/A relations with southern civil society would now take form. But in the end the convention did not accomplish much. Garang's opposition to institutionalization continued, accountability remained weak, genuine local governments never developed, no further conventions were held during the lifetime of Garang, and the appointed National Liberation Council only met four times between 1994 and 2000 (Rolandsen 2005: 153). Moreover, Garang continued to discharge most officials in the movement, army, and civil authority, and under the draft constitution he could only be dismissed by a 75 percent vote of an extraordinary national convention called for by 75 percent of the National Liberation Council membership, thus making him 'virtually irremovable' (153). Two years later Africa Rights found that southerners had concluded that 'the Convention had been a charade' (Africa Rights 1997: 309); while Rolandsen's more nuanced conclusion was that 'The implementation of the reforms at the national level stagnated soon after the Convention' and that the most striking change in the six years after the National Convention was the SPLM/A's adoption of a new rhetoric which stressed democracy, even if it was never realized (Rolandsen 2004: 166–7).

However, continuing failures of local governance in the 1990s led to the need for change. This was expressed in the SPLM/A's *Peace through Development: Perspectives and Prospects in Sudan*, published in February 2000, which called for participatory democracy and good governance and the establishment of the Civil Administration of New Sudan (CANS). But the organization came about virtually on the eve of the peace process, never operated independently of the SPLM/A, and had little political weight. It was meant to gain legitimacy for the SPLM/A by shifting its focus (or appearing to do so) from the military to a concern with governance and development, and thus attract donor funds. But most CANS officials were ex-SPLA soldiers, and this led to an intermeshing of civilian and military spheres through personal ties and influence, and a military ethos always dominated (Johnson 1998: 60). Indeed, the SPLM/A's early administration combined military, executive, judicial, and legislative powers while a five-man high command conducted the war and ran liberated areas with a pyramid of political commissars, officers, and military judges (Fegley 2009: 4) Their primary mandate was to mobilize resources for the war, including forced conscription, provision of rations, and porterage, all of which were greatly resented by the local people, while they failed to establish accountable institutions that met the needs of the civilian population.

But the most striking feature of local government in the SPLM/A-occupied southern Sudan was the lack of government provision of services and the extent to which foreign NGOs filled the gap. Without the capacity either to deliver services or to administer effectively those who were delivering services, the SPLM/A had the international agencies operating in a political vacuum, subject to arbitrary edicts and coercion, or according to their own objectives. The result was often poor delivery of services, and in the absence of effective oversight the NGOs often became wasteful and inefficient. SPLM/A functionaries also manipulated these agencies for both personal gain and the advantage of the movement. Food diversions were common and in many cases done with the acquiescence or even design of foreign donors as a means of supporting the SPLM/A. Without direction from the leadership (Garang) the SPLM/A did not accept its responsibilities as a government and looked to the international community for the provision of resources and skilled personnel. As a result the SPLM/A never acquired the necessary skills to run a government, as became painfully evident in the post-2005 period.

The rampant corruption that characterized CANS, which carried over into the post-conflict Government of South Sudan (GoSS), was due in large part to the opposition by Garang to accountability, transparency, and institutionalization, and his unwillingness to punish the guilty. An SPLM official told me: 'Garang and later Salva accepted corruption as a means to stop dissent.' The low level of modernization and the strength of primordial attachments in southern Sudan figured in an acceptance of corruption, but it was the failure of the SPLM/A leadership to inculcate among its members an ethos of serving the people that made it hard to control. Corruption in the army was particularly identified with the Bor officers, whose interest in business became a major source of grievance among the other tribes. An early member of the SPLA remarked to me that, under Garang, 'it became a wealth-generating project.' Indeed, despite their responsibilities, SPLM/A leaders and even soldiers were not discouraged from pursuing private business activities, and many did so in South Sudan, Kenya, and Uganda, while others bought property in the UK and Australia, where they sent their families.

That the SPLM administration was weak and generally incompetent is not denied, but the usual explanation is that it was underfunded (Johnson 2003; Rolandsen 2005). That was certainly true, but the resources were equally limited for revolutionary groups in Eritrea, Ethiopia, and Uganda and they still managed to establish rudimentary systems of local government, provide minimal services, and implement programs of social transformation. But the political culture of the SPLM/A was based on the gun and only late in the day did it copy the EPLF, TPLF, and MNR and create a humanitarian wing, the South Sudan Rehabilitation Commission (SSRC), for the delivery and distribution of Western-supplied food to the regularly famine-afflicted population. While other revolutionaries managed to carry that out in ways that gained them political support, this was not so in the case of the SPLM/A, which was only able to use food relief to feed its own army (Johnson 2003).

As a result of this militaristic approach, relations with the civilians in the liberated territories were often tense. SPLA Lieutenant

General Alfred Ladu Gore (rtd) observed that 'the abuse of civilians and the failure to develop a democratic culture in the liberated territories was the biggest weakness of the SPLM/A and this legacy still carries over to the present' (interview, 23 March 2011). The abuse of civilians was common in areas occupied by the SPLA, and this often led to the emergence of local self-defense militias, particularly in Equatoria, where the SPLA often arrived with their extended families and cattle. Khartoum was not slow to take advantage of the rise of these groups and began providing them with supplies, and later helping them to integrate into the SSDF (Young 2004). De Waal concluded that at its best the SPLM/A's administration 'represented benevolent paternalism, at its worst it was violent and extractive' (de Waal 1997: 96). With the emphasis on armed struggle, the SPLM cadres who went into local governance were usually of a lower calibre, had more limited career prospects, and fewer financial resources to draw upon than their counterparts in the army. Until 1991, local administrative structures were rudimentary, and the SPLM/A largely used 'indirect' forms of rule and a small number of civil/military administrators, who provided a link between local commanders and chiefs (Rolandsen 2005).

As a result of its Ethiopian links the SPLM/A was initially suspicious of Western and Christian agencies, but after the Derg collapsed in 1989 it was in need of new benefactors and its attitude changed. The Norwegian People's Aid became a close ally, but it was only due to weakness that the Sadig government agreed to the formation of Operation Lifeline Sudan (OLS), which embraced most of the INGOs and to some extent filled the gap created by the loss of the Derg. Indeed, the OLS was crucial to the survival of the SPLA when it did not have the capacity either to mobilize its own people for purposes of extraction or to mine or control minerals as a source of financing, as was done by other revolutionary groups. The OLS in turn needed local interlocutors, and this served as the impetus for the SPLM to establish the New Sudan Council of Churches (NSCC) to work with the international agencies. Thus a southern Sudan civil society took form, but it was largely Western-funded, beholden to Western agencies, and service-oriented, and it continued to be so at the end of the peace process.

Traditional authorities in the south have historically been responsible for maintaining peaceful inter-ethnic relations and organizing self-defense, arbitrating disputes on account of their legitimacy and understanding of traditional laws and practices, and distributing food relief. While the chiefs' authority is based on popular approval at the local level, the legitimacy of the SPLM/A was based on the gun, and as a result the relationship between the traditional authorities and the SPLM/A was often contentious. During its early years the SPLM/A followed a primitive Marxism–Leninism in which chiefs were defined as a feudal class enemy who had to be either politically marginalized or liquidated.[12] Considered as competitors for authority and legitimacy in the rural areas, the chiefs were replaced by military administrations, which were not only ineffective but alienated the people. Other chiefs were forcefully recruited into the army where they were given low ranks designed to humiliate them. Typically these local administrations were led by Dinka officers, which had the additional effect of encouraging anti-Dinka sentiment. It was not until the overthrow of the Derg that the SPLM/A attempted to develop better relations with civil society, including the chiefs. However, by then many chiefs had been displaced and were living in internally displaced persons' (IDP) camps in the north and had developed relations with the government. The NCP appreciated the value of luring the chiefs away from the SPLM/A; this not only gave them salaries and other benefits, but also vastly expanded their number. The SPLM/A typically viewed these chiefs as fifth columnists.

Conclusion

For parties with almost polar opposite ideologies and very different ways of operating, the NCP and the SPLM nonetheless shared a number of common features: ruthless devotion to their cause, contempt for those who did not share their vision and for democratic decision-making generally, a singular focus on attaining state power, and no hesitation about using violence to attain their ends. In addition, both parties were completely dominated by highly intelligent, charismatic leaders, who were in the end largely rejected by their parties. Turabi's downfall came about after he attempted to launch what amounted to a coup against his own government and as a result was put down by his agent, Omar al-Bashir. But Turabi did not go quietly into the night, and instead continued to be both an irritant and a threat to the NCP government.

The extent to which Turabi was prepared to challenge his former colleagues was made clear in the Memorandum of Understanding on shared principles and approaches reached between his Popular Congress Party (PCP) and the SPLM in Geneva on 21 February 2001. This agreement caused a mixture of outrage and fear among his former colleagues and he was immediately jailed. The government was always fearful of alliances between the northern opposition and the SPLM/A, and, having just put the NDA to rest, it did not want to see an alliance involving the PCP, on account of its supposed loyalists in the security services and links to the Darfur-based Justice and Equality Movement (JEM). But, more than that, Turabi made clear that an agreement with Garang was possible and could be reached by committed Islamists. That was the real threat to the NCP, and it may well have served – as the PCP argued – as a stimulus to the ruling party to reach an agreement with the SPLM shortly thereafter.[13] Garang was always looking for ways to divide northerners, and in this thrust he went to the weak underbelly of the regime. That the initiative on the SPLM/A side came from Garang alone was made clear when I questioned Salva about it four weeks later in his headquarters in Yei: he said that he had never seen the agreement and requested that I provide him with the copy I had downloaded from the Internet.[14] Nothing in the end came of the agreement, although the PCP and SPLM/A continued to meet and Turabi regularly called for a popular uprising against the regime he had given birth to, and just as regularly was placed in prison or under house arrest.

But Garang also faced opposition within the movement he had given birth to, and on the eve of independence and less than a year before he died, he was almost overthrown by his compatriots. The episode began when rumors circulated in late November 2004 that Garang intended to arrest and dismiss his deputy, Salva Kiir. Within days virtually everyone in the SPLM/A leadership had heard them, and Salva – who was based in Yei in Equatoria – was joined by senior SPLA commanders from his home area of Warrap to protect him. A stalemate ensued, which only ended after Riek Machar carried out shuttle diplomacy that led Salva and Garang to agree to hold a conference of all senior members of the SPLM/A immediately in Rumbek. And during three extraordinary days between 29 November and 1 December the leadership effectively voted to express its lack of confidence in Garang. The details of the meeting are well known because the minutes were promptly leaked to the government-supporting *Al Ria Al Aam* newspaper in Khartoum and very quickly thereafter posted in their entirety on the Web.[15] Garang was not alone in being verbally attacked at this meeting (for example, James Wani Igga accused Deng Alor of diverting funds received from Nigeria), but the focus of the anger was largely directed at Garang, and even his closest confidantes heaped abuse on him.

Allegations of rampant corruption by Garang and many commanders, a lack of transparency and accountability, a lack of cohesion within the SPLM/A leadership structure, an absence of command structure and delegation of power, failure to develop a political system for the future governance of South Sudan, the absence of rule of law, and equitable regional representation – the list of complaints went on and on. Arthur Akuen, who was officially the SPLM/A's finance minister and would himself soon be accused of stealing $60 million of GoSS funds, said that he did not have the funds to manage because the chairman was also the finance officer and that 'Garang's leadership is bad and cannot be corrected.' Southerners, along with the entire country, were shocked. As one correspondent said, 'the clear message sent to Garang is that South Sudan will not tolerate his despotic rule and a leadership built on a delusional personality cult with an aura of invincibility and infallibility.'

But the correspondent was wrong: Garang survived, apparently because his comrades were too dependent upon him ('he carried the SPLM in his brief case' was how Salva put it), they could not agree on an alternative, and everyone feared division on the eve of the signing of the CPA. Thus Garang accepted the formation of three committees under Riek Machar, Salva Kiir, and James Wani Igga to put forward a package of reforms in the spheres of administration, military and governance (Young 2005b). These initiatives were premissed on the need to develop accountable institutions and restrict Garang's arbitrary decision-making. But almost as soon as the Rumbek conference was over Garang resorted to typical favoritism in the selection of disproportionate numbers of Bor Dinkas to attend senior administration courses in South Africa and in the selection of state advisers. Salva was replaced as chief of staff by Oyai Deng Ajak, promoted to lieutenant general, retired from the army, and given the considerably less powerful position of vice president of southern Sudan. Garang then went on to abolish the National Leadership Council. Nothing was done by Garang's Rumbek critics to rein him in, presumably out of fear that their actions could impede or even end the prospects of an agreement with the north, and thus it is safe to predict that had he lived it would have been only a matter of time before the next confrontation, revolt, or even (his) assassination.

Garang was a man who gave the impression that he could deliver more than was the case, when he could not even reconcile the contradictions within the SPLM, and as a result he left the organization and southern Sudan dependent on the international community. But with his death even his enemies in the SPLM/A elevated Garang to the status of an 'African hero' and loudly proclaimed that his vision would never die. But in practice, Garang's call for democracy had already been fatally tarnished before he died, and his appeal for a united reformed Sudan would die with the January 2011 referendum. It was only his legacy of militarism, authoritarianism, and weak government that would continue.

TWO

A FLAWED APPROACH
TO PEACEMAKING

The overthrow of Jafaar Nimeiri and the coming to power of a transitional military government and later an elected Umma Party government set the stage for peacemaking efforts, but the most promising attempt at achieving peace was the DUP–SPLM agreement, which was aborted when the National Islamic Front overthrew the Sadig al-Mahdi government. With the NIF committed to making the war against the SPLA a jihad, peacemaking efforts by ex-US president Carter and Nigerian president and OAU chairman Ibrahim Babangida had no chance of success. But their failure and the growing threat Sudan's war posed to regional security led the regional-based Inter-Governmental Authority on Development (IGAD) to assume a leading role in the peace process.

Although there is little indication that IGAD's peacemaking efforts were explicitly guided by the theoretical literature considered above, in practice they closely followed it. Confronted with war, the peacemakers never gave any indication that they considered proposing the structural changes of a 'positive peace' over a 'negative peace' of simply stopping the conflict. Faced with conservative peace partners anxious to protect their narrow interests, the peacemakers fell in line and supported a top-down process that precluded the involvement of other parties and civil society, and treated the entire exercise as a military-like operation that necessitated secrecy. Faced with the artificial distinction between democracy and peace, they came down firmly on the side of peace, and got neither. Responding to the fears of the NCP and SPLM, they refused to accept the presence of the Darfuri and eastern Sudan rebel groups and the NDA at the negotiating table, thus ensuring that their claimed comprehensive peace agreement was nothing of the sort. But perhaps the biggest misrepresentation was the claim that their efforts were dedicated to achieving a united Sudan when most of the negotiators on both sides of the table were separatists.

Pre-IGAD Efforts at Peacemaking

President Nimeiri holds the distinction of both ending Sudan's first civil war and ushering in the second war by undermining the Addis Ababa Agreement, and thereby ultimately digging his own political grave. The incoming Transitional Military Council appealed to the southern rebels to join the government and resolve their grievances peacefully, but it was not prepared to accept the SPLM/A as a national party or its demands to restructure the country, freeze sharia laws, end defense agreements with Arab countries, and hold a constitutional conference (Lesch 1998). As a result, this early effort at peacemaking collapsed. Two points should be noted here: first, sharia was to prove to be an enduring and difficult issue in successive attempts at resolving the conflict; second, southern self-determination, which was to be crucial to the eventual resolution of the conflict, was not raised at this time by either party.

The next internal effort at peace-building took place in a meeting between the National Salvation Alliance and the SPLM/A in March 1986 at Koka Dam in Ethiopia, where an agreement was reached on all the SPLM/A's demands. However, the refusal of the DUP and the NIF to participate in the discussions undermined this achievement. In July 1986, after the holding of national elections, Umma Party leader and prime minister Sadig al-Mahdi met SPLM/A leader John Garang and agreed to the Koka Dam recommendations: the meeting 'ended in a note of guided hope,'[1] but this hope was not to be fulfilled.

DUP leader Osman al-Mirghani then tried his hand at peacemaking and on 16 November 1988 signed an agreement with the SPLM, but the then Umma–NIF coalition refused to accept it. However, as a result of losses on the battlefield, declining SAF morale, and the way out provided by the DUP–SPLM/A agreement, the commander-in-chief of the army, Major General Fathi Almad Ali, presented Sadig with an ultimatum on 20 February 1989 signed by 150 senior officers demanding he form a national government (by which it was meant to bring the DUP on board) and accept the DUP–SPLM/A agreement, or provide the necessary weapons and supplies to win the war, and reverse the declining economy (Collins 2008: 169). This set in motion the NIF-led coup of 30 June 1989 and another and more violent phase of the war.

In such an unlikely environment, the SPLM/A held two rounds of talks with the new government in August 1989 in Addis Ababa and in December in Nairobi under former US president Jimmy Carter, but they quickly collapsed. Indeed, the NIF came to power to stop the peace process, but quickly began devoting increasing human and material resources to the war. Were this not enough, the SPLA suffered two further blows in 1991: the loss of its key ally, the Derg, and a revolt in the SPLM/A leadership.

Concern that the SPLM/A was near collapse led Nigerian president and OAU chairman Ibrahim Babangida to hold peace talks in Abuja in May–June 1992 (Young 2004). With a weakened rebel movement represented by factions led by Riek Machar and

John Garang, an increasingly confident NIF proposed that the constitution should be based on sharia, although the south could be exempt from *hudud* (the Islamic code of punishments). Both rebel factions pressed for a secular democratic system and the right of the south to a referendum on self-determination. This was the first time the SPLM/A proposed self-determination; it is not clear whether that was due to the fact that since he was no longer beholden to Mengistu, Garang could now endorse it, or that the party's negotiators had taken their own initiative. However, with Khartoum rejecting rebel proposals for secularism and a referendum, the talks collapsed.

A year passed and Babangida called for a second round of talks at Abuja, by which time the SPLM/A was militarily even weaker. Assuming a similar stance to that of the first round, Khartoum proposed power-sharing and balanced development, rejected secession, proposed a constitution that did not refer to Islam as the state religion, and exempted the south from certain provisions of sharia (Lesch 1998). The SPLM/A rejected Khartoum's federalist approach and called for confederation and a secular, democratic New Sudan, and held that if the government could not commit to them, the south and the 'marginalized territories' (the Nuba Mountains and southern Blue Nile), together with Abyei, should have a vote on confederation or separation. The critical issues of the separation of state and religion and self-determination again brought about the collapse of the negotiations. Such was the state of affairs on the eve of IGAD's first attempt to resolve the conflict.

The First Sudan IGAD Peace Initiative

The failure of the Nigerian efforts at peacemaking opened the door for the region to take up the gauntlet, but first a suitable mechanism had to be established. The impetus came from outside the region. The formation of the Inter-Governmental Authority on Drought and Development, the forerunner to IGAD, was largely due to pressure from aid agencies and international donors, while its subsequent assumption of responsibilities in the fields of peace and security followed new thinking on the role of regionalism and regional cooperation in safeguarding the international order (El-Affendi 2001). Thus IGADD launched a peace initiative at its Addis Ababa summit of 7 September 1993, and a Peace Committee made up of the heads of state of Ethiopia, Eritrea, Uganda, and Kenya was established, with President Daniel Arap Moi serving as chairman. The mediation process was handled by a standing committee comprising the foreign ministers from the same countries and chaired by Kenya. In addition, the Friends of IGADD was formed by leading Western countries and promised support for IGADD's peace-keeping role.

Against this background Sudan's president, Omar al-Bashir, proposed that IGADD take up the peace process. The reasons for Bashir's proposal included the desire to pre-empt any UN initiative, fear that in the absence of a viable peace process US military engagement under way in Somalia could spread to Sudan, and anticipation of a sympathetic hearing from the former Ethiopian and Eritrean rebel groups that his government had supported. The NCP considered the SPLM/A largely a proxy of Haile Mengistu Mariam and Uganda's President Museveni, but with the overthrow of the Ethiopian military regime it hoped for better relations with the new governments that came to power. Indeed, the incoming Ethiopian government strongly supported good neighborly relations and oversaw the expulsion of the SPLM/A from its territory as part of that commitment. But if Bashir had concluded that the leaders of Ethiopia and Eritrea would be sympathetic to Khartoum, he was soon to be badly disillusioned.

Counterbalancing the Eritreans and Ethiopians, the NCP assumed that Uganda was completely on the side of the SPLM/A, and while Djibouti as a fellow member of the Arab League and Organization of Islamic States would probably support Khartoum, it was not a member of the conflict committee. Kenya thus became the obvious regional candidate to lead the process. In the assessment of a NCP respondent, it was only peripherally involved in the provision of weapons and equipment for the SPLM/A and had few connections with the rebel leadership. Negatively, Kenya was the most subject to Western, and particularly British and American, influence and – in the view of the Khartoum government – its officials had less knowledge of the conflict in Sudan than their counterparts in Ethiopia and Eritrea. According to a NCP official, although IGADD was not the best forum and in any case was viewed as 'a platform,' it was the only group that could convince the SPLM/A to accept peace. The NCP also could not refuse an African initiative and it was assumed that IGADD would provide some protection against the partisan US, the 'number one player.'

As would soon become apparent, the countries of IGADD shared a collective interest in containing Sudan's civil war, and with the elevation to power of President Isias Aferworki of Eritrea and Prime Minister Meles Zenawi of Ethiopia in 1991, the organization had two dynamic leaders ready to assume the task. A Standing Committee on Peace in Sudan was established with Kenyan foreign minister Kalonzo Musyoka as chairman, and in March 1994 peace negotiations were officially launched in Nairobi. To the surprise of the parties, IGADD – largely as a result of the efforts of Ethiopian foreign minister Seyoum Mesfin – proposed a Declaration of Principles (DoP) that acknowledged the right of the south to self-determination, but made this contingent upon the failure of the NIF to introduce democracy and secularism. It also stipulated that Sudan must respond to the needs of a diverse population for social and political equality. Although implying that other groups besides the south suffered oppression in Sudan, the DoP reflected the SPLM/A–Mainstream and SPLM/A–United bargaining positions during the second round of negotiations in Abuja. Khartoum was shocked that the leaders of two parties which it had assisted in coming to power – the EPLF and the TPLF – would make a proposal so repellent to the government. The southern rebels of the SPLM/A–Mainstream and the SPLM/A–United accepted the DoP, but after considerable confusion in the government camp it was rejected, and a stalemate ensued for the next four years.

In response to the failure, the SPLM/A and the government turned their energies to fighting political and military battles and positioning themselves for what would inevitably be another encounter at the negotiating table. The SPLM/A built up its relations with the NDA, a loose grouping of northern opposition forces based in Asmara, as a means of bringing further pressure to bear on the government, dividing the north, and gaining acceptance from parties which arguably represented the majority of the Sudanese people. Politically this was expressed in the Asmara Declaration of June 1995, which included acceptance of self-determination for the south and other disputed areas, and separation of state and religion. But the self-determination endorsed by the Asmara Declaration followed from the IGAD DoP. Thus the Asmara Declaration gave priority to the establishment of democratic government and the removal of all remnants of the NIF, and agreement on a new constitution, after which the vote on self-determination would take place. All parties, including the SPLM, were committed to supporting unity in the resulting campaign.[2]

The NDA also gained considerable international support, particularly from the US, which at the least saw it as a means of weakening the NIF, and at most as an instrument for overthrowing the government. And in response to what was held to be an Islamist threat to their sovereignty, Ethiopia, Eritrea, and Uganda stepped up their military assistance to the SPLM/A, and by late 1995 were sending their armed forces deep into Sudan. In the wake of the attempted assassination of Egyptian president, Hosni Mubarak, by what were believed to be agents of the NIF in June 1995 in Addis Ababa, the US began assisting these 'frontline states' with US$20 million to protect themselves from Khartoum. This policy reached its height with the August 1998 US bombing of the El-Shifa plant in Khartoum and the October 1998 meeting of Secretary of State Madeleine Albright with the NDA and SPLM/A leadership in Kampala, where she made clear that the US favored regime change. Time was to prove that the NDA was a paper tiger, but that was not clear in the late 1990s. With considerable support from the region and indications that the Clinton administration was prepared to give increasing assistance to the NDA and the SPLM/A, the NIF had good reason to be concerned. ✓

Meanwhile, the Khartoum government pursued a strategy of 'peace from within' that led to the signing of the Khartoum Peace Agreement in 1997 with the South Sudan Independence Movement (SSIM) of Dr Riek Machar and a handful of smaller liberation groups, and the Fashoda Agreement with Dr Lam Akol of SPLM–United (Young 2006). Critically, these agreements acknowledged the right of the south to self-determination, a principle that was then enshrined in Article 113 of the 1998 constitution. Although the Khartoum Peace Agreement in many ways served as the model for the CPA, it did not gain regional or international legitimacy, and that made clear to the government that such efforts would never prove effective. This conclusion, together with the weakening of the regime in the divide over Turabi's expulsion, led the NIF to return to the IGAD bargaining table in October 1997, and in May 1998 it accepted the DoP as a basis for negotiations. However, with the outbreak of the Ethiopian–Eritrean war in the same month, the energy of the mediators and the incentive of the NIF to accept a process based on the DoP markedly decreased, and the IGAD Peace Initiative began to falter.

Against this background the IGAD Partners Forum and civil society groups got the IGAD states to agree to the establishment of a permanent secretariat and the appointment of a special envoy. In addition, IGAD turned its attention to gaining Western financial and political support and ensuring that other peace processes were not endorsed by the international community. The 1991 mandate was renewed in July 1999 with the support of the parties to the conflict, and a secretariat based in Nairobi was established to carry out mediation. It was also decided to have a special envoy appointed by the president of Kenya and for the other subcommittee members of Uganda, Ethiopia, and Eritrea each to appoint a full-time envoy to the peace process, although in practice their ambassadors to Kenya served as peace envoys. Ambassador Daniel Mboya, a veteran diplomat, was appointed special envoy and set about establishing the secretariat and conducting the mediation. However, despite this revamped system the July 1999 talks in Nairobi did not make any substantive progress; nor did two further rounds in 2000.

In response to the perceived weaknesses of the IGAD process, a number of other peace efforts were launched. Foremost was the Joint Libyan Egyptian Initiative (JLEI), which was concerned with the absence of the northern opposition, African domination of the peace process, and the lack of a formal role for Egypt, given its considerable interest in Sudan. This initiative also reflected Libyan and Egyptian opposition to self-determination for southern Sudan, which was seen as a threat to Cairo's access to the waters of the Nile. Khartoum and the SPLM/A both agreed to the JLEI principles, but the latter made clear it wanted the document revised to include self-determination, secularism, and coordination of the JLEI with the IGAD peace process; in other words it rejected the document. The JLEI largely withered, but it represented a strong statement of Egyptian fears about southern Sudan self-determination as well as the absence of the northern opposition forces from the negotiations.

Out of fear of the imminent collapse of the IGAD peace process Nigeria again attempted to promote peace in Sudan. This effort came to nothing, but it brought to the fore the issues at the heart of the conflict – religion, race, and regional disparities. This had resonance far beyond the country's borders. Moreover, the focus of this effort, in contrast to IGAD, was a more inclusive process that involved the engagement of the major political forces of the north and the south. Another weakness of the IGAD peace process was attributable to tensions between the countries of the region. These tensions reached their height with the outbreak of the Ethio–Eritrean War in 1998.

The Second IGAD Peace Initiative: May 2002 to January 2005

American supporters of Garang worked to reconstruct his image from that of a communist in league with the Derg and Eastern Bloc to that of a heroic leader of an African liberation movement. This began to change American conceptions of Sudan's civil war. This was made clear in November 1997 when President Clinton signed an executive order imposing comprehensive trade and economic sanctions on the Khartoum government, followed on 29 November 1999 by Clinton authorizing the US to supply food directly to the SPLA, even though this contravened previous laws forbidding funding of belligerents in conflict. The provision was proposed by Secretary of State Madeleine Albright and Assistant Secretary Susan Rice and supported by familiar names like Representative Donald Payne, Roger Winter of the Committee on Refugees, and Baroness Caroline Cox of Christian Solidarity International. The measure was, however, strongly opposed by

many, including former president Jimmy Carter, who had been
working for reconciliation between Bashir and Museveni and was
known to be at odds with the policies of Clinton, and later Rice,
on Sudan. A *New York Times* editorial also opposed the measure,
concluding that 'One of the tragedies of Sudan's war is that John
Garang's SPLA has squandered a sympathetic cause. Though its
members claim to be "Christians" resisting Islamization, they
behaved like an occupying army, killing, raping and pillaging'
(*New York Times* 1999).

President George W. Bush's appointment of special peace
envoy Senator Danforth, five days before the 11 September attacks,
demonstrated growing US concern about the faltering Sudan
peace process and the danger of 'failed states.' Additional pressure was brought to bear by Sudan being identified as one of
seven countries on a State Department list of state sponsors of
terrorism. Interest in Sudan by a number of key constituencies
– the Congressional Black Caucus, the Christian right, liberals,
human rights activists, American humanitarian agencies, and the
oil lobby (upset at being denied entry into the potentially lucra-
tive Sudan market because of American sanctions) – combined
with heightened concerns about international terrorism after 11
September, and contributed to demands for increased US involvement in Sudan.

Sudanese government officials, however, denied claims that US
pressure was decisive in bringing them to the table and forcing
concessions. They point out that President Bashir was clear that
the government 'was compelled to fight but did not want to fight,'
and that a 'strategic decision' had been made to embrace peace.
Certainly, on the eve of the last IGAD attempt at peacemaking
the government's security position was improving as it appeared
to be in control of the oilfields and was able to use the windfall
revenues to buy increasingly sophisticated military hardware.
Moreover, even with the end of the Ethio–Eritrean War, Addis

Ababa continued to have cooperative relations with the regime. And internally, although the split in the regime with the departure of Turabi and his followers was a major shock, by 2002 it appeared to be weathering the storm. Nonetheless, the government's assessment was that even if the SPLA were defeated, there would still be a major problem in the south that had to be confronted, and although the threat posed by the region had declined it could again be resurrected.

This reasoning was not without foundation, but does not explain why the NIF opposed the peacemaking efforts of the Sadig al-Mahdi government and why it refused to implement the provisions of the Khartoum Peace Agreement. It would seem that the NIF feared the US would significantly increase support for the SPLA and other armed groups. And this would explain the rapid jettisoning of its expansionist Islamist policy in the region, the offer to turn Osama bin Laden over to the US, and cooperation with the Americans in the field of intelligence. However, entering a peace process, particularly one which restricted participation to the NIF and SPLM/A and defined Sudan's conflict in exclusively north–south terms, was attractive because it would undermine the alliance between the SPLM/A and its northern allies and make survival of the agreement dependent upon its signatories, thus providing a new lease of life for the embattled regime. Providing further encouragement were signals sent by the incoming Bush administration that, contrary to the Clinton administration's focus on regime change, it would attempt to engage the regime constructively.

The starting point for heightened US engagement in the peace process was the report by Senator Danforth which proposed a series of confidence-building measures, including a ceasefire in the Nuba Mountains, zones and times of tranquility in which vaccinations and other humanitarian interventions could be carried out, a commission to report on the issue of slavery, an end to attacks on civilian targets, and the formation of an organization on the ground to ensure that allegations of such acts by both armed groups were impartially investigated (Danforth 2002). In October 2002 the Sudan Peace Act was passed, which called for further sanctions if the Government of Sudan was found to be not participating in the peace negotiations in good faith. Whether or not these measures increased mutual confidence between the government and the SPLM/A is doubtful, but they did suggest the US was prepared to use power to achieve its ends. Significantly, Danforth never mentioned any need for a democratic transformation as part of the peace process. Also significant was that, despite appeals from various sources that it fashion its own peace initiative, the US administration made clear that it supported regional efforts led by IGAD and would not lead a separate peace process.

The rejuvenation of the peace process in its final phase was thus a response to growing US interest in Sudan's conflict and its support for IGAD's efforts. IGAD meanwhile replaced Ambassador Daniel Mboya with General Lazaro Sumbeiywo as special envoy while the Sudan IGAD secretariat was legalized under Kenyan law, which gave its members diplomatic status and conferred on Sumbeiywo the dual status of special envoy and Kenyan ambassador for peace. Further strengthening the position of General Sumbeiywo was his relationship with President Daniel Arap Moi, with whom he had worked closely for more than a decade. The increasing engagement of these officials in the peace process reinforced the growing sense of Kenyan government ownership of the process, but at the same time weakened the link with the IGAD secretariat. While the IGAD link weakened, that between Nairobi and Washington strengthened.

In the wake of the 9/11 attacks on the US, the Americans increasingly called upon Kenya to assume a major role in the war on terror because of the strategic location of its large Muslim population living on the coast across from the volatile Gulf. The terrorist bombing of the US embassy in Nairobi in August 1998 served further to link Kenya to the US and its policies in the region, whereupon it became a major recipient of security assistance. In addition to British bases that had long been in the country, land was granted to the US military in north-eastern Kenya, Mombasa became a major centre for Western warships patrolling the Gulf, and intelligence cooperation expanded. And, with the link being drawn in the US between national security and the Sudan peace process, the Americans would be reassured that Kenya was designated to play a dominant role, and that the negotiations would be led by General Sumbeiywo, who had received his education in the US, had previously directed the Kenyan intelligence service, was the head of the army, and had developed relations with the leadership of the SPLM/A during the retreat from its bases in Ethiopia in 1991.

The first session of what would prove to be the last phase of the Sudan peace process began at Karen on the outskirts of Nairobi in May 2002. The NCP negotiating team was led by Idris Moham-med, a state minister in the Office of the Presidency, and the SPLM team was headed by Elijah Malok, an uncle of Garang. The first concern was to gain acceptance of a framework agreement, but the Karen meetings ended with only minimal progress.

The next round began at the town of Machakos on 17 June 2002, with Idris still leading the government delegation; in the SPLM camp Elijah was replaced by another Garang loyalist, Nhial Deng Nhial. In an attempt to speed up the slow pace, Sumbeiywo and the mediators drafted a single negotiating text, but crucially it did not stipulate the right of south Sudan to self-determination. Not only was the SPLM furious, but the US envoy walked out of the talks in frustration, although Senator Danforth also viewed self-determination as beyond the accep-tance of the NIF (Waithaka Waihenya 2006). In the wake of this setback, Sumbeiywo arranged for the parties to express their anger through a series of workshops and plenums dealing with such issues as African identity, slavery, and self-determination. The mediators considered this exercise useful, but the Americans viewed it as time-wasting since it did not lead to a return to the actual negotiations.

In Khartoum the ruling party was struggling with the issue. A southern minister in the national government told the author how he warned a cabinet meeting that if it could not accept self-determination at Machakos then it would cast doubt on its commitment to the Khartoum Peace Agreement, and that could encourage defections to the SPLA. The same minister and another minister told me they urged the SPLM negotiating team not to oppose the NCP's desire to retain sharia, as doing so would serve to encourage southerners to vote for secession. They noted that the Khartoum Peace Agreement accepted sharia and instead focused on the commitment to self-determination. Underlying their concern was that, at Garang's behest, the SPLM negotiating team would agree to an acknowledgement of the right to self-determination, but it would be realized by a referendum in which the choice would be limited to unity, confederation, or federation, and not secession. Meanwhile, others were telling Danforth and the Americans that there could be no peace agreement without a commitment to self-determination. And, to drive the point home, a number of southern officials in Khartoum organized a demonstration at Machakos, calling for self-determination.

Eventually the parties reached agreement on what would become known as the Machakos Protocol, which was signed by General Salva Kiir on behalf of the SPLM/A and Dr Ghazi Salhudin on behalf of the NCP before President Moi at State House on 20 July 2002. Significantly, the Protocol fully embraced self-determination. The first response of the Americans was to reject it out of hand on the grounds that Sumbeiywo had

not first consulted them (Waithaka Waihenya 2006). Almost
certainly they were caught off guard by the agreement on self-
determination given that their understanding of the negotiating
position of the SPLM derived from their meetings with Garang,
who opposed such a forthright commitment. Indeed, Garang was
also caught off guard by the commitment of Salva on behalf of
the SPLM. According to one person close to him at the time,
'Garang went berserk.' There was little doubt as to Salva Kiir's
separatist thinking then and later, but the loyal deputy for once
took the initiative and was widely applauded in the SPLA, which
was always a separatist organization, the rhetoric of Garang notwithstanding. There is little doubt that this pivotal action was
the starting point of the tensions between Garang and Salva that
would come close to bringing about the collapse of the SPLM/A
a few years later.

Garang soon appreciated that he could do little about an agreement already signed, and to berate Salva publicly would make
clear that he was not in control and would set him at odds with
the rest of the movement, which strongly endorsed the Machakos
Protocol. But Garang promptly replaced Salva with Nhial Deng
and the commitment to self-determination in the form of a referendum was never again considered. After due consultation with
Garang and testing the political waters, the US endorsed and
even praised the Machakos Protocol. Dr Ghazi was also roundly
criticized in the NCP for signing the document, and he too was
removed from the negotiations. The NDA were likewise shocked
by the Machakos commitment to southern self-determination,
which went much further than that in the Asmara Declaration
and was in complete contradiction to assurances Garang had
given the organization.

While both the Communiqué of the IGAD Ministerial Sub-
Committee on Sudan of 19–23 July 1999 and the Joint Communiqué of the First Session of the Political Committee Task

Force of 20 July 2002 emphasized their commitment to the DoP, the Machakos Protocol – which provided the framework – bears only superficial resemblance to it. Special Envoy Sumbeiywo described the DoP as a 'complete analysis' (quoted in Waithaka 2006). He said that he 'translated the DoP into a single text and then zeroed in on the two main issues of self-determination and separation of state and religion' (84). In other words, Machakos was intended to be a simplification, but in practice it ignored key principles of the DoP. Although only a page in length, the DoP endorsed the right of the south to self-determination, but at the same time was designed both to ease the concerns of President Bashir and to mesh with Garang's vision of New Sudan, which emphasized the need to overcome broader inequities in the Sudanese state and did not reduce the problem to merely a north–south dimension. Indeed, the DoP stipulated:

> 3.4 A secular and democratic state must be established in the Sudan. Freedom of belief and worship and religious practice shall be guaranteed in full to all Sudanese citizens. State and religion shall be separated. The basis of personal and family laws can be religion and customs.
>
> 3.5 Appropriate and fair sharing of wealth among the various people of the Sudan must be realised.

While the DoP called for the separation of state and religion, Machakos only endorsed this principle in the south. As a result, Machakos moved from a broader vision of Sudan's ills to meeting the immediate needs of the parties. Moreover, while the DoP made the right of the south to self-determination subject to the failure of the national government to introduce democracy, secularism, and the fair distribution of resources, Machakos granted the south the right to self-determination after a transitional period, irrespective of any changes within the central state. Thus, despite IGAD's contention that the DoP formed the basis of the Sudan peace

progress, the widespread view at the time held Machakos to be
a breakthrough, contradicting the assertion (above) by General
Sumbeiywo that Machakos was the distilled political essence of
the DoP. In reality the Machakos Protocol entered very different
political waters. Indeed, a SPLM respondent involved in the
negotiations concluded there was 'no real link between the DoP
and the Machakos Protocol,' and a NCP negotiator informed me
that 'Machakos was completely different than the DOP,' although
not everyone shared this assessment. Moreover, given the fact that
much of the later period of the IGAD peace process took place in
the shadow of the humanitarian disaster in Darfur, which made
clear that Sudan's problems could not be reduced to a north–south
conceptualization, much less a Muslim–Christian conflict, the
analysis that underpinned the DoP looks more convincing than
the reductionism of the Machakos Protocol. Even at the time the
Machakos Protocol looked like a road map for the secession of
southern Sudan and not the comprehensive agreement that its
backers claimed.

In any case the government's concession of self-determination
had already been accepted in a number of forums, while the
SPLM/A leaders at the time said they did not expect the NCP to
carry out the self-determination clause. What appears to have been
the case is the SPLM/A lacked trust in the NCP and needed yet
another promise of self-determination, this time before the international community. It also did not want to acknowledge either
the legitimacy of the Khartoum and Fashoda Peace Agreements
(while one SPLM/A negotiator concluded that they 'laid the basis
for the CPA,' another told me these agreements were 'documents
signed and meant to die') or the 1998 Constitution, and wanted
to claim credit for gaining this concession. Meanwhile, the NCP
attempted to present self-determination as a great compromise
and convince themselves that with Garang committed to unity he
would eventually bring the SPLM/A and southerners around to

his view. Against this background the 'compromise' at the heart
of the Machakos Protocol seems far less significant than it was
made out to be.

Another issue generating considerable controversy in the southern camp during negotiations was the status of Abyei, Nuba
Mountains, and South Blue Nile. Garang insisted on pressing
for the inclusion of these territories in the Protocol. The fact that
some of his closest colleagues in the SPLM/A were from Abyei,
as was Sudan's best-known son, Francis Deng, another Garang
loyalist, made it difficult to leave these territories outside the
negotiations. But many southerners contended that the Abyei
chiefs who decided to link their territory to the north had to
take the lead in resolving the problem, and the other areas were
constitutionally part of the north, and thus the inclusion of these
three territories in the peace process would be opposed by the
NCP and unduly complicate the negotiations. In the face of
considerable opposition Garang had to relent and there was no
mention of the territories in the Machakos Protocol.

The result, however, was that the SPLM/A leaders from these
territories faced a near uprising from their followers. Malik Agar
Eyre from South Blue Nile and Abdel Aziz al-Hilu from the Nuba
Mountains demanded that the marginalized territories be consid-
ered part of the south and granted the right to self-determination.
Indeed, dissatisfaction ran so high among SPLM/A ranks after
the South Blue Nile and Southern Kordofan Protocol, particularly
among Nuba Mountain supporters, that the party almost split.
This appeared to be another reason why Garang removed Salva
Kiir as head of the SPLM negotiating team.

Apart from the issue of self-determination for the south, probably the key condition in the Machakos Protocol was the commitment by both parties 'to make unity attractive,' a provision
which was assumed to mean that southern Sudanese should be
convinced that their rights and culture would be protected in

Sudan and they would be treated as valued citizens. However, the SPLM contended that provision only applied to the NCP, and in any case no one on the SPLM negotiating team believed the government would live up to this commitment. As a result, this provision was effectively held as a 'get out of Sudan' card since the SPLM leadership remained convinced through to the referendum that the NCP would not establish the democratic conditions that would make unity attractive for southerners. One former SPLM negotiator remarked to me, 'unity is a danger to the survival of the NCP' because a genuine democratic system would be its undoing, and noted that even before the start of the IGAD peace process senior members of the ruling party had agitated for an early separation of the south to ensure their continuing control over the Muslim heartland in the north.

But the contradictions were not restricted to the government camp. While formally committed to a united 'New Sudan,' the commanders and soldiers of the SPLA were motivated by the desire for southern independence, and this bedevilled the negotiations and complicated the peace process. A NCP respondent said: 'Garang had his own understanding of unity and it was not that of the people.'

Nonetheless, the preamble of the Machakos Protocol refers to the 'commitment to a negotiated, peaceful, comprehensive resolution to the Sudan Conflict within the Unity of Sudan' (Machakos Protocol 2002: Preamble). The first principle of the Machakos Protocol in turn is 'That the unity of the Sudan, based on the free will of its people to democratic governance, accountability, equality, respect, and justice for all citizens of the Sudan is and shall be the priority of the parties and that it is possible to redress the grievances of the people of South Sudan and to meet their aspirations within such a framework' (Machakos Protocol 2002: Principles, 1.1). Many more references in a similar vein can be found throughout the CPA, thus making clear the commitment to unity and the fact that both parties shared that commitment. And yet it is clear that many members of the SPLM negotiating team were separatists, including Salva Kiir, who signed the document on behalf of the SPLM.

Support for southern separatism was not restricted to the SPLM. This is suggested by the unwillingness of the NCP to permit other rebel groups to participate in the negotiations, which would give them a more country-wide character; the NCP insistence that the negotiations be understood solely as a north–south affair, an ideology that repeatedly put the commitment to Islam above the integrity of Sudan; and – as will be seen later – the party's less than robust support for the unity campaign during the referendum. And it is equally hard to believe that the mediators, ambassador/envoys, and the US and its allies also did not know, or did not suspect, the hypocrisy of the commitment to unity. It is almost as if there had been a collective effort to delude the Sudanese public and international community as to the nature of the agreement that was being reached.

The Machakos Protocol is equally forthright in its commitment to Sudan's democratic transformation, although there is good reason to question the sincerity. The mediators and belligerents appeared to appreciate that the legitimacy of the peace agreement was dependent upon a commitment to democratic transformation. The Protocol is replete with reference to 'democratic governance, accountability, equality, respect, and justice for all citizens of Sudan' (Section 1.1), asserting 'that the people of South Sudan have the right to control and govern affairs in their region' (Section 1.2), and that Sudan 'establish a democratic system of governance' (Section 1.6).

It is thus striking that a NCP negotiator told me that 'there was no real democratic conviction on either side.' A southern SPLM negotiator contended that 'all the protocols were signed in bad faith' and most of his colleagues appeared to share this sentiment. Many SPLM negotiators also felt that, despite promises to the contrary, a southern Christian would never be accepted as president of Sudan, and that included Garang, had he lived. Not only did the parties apparently not believe in the exercise they were pursuing, but it would soon become apparent that a major weakness of Machakos lay in the gap between the democratic phrases and the means to give this language concrete expression. Just as there was a disjunction in the process between the broader vision of the DoP and Machakos which was designed to meet the concerns of the ruling parties of the north and south, so there was another gap between the democratic claims of Machakos, the utilitarianism of the protocols that followed, and the less than democratic approach utilized.

From Two-Party Dominance
to the Dominance of Two People

Machakos was important because even if it revisited old ground, it nonetheless involved the two parties making commitments to one another, to their constituencies, and – through the mediators, ambassador/envoys, and observers – to the world that they would seriously attempt to reach a peace agreement, or at least such was the image being projected. Another statement of this commitment was a meeting between John Garang and President Omar al-Bashir in Kampala immediately after the signing of the Machakos Protocol. While numerous leaders attempted to host this meeting, the SPLM/A decided on Kampala as a means to thank President Museveni for the support he had given them. Perhaps Garang also wanted to embarrass Bashir, since the latter reviled Museveni.

But before the negotiations could move forward, there was a major controversy over the SPLM/A insistence that deliberations over a ceasefire agreement be left to the final stage of the peace process because it was their principal means to bring pressure against the government. The NCP was equally adamant that if the negotiations were to be treated seriously there needed to be agreement on a ceasefire. Much to the anger of the government, Sumbeiywo accepted the SPLM/A contention that simultaneous fighting and talking would prevent 'the frozen status quo of the battlefield being interpreted into an unjust agreement at the negotiating table' (quoted in Martin 2006: 64). Whether as a means to advance its position at the bargaining table or for Garang to undermine the entire peace process in light of his unhappiness with the Machakos Protocol,[3] the SPLA captured the strategic Equatorian town of Torit in September 2002. The reason to suspect the latter is that since the outcome of the peace process would inevitably result in all of the south passing to the SPLM, there could be no military advantage in capturing more territory.

NCP anger at the capture of the town was also due to the large number of senior military officials killed in the attack, as well as Mulla Ahmed Haj, a close friend of President Bashir and a leading Islamist. The NCP walked out of the negotiations, and six weeks later Torit was retaken by the SAF, heavily supported by the SSDF, without much of a fight since the town was largely defended by youngsters, some brought in from the secondary school in Rumbek and others just returned from training in Cuba. The government returned to the negotiations and insisted on a comprehensive cessation of hostilities, which was supported by the Americans and General Sumbeiywo. An agreement was quickly reached that, in the Special Envoy's words, continued 'more than less' until the signing of the CPA.

With the ceasefire under their belt the mediators attempted to produce an all-encompassing proposal that would resolve the outstanding issues arising out of the elaborations of the Machakos Protocol. Although assured that it could be revised, the NCP nonetheless contended that the proposal – called the Nakuru

Framework – abandoned the language of the Machakos Protocol, deviated from the unity in Sudan, and gave too much autonomy to the south. In the view of the NCP negotiating team the Nakuru Framework was an unwelcome level of engagement by the advisers, and their quick and emphatic rejection of it was meant to send the powerful message that they, and not the mediators, were in control of the process. The SPLM/A were largely sympathetic to the Nakuru Framework and accused the NCP of attempting to 'derail the process.' Likewise the Nakuru document ruled out participation by the liberation movements that signed the Khartoum and Fashoda Peace Agreements in the interim security arrangements, which caused 'a lot of unease among the parties' (Akol 2009: 308).

While some of the elements that most upset the NCP, like the proposal for maintaining a separate SPLA army, were eventually accepted in the Security Arrangements Agreement, the government's threat to leave the negotiations proved effective. The mediators backed down and did not again attempt to put before the parties a holistic approach to resolving outstanding problems. Instead they followed the parties that preferred a piecemeal approach.

The NCP had complained from the inception of the peace process in the mid-1990s that even through rarely present, John Garang micro-managed his negotiating team. It also concluded that Garang only wanted to use the various negotiations as forums to strengthen his political position, and remained committed to a military victory. Garang made clear he would only sit at the table if President Omar al-Bashir joined him. But although known to be under some pressure from his negotiating team, Bashir never agreed to participate in the Naivasha negotiations. Garang's reasoning was apparently twofold: first, he would suffer a loss of dignity by going face-to-face with someone of a lesser standing than the Sudanese head of state; second, should the negotiations break down, they would be that much more difficult to restart. And, for his part, President Bashir never agreed to negotiate directly with Garang and thereby give him the status of an equal. Thus those anxious to bring dynamism to the flagging peace process began to propose that first vice president Ali Osman Taha, widely believed in the international community at the time to be the real power-holder in the north, lead the NCP negotiating team.

Ali Osman Taha's leadership of the negotiations was the result of a number of factors. Although Bashir met Garang for the first time in Kampala on 27 and 28 July, in the wake of the signing of the Machakos Protocol, they apparently agreed to take the talks to a higher level. Second, there was growing disenchantment by the US and its allies with the slow pace of negotiations, which was in part put down to Ghazi Salhudin's leadership of the NCP negotiating team. Third, it was known that Ali Osman had reservations about the peace process; because of his seniority in the government many people involved in the negotiations concluded that he must be brought on board to win his support. Although Ghazi was a very senior member of the government, with the agreement on the Machakos Protocol the negotiations had raised expectations of a final peace agreement and this necessitated the highest level of support from the government.

Against this background, various individuals started pressing for Garang and Ali Osman to lead their respective negotiating teams. Kenyan foreign minister Kalonzo Musyoka took the message to President Bashir in Khartoum that a negotiating team led by the first vice president would be welcome, and the Americans invited Ali Osman to a private meeting at the US embassy in London. There he was pressed to lead the NCP negotiating team and in return was assured that the achievement of peace would lead to improved relations with Washington, and on that basis he accepted.

Garang was equally reluctant to sign up to the idea of going head-to-head with Ali Osman in negotiations. One particularly influential voice in favor, however, was that of Abel Alier, leader of the first autonomous government in southern Sudan and a confidant of Bashir. Although Garang eventually relented, he did not believe these negotiations would actually materialize. And while Ali Osman agreed to lead the negotiations, he and his government were convinced that Garang would not meet with him because he had failed to meet with him on three occasions previously. As a result, although a date for their meeting was planned, Garang went ahead with a conference of his military commanders in Rumbek and was surprised to find that Ali Osman was in Nairobi waiting for him. A series of phone calls took place with SPLM/A allies in Khartoum, who told Garang that Ali Osman was on his way out of the leadership and held that it would be a mistake to meet him. Moreover, according to a senior official close to these events, apart from his deputy Salva Kiir and Pagan Amum, virtually all the rest of his advisers and the 3,000 commanders in Rumbek advised him not to meet Ali. But with Ali Osman waiting in Kenya for the meeting, Kalonzo Musyoka told SPLM official Dr Justin Yac that if Garang did not attend the meeting his party would have to leave the country. In the end Garang was convinced by the arguments of Yac and others that if he did not meet the first vice president the government would be able to argue convincingly before the international community, and particularly the US, that he and the SPLM/A were not serious about the peace negotiations. More ominously, the stakes had been raised so high that if this meeting did not take place there was a real danger that the entire peace process would collapse.

Although appearing reluctant to enter such high-level negotiations, the proposal was timely for the government, as the SPLM was widely perceived as not being genuine in its commitment to the peace process, and by taking the negotiations to a higher level it would do much to strengthen this view. And if Garang did not show up for the first face-to-face meeting, and that was the government's assumption, the latter would gain the high ground in the propaganda war. But Garang still hedged his bets and Ali Osman had to wait four days for him to show up. Moreover, for a great strategist like Garang, who was constantly trying to create divisions in the northern camp, it would be difficult not to engage one of the most senior officials in the NCP in the hope that it would breed suspicion in the enemy camp.

Although they were initially very wary, their relations improved and soon the SPLM–NCP negotiations were largely reduced to Garang–Ali Osman negotiations. The international diplomats and others following the process were almost delirious with joy at their achievement and were convinced it heralded a successful outcome. Indeed, both Washington and Nairobi would claim the achievement was due to their particular efforts. The result, however, was clear: first, peacemaking was reduced to two parties and then it was further narrowed to only two individuals. There is no doubt that the presence of Garang and Ali Osman at the negotiations had the desired effect of accelerating the pace of the negotiations since all disputes between the parties were referred to the mediation team and then sent on to the leaders, who were fully authorized to decide on them. That is to say, Garang had almost unlimited authority to decide, while Ali Osman was known to have phoned Khartoum and on a few occasions fly to the capital for consultations. Ali Osman appeared to have a wide mandate to negotiate, and as a result took initiatives that later produced resentment among leading members of the government. One area of particular concern in Khartoum was Ali's agreement that the Sudanese national army be entirely removed from southern Sudan by July 2007, acceptance of which appeared to acknowledge that it was an army of occupation, the removal of which would pave the way for the south's independence. This was not understood by the mediators and analysts, who considered the domination of the peace talks by John Garang and the first vice president a great achievement and signalled the impending success of the effort.

However, with the death of John Garang in a helicopter crash on 30 July 2005, and the fact that first vice president Ali Osman did not lead the NCP government, as was assumed by many at the time, there is good reason to doubt whether leaving the leadership of the peace process to two people was the great achievement its promoters proclaimed. The arguments in favor of Garang and Ali Osman leading the process included: raising the level of the negotiations, putting people at the table who had the highest authority in their respective parties, making clear the seriousness with which both parties viewed the negotiations, and giving hope that the negotiations would be successful. But the arguments against this approach are in retrospect equally compelling: it left the fate of the peace process in their hands and assumed (wrongly as it turned out) they would continue to be in positions of authority to implement the agreement they reached, risked a complete breakdown of the negotiations if their talks failed, and played to the institutional weaknesses of Sudan by making the process dependent upon two personalities. That is, since a major weakness of Sudanese governance in both the north and south, but particularly the south, was the role of key individuals at the expense of institutions and accountability, then the final phase of the negotiations only reinforced this weakness.

The Garang–Ali Osman talks also produced secrecy and rumors that they were making private deals, which even some of Garang's closest colleagues thought was possible. We cannot know if there were any secret deals or if the talks represented the inauguration of Ali Osman's proposal for a 'political partnership' between the NCP and the SPLM/A, but some of the decisions that came out of the talks suggest it. Thus while the strong resistance of the NCP to proposals for international guarantees of the peace agreement were predictable, Garang's opposition to them was harder to understand. People close to the meetings report that Garang also opposed the formation of a Truth and Reconciliation Commission and did not accept that the proposed Assessment and Evaluation Commission should have a strong mandate and report back to IGAD or another international body. One mediator speculated that Garang was comfortable abusing the NCP for its undemocratic practices, but would not want the AEC probing matters of governance or overseeing elections in a south Sudan that might well not meet international standards. Also not easy to understand was Ali Osman's agreement that the Sudanese national army be entirely removed from southern Sudan by July 2007. While Garang alternately entertained the possibilities of a political partnership with either the NCP or the NDA, Ali Osman's proposal was ultimately more attractive because, first, the NCP would be the signatory to the CPA while some leading members of the NDA were known to oppose elements of it, and, second, the NCP held state power, and the best the NDA could hope for was to ride to power on the backs of the SPLM/A.

Although Garang kept his options open on a full-fledged political partnership with the NCP, he and Ali Osman both operated as if they would hold the presidency and could work out the inevitable problems of the agreement's implementation. Thus the two agreed that critical issues ranging from Abyei to border demarcation would ultimately be deferred to and resolved in the presidency. In the event, many of the most intractable problems facing the implementation of the CPA were left to the presidency; however, with the death of Garang and his replacement by Salva Kiir these problems remained unresolved. What appeared to be a useful expedient at the time soon haunted the implementation of the CPA.

Simultaneous with the domination of the peace process by Garang and Ali Osman was the growing role of the foreign, and largely American, experts and think-tanks, which prepared a range of papers and proposals. Probably most significant was the notion of 'two systems, one state.' These documents and the deferral to Garang and Ali Osman served to undermine the efforts of the two negotiating teams to reach common understandings and agreements. As one NCP respondent put it, the foreign experts 'did our homework for us' and increasingly that had the effect of sidelining the negotiating teams. Indeed, the relevance of the meetings of the negotiating teams declined in tandem with the rise of the foreign experts and the focus on Garang and Ali Osman. The role of Special Envoy Sumbeiywo and the mediation team also declined; indeed, they largely lost control of the process and were reduced to a formal presence, repeatedly going to Garang and Ali Osman for updates, according to NCP and SPLM negotiators.

The death of Garang left a major gap in the peace process. It quickly became apparent that Salva Kiir and his supporters had a different approach. Meanwhile, Ali Osman was, as one SPLM respondent put it, 'a victim of the CPA.' With the death of his partner Garang he lost considerable authority, and his policy of making concessions in the peace process to normalize relations between Khartoum and Washington did not bear fruit. While Senator Danforth repeatedly held that the NCP would only move away from its hardline approach if the US could provide positive incentives to the regime, the Bush administration concluded that it had little room to maneuver in the face of the mounting tragedy in Darfur and rising domestic demands for stronger action against Khartoum. As a result, Ali Osman was increasingly attacked by NCP hardliners led by Nafie Ali Nafie, who held that he gave away too much at Naivasha and was naive to believe American promises.

The Challenge of an Inclusive Peace Process

While the NDA, other political groups in both the north and south of the country, and civil society organizations repeatedly requested formal or observer status in the negotiations, they were rebuffed. And this failure to widen the peace process contributed to many of the problems that emerged in the post-CPA period. General Sumbeiywo opposed civil society having a role: 'In this negotiation there is inclusivity. We have attempted to include other people in the south and the north so it is not a monopoly of the SPLM/A and the government' (quoted in Waihenya 2006). While some political parties and elements of civil society were consulted by the parties, the evidence for his claim is lacking. Sumbeiywo then went on to say that the process would be tested at the ballot box, which, as will be seen below, did not occur.

Although both the SPLM/A and the NCP appeared sympathetic to the interests of some of the other parties, they did not want them to have a role in the peace process, and that included their closest allies. The NCP opposed bringing the NDA to the negotiating table because it feared being ganged up on, while the SPLM/A in turn feared that members of the NDA might make common cause with their northern brothers and their participation would detract from the north–south focus of the negotiations. Meanwhile, the South Sudan Defense Force, which was of comparable size to the SPLA, was not brought into the negotiations. On the one hand, the NCP feared that the SSDF might make common cause with their southern brothers in the SPLA; on the other hand, the SPLM viewed them as NCP dupes and feared their presence would disprove the SPLA's claim to control militarily most of rural southern Sudan. The failure to engage the SSDF continued to be a problem even after South Sudan's independence.

NCP negotiators held that the political parties were not ready for inclusion, although if that was the case it was due to years of government repression. It was also alleged that the major political parties did not press strongly for a place at the negotiating table because they did not believe the peace process would be successful and their participation would give the government a measure of legitimacy that was not warranted. Umma Party leader Sadig al-Mahdi was supportive of the process from the beginning, but concluded it would only reach a bilateral agreement, after which there would be need for wider consultation leading to a national agreement. The DUP's Osman al-Mirghani did not believe the peace process would be successful and supported the party's continuing links with the SPLM/A through the NDA and hence did not demand a place at the bargaining table. However, in the event, one opposition respondent informed me that 'Garang forgot his NDA membership and told Mirghani that the SPLM would represent their interests.'

A negotiator for the NCP claimed the government 'took on board' the principles behind the Asmara Declaration and 'in substance these opposition parties were involved,' but their physical presence would have been more convincing than such professions. It is also true that the NCP encouraged fractures in the Umma Party and DUP and then gave members of these dissident groups positions within the government. In addition, it gave positions to a number of fledgling southern groups and to the United Democratic Salvation Front, in theory the political wing of the SSDF, and the NCP team regularly contained southerners (Young 2006). The notion, however, that the government was a coalition, as was sometimes argued, is disingenuous.

Civil society was also denied participation in the negotiations. Northern Sudan had one of the most developed and politically active civil societies in Africa in the post-colonial era, but by the late 1980s it had followed the general pattern of becoming service-oriented and heavily dependent on funding from the international community. In the south much of civil society was a creation of the international community to facilitate its humanitarian interventions, and as a result did not have deep roots (Young 2002). With the rise to power of the NIF in 1989 severe restrictions were placed on their political activities in government-controlled areas. The SPLM/A was only marginally more accommodating to civil society in areas under its control. By the time the IGAD peace process began taking off there was some easing of pressures on civil society. But this led to the emergence of a civil society in the north which was sometimes a thinly veiled instrument of the NCP, while in the south a parallel but much weaker process was under way.

In the final stages of the negotiations the mediators, the NCP, and the SPLM/A became increasingly aware that to achieve acceptance the peace settlement needed the support of the Sudanese public. While the SPLM/A attempted to allay the fears of civil society that it was not consulted during the negotiations, the NCP was more active in briefing non-governmental groups, the leading opposition parties, nationally known figures, tribal and religious leaders and took some of them to Naivasha. However, in both cases their role was limited to providing legitimacy for an agreement that had almost been finalized; as one member of the NCP admitted to me, 'it was largely an exercise in public relations.' At no point did either the SPLM/A or the NCP accept the principle that they were accountable to constituencies beyond their parties for the positions they took in the negotiations. There is no indication either that those leading the peace process considered the lack of broader participation a critical obstacle to the peace process.

According to one diplomat close to the process, both the SPLM and the NCP 'viewed civil society as the enemy,' although it would be more accurate to conclude that they viewed their own civil society as an enemy and that of their opponents as potentially an ally. Thus the SPLM welcomed elements in the north that called for secularism, while the NCP encouraged southern civil society that challenged Garang's hegemony. The mediators were just 'not particularly concerned,' as one member of the secretariat put it. They feared, however, that the presence of civil society groups would serve to harden the positions of the parties.

The mediators' negative view of civil society failed to appreciate that the engagement of civil society was an antidote to the hegemonic claims of both parties and it could serve as ally to the mediators. There was also a general lack of appreciation of the need for the two parties to communicate with their constituencies, since without that consultation reaching a quick agreement between the parties would only serve to delay, and probably intensify, problems at a later stage. Thus the failure of the SPLM/A to listen to their supporters in the Nuba Mountains and South Blue Nile made for an easier passage at Machakos, but as a result the political explosion took place outside the formal negotiations. Likewise, agreement was reached on the Abyei dispute, only for the government to refuse to implement the Abyei Boundary Commission's report and that of The Hague Arbitration Tribunal when they caused outrage among its Misseirya supporters.

Moreover, the need for north–south reconciliation, if the supposed commitment to a united Sudan was to be achieved, could only be realized by involving the Sudanese people, and the starting point was civil society. Although the IGAD secretariat proposed a reconciliation component to the CPA, it was opposed by the NCP and later by the SPLM. Both parties knew they had committed major crimes during the course of the civil war, which would be discussed in public forums, and they were reluctant to see that happen. Indeed, at one point there was an agreement between the SPLM and the NCP to give themselves a blanket amnesty for crimes committed during the course of the war, but the mediators convinced them that such an agreement was illegal under international law and could not be enforced. Even when it was entertained, however, reconciliation was viewed as an 'add-on,' and when it faced opposition was largely dispensed with. This failure would turn out to have particular significance for the one-third of north and south Sudanese who lived in the border area and whose lives were highly interdependent. Many of these people were nomads from the north who spent as much as seven months a year in the south; their problems were exacerbated during the war and not addressed in the CPA or in the following six-and-a-half-year interim period.

In talks with the mediators and diplomats engaged in and following the negotiations the argument for narrow-focus talks was based on a number of contentions. First, it was held that the all-encompassing nature of the negotiations made the process very complex, and hence the participation of additional actors might make the process unworkable. No doubt it was also feared that if the door was opened to additional participants in the negotiations, it would be difficult to close it. Second, there was fear that enlarging the numbers around the bargaining table would inevitably increase the leaks of what was held to be confidential information, and this in turn could be used to galvanize dissent that could disrupt the process. Indeed, this also explains the secretive nature of the negotiations and the strict means by which the media were controlled. Third, Sumbeiywo and the secretariat strongly believed that 'small was good,' and hence wanted to keep participation at a 'manageable' level where it could be better controlled. As one observer told me, 'it was hard enough trying to broker a deal between two parties, and the addition of others would have made things impossibly complicated.' Indeed, in hindsight there is a tendency to justify the exclusion of other groups by comparing the situation to the Darfur talks at Abuja where large numbers participated and the result was chaotic.

Engaging civil society in the peace process, either formally in the negotiations or, more plausibly, through a parallel process would have been messy and, as its critics assert, would have complicated an already difficult process. It would also have meant that there would be less secrecy surrounding the talks. Engaging civil society would also have necessitated serious research to determine the authenticity of the various organizations considered for participation and to make proposals on the best way to involve them in the process. However, contrary to claims of chaos at a negotiating table encumbered by countless members of civil society, most of these were simply calling for participation in a broader peace process. Accepting that civil society was necessary to the success of the peace process and having its members at the table were two very different things.

Notwithstanding the weaknesses of Sudan's civil society, it could still have played a constructive role in the peace process and served to reduce or eliminate some of the problems that increasingly have come to light in the post-CPA period. High on this list would be overcoming the lack of democratic legitimacy of both parties, a problem that was particularly pertinent given the failure of the Addis Ababa Agreement of 1972, which foundered because opposition parties were able to contend that the agreement did not have the support of the Sudanese people (Lesch 1998). The engagement of civil society would also have brought women into the peace process. Their absence was striking, and further undermined the legitimacy of the process; they could have brought an important perspective to the talks. Moreover, the lack of ownership by the northern population was a major weakness of the IGAD peace process, which could have been overcome by involving civil society. As one opposition respondent noted at the time, 'no one is defending the CPA in the north'; and that remained the case through to the end of the agreement in July 2011.

By failing to make the Sudanese people feel part of the peace process, the IGAD mediation had the wholly non-constructive effect of giving life to the top-down, illegitimate political culture of the country. In the south a great number of political factions and tribal and regional-based organizations had taken form, but only a small number could be considered genuine political parties. In conditions of war and extreme underdevelopment power grew out of the barrel of a gun, and the focus of the struggle had been as much about achieving a hegemonic position in the south as in challenging northern governments and the inequitable distribution of power and wealth. As a result, there have always been two wars under way in the south: south–south and north–south, although it was sometimes hard to distinguish them in practice. The second war (north–south) was the focus of the IGAD mediation, which completely ignored the first (south–south) war, but it was the first war that probably caused the most suffering to the people of southern Sudan and that continued even after the south gained independence.

It was on these increasingly discredited elites from the north and south that the IGAD based its mediation. While their demonstrated military muscle meant they could not be ignored, the peace process served to give them a stature internationally that they had lost in Sudan. Just as participation in international bodies and organizations has given states in the developing world a measure of legitimacy despite their fragility, mediations such as that of IGAD have served to raise declining elites and cast them into the esteemed role of peace-makers and statesmen. Broadening the peace mediation would not only have given a measure of legitimacy to a process that was discredited in many circles simply because it relied entirely on northern and southern elites, but it would have given the mediators a much needed basis from which to assess critically their rhetoric and analysis. Just as IGAD is by definition a state-centric organization, the peace

process that it oversaw was elite-centric, inherently conservative, and had the effect of giving legitimacy to parties that were
increasingly being passed over by their own people. Moreover,
as one observer in the negotiations noted, the mediators 'never
quite got to the conclusion that the parties were too exclusive to
achieve sustainable peace in Sudan.'

A Peace Process without Trust

Contrary to traditional African approaches to resolving conflicts,
which emphasize trust-building, the Sudan peace process made
no attempt to build trust between the parties. While it is unlikely
that trust could ever have developed between the parties, it is
clear that it could only come about through extensive meetings
and debates, and not through mediators resorting to legalese,
the imposing of strict timetables, and establishing a vast array of
commissions and other bodies. The difference is best illustrated
by comparing the Naivasha process and that of the New Sudan
Council of Churches' People to People conferences of Wunlit
between the Nuer and Dinka in 1999 and the Liliir Covenant
between the Anyuak, Dinka, Kie, Kachip, Murle, and Nuer in
2000. Emphasizing dialogue and building trust through the
airing of grievances and the introduction of healing processes
contributed enormously to reconciliation between the two tribes.
Although weakened as a result of modernization, indigenous
modes of conflict resolution and their emphasis on reconciliation
are frequently highly effective (Cliffe and White 2002).

However, neither the SPLM nor the NCP wanted civil society
and the traditional authorities, who would have highlighted the
issues of trust and reconciliation, to have a role in the peace
process, and the mediators and the US-led quartet appeared to
share these sentiments. A Truth and Reconciliation Commission
along the lines of that in South Africa was widely supported by

civil society, but in the end it was written off by Garang and Ali Osman, who held that it would undermine the peace process and clearly did not think they had to play the role of democratic politicians and sell the agreement to their constituents. Not only did the parties not trust one another; they also did not trust the people of Sudan. As a result, no constructive efforts were made during the course of the peace process or since the signing of the CPA to confront seriously the pain, trauma, bitterness, and distrust that the war had inflicted on the population.

The insistence from the beginning by the SPLM/A that they needed to maintain their army through the entire peace process was a stark statement of their distrust of the NCP, which was almost certainly warranted. Indeed, in rejecting the notion that the UN would protect the south from any violation of the CPA, John Garang said:

> Our guarantee is organic. The fact that Southern Sudan will have its own separate army during the interim unity period in addition to the integrated forces and other security forces, is the only fundamental guarantor and indeed the cornerstone for the survival of the Comprehensive Peace Agreement. (cited in Madut-Arop 2006)

The SPLM/A viewed the NCP as the worst in a long line of northern governments that had lied to southerners and dishonored agreements. As a consequence, they were constantly on their guard and suspicious. The NCP in turn viewed the SPLA as untrustworthy and in evidence pointed to the capture of Torit during the negotiations as indicative of their lack of commitment to the process. They also pointed to the rising power of the Darfur-based Sudan Liberation Movement/Army (SLM/A), which was supported by the SPLA, as proof that it was talking peace but had not disavowed the option of overthrowing the government. Moreover, they never doubted the separatist sentiments of most of the SPLM negotiating team, and in that they were right.

But significantly there was also distrust within the peace partners' own camps. Most evident in the SPLM/A was Garang's
insistence from the outset that he monopolize all power in the
south – president of the Government of South Sudan, president
of the SPLM, and leader of the SPLA – and further that as
first vice president he be the leading representative of the south
in the national government. Likewise, Garang decided on his
own volition that Juba was not a suitable capital because of his
distrust of Equatorians and instead selected Ramkiel, homeland
of the Aliab Dinka in eastern Bahr el Ghazal. The lack of trust
between Dr John and different elements of civil society and other
southern parties largely explains the SPLM/A's opposition to
their participation in the peace process. And that also applied
to the NDA.

Distrust was equally apparent on the NCP side. Not only
did they have a large number of negotiating team leaders over
the course of more than a decade, each with their own style of
leadership, but they also had markedly different approaches to
fundamental issues. That was most apparent when the NCP's Ali
al-Haj came close to endorsing self-determination for the south
and entertaining a compromise on the issue of sharia during the
first rounds of negotiations in the mid-1990s, only to be withdrawn
from the talks and for the government to reject emphatically self-
determination and any compromise on sharia. And during the
late 1990s the NIF divided between the Bashir and Turabi wings,
which had different approaches to these issues. There were also
markedly different attitudes to basic issues between Dr Ghazi
Salhudin, who oversaw the agreement on the Machakos Protocol,
and first vice president Ali Osman Taha over elections (the former
preferred them sooner and Ali Osman later), security arrangements (Ghazi Salhudin preferred a continuing role for the national
army throughout the interim period and Ali Osman accepted its
withdrawal in the second year), a political agreement with the

SPLM/A (Ghazi Salhudin was opposed, while Ali Osman supported it), and other issues. And just as al-Haj was condemned by his colleagues for his concessions, Ali Osman would be accused of giving away too much in the negotiations.

Distrust not only affected relations between the various actors in the peace process, but was also reflected in their output, the protocols. Indeed, the peace process was shaped by the Anglo-American legal culture, where law is emphasized in the absence of trust; indeed, one SPLM negotiator remarked to me that trust was not necessary to reach an agreement. Seemingly every issue and contingency was identified and catered for in the protocols; the result was a massive and complex document which was hard to understand, and its implementation extremely difficult to assess. Within the Anglo-American legal culture alleged breaches of an agreement are referred to accepted judicial bodies which have the capacity both to rule on the complaints and to order policing authorities to ensure their rulings are implemented. However, no such accepted judicial organs or authorities existed in Sudan, none took form during the interim period, and hence the resort to this sophisticated legal culture in the absence of trust was misplaced. In retrospect one of the observers told me this emphasis on legalism was a 'waste of time' and held that more time in the negotiations should have been devoted to agreeing on principles.

While trust cannot be expected at the start of negotiations between parties that have long been at war, the experience of the Sudan IGAD peace process showed that if trust is not developed at some point, the deliberations and resulting agreement will remain highly unstable. In this light a consideration of the problem of the SSDF in the peace process is instructive. Although international intervention in the peace process was premised on the desire to end human insecurity in southern Sudan, by stipulating that the Other Armed Groups (OAGs) in the south had to be disbanded

within one year of the signing of the CPA (and that largely referred
to the SSDF) the Security Arrangements Protocol of the CPA had
the initial effect of raising tensions between the SPLA and the
SSDF (Young 2006). While the NCP wanted to use the SSDF to
undermine the peace process and appeared to know that it could
not be dissolved within one year, Garang consistently opposed the
integration of the SSDF into the SPLA. A Kenyan and Sudanese
respondent quoted a senior SPLM/A official at the time as saying
that 'Garang wants a minor insurgency' as a means to maintain
control in the south, an approach not unknown in the Horn.
However, since the SSDF posed a far bigger threat than that, it is
more likely that Garang saw a much larger challenge facing him
politically with the integration of the SSDF into the SPLM/A, and
concluded the problem could be contained by appealing to his
American friends to bring pressure on the NCP when the SSDF
would likely still be on the ground after one year.

    With Garang vehemently opposed to bringing the SSDF into
the peace process, and given strong backing by the US, there was
no prospect that the problem would be acted upon. While some
at the negotiating table foresaw the impending danger, they did
nothing and the result set the organization on a collision course
with the SPLA. The only reason this did not happen is that with
the death of Garang, Salva Kiir came to power and he moved
quickly to agree to the 8 January 2006 Juba Declaration. The Juba
Declaration was in the first instance a response to the widespread
demand of southern Sudanese that their leaders resolve their
differences peacefully and end the insecurity that made their lives
intolerable. With only minimal input from the Kenya-based Moi
Foundation, Salva Kiir and SSDF leader Paulino Matieb came
together and quickly established a relationship of trust and agreed
on the principles underlying the agreement (Young 2006). The
Juba Declaration is short, easily understood, without legal jargon,
almost immediately led to a marked decline of insecurity, and – as

the author, who was in Khartoum at the time of the agreement, can testify – almost overnight the negative SSDF references to Salva and the SPLA ended. The first lesson to be drawn was that the trust that underpinned the Juba Declaration is a more effective means to overcome tensions and disagreements between former enemies than resorting to legalese and institutions, which was the course followed in the IGAD peace process. The second lesson was that trust must be renewed. The subsequent poor implementation of the Juba Declaration, caused by mistrust in the senior ranks of the SPLA of the largely Nuer soldiers being integrated, led to tensions emerging once again and taking form in a series of revolts.

People in the north had trouble identifying with the peace process and the CPA because they saw few benefits accruing to them. Likewise the negotiating partners rejected measures which would have engaged the broader population in a collective healing exercise and encouraged trust. The dangers of this omission were made patently clear when in the wake of John Garang's death on 30 July 2005, Africans rioted in Khartoum, while the Arab population of the city cowered in their houses, with some later joining the state security apparatus in revenge attacks on Africans. Not for many years had the divisions in Sudan seemed so wide, and this only six months after the signing of the CPA, an agreement designed to build a new basis of unity and mutual trust in the country.

The US and Its Allies

Critical to the unfolding peace process was the role of the US and its allies, usually called the 'Quartet,' the four countries that provided the political backing for the peace process and sat in on the negotiations as observers. Norway and Italy derived their membership from being co-chairs of the IGAD Partners'

Forum (IPF), while the US and Britain appear to have assigned themselves leading roles in the process. The SPLM/A welcomed the US playing a leading role in the peace process because Garang had forged close relations with Washington and looked to the Americans to provide needed pressure to move the peace process forward and later to help with the implementation of the agreement and provide financing for post-conflict reconstruction. But the NCP also supported this major role of the US for a number of reasons: first, it felt that it was the only country that could bring the needed pressure to bear on Garang to sign an agreement; second, Khartoum wanted to improve relations with Washington. Moreover, it feared that without an improvement in relations Washington might increase assistance to the SPLM/A or even attempt to carry out regime change.

Appeasement was easier to accomplish after the expulsion of the more aggressive Turabi wing from the party in the late 1990s. This change in policy largely coincided with the advent of George Bush to the US presidency. While the human rights activists and the Black Caucus attracted most attention within the Clinton administration, under Bush it was the Christian right, to a lesser extent the oil industry, and, most significantly, security and intelligence interests. The Christian right had long sympathized with the plight of the southern Sudanese, who were turning to Christianity in growing numbers, and by extension the SPLM/A, which in turn saw these politically well-connected Christians as valued allies in Washington. President Bush himself drew inspiration from religious groups in his home town of Midland, Texas, where church leaders pressed him to deepen the US engagement in Sudan. Bush also had a close personal friendship with the evangelist Billy Graham and his son Franklin, who operated their own NGO, Samaritan's Purse, in Sudan.

The US oil industry was well placed to influence the Bush administration since the president and a number of his leading colleagues had close links with the industry. The oil industry was upset that the benefits of its efforts at establishing the industry in Sudan were being reaped by a handful of Asian companies and Talisman Company of Canada. Thus it can be surmised that the oil companies urged Bush to achieve a peace agreement in Sudan that would permit the embargo to end and provide the necessary security for them to consider operating in Sudan. The oil industry's interests thus dovetailed with government policy, which linked US security to diversifying its energy sources away from the unstable Middle East and increasing its share of oil from Africa.

However, in the wake of the Islamist attacks on the US, acquiring information on groups through cooperation with the Sudanese security services, protecting allies in the region from Islamists, and deepening engagement in the Sudan peace process all flowed from the growing perception that America's security was linked to the course and outcome of conflicts like that in Sudan. And all of these endeavors could be subsumed as part and parcel of the 'war on terror.' Concern with human rights, humanitarianism, and outlets for American stockpiles of grain for needy Sudanese figured in US calculations, but 9/11 had the effect of making security, the closely linked concern with failed states, and the pursuit of the war on terrorism the major objective of US foreign policy. This was most graphically indicated when Salah Gosh, the NCP's top security official, with a heavy involvement in human rights abuses, including the organization of the country's 'ghost houses' where perceived enemies of the regime were tortured, was so integral to US security concerns that he was flown by a CIA plane to New York and Washington in April 2005 to be thanked for his role in assisting the US government in its war on terrorism (*Los Angeles Times* 2005). But this link between the supposed enemies was a double-edged sword for the NCP because it also led to the USG assuming a high-profile role in the country's faltering peace process. Referring to 9/11, minister of the GoSS Gabriel Changeson observed that 'the terrorist attack on the US liberated us, it rescued us, because without it Bush would never have got involved' (interview, 30 March 2011).

The US heightened its engagement in the peace process by, first, utilizing the framework of IGAD; and second, operating through a quartet of loyal allies, and accepting the local management of the process by Kenya, which had long done the bidding of Britain and the US. What had been a genuinely regional peace initiative became, with trappings to provide the necessary legitimacy, an American-sponsored and -led process. All the parties acknowledged this with the exception of Kenya, which continued to think against all the evidence to the contrary that its minuscule diplomatic weight carried the process forward. The significance of the US to the peace process was, in the words of one diplomat, 'inevitable given its status as the sole super-power' and also given the timing of its intervention, while presidential adviser Ghazi Salhudin said that the US was as integral to the peace process as the SPLM/A and the NCP (interview, 26 May 2004).

Corresponding to the rise in significance of the US and its allies was the virtual withdrawal of Ethiopia from the peace process and the increasing marginalization of Eritrea in the region, the two countries that had taken the lead in the earlier phase of the IGAD peace initiative. While the Ethiopians and Eritreans used both political and military means to press forward a resolution to the Sudan conflict in the mid-1990s, the US under the Bush administration believed it could work with the Islamists and achieve its ends through negotiations. And while the regional powers pursued their objectives at a country-wide level and saw a role for the northern opposition in the process, the Americans focused almost entirely on the south and looked for a quick buy-in of the northern opposition after successful peace negotiations between the NCP and the SPLM/A. That buy-in never came, and indeed was never on the cards. The American assessment was strongly influenced by John Garang, in whom they had enormous confidence and to whom they looked to play a leading role in post-conflict Sudan. This approach meant that the US found it very difficult to respond constructively to the rapidly developing Darfur crisis, and when Garang died their policy virtually collapsed.

While the UN secretary general concluded that the war in Darfur had produced the greatest humanitarian disaster in the world and the US State Department found that the NCP had carried out acts of genocide in Darfur, the Americans were slow to suggest any policy initiatives and indeed were anxious that nothing be done that could threaten the ongoing IGAD peace process or their valuable intelligence links with Khartoum. In the lead-up to the signing of the CPA the government overrode the ceasefire and launched major attacks on rebel positions in Darfur, which deepened the humanitarian disaster. Nonetheless, the US and its allies were consistent in supporting a narrow-based peace process that excluded wider participation, including that of the Darfuris. And, having supported a peace process that involved turning over virtually all power to the NCP and SPLM/A, the US insisted that the grievances of others in Sudan be taken up through equally narrow-based processes to ensure that they did not threaten the CPA.

US policy on Sudan was also strongly influenced by the close personal relations of three of their leading officials with Garang – Brian de Silva in the Department of Agriculture, Roger Winter at USAID, and Andrew Natsios, formerly in USAID and subsequently the special envoy of President Bush. Strongly committed to Garang over many years, they were instrumental both in advising Garang on how to win the acceptance and later support of the USG and in convincing the American government that a rebel leader widely considered a communist because of his links to the Derg could become a valued ally. They boosted the image of Garang to the point that he had inspired a personality cult in some circles of the US by the late 1990s, and this in spite of his record of systemic abuse of human rights and murder of numerous colleagues, and his refusal to share power.

Despite the influence of de Silva, Winter, and Natsios on US policy and their attachment to the plight of the people of the Nuba Mountains and Abyei, they were not able to have the concerns of these areas acknowledged in the Machakos Protocol, or through the parallel peace process led by the Special Envoy to ensure that SPLM/A promises of self-determination for Nuba Mountains and South Blue Nile were kept. On Abyei the three Americans worked from the commitment made in the Addis Ababa Agreement of 1972 that the people of the region would get a referendum on whether they wanted to be part of the north or the south, and were able to achieve the same provision in the CPA, and to gain agreement this vote would take place simultaneously with the southern referendum on self-determination. However, the parties were not able to reach an agreement on the borders of Abyei (and hence who could vote in the referendum) and instead left it to a commission where foreign experts would cast the deciding vote. Not surprisingly, the stipulations of this protocol were not realized, in particular the call for a referendum, and at the end of the peace process there was little prospect that they would soon be fulfilled.

The NCP assumed the US had concluded that the balance of power was shifting against the SPLM/A as Khartoum was able to devote increasing oil-derived resources into buying sophisticated military technology with which to fight the war. As a result, the peace process was a last and best chance for the SPLM/A to win in negotiations what could no longer be won on the battlefield. (The outbreak of a major war in Darfur would change that assessment, but by then the die had been cast.) Indeed, the impact of rocketry, fighter jets, and the home-grown production of small arms and even artillery was having an impact on the war. Malik Agar Eyre, SPLM/A governor of South Blue Nile, concluded that if the movement failed to disrupt the oil flow and Khartoum was to use this financial windfall for the next three to four years, 'the SPLA would lose the war.'[4] His projection fits closely the shift of the SPLM/A from a focus on the military front to the peace process. As a result, although there was scepticism in the NCP about US promises to move toward establishing normal bilateral relations with Sudan if it promised to cooperate on terrorism and reach a peace agreement, Khartoum felt that it did not have any option except to engage in the peace process and support the US playing a leading role in it.

Norway came second to the US in terms of influence, which was largely due to the energy of its personnel, in particular international development minister Hilde Johnson, although this view was not shared by those in the government camp who resented her blatantly pro-SPLM/A stance. According to one NCP respondent, 'Norway was completely biased to the south and viewed its role as a crusade.' To the surprise of many, given its long engagement in Sudan, it was generally agreed that Britain did not have much influence over the peace process. Britain was held to be more sympathetic to Khartoum, an assumption that only bears up if compared to the other countries. Former British ambassador to Sudan and appointee observer Alan Goulty was accused by the SPLM/A of being sympathetic to Khartoum, but the fact that he was subsequently forced to leave the country suggests the NCP did not share this view. Italy was the odd man out: while it was a major financial contributor to the peace process, it was widely viewed as the least active.

The self-promotion of these four countries in the peace process, however, was not without controversy. The IPF countries felt they collectively should be recognized as the backers of the IGAD peace process, but instead found they were largely sidelined. However, they could do nothing except serve as a cheering squad and contribute to the financing of the negotiations.

Limits of Mediation

Critical here is the question of whether mediators are completely bound by the demands of the parties to the conflict, or do they have the capacity to strike out on their own? If they are bound by the requirements of the parties, they may give legitimacy to a process leading to disaster, while if they strike out on their own they will at the least be accused of denying the parties ownership of the process and possibly bringing about its collapse. The IGAD mediation team chose to be bound by the parties. Special Envoy General Sumbeiywo asserted: 'The conceptualisation has to come from the parties themselves rather than from without ... you have to get them to have ownership of the agreement' (quoted in Accord and Concordis International 2006). Ownership, as defined by Sumbeiywo, was ownership by the parties, not by the communities they professed to represent.

Accepting this limited role, however, reduced the task of the mediators to finding the lowest common denominator linking the positions of the two protagonists, as was done in the Machakos Protocol. Moreover, a wider perspective in the circumstances was not possible because civil society and other parties – which would have provided for or insisted upon it – were not permitted to participate in the peace process. In addition, there were constraints on public opinion since the negotiations were shrouded in secrecy and the media kept at arm's length.

Indeed, the resilience of Special Envoy Lazaro Sumbeiywo in the peace process does not lie in his vision, because there is no indication that he had one. Rather, it lies in the fact that he successfully adapted to the interests of the SPLM/A and NCP, which did not want vision, aggressive leadership, intellectual grandstanding, or the production of grandiose proposals. Instead they wanted – and got – a go-slow, piecemeal, unimaginative process and the environment to carry out their endeavors largely free from the overt pressures of outside interests. It is striking how often negotiators (particularly those from the NCP) voiced their appreciation of the strong role Sumbeiywo played in containing the observers and other outsiders. And when in the final months the Sudanese actors led by John Garang and Ali Osman took charge, the Special Envoy faded into the background. There is no doubt that this simple but always clear and disinterested approach contributed significantly to moving the process ahead and reaching an agreement where few could have expected one when the process began.

However, many problems followed from this limited view of the mediators' role, the most dangerous being that at the least it made the resolution of conflicts elsewhere in the country much harder to resolve, and may have even exacerbated them. Put differently, in the end the IGAD mediation team and the US and its allies were successful in reaching a signed agreement, and since that was the task they were assigned they were given considerable credit. But if they cannot be accused of causing the intra-south conflicts, and those in the west and east of the country, their mediation did nothing to resolve them, and arguably it exacerbated them and made their ultimate resolution more difficult.

Moreover, the claim that there would be a second stage to Naivasha, which was also widely maintained by diplomats close to the mediation at the time, was false. And the further contention that the CPA provided the framework and the incentive for the peaceful resolution of conflicts elsewhere in the country, and notably in Darfur, has not been borne out. Sumbeiywo observed that 'If the agreement [i.e. the CPA] is properly implemented it will resolve the other conflicts in Sudan. The agreement means there is somebody else joining the government in the centre, which in turn means the government will not be able to continue marginalizing other areas of the country as it has done in the past' (quoted in Potter 2006). That contention has been proven wrong, but most analysts followed Sumbeiywo in concluding that the best means to resolve the conflict in Darfur was to reach a rapid agreement in the south.

Furthermore, the power-sharing protocol made the achievement of a comprehensive peace agreement all but impossible. By leaving only a 14 percent share in national power to be divided (after assigning 52 percent to the NCP, 28 percent to the SPLM/A and a further 6 percent to southern parties in the north) among the large majority of the population in the north, rebels in the west and east had no room to buy into the central government. Not only was this result not accepted by the rebels of the periphery, but it strengthened secessionist tendencies that could eventually bring about the dismemberment of the country. In the wake of the signing of the CPA, former prime minister Sadig al-Mahdi summed up the situation when he said that the parties had 'clad themselves in a kind of iron jacket that is not capable of accommodating others.'[6]

The question that cannot be satisfactorily answered is whether the mediators and the US and its allies understood the likely dangerous consequences of such a narrow mediation and the constraints imposed on any peace processes that would follow in its wake. General Sumbeiywo took an extensive tour of Sudan in the aftermath of the Machakos Protocol, where he met leaders of the opposition parties and the SSDF. And when asked what he would do differently, the Special Envoy said: 'I would go earlier in the negotiations to the ground, to find out what the people want, which is not necessarily the same as what the negotiating team is presenting' (quoted in Accord and Concordis International 2006). This begs the question of why he should have gone 'to the ground' if the mediators were bound by the parties, as he has also said. And if he was so interested in ascertaining 'what the people want,' why was he adamant about restricting the negotiations to the NCP and the SPLM/A? There can be little doubt that the people of southern Sudan, and particularly those in Greater Upper Nile, would have pressed for a resolution of the SPLA–SSDF conflict. And had the Special Envoy met with northern Sudanese outside the ruling party they would have made him aware of the potentially disastrous consequences of the southern peace process for the resolution of armed conflicts in the east and west of Sudan, and demanded a genuinely comprehensive peace process with a clear emphasis on democratic transformation. There is also no indication that the outbreak of war in Darfur and the ensuing humanitarian crisis that took place during the last year of the IGAD mediation in any way affected the course and content of the negotiations. Indeed, as one analyst pointed out before the signing of the CPA, 'The price of the agreement in the south has been the exclusion from the peace process of all but two parties, the government and the SPLM' (Ryle, 2004). There is also no evidence that the IGAD mediators drew the same conclusion as most analysts, namely that the same conditions that produced the conflict in the south were producing similar conflicts in the west and east.

Conclusion

Even with enormous support from the region the SPLM was unable to defeat the northern army militarily, and hence it looked to the international community to achieve at the negotiating table what it could not achieve on the battlefield. Meanwhile, regionally and internationally isolated, the NCP made the best of a bad situation and never refused requests to participate in peace processes. Indeed, the NCP understood that the more peace processes there were, the more means there were to divide its opponents. The proposal for a US-backed IGAD peace process presented particular challenges, but the NCP could not refuse the Americans without running the risk of military attack or having them throw their weight behind the SPLM. What was needed, then, was a peace process that narrowly focused on north–south issues, did not permit the rebels from other parts of the country or civil society groups to make common cause with the SPLM, and did not threaten sharia, which was crucial to holding together the NCP's constituency. Neither the SPLM nor the peacemakers could have been more cooperative in responding to these NCP concerns. And with the peacemakers far more interested in reaching an agreement than contending with sticky issues like Sudan's unity and democratic transformation, these concerns could be pushed down the road where they could later be derailed or provide assurance that having got that far along the peace track, the international backers of the process would not pull out. In this, as in many other cases, the logic followed by the SPLM leadership was not very different from that of the NCP.

Meanwhile, the Security Council's assessment, as indicated by its press release in the wake of the signing of the peace agreement, devoted almost as much space to the war in Darfur, which was then filling the world's television screens, as it did to the CPA.[5] The press release quoted Ali Osman as calling on the international community to lift economic and trade restrictions or sanctions, write off all foreign debt owed by Sudan, and for countries to donate generously to the upcoming donors' conference. In the same press release Garang praised what he called a 'one country, two systems model,' which presumably would serve as a post-referendum blueprint for a united Sudan. But the

Security Council itself gave more attention to Garang's comments on resolving the Darfur war.

Ali Osman, Garang, and the Security Council would all be disappointed. Peace did not descend from the sky on southern Sudan, and in the wake of the signing of the CPA war loomed between the SPLA and SSDF, in addition to the outbreak of a multitude of local conflicts suppressed by the war. Garang did not live to learn that southerners would vote overwhelmingly for secession, thus ending his dream of 'one country, two systems.' The Darfur war dragged on with no end in sight. Ali Osman was still waiting at the end of the CPA for Sudan to be taken off the US sanctions list. Democracy did not develop with the signing of the CPA and was not in evidence when the agreement ended in July 2011. Indeed, far from setting the country on the road to resolving its problems, the CPA became part of the political baggage borne by the country. The crux of the problem remained the structural inequities of the Sudanese state, which the international community, the SPLM, and the NCP could not agree to resolve.

THREE

DISPENSING WITH DEMOCRACY:
THE APRIL 2010 ELECTIONS

Elections are considered a key element in liberal notions of peacemaking and good governance, and are among World Bank and
IMF political conditionalities for countries seeking credit or
economic reform assistance. But under the conditions considered above, where the Sudanese state has been reduced to being
an instrument of the NCP, with the SPLM well on the way to
achieving the same end in the south, the possibility of free and
fair elections was extremely remote. In this situation elections
'may be a strategy for maintaining power and many African elections ... have been clearly intended to forestall change, or even
strengthen the status quo' (Villalón 1998: 16). In consequence,
international participants in these exercises largely exclude any
notion of people empowerment and instead focus almost exclusively on the form and not the content of the exercise. Writing
about West Africa, Adelaja Odukoya has concluded that the West
favors elections that do not address structural problems because
it helps to demobilize any opposition contemplating violence
and secures the cooperation of the favored ruling elite (Odukoya
2007: 147–60). And Paul Collier observes that autocratic rulers
adapt themselves to the 'democratic' circumstances and develop

various strategies including lying, bribery, and various means of electoral fraud to ensure that elections do not threaten their hold on power, and as a result elections are more likely to undermine the reform of economic and governance policies (Collier 2009: 5). Indeed, the international community was anxious to see the power of the NCP and SPLM maintained because they were held to be essential to keeping the peace process on track, bearing in mind that this was a one-track affair directed at achieving a smooth independence for southern Sudan and not achieving a democratic transformation.

Sudan's elections were repeatedly postponed, and when finally held, in April 2010, were dominated by the NCP and SPLM, which alone had access to the necessary state resources and personnel to conduct campaigns effectively. Despite those advantages the ruling parties carried out widespread rigging and harassed the opposition parties in the north and the south, which had in any case been weakened by years of oppression. The NCP and SPLM, which had initially opposed the elections, viewed them as a great success; having previously based their legitimacy on Islamist and liberation philosophies, respectively, they could now pose as democratic governments with the endorsement of the international community. The outcome of the elections was almost completely negative as they increased the representation of the ruling parties in their respective assemblies, further marginalized the opposition parties in both the north and the south, and created a de facto independent south.

Democratic Accountability and the National Elections

Although the NCP held elections in 1996 and 2000, they had little credibility; the last generally accepted elections in Sudan were held in 1986. Liberal peacemaking, however, demands at least the appearance of democratic accountability, and that was supposed to be a consequence of the CPA-stipulated elections. ⌐ Special Envoy Sumbeiywo asserted: 'After three years all the parties will get the chance to compete for power through the electoral process' (quoted in Potter 2006). The SPLM/A took a similar position, arguing that, instead of criticizing the CPA, civil society and the political parties should exploit the new freedoms to organize and prepare for the forthcoming elections. Although the US consistently opposed broadening the peace process to give it democratic legitimacy, it nonetheless supported free and fair elections. The international community also contended that the elections would open up the political space imposed by the power-sharing formula of the CPA, which granted the SPLM and NCP the lion's share of power in north and south Sudan, but, as will be seen, that hope also was not realized.

At the time of the elections, interference with the press was common in both the north and south; freedom of association was limited; non-government political parties faced periodic harassment; civil society was interfered with, particularly in the north (in the south it was largely absent); and the security organs in north and south Sudan continued to play a leading role in the state. Thus the elections took place in an environment in which democratic freedoms and respect for human rights were limited and political repression was common.

In the wake of the Machakos Protocol, Dr Ghazi Salhudin proposed moving quickly to national elections. While his proposal probably had more to do with the partisan advantages he saw for the NCP, which he assumed was better prepared than the SPLM, the proposal had the merit of rapidly placing in power governments in the north and south with the legitimacy to carry forward the peace process. There is no denying the organizational and political difficulties of moving so quickly to an election, but it was not these concerns that led both the SPLM/A and NCP to reject the proposal. Very simply, neither party wanted to test its support before the Sudanese electorate and instead favored not holding elections until after the 2011 referendum on self-determination. In the face of the mediators' contention that elections were necessary to give the peace process legitimacy, the SPLM argued – in the words of one negotiator at the time – that it was a liberation movement and did not need a mandate. Another negotiator asked, 'What would be the effect on the peace process if the SPLM lost?' A number of southern intellectuals, including Abel Alier, argued forcefully against the holding of presidential elections either on a Sudan-wide basis or just in the south, because it was feared they would be too destabilizing. However, the mediators and observers were adamant that there could not be an agreement without a commitment to hold elections.

During the negotiations concerns were raised that given the lack of trust between the parties to the agreement, the deep divisions in the country, and the high stakes involved, elections would more likely precipitate conflict than bring the disparate communities together and lay the basis for Sudan's democratic transformation. However, it was widely assumed that no matter how the Sudanese cast their votes, the SPLM/A and the NCP would determine the power-sharing arrangement, just as they had during the peace process.

Part of the rationale for holding elections during the period of the peace process was that since the political parties and civil society had been denied the right to participate in that process, they should be given the opportunity through elections to express their views, albeit indirectly, on the CPA. But in early 2007 the National Assembly made it illegal for parties to contest the election unless they supported the CPA, thus eliminating the opportunity for Sudanese to express their views on the peace agreement. While most of the parties in the country endorsed the broad thrust of the CPA, some in the Umma and DUP argued that the agreement ventured into areas beyond its competence and they opposed the fact that it was solely a bilateral creation. But under the Political Parties Act parties could be dissolved which did not accept the country's constitution, which was based on the CPA.

In 2005 Sadig al-Mahdi posed what he called a 'worst case scenario' in which the SPLM/A and the NCP would claim to have a comprehensive agreement and form a national unity government, and whoever opposed them would lose their rights, thereby creating a confrontational situation (IRIN 2005) – a not unreasonable conjecture as it turned out.

Other difficulties arose from the CPA sequencing, which called for border demarcation, national census, and then the election. In the event, the border demarcation had not been completed before the peace process officially ended in July 2011. Both sides blamed the other for the delays, but the SPLM was more forthright. Thus, one commissioner of a border area in dispute told me that 'the party did not want border demarcation to interfere with the referendum and that the problem would be better resolved when the south was independent and could get support from outside countries.' Sudan's fifth census in its history was conducted throughout the country from 22 April to 1 May 2008, but the SPLM rejected it, insisting that it would not accept any results for the south showing fewer than 11 million people; and this in spite of the fact that in the south the census was carried out by an agency of the GoSS. As it turned out, the Central Bureau of Statistics produced a gross figure of 39.15 million for the entire country and gave a figure of 8.2 million for the south.[1] Many people reported they had not been counted. Problems seemed particularly severe in Darfur and Southern Kordofan.

Just as the initial division of seats in 2005 between the parties in the north and south was based on an agreement and not any objective basis or elections, the parties agreed in February 2010 to add 40 seats for southern Sudan in the National Assembly, to give Abyei 2 additional seats, and Southern Kordofan 4; again it was the parties and not the citizenry that took these decisions. The 40 seats for the south were to be designated after the elections based on the performance of each political party, although, again, that never occurred. This was the key number of seats that would raise southern representation in the national parliament to 27 percent, enough to block any potential constitutional amendments that could prevent the referendum from moving forward. The parties further agreed in the case of Southern Kordofan to repeat the census and voter registration in preparation for the state assembly and gubernatorial elections, which were rescheduled for April and then May 2011.

Critical to the conduct of the elections was the establishment of the National Elections Commission (NEC), a product of the National Elections Act passed by the National Assembly on 7 July 2008. Although headed by Abel Alier, an eminent lawyer with close ties to the SPLM, and agreed upon by a unanimous vote in the Assembly, the opposition from the outset viewed the NEC as an adjunct to the NCP. Indeed, although Alier was widely respected internationally and among some sections of the northern elite, southerners had very mixed views about him, a man many viewed as a pawn of Nimeiri and later of Garang, and as having overseen a Dinka-dominated corrupt regime when he served as president of the High Executive Council in southern Sudan during the first autonomous period. But the main concern was that Abel Alier was now elderly, and it was feared that he would be manipulated by the other commissioners.

From the outset the opposition parties complained about the legal framework. Their complaints were echoed by the observation missions, which concluded that a number of Sudan's laws were overly restrictive (Carter Center, 17 April 2010: 6). Also of concern were fears that state institutions such as the National

Intelligence and Security Service and the Humanitarian Affairs Commission (HAC) would interfere in the elections, as indeed the former did. The NCP, however, refused appeals by the parties and the international election missions to cancel any of these laws for the period of the election and to end the state of emergency in Darfur, but it did agree not to apply the laws during the elections.

The April 2010 elections must rank as among the most complex ever held: people in the south had to fill out twelve ballots, those in the north eight. The ballots in the south were for the president of Sudan, the president of South Sudan, state governors, and geographical constituencies, party lists, and women's lists at the national, regional, and state levels (National Elections Act, Article 31, 2010). The presidency called for an absolute majority of 50 percent + 1, while gubernatorial races were based on the majoritarian principle that the winner takes all. Legislative elections were based on the combination of majoritarian and proportional representation. In the National Assembly, 60 percent of seats were majoritarian, 25 percent proportional representation of women candidates put forward by political parties, and 15 percent from state-level candidates chosen by political parties. This complexity was in part due to the compromises that needed to be reached by the NCP and SPLM, and also carried over to the delineation of the constituencies. The NEC decreed that no constituency should exceed the national dividend by more or less than 15 percent, giving a 30 percent margin, but there were constituencies which varied in size by as much as 150 percent and there were cases of constituencies being added in areas of strong NCP support and removed in areas with little support (African Centre for Justice and Peace Studies, May 2010: 9). As a result, the Carter Center concluded that the boundaries of the constituencies were 'vague, unmapped and difficult for observers and election officials to comprehend' (Carter Center, 17 April 2010), and as a result some

800 complaints were made, less than a quarter of which received an official response from the NEC. In the event, 16,000 candidates contested 1,841 parliamentary and executive seats.

While southern Sudanese typically saw the elections as a critical step on the way to achieving self-determination, northern Sudanese initially hoped they would start the long-promised democratic transformation. In the event, the international community supported the southerners and the SPLM/A and abandoned the northerners. Indeed, Salva maintained that no delay in the national election should affect the January 2011 referendum, and further asserted that 'the conduct of the elections is not a prerequisite to the conduct of the referendum.... The people of southern Sudan attach more importance to the referendum than the elections' (Agence France Presse, 9 March 2010). Salva needed the GoSS presidential election and the federal and state elections to go ahead to ensure he could carry forward the referendum, but other elements of the election were negotiable. Not surprisingly northern Sudanese viewed Salva with considerable suspicion; as the NCP's Sana Ahmed said, 'People looked upon Garang as a Sudanese, not a southerner, like Salva' (interview, 20 June 2011). The NCP leadership meanwhile was adamant that the presidential and parliamentary elections should go ahead, because they were needed for it to gain the legitimacy for which it strove. Generally the NCP was prepared for elections, the SPLM was hesitant, the northern opposition parties were caught by surprise as they did not think the elections would be held, while the southern opposition parties were enthusiastic but had no resources, experience, or, in many cases, members.

All the parties paid lip service to democratic transformation, but for the NCP the elections meant overseeing a tightly controlled electoral process that would ensure its continuing hold on power and gain it a measure of international legitimacy. Loss of power was never considered a possibility. For the northern opposition,

the elections meant making progress toward overthrowing a totalitarian regime and using the political opening to connect with
its bases. For the SPLM the elections were a means to weaken the
NCP while not threatening the realization of self-determination,
its primary objective. The southern parties viewed the elections
as a way to exert some influence on a process hitherto completely dominated by the SPLM. The northern opposition parties,
including the SPLM, began the election loosely linked as the
anti-NCP Juba Alliance.

The CPA had already led northern opposition politicians to
increasingly doubt the SPLM/A commitment to New Sudan in
favor of southern secession. The elections would provide further
evidence to reinforce that suspicion, and the ties that bound them
to the SPLM increasingly weakened. This question should have
been conclusively resolved at the SPLM's second national convention in Juba in July 2008, but it was not, and the convention
instead exposed serious divisions in the party leadership.

Two candidates, Riek Machar and Nihal Deng,[2] declared their
intention to challenge Salva for leadership of the party, but widespread opposition to any displays of division precluded an election
and led to a unanimous endorsement of Salva's leadership. Salva
then surprised many by his efforts to overturn the SPLM policy
of having three deputy leaders, in favor of only one, and for that
to be Assembly Speaker, James Wani Igga, a person widely held
to be a Salva sycophant. Considerable time at the convention was
devoted to this issue before Salva was forced to backtrack. He
also signaled that he was not happy with Pagan Amum, but again
in the face of considerable opposition he relented and Pagan was
again endorsed as the party's general secretary.

As expected, the party endorsed the commitment to New
Sudan, but it was by no means clear this involved a commitment
to struggle for a united Sudan in either the upcoming national
election or in the 2011 referendum. Nor was it clear who would

serve as the SPLM's presidential candidate in the national election. The US had supported Garang's run for the presidency as the best means to effect regime change, a strategy that was believed to have been formalized when the SPLM leadership flew to Washington in early 2006 and met with Condoleezza Rice. With Garang's death on 30 July, Salva Kiir reluctantly inherited this approach.

However, the 2008 Elections Act precluded candidates from running for more than one executive position (president in either the north or south or for a governorship); this meant that if Salva lost the national presidency he would be powerless. At the same time, if another SPLM candidate ran for and won the national presidency while Salva took the southern presidency, he would become his junior. Moreover, should Salva step aside for another candidate from the SPLM to run for president of the Government of National Unity (GNU), and should that person win, Salva would automatically lose his position as first vice president since that position constitutionally had to be filled by a northerner. Pagan and Yasir repeatedly announced that Salva would run for the national presidency, but he feared their appeal was meant to sideline him. At the end of the convention it was announced that he would run, but very soon after that he began having second thoughts.

The initial announcement that Salva would run for the presidency angered the NCP, which held that the SPLM should support Bashir as leader of the GNU and in recognition of their partnership, but in the event Salva backed down. As well as the problem of who would run for the national presidency being ignored, also left undecided at the convention, and indeed up to the eve of the election, the SPLM election strategy was left unresolved – whether it would it run on its own, build an alliance of like-minded parties, go into an alliance with the NCP, or agree with the NCP to only focus on their home turfs. Although an alliance with the NCP would likely ensure a peaceful election outcome, and this

was the preferred option of the NCP, it would run afoul of the
US, could cause a revolt among the party's northern sector, and
and looked bad internationally at a time when ICC warrants were
likely to be issued for Bashir. A milder version of this scenario,
and the fallback position of the NCP, was for the SPLM to leave
north Sudan to NCP domination while south Sudan would be left
to SPLM domination. This latter version was possible, although
the SPLM leadership would have trouble convincing the northern
sector of the party to accept such an arrangement. Ultimately the
Juba leadership did opt for this option, and it was electorally
successful, but it produced a split in the party.

Elections

Formally the election process began with voter registration from
1 November 2010 to 7 December, a week being added to reach
logistically difficult areas in south Sudan and made necessary
by the failure of both the NEC to fully inform people and of
the SPLM officials to mobilize their people. The African Centre
for Justice and Peace Studies concluded that 'the registration
period was a precursor to the elections in the irregularities and
violations that occurred (2010: 10). According to the NEC, 71
percent of eligible voters in the north registered and 98 percent
in the south; indeed in the south, figures were sometimes higher
than 100 percent after SPLM leaders endeavored to prove in the
final weeks that the census figures were mistaken.

Virtually all the observer missions emphasized the NEC's
failure to educate people about voter registration which 'negatively impacted the level of participation as well as understanding
of the process for Sudanese at large' (Carter Center, 17 March
2010). It says a lot about the NEC that it used the tree, which
was the symbol of the NCP, and the same slogan as President
al-Bashir in its voter education material. Numerous cases came

to light of citizens being blocked from registering, of registering inappropriately, of under-aged registration, and of harassment of observers. Popular Committees and native and traditional authorities were empowered by the NEC to authenticate personal identification documents for voters according to Article 22(b), despite the fact that in many cases these organizations had close links to the NCP. Officials often permitted individuals to register who did not live in the area, did not have proper documentation, or did not provide all the information required. While there was a need for flexibility in dealing with those of questionable age given the general lack of birth certificates, there was reason to believe the process was manipulated, as demonstrated in cases such as girls not more than 12 years old in a video seen by the author happily waving their registration slips. Most military and paramilitary officials were registered in their place of work instead of their residence, which was in contravention of Article 22 of the 2008 Election Act. When complaints were made, the NEC issued a statement, on 24 October, permitting the practice. This raised two possibilities: military personnel may have been able to register in more than one place, and/or the government could direct or coerce these government employees to areas where its support was low.

There were also problems, particularly in the south, of registration centers opening and closing without prior notification. South Sudan used mobile registration centers, but few knew of them in advance. Under the CPA, residents in Abyei could register in either Southern Kordofan or Warrap, but people in the territory were poorly informed. One observation mission concluded that, 'Given Sudan's historical imbalances, marginalisation, and regional inequities in the countries' peripheries, the uneven results risk reinforcing traditional differences and the perception or reality of marginalisation, rather than building a truly inclusive political process' (African Centre for Justice and

Peace Studies 2010). Unity, Western and Northern Bahr el Ghazal states, Blue Nile and Southern Kordofan states all suffered from a shortage of registration materials. Registration of pastoralists was low, and others found it difficult to register because of long distances to the centers and insecurity, particularly in the south. The NCP's Dr Gutbi Mahdi claimed that registration in the south was characterized by massive fraud, which was not fully exposed because NCP cadres were routinely arrested and there were too few international observers to be effective (interview, 17 March 2010). All observers were aware of NCP officials operating through party-affiliated popular committees or tents outside registration centers, collecting voter registration cards, supposedly for safekeeping.

The Darfuri liberation movements did not participate in the elections because they had objected to their being held, and it was also contended that as armed groups they were not eligible. In addition, until virtually the end of the campaign they urged a boycott of the process. The SCP and Umma Reform and Renewal Party decided at the outset that they would not participate in Darfur, given conditions of war, problems with voter registration, denial of rights of IDPs, lack of access to the election of those living behind rebel lines, the appeals of a range of civil society Darfuri actors, and the desire to establish peace first and then bring the armed groups into the political contest.

Despite these problems the only international mission that observed the registration, the Carter Center, concluded that the voter registration process was mostly peaceful and orderly, excepting Darfur. Most analysts later decided that some of the worst abuses of the election occurred in this phase and went largely unrecorded. In the end, some 16.35 million voters were registered in Sudan and a further 100,000 overseas. Some seventy-two political parties nominated candidates in the elections, although only two, the NCP and SPLM, had sufficient financial and human resources to contest the elections in many constituencies.

Problems during the campaign period included the requirement that parties give seventy-two hours' notice of their intention to hold rallies, even rallies on their own premises – a provision that was ignored in some areas and involved notifying a number of security agencies in others. There were problems about media access, and in one instance a prerecorded speech by Sadig al-Mahdi on state Radio Omdurman on 3 March was pulled because it was alleged that he was 'inciting hatred,' which the Carter Center later found to be unsubstantiated. Because of perceived bias, the northern Juba Alliance subsequently withdrew from participation in the government-established media council. Two radio stations in Juba, Bakhita Radio and Liberty FM, were briefly closed down by southern security agents because of objections to the content of their broadcasts, and journalists throughout Sudan were harassed and threatened. The Juba Alliance parties complained about the use of government property for campaigning, demanded that the state of emergency in Darfur be lifted, insisted that an agreement be reached to allow armed groups in Darfur to vote, and further questioned the impartiality of the NEC in a submission to the Commission on 6 March. NISS was particularly ruthless in arresting and beating members of Grifna (Arabic for 'we are fed up'), in its attempt to question the legitimacy of the election through street dramas and its appeal 'to reinstate a democratic nation-state eliminating the party-state.'[3]

Efforts were made by the AU team, led by former South African President Thabo Mbeki, to gain the acceptance of the political parties of a party code of conduct, but in the north the opposition parties attempted to use the negotiations to further open up the political process and provide them with government funding (based on Article 67c of the National Elections Act), but the NCP refused and the effort collapsed. One member of the Mbeki team placed the blame for the failure to get a code of conduct on the efforts of two men: Siddig Yousif of the Sudan Communist Party and Mubarak al-Fadil al-Mahdi of the Umma Reform and Renewal Party. In the south the opposition parties and the SPLM did agree on a code and also for the government to provide funding. The SPLM acceptance of the code of conduct was largely symbolic, as its systematic abuse demonstrated, while the funding was only provided late in the day and to two parties for subsequent dispersal; in the event most of the parties did not receive anything.

More problems ensued with the nominations, although they could be attributed largely to the lack of party rules on procedure rather than to the NEC. Thus large numbers of SPLM and NCP members, and particularly the former, did not accept the party selected candidates and instead ran as independents. Some of the defectors in the north ran in the expectation that they would be bought off by the party and withdraw.[4] But that was not the intention of most southern SPLM dissidents, and as a result 357 ran as independents in opposition to officially sanctioned party candidates, including Angelina Teny-Dhurgon, SPLM state minister in the GNU and wife of Vice President Riek Machar, who ran for the governorship in Unity state. She decided to run after the incumbent, Taban Deng Gai, was forced on the state party and people.[5] Taban had lost the position of chairman of the state party in a party election to a former governor and then GoSS minister of health Dr Joseph Babiny Monytuil, who was then selected by the party to run as its candidate, only to have the Salva-appointed Electoral College overrule the decision and insist on the highly unpopular Taban.

Taban Deng Gai had created a virtual gangster dictatorship in Unity state based on the 2 percent oil revenues that the state received as part of the wealth-sharing protocol of the CPA. This

money was handled by his personal agent in Khartoum for purposes that were not known even to his minister of finance, while
everyone in the state went about in fear of the governor. He
managed this regime on account of his close relations with the
SPLA chief of defense staff, James Hoth, and what amounted to
a private army, which he used in 2009 to attack and kill sixteen
bodyguards at the Bentui house of the deputy leader of the SPLA,
Paulino Matieb, whom he viewed as a competitor in the state.[6]
Taban was also supported by Salva, probably as a means to
curtail the ambitions of his vice president, Riek Machar. As a
result of these actions Paulino, Machar, Babiny Monytuil, Major
General Peter Gadet and many leaders in the state SPLM joined
together to oppose Taban Deng Gai and support Angelina Teny-
Dhurgon's candidacy. Unity state stood out for its corruption and
maladministration, but other states experienced similar problems.
That encouraged dissidents at all levels in the south to run as
independents.

Initially the SPLM leadership wanted to disown and punish
the independents, but because of their large number, Salva was
forced in the end to take a conciliatory approach. This was
reinforced by many of them saying they would return to the
party should they be elected. The clearly failed process caused
the Political Bureau embarrassment and led SPLM secretary
general Pagan Amum to offer his resignation. The emergence of
these independents added to the confusion in the south, and the
NCP claimed that with the SPLM in such disarray it would be
difficult to partner with it and take the peace process forward
after the election.

The NCP faced similar problems in the nomination of its
candidates, without, however, the situation becoming quite as
divisive because local constituencies had more control over the
process than in the south. Struggles over nominations in Northern and Southern Kordofan produced divisions, fisticuffs, and

lawsuits, while in Gezira, Dr Nafie Ali Nafie, one of the most powerful men in the NCP, was rejected by the local constituency and forced to seek a nomination in his home area of Shendi in the north. As leader of the NCP campaign Dr Nafie frequently overruled local bodies of the party in the selection of candidates. This produced widespread anger, which turned on him.

The controversies were particularly tense in the competition for nominations for governor. While the outgoing state legislatures and governors had little power under the 1998 NCP constitution, and were regularly replaced by Khartoum and Juba, as a result of the CPA-informed interim constitutions in the north and south they had considerably more powers. The NCP was faced with the dilemma of opting either for party loyalists who might not win popular support, or for candidates who had strong popular bases but who could become difficult to control if elected. The emergence of the independent candidates did not represent any fundamental ideological or political disagreements in either the north or the south, but rather were largely a response to the overbearing selection approaches of the SPLM and NCP and local-level tribal issues.

While the rise of independent candidates caused internal party frictions, the SPLM selection of Yasir Arman as presidential candidate was highly controversial, in part because he was not chosen by the 2008 SPLM National Convention but instead by the party's Political Bureau in December 2009. As a long-term party activist Yasir was undoubtedly a qualified candidate, but his selection posed a number of problems. First, the decision to run Yasir instead of Salva as leader of the party was a powerful signal that, despite the SPLM's commitment to a united New Sudan, Salva was positioning himself to be leader in an independent south. Moreover, because it was initially assumed that Yasir could not win, many observers held that his candidature was designed to rally support for a post-referendum northern SPLM after the south separated.

Second, the Political Bureau's selection of Yasir Arman appeared to throw up a major obstacle to achieving a workable post-election partnership with the NCP, because they viewed him as a northern turncoat, a communist, and a strong exponent of the New Sudan ideology, which was based not only on unity, but crucially on secularism, a notion the NCP wanted to bury.[7] The NCP claimed that it did not run a candidate against Salva in the south, but Dr Lam Akol Ajawin, former SPLM foreign minister in the GNU and leader of the recently formed SPLM–DC (Democratic Change), did run as a presidential candidate and the SPLM contended that he was effectively the NCP candidate.

Third, Yasir's selection was expected to create divisions within the SPLM's southern constituency for those who would find it difficult to vote for a *jallaba*, albeit a *jallaba* of a different kind. When he was arrested and beaten along with Pagan Amum at a demonstration in Khartoum in late December 2009, Pagan reported that a SAF colonel said, 'Yasir should be killed because he brought these slaves to Khartoum' (interview, 28 March 2010). Indeed, part of the NCP's hatred of Yasir was because he was a Jalien, from the same tribe as Bashir (and reputedly a distant relative), and thus viewed as a racial traitor. Nonetheless, the more cynical (and this apparently included Riek Machar) suggested that Yasir was selected as a 'sacrificial lamb' who could be withdrawn as part of a bargain with the NCP.

Soon after Yasir's nomination, second vice president Ali Osman Taha visited Juba, where an NCP insider told the author that he proposed to GoSS president Salva Kiir that he be dropped to keep the SPLM–NCP partnership on track and ensure satisfactory agreements on outstanding issues like the census and additional seats in the south. This report is believable because the

NCP made no secret of what they considered to be the SPLM's betrayal of their partnership by running a candidate against Bashir. Salva and Riek apparently agreed, but were over-ruled in an acrimonious SPLM Political Bureau meeting – though that was not the end of the matter. One NCP leader told me that Yasir was not a threat, but the party wanted a flawless election and to display unity between the peace partners, but another official acknowledged that Yasir appeared to have most southern votes locked up, and in a second ballot situation the northern opposition could be expected to gravitate to him and pose a real threat to Bashir.

Salva personally ran afoul of the rules by continuing to wear his military uniform and being addressed as Lt General, which the chairman of the Registration Committee of the National Elections Commission, Mukhtar Al-Asam, said made him ineligible to run (*Sudan Tribune*, 16 January 2010). Salva had of course been forcibly retired from the SPLA by Garang in 2005, and he quickly fell in line.

The election campaign began on 20 February 2010 with all the major parties holding rallies and press conferences. Large posters of Omar al-Bashir appeared on nearly every street corner in central Khartoum, and as a result local wags said that the winner of the election would either be Bashir or the local soft drink Champion, which competed with the president in the number of signs. Juba began with few posters of Salva Kiir and none of his arch rival, Lam Akol. Salah Gosh, the former intelligence chief, launched the NCP campaign in Juba on 23 February and Salva launched the SPLM campaign on 24 February with the SPLA ordering the closure of commercial establishments in the city to ensure attendance. Although a ceasefire was announced in Darfur between JEM and SAF, it did not apply to other armed groups and in the event did not open up even JEM-controlled areas to campaigning.

In Northern Bahr el Ghazal, Governor Paul Malong stopped opposition candidates from holding public rallies. Carter Center observers and the media reported that Unity state governor Taban Deng Gai ordered the arrests of some of Angelina Teny-Dhurgon's officials and closed the bridge between Bentiu and Rubkona to stop a cavalcade. Carter Center observers also reported the use of SPLA vehicles at Taban Den Gai's rallies, SPLA members tearing down opposition posters and a speech by Taban contending that Angelina was unsuitable to be governor because she was a woman. At one point during the election an all-party delegation, including some members of the SPLM, presented the author with hundreds of marked ballots they claimed were literally thrown out the window by election officials because the electors had voted for candidates other than Taban.

From the outset the Juba Alliance parties tried to use the threat of their withdrawal from the elections to pressure the NCP to agree to a postponement and the formation of an all-party government to oversee the elections. In the midst of this debate and without any consultation with their Juba Alliance compatriots, Yasir announced the SPLM's boycott of the presidential and Darfur elections, although the party would continue participation in the rest of the north, including Blue Nile and Southern Kordofan. This threw the Juba Alliance parties into disarray. It had three immediate impacts: first, it led many in the north to conclude this was in effect a SPLM declaration of southern independence; second, it led to deep suspicions that the Yasir campaign had been sunk because of a backroom deal between the Juba SPLM and NCP; and lastly, it encouraged northern opposition parties to resolve their positions on boycotts. Indeed, after the SPLM made the first move, the Umma Party and the DUP in short order announced their boycott of the presidential elections, thus joining the earlier boycotts of the SCP and the Umma Reform and Renewal Party.

It became clear that the SPLM was being pulled between New Sudan advocates in the north, who did not think they could win the legislative or state elections but thought they just might win the presidency, and southern separatists, who were becoming alarmed at the success of Yasir's campaign, which was also setting off alarm bells for the NCP. And within the northern sector of the SPLM the division deepened between those who wanted a complete boycott and those who wanted full participation, although still excluding Darfur and Blue Nile (the latter was for SPLM purposes considered part of the south). The complete boycott section won, and the party's secretary general, Pagan Amum, announced the official decision at a press conference. This decision looked solid because it was largely based on the withdrawal of candidates in the region, but there was opposition to it by those who viewed it as a threat to the party's partnership with the NCP and by Malik Agar Eyre, deputy leader of the SPLM and head of its northern sector, and who was running for the governorship of Blue Nile state.

But the question remained as to why Yasir was withdrawn. The official reason given was that conditions were not suitable for the conduct of the election, and that after the SPLM failed to use its partnership with the NCP to make changes to the electoral procedures and end its control over the NEC the party decided to withdraw. The reason given in private was different, but equally unconvincing, even bizarre. Yasir and Pagan made two arguments in support of the withdrawal: first, they said that they initially believed there could be a democratic transfer of power and only recently realized that was not possible; and, second, they claimed that to continue the SPLM campaign risked bringing about a large-scale racial massacre because the regime felt threatened. However, it strained credibility to think that the SPLM could imagine a peaceful transfer of power. The second argument had a little more going for it, but not much.

It noted the racial epitaphs directed at Yasir personally for his support of southerners, registered the racial hatred on the pages of *Al-Intibaha* newspaper published by Tayyib Mustafa, an uncle of Bashir's, and said that tensions surrounding massive election rigging could lead to a 'racial conflict' and that the SPLM's withdrawal was designed to ensure this not take place. Indeed, it was contended that the international community should appreciate the SPLM's withdrawal to ensure peaceful elections. How meaningful elections could be possible in the absence of the only candidate that posed a serious threat to Bashir was never answered.

Violence would almost certainly have resulted if Yasir were denied the presidency (were he to win it) at the ballot box, but the two individuals making the argument were not known previously to have been intimidated by threats of violence by the government. Moreover, the claim that the violence would be racial, when to have that victory Yasir would have had to garner many votes in the north, was not credible. Riek Machar, who supported the presidential boycott but strongly opposed the decision of SPLM North to boycott the other areas, said that Yasir repeatedly begged the Political Bureau to withdraw his candidacy, and only late in the day it agreed. This too was not credible: Yasir gave every impression of enjoying his run for the presidency. What is known is that the NCP had good reason to fear that Yasir could either beat Bashir or ensure, along with other presidential candidates, that Bashir was denied a first-round victory and thus force a second round, when the other opposition parties could be expected to rally around Yasir.

A week before the election the author was at the SPLM offices in Khartoum and was told by officials that the party's boycott was complete except for Blue Nile state. During the course of the meeting a siren rang announcing the arrival of Dr Riek Machar. In a brief interview a few minutes later he told me there would be no SPLM boycott in the north, except for the presidency, and rejected suggestions of any deal with the NCP on that. He left and SPLM officials assured me that, despite what he had said, the boycott was definitely on.

The most convincing explanation therefore is that either at the Salva–Ali Osman meeting in Juba or shortly thereafter a decision was made by the SPLM leadership in Juba to end Yasir's campaign in the interest of keeping the NCP partnership alive and not upsetting the march to southern independence. Coming in the wake of what were perceived as sell-outs of their supporters in the northern states of Southern Kordofan and Blue Nile during the CPA negotiations and many trade-offs in the National Assembly over democratic measures to keep the southern secessionist project on track (and these were supported by Yasir in his role as leader of the SPLM parliamentary bloc), this would not be surprising. There may also have been agreement at the Ali Osman meeting with the SPLM leadership to ignore the rigging by each party on their respective turfs.

In retrospect Salva would probably agree that the selection of Yasir Arman as the SPLM national presidential candidate was a mistake; not because he was an ineffective candidate, but precisely because he was effective and demonstrated a surprising capacity to mobilize people in the north, particularly in marginalized areas like Darfur, and among southerners resident in the north, as well as gaining the support of southerners in the south. Yasir was living proof that the ideal of New Sudan had a concrete political basis with the potential of winning mass national support. However, and in a rare commonality of interests, Salva and Riek came together to press through the Political Bureau the decision to withdraw Yasir on the grounds that he and Pagan had long contended that either the elections would not take place or they would be rigged, and thus it was not consistent to withdraw only from the other elections and not the presidential campaign as well.

It was precisely at that point that New Sudan was sacrificed for the achievement of southern separation.

The Umma Party was completely split on the decision to boycott, with Sadig al-Mahdi opposing it while some of his closest colleagues, including his daughter, Dr Maryom, called for a boycott. When his attempt to pressure Bashir to make concessions failed, his party went into non-stop internal debates, the outcome of which was the complete withdrawal of the Umma Party from the election. While the decision to boycott was officially based on the conviction that the elections were rigged and the party had suffered enormously from years of NCP repression, it is also true that the Umma Party was in historical decline and would have performed poorly in the elections. Sadig al-Mahdi saw a horrible conundrum: if Bashir was elected there would be 'great trouble,' while if Yasir was elected he would not be accepted by the army.

DUP leader Osman al-Mirghani, who exerts more control over his party than Sadig al-Mahdi does over the Umma Party, joined the Juba Alliance late, but quickly announced the withdrawal of presidential candidate Hatim Asir. Mirghani left open the possibility of a wider boycott, but soon even the boycott of the presidential election was cast in doubt. Three factors were at play. First, the party was split like the Umma over participation. Second, there was heavy bargaining between Mirghani and the NCP leadership, including Bashir, and while some of this focused on electoral reforms, it also included Mirghani's demands for compensation for his property confiscated by the government. Third, with its historically close relations to Egypt, the DUP was subject to pressure from Cairo, which called for both an extended postponement of the election and the referendum. Because of fears of even more instability in Sudan, Egypt pressed its ally to stay in the election, and in the end the DUP ran candidates at all levels. However, when they were badly defeated, the leadership stated that it did not recognize the outcome of the elections. Like the

Umma Party, the present DUP under Mirghani is a pale imitation of its once powerful self.

Turabi and the PCP said from the outset that they would participate fully in the elections because he viewed them as an opportunity to capitalize on what he saw as the disarray in the Umma Party and DUP and become the parliamentary leader of the opposition in the post-election period. Turabi, however, was held by most people in Sudan to be the author of most of the country's misfortunes, and they could never vote for him or his party. Abdullah Deng, a Dinka Muslim, ran as the PCP candidate for the national presidency. Turabi no doubt thought that as a member of the two majority communities – African and Muslim – he could make his mark, but that did not prove to be the case.

Probably the most effective party leader was Mubarak al-Fadil, who broke from the Umma Party after the refusal of Sadig al-Mahdi to modernize and hold competitive elections for the leadership, a route that Mubarak hoped would take him to power. He then formed the Umma Reform and Renewal Party, which by its name suggested that his ultimate objective was to return to the mother party. The election provided an opportunity for Mubarak to cast himself on the national stage and he proved that he had the resources and drive to be nominated for the presidency. Moreover, his performance, especially on television, where he talked openly about the corruption in the ruling party, was one of the few events that got the otherwise largely withdrawn citizenry of northern Sudan talking.

The SCP nominated candidates throughout the north, including Ibrahim Nugud for the presidency, but from the outset refrained from participating in Darfur. Initially the party used the opportunity of greater freedom to campaign, reconnect with its base, work through the Juba Alliance to bring pressure on the NCP to further open up the political process, and, when that reached its limits, to support the SPLM North's call for a boycott. Nugud warned early in the campaign that the election results would probably not be accepted – and his prediction proved correct.

Despite the withdrawal of the big five opposition parties (excepting the DUP), their names would still be on the ballots and that meant that registered voters could still cast their votes for them. Indeed, while party leaders distanced themselves from the exercise, some quietly told their supporters to vote for them anyway. However cynically they approached the election, the northern opposition parties felt they had made a convincing case that the electoral process was deeply flawed and were angry that the US, the UK, Norway and other Western countries which gave so much rhetorical support for democracy found it easy to ignore the systemic abuses on display during the Sudanese elections.

Salva identified flaws in the elections similar to those singled out by the northern opposition: a faulty census, biased NEC, and restrictive laws. He was also fearful that if the NCP gained a majority in the National Assembly, it would change the peace agreement and force the south back to war. During the campaign Salva consistently rejected the allegations by the opposition parties of SPLM abuses and held that these parties only complained because they had no prospects. For years during the war the SPLA controlled the countryside, and as a result the SPLM was the only party people in the rural areas knew. He also insisted that he 'faithfully remained guided by the SPLM Vision and Mission for the people,' which would seem to mean endorsing Sudan's unity, but he also said that he would 'accept whatever choice was made by the people in the referendum' (campaign booklet, 2010: 2–3).

The southern opposition party leaders agreed with Salva about the NEC, but did not accept his view that they were free to campaign. The SPLM–DC reported that its political activities were curtailed and complained about government control of the media; its chairman in Wau had been held under house arrest for the previous six months, his deputy detained, officials of the party in Lakes and Jonglei states were arrested, and its offices in Bentiu and Wau were closed down by the security forces. Most of the DC's members in Unity state had been arrested even before the start of the campaign and the others could only operate covertly. The Union of Sudan African Parties (USAP) said that its complaints of illicit actions, made to senior members of the SPLM, were ignored; officials of the South Sudan Democratic Forum were arrested during the voter registration; the United Democratic Front (UDF) and its veteran leader Peter Sule reported arrests and abusive treatment of party agents and of an election being 'stolen'; and the United Democratic Salvation Front complained that while the election was supposed to implement democratic transformation, the abuses of the SPLM and SPLA ensured that would not happen.

Dr Lam Akol, leader of the SPLM–DC, launched his campaign in Malakal, home to his core Shilluk supporters, but operated out of Khartoum for the duration of the campaign as much for his personal safety as for convenience. By far the most cerebral campaigner, he was virulently hated by the SPLM, which insisted he was a militia leader in the pay of the NCP. Indeed, given conditions in Sudan it was clear that parties could only compete if they received state or foreign funding, and the latter was illegal under the Elections Act even if there were strong suspicions it was abused. Dr Lam launched his party on 6 June 2009 as 'a wind of change and reform of the situation in the SPLM which lost direction after the loss of its first leader, Dr John Garang de Mabior.' Committed to the CPA, SPLM–DC produced a manifesto for the election which covered most policies, but was less than clear on southern secession and called for both 'the right to and exercise of self-determination' and at the same time 'the realization of voluntary unity between the various peoples of the Sudan' (SPLM–DC February 2010: 3).

Egypt and Eritrea viewed the situation with increasing concern, with the former in favor of postponing the elections and the referendum because of insecurity and the unfulfilled conditions of the CPA. Ethiopia's Meles Zenawi was known to oppose southern secession, but was publicly very discreet. Nonetheless, according to one NCP informant he told the government that in his heart he supported unity, particularly in light of the problems associated with the secession of Eritrea, but he would not directly interfere in the debate in Sudan. Kenya and Uganda were clearly rooting for the SPLM and southern secession. NCP officials invariably singled out Ugandan president Museveni for condemnation. One official told me Museveni seemed to think that his role was to defend the south and that he sometimes took stronger positions on issues than the SPLM. Muammar Gaddafi had a long record in meddling in just about everyone's affairs in the region and, while he remained silent on the election, it was believed that he provided financing to a number of parties.

Before the start of the election campaign, the NCP's lead Darfur negotiator, Dr Ghazi Salhudin, announced that the NCP and JEM had reached a framework agreement and that he expected a comprehensive agreement between them to be signed shortly. Indeed, Bashir promptly went to Darfur where he launched his party's campaign by announcing that the war was over. Speculation was rife that since it was widely believed that JEM was under the influence of Turabi, and the PCP had opted to stay in the election, unlike most of the other opposition parties, the election would have the effect of bringing these three key elements of the Islamist community in Sudan together. But that was far from the case: the framework agreement did not open the door to a broader agreement, conflict in Darfur continued during the elections, and the PCP later concluded that the elections were completely fraudulent and rejected the results.

Campaigning was more vigorous and chaotic in the south

and provided more examples of SPLM and SPLA abuses than in the north, but despite this none of the southern parties called for withdrawal. In Northern Bahr el Ghazal, where Governor Paul Malong ran a fiefdom along similar lines to that of Taban Deng in neighboring Unity state, one local NEC official had to seek refuge in the UNMIS compound after the governor publicly threatened to shoot her. This official described to me how SPLA forces operating at the governor's behest surrounded a number of rural polling stations to ensure that only SPLM supporters were permitted to vote.

As much as Yasir Arman's candidacy upset the NCP, the decision of Lam Akol to run for the presidency of South Sudan angered the leadership of the SPLM, which repeatedly threw up obstacles to his campaign, even questioning the right of his party, the SPLM–DC, to run. Lam responded by appealing to the Constitutional Court, which on 6 January 2010 voided the unconstitutional restrictions imposed by the GoSS on the activities of the SPLM–DC (*CPA Monitor*, May 2011). But the decision made little difference, and Lam later complained that he was effectively not permitted to campaign in 40 percent of southern Sudan.[8] During the course of the campaign SPLM–DC officials were arrested and beaten, campaign material was confiscated and posters were torn down by the SPLA, meetings were arbitrarily cancelled, and in one case the police failed to protect the party's leader from stone-throwing citizens in Wau. As a Shilluk, Lam's best prospects were in the Upper Nile home of the tribe, which became very polarized between the Shilluk and Dinka after the latter – with the support of the SPLA – began on the anniversary of the CPA on 9 January 2009 to try and force the Shilluk from their ancestral lands on the east bank of the Nile and to claim ownership of the capital, Malakal.

Darfur predictably experienced the most problems; indeed the EU Election Observation Mission withdrew from Darfur on the grounds that it was impossible to fulfill its mandate due to general insecurity and lack of access to rural areas. The Carter Center did have observers in Darfur, but their movement was restricted and they reported under-aged voting, harassment, arrests of party agents, and in the end concluded that the election in the region could not be considered free and fair.

The printing of ballot papers at the government printing factory was widely deplored – 'it may weaken the security of the ballots' was how the Carter Center put it (Carter Center, 17 March 2010). Names and parties on the ballots were sometimes mixed up, while some candidates were not listed. Voter lists were problematic, with many names left off or incorrectly spelt; difficulties arose from voters being told that they would be voting at the same location in which they were registered and that not being the case; and at the last minute the number of polling stations was reduced, ostensibly for security reasons, but more likely due to gaining party advantage. The EU concluded that 8 percent of voters were left off the voting lists, while the Carter Center found that flaws in the voter registry had led to the disenfranchisement of many. Operational hours at the polling stations were not consistent, and many did not open on time or, in some cases, at all during the first day of the election. Illiterate and incapacitated voters required assistance, but there were widespread reports that party observers and NEC officials directed rather than aided these people.

While international observers experienced few problems with the security agencies, that was not the case with domestic observers and party agents, particularly in southern Sudan. The NCP complained about the activities of the TAMAM al-Khatim Adlan Center for Enlightenment, which they accused of being communist (as if being a communist was illegal). Numerous instances were noted by all the major observation missions of restricted access, intimidation, harassment, beatings, and the arrest of party agents and domestic observers, in most of the southern states, although problems were particularly severe in Central Equatoria, Western Equatoria, Western and Northern Bahr el Ghazal, Lakes, and Unity state. In consequence, many southerners did not accept the officially announced results, particularly for the gubnatorial positions. Security conditions were so bad in Western Equatoria that the EU Observation Mission withdrew. There were many cases of SPLA involvement in the abuse of opposition candidates and their agents. The Carter Center found that in Northern Bahr el Ghazal soldiers marked ballot papers and forcefully replaced police and party agents at polling stations (Carter Center, 17 March 2010). In Hameshkoreb, Kassala state, a local big man and traditional ruler, Sultan Ali Bitai, ran on an NCP ticket and used his militia forces to bar DUP observers from monitoring the election.

The observation missions noted discrepancies in the amount of money available to the parties to conduct their campaigns and issued mild rebukes for those exceeding the limits approved in the Elections Act. However, they never came close to understanding the extent of the problem, which permitted a handful of parties to receive vast funding and seriously call into question the competitive nature of the elections. Along with Gaddafi, it was widely believed, and reported by some GoSS ministers, that the US government had provided direct funding to the SPLM since at least 2006.

Observing the Observers

Monitoring by international missions has become part of the accepted arrangements for the conduct of Third World elections and part of the peace-building package. Thus for the April 2010 Sudan elections there were five major international monitoring missions – the European Union, the Carter Center, the African Union, the Arab League, and IGAD – as well as a host of smaller bodies, and embassies. There was also a much larger group of domestic observers, many of which, however, were affiliated with the Carter Center or the National Democratic Institute. Although there was no official coordination, the approaches and the final statements of all the groups were remarkably similar, which is not surprising given how often they work together, that they are influenced by the same set of assumptions and political concerns, and they exchange personnel. In theory monitoring boosts confidence in the fairness of the electoral process, helps deter fraud in the balloting and counting procedures, reports on the integrity of the election, mediates disputes resulting from the election, and vouchsafes democratization (Bjornlund et al. 1992).

The experience of election observation in Sudan did not for the most part confirm this theory. First, neutrality was compromised by the fact that the leaders of the observation missions had informally decided at the outset that the elections should not undermine the overall peace process and, in particular, the upcoming referendum and the march to South Sudan's independence. It was assumed by virtually all those leading these missions that a critical appraisal of the abuses, particularly those of the NCP, could lead to the peace process being disrupted or aborted. The contrary view, that a whitewash would convince the guilty parties that they were effectively being given free rein, was never seriously considered. There were many references to this being the first genuine multiparty election in twenty-four years and thus it was natural to expect problems. This glossed over a couple of key points: first, the NCP had overthrown a democratically elected government in 1989, and any ignorance by the Sudanese about elections was due to the refusal of the ruling party to hold them; and second, the last accepted election in 1986 proceeded with far fewer problems and allegations of abuse than the election in 2010, even though it was the first genuine election in eighteen years and did not have the benefit of massive engagement by the international community.

The technical approach of the observation missions, which appeared designed not to understand the political developments, was also not capable of exposing many of the abuses. Elsewhere in Africa it has been noted that politicians exploited observation missions to gain electoral respectability, knowing that they posed little threat to any manipulation of the electoral process (Anglin 1998). The concern of the election-supporting agencies and the observation missions was to ensure that the process was technically proficient, and this became the critical criterion for determining whether the elections were free and fair. Other analysts have also noted the gap between the intensity of election observing and the failure of the approach to detect major abuses; this led Soremekun to describe the activity as 'disguised tourism' (Soremekun 1999).

Also noteworthy was the attempt of leaders of the observation missions to try to influence the course of the election campaign. Thus in northern Sudan, Umma Party leader Sadig al-Mahdi, DUP leader Osman al-Mirghani, SCP leader Ibrahim Nugud, and Umma Renewal leader Mubarak al-Fadil al-Mahdi repeatedly argued that, first, the NEC was dominated by NCP loyalists who could never deliver free and fair elections, and, second, that they wanted a seven-month delay in the election and the formation of an all-party government in the interim to oversee the elections and ensure they were fair. Ex-president Jimmy Carter responded, on the basis of a 45-minute meeting with NEC officials, that he was confident of their neutrality and competence, and he held to that position publicly and privately until the eve of the elections. In response to the appeal that the elections be postponed, Carter refused to entertain the idea, noting that since the international community had paid $500 million for the elections (where that figure came from has never been determined) they could not be postponed. Later in the election campaign members of the northern opposition attempted to organize a boycott, and Carter argued forcefully against the proposal, making a number of public statements that the boycott was failing when it clearly was not. Carter's position on this and other key issues corresponded with that of the US government, and in particular with US Sudan special envoy General Scott Gration.

Indeed, Gration inserted himself in the election in ways that repeatedly caused controversy and anger. While he became enormously popular in NCP circles (Bashir was quoted at a rally as saying with respect to him, 'Even America has joined the NCP'), he was reviled by the northern opposition, including the SPLM. What angered them was his strong support for facilitating the holding of the referendum, which was widely believed in the north to be a US endorsement of the separation of southern Sudan, his lack of neutrality, and his four key positions on the election: first, that the NEC was a competent and fair body to conduct the election; second, that there could be no postponement of the election; third, dismissal of the concerns of the opposition; and lastly, the assumption that the elections would be as 'free and fair as possible.' A senior member of the SPLM told the author that 'the job of Gration, as he sees it, is to facilitate the departure of South Sudan. This is the only thing that can be salvaged from this deeply flawed election.' Gration also followed the NCP in condemning the Darfur liberation movements, and Abdel Wahid in particular, for not participating in Sudan's 'big election.' He said,

> This election is the first time in 24 years that the people in Sudan can express their will through the ballot and I think this is very important, because the process[es] that are put into place now, the political transformation, the democratization that is happening right now might set the future generation a way of expressing their will through the ballot and not the bullet.[9]

While opposition leaders were careful not to condemn the US for the actions of Gration, the election did lead to a growth in anti-Americanism. Although Bashir welcomed Gration's involvement in the election campaign, even he could not resist taking a few pokes at the Americans to capitalize on this sentiment. The UK and Norway, the closest allies of the US, however, also gave strong support to the elections. That foreign election observers openly attempted to direct the course of the election contributed to the widely held view that they were in league with the ruling parties to fix the result. Indicative of this suspicion, at the EU press conference in Khartoum on 17 April 2010, attended by the author, three journalists asked the Observation Mission leadership whether their report had been prepared in Brussels before they came to Sudan. The answer they received was that the information had been forwarded to Brussels, which had indeed produced the final draft.

If the public sometimes viewed observation missions as supporting the ruling parties, the NCP and SPLM did not. When one of the Carter Center's reports asked the NEC to consider a brief delay on technical grounds to ensure the election would be competently organized, the government came down hard on the organization for supposedly making common cause with the opposition parties, which were calling for a seven-month delay for political reasons. President al-Bashir slammed the organization, saying at a campaign rally that the Mahdi had killed interfering foreigners and that 'any foreigner or organization that demands the delay of elections will be expelled sooner rather than later. We wanted them to see the free and fair elections, but if they interfere in our affairs, we will cut their fingers off, put them under our shoes, and throw them out' (*Sudan Tribune*, 24 March 2010), all to cries of 'Allah Akbar' from his audience. That abuse passed almost unnoticed, but when on the eve of the election Bashir issued a similar statement, the Carter Center quietly asked for an apology and implied that if it was not forthcoming that it might withdraw from observing the elections. The apologies came thick and fast from Ali Osman, Ghazi Salhudin, and Bashir in both a phone conversation with Carter and at a public rally the next day. The theme of the apologies was to praise Carter and thank him for his support to Sudan over many years. In fact Carter was in Atlanta at the time; the Center's staff and observers who were in the country at the time of the threat were the ones potentially at risk.

The question that must be asked is whether the elections did anything to empower the Sudanese people, which after all is what the CPA-stipulated transition to democracy means. Were Sudanese citizens able to have their interests better represented and to have more control over the political leaders than before the elections? Did they have more control over *their* peace process? The answers to those questions are obviously negative, and in that light the only conclusion that can be drawn is that the elections were a failure. Indeed, the elections actually reduced the power of the Sudanese people over their political leaders and the political environment in the north, and in the south conditions considerably deteriorated after the elections.

The repeated refusals of the GoSS and the GoS to deal constructively with their respective opposition parties after the elections was invariably backed up with the claim that they held power through the legitimacy of elections, and unstated was that the international community through the auspices of the international observation missions confirmed this. Thus President al-Bashir noted: 'This election was monitored by local, regional, and international observers. They all witnessed the honesty and the transparency of these elections in Sudan' (*Guardian*, 20 April 2011). Of course the observation missions drew no such conclusions. However, when this claim was constantly repeated by politicians and in the media many ordinary Sudanese did indeed

think that these missions had fully endorsed the elections, and
were as a result frequently very angry. Against that background a
case can be made that it would have been better if there had been
no observation missions. There could hardly have been more
rigging, since the NCP won virtually all the seats and governor
positions in the north, and the SPLM did the same in the south,
so the presence of the missions in that respect was irrelevant. But
without the international missions, the NCP and SPLM would
have been on far weaker ground to claim legitimacy for their
victory and just might have had to be more accommodating of
their oppositions.

In the wake of the elections the SPLM and NCP spoke of their
commitment to forming 'broad-based governments,' but at the end
of the peace process that had not happened. In any case both
governments claimed that the proposed power-sharing was due
to their generosity, since they alone had been shown to represent
the will of the people based on internationally endorsed election
results. Moreover, the hope of the international community that
the elections would broaden the base of governance and bring
other parties directly into the national assemblies in Khartoum
and Juba, and into the hitherto NCP- and SPLM-dominated peace
process, proved to be a pipe dream since the ruling parties in
Khartoum and Juba held more seats in their respective assemblies
than before the elections. The opposition parties in both the north
and the south meanwhile condemned the elections and refused
to accept the results, although in their weakened condition that
did not mean much.

However, the biggest failing of the international community
was to ignore the link between democratic transformation and
peace and stability. Democracy was traded off in the elections,
just as it was countless times during the peace process interim
period, in the interests of political expediency. And the price was
paid not just in the arrogance and hypocrisy of the leaderships

of the NCP and SPLM, but in multiple threats to the peace process and the continuing absence of stability. A pragmatist might contend that it was not so bad to compromise on principles if the end result was satisfactory, but in fact it looked distinctly unsatisfactory. Just as in the Middle East, the US and its Western allies in Sudan demonstrated a complete disconnect between their rhetorical support for democracy and their support for autocratic regimes. When push came to shove, the international community was more concerned about stability than democracy – and in the end got neither. And this in practice meant support for the power holders in Khartoum and Juba irrespective of how they acquired that power, a pattern evident over many years throughout the world and facing its most serious challenge in the Middle East.

Conclusion

In a study published just before the 2010 national elections the authors concluded that 'If the election should lack credibility, it is hard to see how the Comprehensive Peace Agreement can survive' (Willis et al. 2009). But the CPA did survive in spite of its lack of credibility; indeed, when democracy is perceived as a threat to peace the international peacemakers invariably ensure that it is democracy that gives ground. This study went on to reject the thesis that

> The ballot ... has been fetishized, encouraging an empty perform-ance of electoral behaviour that leaves the fundamentals of politics unchanged. It is possible, according to this argument, to have a ballot yet still deny the population the essentials of democracy: access to justice, governmental transparency, and freedom of expression and association.

The thesis rejected by the authors was in fact an accurate summary of the April 2010 Sudan general elections.

The Carter Center and the European Union observation missions engaged in serious internal debates over how to approach the abuses due to fears that to call the parties to task might threaten the unfolding peace process. In the event, the observation missions tended towards the latter view and ultimately reached the conclusion that the elections did meet international standards. But they pulled their punches, while the NCP and SPLM ran roughshod over the opposition and used the opportunity to divide the country along north–south lines that roughly corresponded to what would soon effectively be international boundaries. Few people actually read the international observation mission reports, and in any case they contained a lot of reflection and analysis about technical issues and other concerns, and as a result it was not too much of a stretch to conclude that they endorsed the elections since they emphasized that whatever the abuses the peace process should continue. Indeed, the Carter Center found that 'the CPA's promise of democratic transformation has not been fulfilled,' that the elections 'will fall short of meeting international standards and Sudan's obligations for genuine elections in many respects,' but nonetheless concluded somewhat illogically that 'the elections are important as a key benchmark in the Comprehensive Peace Agreement.' The US government's public statement on the Sudan elections largely mirrored those of the observation missions and also their emphasis, the first line of the statement asserting that 'The elections held recently in Sudan were an essential step in a process laid out by Sudan's Comprehensive Peace Agreement' before noting that they did not meet international standards.[10]

The breakdown of seats in the National Assembly (excluding the 17 rescheduled Geographical Constituency elections and one Red Sea constituency whose results were not released) had the NCP winning 312 seats, comprising 180 Geographical Constituency, 50 Party List, and 82 Women's List seats, equating to 72 percent of the total. The SPLM won 99 seats, made up of 56 Geographical Constituency, 17 Party List, and 26 Women's List seats (23 percent of the total). The PCP won 4 seats – 1 Geographical Constituency and 3 Women's List seats – while the Federal Umma Party obtained 2 Geographical Constituency and 1 Women's List seats. The following garnered Geographical Constituency seasts: DUP 4, DUP–Original 1, SPLM–DC 2, Umma Reform & Renewal 2, National Umma Party (NUP) 1, Independent candidates 3, and the Muslim Brotherhood 1 (*CPA Monitor*, May 2011). NCP candidates won 91 percent of the state assembly seats in the north, while the SPLM took 87 percent of the seats in the south.

Although NCP cadres had widely predicted that Bashir would pick up 80 percent or more of the vote, even after Yasir withdrew, his final total was only 68.15 percent; there were many doubts as to the accuracy of that number among the observation missions, but in the absence of supporting evidence there was no public questioning of Bashir's count in their reports. Yasir picked up 21.64 percent of the vote, as his name was still on the ballot even though he had withdrawn from the election, and southerners voted en masse for him (at the direction of the SPLM). Salva Kiir meanwhile picked up 93 percent of the vote against Lam Akol's 7 percent; these figures too were questioned privately, but not challenged publicly.

The southern assembly was harder to call given the importance of independent candidates, but in the end the SPLM won all but 16 seats: 4 seats to SPLM–DC, 1 to the NCP, and 11 to independents, although most of the independents eventually returned to the SPLM. The NCP won all of the governor positions in the north except Blue Nile state, which was won by the SPLM's Malik Agar Eyre after negotiations and threats of violence, while in the south the SPLM swept all of the governor positions after Colonel Bagosora, who had run as an independent in Western Equatoria, abruptly announced his return to the SPLM. Although it can never be fully ascertained, it was widely believed that as well as Western Equatoria the SPLM lost the governorships of Central Equatoria, Upper Nile, Unity, Lakes, Northern Bahr el Ghazal, and maybe Jonglei – that is, six of the ten states in the south.

Since most southern Sudanese seemed convinced that the SPLM governors in these states were defeated – and none of the observation missions was able to confirm this – there is a need for explanation. As a participant in the exercise I can say that there was no overt political pressure on the observers or any attempt to cover up the rigging, but it does seem in retrospect that the methodology of the observation missions was inadequate in detecting many of the abuses that took place. The inability of the observation missions to carry out the necessary analysis of campaign funding is one example. There was also, and this is no doubt typical in such exercises, considerable pressure to produce a statement immediately upon completion of the election process, due in large part, as one senior observer explained, to the desire to reassure the public that despite the problems they should accept the results and not resort to violence. As a southern politician put it, the job of the observers was 'to legalize the status quo.' In the event, the two lead missions – the Carter Center and the EU – both released their statements and held press conferences on 17 April, while the counting was still under way; and the other missions fell in line. This anomaly was due solely to the fact that the heads of the two missions had other engagements on the 18th.

It seems likely that many of those in the south who voted for the SPLM did so not out of respect for the party, appreciation of its achievements in government, or expectations of future good performance, but simply because a vote for the SPLM was seen as the best means to keep the peace process on track and ensure the holding of the referendum and the eventual secession of southern

Sudan. While Yasir received most of his votes from southerners, those in the north voted for the SPLM because of their belief in the ideology of New Sudan. They were among the biggest losers in the election.

But if the international peace-builders and the observation missions hoped quickly to put the embarrassment of the election behind them, they failed to appreciate the legacy of bitterness it created among the opposition parties and the cynicism it produced among the general population. Indeed, as will be seen, some of the most severe political and security problems in the south would occur in those states where rigging was the most prevalent. Finally, the April 2010 national elections served to put to rest CPA commitments to democratic transformation and the unity of Sudan and to dispel any illusions about the democratic credentials of the SPLM. The veteran northern SPLM leader, Dr Monsour Khalid, concluded that 'a weakness of the CPA was its dependence on the partnership between the NCP and SPLM, but the real problem was due to the failure of both parties to broaden the process and thus produce the promised democratic transformation' (interview, 22 October 2011). Dr Monsour made clear that the international observers also bore responsibility for the failed elections.

It was only on 10 May, after the peace partners and the international community had tired of congratulating themselves on a job well done, that the Carter Center issued a post-election statement on vote tabulation which concluded that the 'process was highly chaotic, non-transparent, and vulnerable to electoral manipulation. As a result, the Center was concerned about the accuracy of the preliminary results announced by the National Elections Commission, and in addition that 'procedures and safeguards intended to ensure accuracy and transparency have not been systematically applied and in some areas have been routinely bypassed' (Carter Center, 10 May 2010). In other words, even setting aside the problems of the registration, the campaign, the unequal playing field, and blatant human rights abuses, on purely technical grounds the Carter Center came close to concluding that the tabulation process was so deeply flawed as to cast the entire exercise in doubt. But by then no one was listening; the focus was on keeping the peace process moving and ensuring a successful outcome to the referendum.

FOUR

CONFIRMING THE INEVITABLE: THE JANUARY 2011 REFERENDUM

The international backers of the peace process, together with the SPLM-led GoSS, were anxious to move beyond the flawed April elections and focus on what they always considered the main objective of the CPA, namely the referendum to facilitate the separation of southern Sudan and to determine whether the residents of Abyei wished to be affiliated to the south or remain with the north. But the bitterness caused by the elections, the failure to make headway in realizing the commitment to democratization, and the lack of progress on a range of issues meant the climate in the lead-up to the referendum suggested conflict and even a return to war. In addition, the SPLM leadership had to overcome the contradiction between its program, which called for a reformed united Sudan, and its support for southern secession, as well as reconcile with an embittered opposition and convince the NCP to accept the inevitability of secession. The NCP was in an equally contradictory position because, while it officially supported unity, most of its leaders were only too happy to see off the troublesome secularists of southern Sudan and their New Sudan ideology as long as they could use recognition of the secessionist vote as a means to extort the GoSS and international community on a range of issues.

Right to Self-Determination

The demand for self-determination flowed from almost six decades of political and armed struggles; it was supported by virtually all sections of an otherwise much divided southern society. The legal right to southern self-determination was prescribed in the Machakos Protocol, which asserted that 'the people of South Sudan have the right to self-determination, inter alia, through a referendum to determine their future status' (Article 1.3). It further stated that, 'At the end of the six (6) year interim period there shall be an internationally monitored referendum, organized jointly by the GoS and the SPLM/A, for the people of South Sudan to: confirm the unity of the Sudan by voting to adopt the system of government established under the Peace Agreement; or to vote for secession' (Article 2.5).

Although there was reason to believe that a confederally organized Sudan would have a solid basis of support in the south, this was not provided as a separate option even though focus groups in the south canvassed by the National Democratic Institute (NDI) found there was strong support for it, albeit much more for secession. Backing for confederalism could be held to be support for unity because it would effectively mean maintaining the autonomous governmental structures in the south bequeathed by the CPA. The SPLM's northern sector leader and governor of Blue Nile state, Malik Agar Eyre, argued for years for such an arrangement. Dr Ghazi Salhudin, the chief NCP negotiator of the Machakos Protocol, said that since the 1950s northern politicians had equated 'extended federalism' with secession and never seriously entertained it.[1] In fact both the NCP and SPLM opposed it, the former because it implied support for a New Sudan vision and elimination of the opportunity for Islamization of the south, and the latter because, despite official support for a united Sudan, the post-Garang leadership favored outright separatism.

The Machakos Protocol was grandfathered into the constitution, but it was the Referendum Act approved by the National Assembly in December 2009 that stipulated the conditions under which the referendums for southern Sudan and Abyei would be held, and that was the product of laborious negotiations, principally between the two vice presidents Riek Machar and Ali Osman, and demonstrations led by Yasir Arman. A cause of particular controversy was the percentage of southerners that would have to vote in order that the results be accepted. In the event, the parties agreed that 60 percent of registered voters must cast their vote in the referendum and that if that threshold was not reached the referendum would be repeated within sixty days (South Sudan Referendum Act 2009: Article 25.41.2), a provision that caused much anger in the south. It was agreed that a simple majority of 50 percent plus one vote would confirm either unity or secession. The Act further called for 'international observation' of all aspects of the process. In recognition of the widespread displacement that accompanied the conflict in southern Sudan, the Referendum Act provided for voting in northern Sudan and eight out-of-country voting (OCV) locations.[2] The Act called for the establishment of referendum centers in all locations where over 20,000 southerners reside and state capitals in northern Sudan. In the absence of 20,000 registered voters, voters were expected to travel to the capital of the state out-of-country location.

The most contentious provision of the Act was its determination of eligibility to vote, which it divided into three categories: one, those born to at least one parent from a southern indigenous community who resided in the south before 1 January 1956; two, those whose ancestry could be traced to one of the ethnic communities of the south, but without at least one parent residing in southern Sudan on or before 1 January 1956; and three, permanent residents who (or whose parents or grandparents) had resided in southern Sudan since 1 January 1956 (South Sudan

Referendum Act 2009: Article 25). The first group could vote in northern Sudan, southern Sudan, or partake in OCV locations. The second and third categories of voter could only vote in southern Sudan. These criteria were intended to include ethnic southerners and long-term southern residents, but no list was provided as to what constituted an ethnic or an indigenous community, or what evidence was needed to demonstrate how these criteria were to be met.

These complicated provisions were a response to SPLM concerns regarding NCP manipulation of voters in the north. Initially the SPLM wanted to deny southerners residing in the north the right to vote, but its parliamentary allies convinced it to back down.[3] In consideration of the parallel Abyei Referendum Act, the SPLM parliamentary bloc went even further in denying basic democratic rights. After an all-party National Assembly committee recommended giving both the Ngok Dinka and Misseirya nomads of the territory the right to vote in the referendum, the SPLM caused such a ruckus that proceedings were stopped and it went into private negotiations with the NCP. The upshot was the introduction of a bill to expand the authority of the National Intelligence and Security Service, with the SPLM agreeing to vote for these measures and the NCP accepting that the Misseirya would be denied the right to vote in the Abyei Referendum (South Sudan Referendum Act 2009: Article 25). The SPLM's opposition colleagues were disgusted and the Misseirya MPs, most of whom were members of the NCP, were deeply aggrieved. Claiming that they had been 'sacrificed' and 'betrayed' the Misseirya MPs marched out of the National Assembly accompanied by a number of NDA and other MPs. One of the dissenting MPs noted bitterly that 'these events seriously undermined our trust in the SPLM.'

The South Sudan Referendum Act also provided for the establishment of the Southern Sudan Referendum Commission (SSRC), an independent government body based in Khartoum to oversee the referendum, and the subsidiary Southern Sudan Referendum Bureau (SSRB), based in Juba, responsible for managing the referendum in southern Sudan. Although the SPLM tried to suggest otherwise, the chairman of the SSRC, the elderly Professor Mohammed Ibrahim Khalil, was a distinguished lawyer, lifetime Umma Party member, and no friend of the NCP; indeed, he had left Sudan and lived in exile in the US since the Islamist coup. The professor and the SSRC came across as being from a different generation – kindly liberal-minded Sudanese trying to do the right thing even if it led to the dismemberment of their country. Justice Chan Reek Madut, who served as chairman of the SSRB, was the deputy president of the Supreme Court of Southern Sudan. A number of the members of the Commission and Board were known SPLM supporters, so that, unlike the April 2010 elections, there could be no accusations of bias unless it was against the NCP. Although the SSRC and the SSRB were faced with a multitude of logistical and financial problems, it was later generally agreed that they carried out their responsibilities professionally and neutrally.

March to the Referendum

Although the SPLM and NCP proved quite skilled during the elections at cutting deals to advance their particular interests, undermining the opposition parties, and making a mockery of the CPA commitment to democratic transformation, the elections nonetheless served to deepen the distrust between them. It also poisoned the atmosphere for considering a range of what became known as post-referendum issues. Consideration of these issues was slow to take off because of delays in realizing most of the objectives of the CPA, political uncertainty, the desire at different times of both parties to delay matters, and also because they were discouraged by the US and other Western countries from addressing matters earlier because it was held that this would pre-judge the results of the referendum. However, the outcome of the April elections divided the country between an overwhelmingly NCP-controlled north and a similarly SPLM-controlled south, and made clear what the outcome of the referendum would be.

With the negotiations making little progress, the head of the AU High Level Implementation Panel (AUHIP), Thabo Mbeki, moved the process to Mekelle, Ethiopia, where on 23 June they agreed on a formal process to consider the issues and who was to be involved. It was decided to break down the various topics into four clusters: citizenship, security, finance, and international treaties and legal issues, and that the negotiations were to be led by the AU with the mandate 'to assist the Sudanese parties in implementing the CPA and related processes,' a process that would be supported by IGAD, the IGAD Partners Forum, and the UN. Lastly it was agreed that the negotiations should involve other political parties and civil society. It seemed like a good start, but a year later there were still no signed agreements.

Citizenship was of particular concern because it produced fears of sudden displacements and loss of basic rights of southerners in the north. Indeed, the specter of the tit-for-tat expulsions in Ethiopia and Eritrea in the wake of their 1998–2000 war remained an example of what could befall Sudan. Although Presidents al-Bashir and Kiir issued reassuring statements, that was not the case with some of their ministers, who found it politically expedi-ent to inflame the situation. The GNU minister of information, Kamal Obeid, said that if southerners vote for secession, 'They will not enjoy citizenship rights, jobs or benefits, they will not be allowed to buy or sell in Khartoum market and they will not be treated in hospitals' (*Al Arabyia News*, 25 September 2010). President al-Bashir promptly rejected the statement and said it was his responsibility to protect southerners in the north. But that did not forestall the firestorm, with southern politicians and the media returning to Kamal Obeid's statement for weeks. In fact his statement was to prove accurate. NCP officials insisted that the situation in Sudan was not like that in Ethiopia and Eritrea in the run-up to the expulsions carried out in those countries, but the author was told by a senior NCP member of the government a year and a half before the referendum that in the event of a vote for southern secession southerners would be expelled. The NCP approach would subsequently moderate, but in early 2012 South Sudanese residents in Sudan still had no assurances.

While some elements in the NCP wanted to threaten or punish southerners for the impending vote on secession, SPLM officials created a climate of fear to encourage southerners to move south for the voter registration and referendum. Indeed, southerners did start to leave in increasing numbers in the belief that there was no future for them in the north, although at the end of the peace process there were still hundreds of thousands of southerners in the north, including those who had returned after facing difficult living and working conditions in the south, some of whom had faced the epithet *jallaba* – 'northern merchants,' a term of abuse. This movement had a discernible effect on the northern economy in spheres such as urban building, and in eastern Sudan, where agricultural production was disrupted because of the reduced number of southern farm laborers available. As well as southerners living in the north, 30 percent of the northern and southern population of both territories reside in the border area, including as many as 3 million northern-based nomads who regularly cross the border, all of whom would benefit from agreement on a system of dual citizenship, a principle that was opposed by the NCP and not pressed by the SPLM.

Under the CPA oil revenues were shared 50–50, but in the event of a vote for independence the south would be legally entitled to all the revenues from oil within its territory, which was estimated to be about 75 percent of total oil production. Both the SPLM and NCP agreed that, should the south opt for independence, arrangements would be made to cushion the revenue blow to the north, but they did not agree on the measures to be taken. The NCP favored a long-term arrangement with a slowly reducing revenue share, while the SPLM wanted to forgo revenue sharing entirely and instead pay for use of the pipeline to Port Sudan for a stipulated period. At this stage the SPLM preferred to pay the north in cash and oil to ensure its soft landing.

The issue of oil necessarily raised the subject of border demarcation – of which there had been no resolution – since most oil deposits are on or near the north–south border. Indeed, the regular pronouncement of the mediators that only 20 percent of the north–south border, amounting to nearly 400 kilometers, was in dispute, was not very reassuring when no progress was made. The NCP attributed the failure to make progress on border demarcation to, first, the desire of the SPLM to push such concerns into the post-referendum period when, they assumed, their bargaining position would be enhanced by a vote for secession, and second, their difficulties in reaching a consensus among themselves on defining the border. The SPLM meanwhile complained that the NCP wanted to use the border issue as a means to bring pressure on other areas, notably oil revenue sharing.

Another area of concern was international treaties, foremost being the Nile River treaties of 1929 and 1959, which effectively divided the waters of the river between Egypt and Sudan. Appreciating that this arrangement was not sustainable, a number of Western countries began supporting the Nile River Basin Initiative (NBI) to build cooperative relations between the Nile basin countries. This initiative was not very successful, as was made clear after failed negotiations in May 2010, when Ethiopia, Uganda, Tanzania, Rwanda, and Kenya signed a new agreement without Egypt or Sudan and tensions steadily grew between the upstream and downstream countries. Into that mix will go South

Sudan, which it is assumed will make common cause with the upstream countries given its close attachment to Uganda and Kenya. The SPLM initially did not highlight the issue of water resources in the CPA, no doubt out of concern that it would anger Egypt, and also because presently the south does not use the Nile waters for irrigation or industrial purposes. However, in the post-referendum negotiations the SPLM did press for a share of the Nile. This has not proven easy to resolve, since with the loss of oil Sudan's development plans depend to a considerable degree on irrigated agriculture, which makes the NCP less willing to relinquish any of its water share under the 1959 agreement.

At the start of negotiations the SPLM contended that since the south received few benefits from the national government, Khartoum should assume responsibility for the entire national debt of $39 billion, but that position proved untenable. Various formulas were explored that involved Sudan assuming the entire debt, but in return for accepting the referendum and its outcome that this debt would be taken over by sympathetic donors. There was an early agreement that southern Sudan would develop its own currency after independence, although by the time of independence this appeared to have collapsed.

The NCP not only wanted the SPLM to pay a price for the independence of the south ('ransom' was the term Pagan Amum used), but it also looked to gain benefits from the US and the international community. In particular, the NCP wanted debt relief, be it directly from the US, or through US influence at the World Bank, or via a US-led group of contributors. It also wanted the US to end sanctions against Sudan (although those implemented as a result of the Darfur war could not be considered), drop the 'state sponsor of terrorism' designation, and, through the Security Council, have the ICC charges against President al-Bashir suspended. In return the NCP would facilitate the referendum process and recognize southern Sudan's independence. The NCP had experienced US broken promises after it signed the CPA, but felt that it had the leverage. Even if the Americans again failed them, they had nothing to lose by trying.

Confronting Party Contradictions

The elections were barely over when the parties started positioning themselves for the referendum. For the SPLM it involved, first, providing justifications for breaking their program's commitment to New Sudan and the commitment under the CPA to national unity; second, keeping the process on track; third, moving forward on the post-referendum issues; and lastly, reconciling with the southern opposition to ensure internal accord in the march to the referendum. For the NCP, which had almost certainly not anticipated that the peace process would reach this stage, there was a need, first, to retain the loyalty of its constituency, which had mixed feelings about the pending loss of southern Sudan; second, it had to position itself to maximize the benefits it expected to accrue from agreeing to the process unfolding and accepting the results of the referendum; lastly, it wished to place some of the political burden that southern secession would entail on the opposition parties.

The starting point of the referendum campaign was a series of meetings held in the US, the highlight being a conference at the UN General Assembly on 24 September attended by vice presidents Ali Osman Taha and Salva Kiir, along with UN secretary general Ban Ki-Moon, US president Barack Obama, Thabo Mbeki as chairman of the AUHIP, and leaders from Kenya, Rwanda, Ethiopia, as well as officials from the UK, France, Germany, and China. The conference underlined the international commitment to the peace process and the need to hold the referendum in a fair and transparent manner and on time. It was in the US that Salva Kiir first said that while unity had been a priority since

the signing of the CPA, it was 'no longer an attractive option' for
the people of southern Sudan (*Sudan Tribune*, 24 September
2010), thus embarrassing his fellow vice president. Ali Osman
meanwhile assured the UN and Salva Kiir that the referendum
would not be delayed. However, he complained about the 'de-
monization' of Sudan, as evidenced by the ICC indictment of
President al-Bashir on war crimes charges, economic sanctions,
the lack of debt relief and Sudan's presence on the United States'
list of state sponsors of terrorism.

Salva Kiir's real debut, however, was among allies and friends
in the Congressional Black Caucus, to which he gave a keynote
address a week earlier, in which he again said that unity had not
been made attractive and predicted that 'the Southern Sudanese
people will vote overwhelmingly for independence.'[4] Obama's
special envoy Scott Gration also organized talks between the
SPLM and NCP delegations on a range of post-referendum subjects, with particular attention given to Abyei. Gration's approach
to negotiations, for which he would be remembered after he left
Sudan to become the US ambassador to Kenya, was summed up
as 'We've got to think about giving out cookies. Kids, countries
– they react to gold stars, smiley faces, handshakes, agreements,
talk, engagement.' Not surprisingly, nothing of any significance
came out of those meetings.

Salva regularly expressed in his US speeches the desire to
resolve the post-referendum issues, but the one he emphasized
most was oil revenue sharing. NCP ministers said their biggest
concern was borders, and indicated that Ethiopia's Meles Zenawi
had pressed on them the need for such an agreement before South
Sudan's independence to ensure they did not find themselves in a
border war like that between Ethiopia and Eritrea. Indeed, NCP
officials began by insisting that there must be an agreement over
north–south borders before they could agree to holding the referendum or accepting its outcome, although as its date approached

that position steadily softened. They continued to maintain, however, that without a postponement of the referendum it was likely to be marred by a lack of preparation. In this they were to be proven wrong. Yet their doubts that the post-referendum issues could be resolved before July 2011 and the formal end of the CPA peace process were justified.

The NCP usually took the position of saying publicly they were committed to holding the referendum on time. However, privately in meetings with the author they suggested the need for a one- or two-month delay. It was understood, however, that the SPLM would have trouble accepting any delays because it was constrained by 'conspiracy theories of its own making,' according to one official. It was subsequently learned that Egypt had pressed the US to call for a four- to six-year delay in the holding of the referendum (*Reuters*, 3 December 2010). Given its apparent concern to protect the NCP government, it was something of a surprise when during the height of the referendum campaign *Al-Ahram*, Egypt's leading semi-official newspaper, came out condemning the NCP government. Mustafa El-Fiqy, who chaired the foreign relations committee at the Egyptian parliament, said that the Bashir government was the 'worst in the country's history' (*SOAS News*, 29 December 2010).

NCP ministers complained to the author that Salva had become more aggressive since his US trip, and by coming out in support of southern secession he was flouting their agreement. They did not attribute this to particular assurances by the USG or President Obama, who was considered at the time not to be overtly supportive of the SPLM, or to Hillary Clinton, although one official complained that she treated the NCP like 'schoolboys' and did not appreciate that the party had a genuine constituency and could not do everything being demanded of it. They also appreciated General Gration's efforts, even if he was sometimes viewed as a lightweight. The problem in relations with the US according to the NCP was due to the negative views of Susan Rice and the Black Caucus. The USG as a whole, however, was criticized for following the SPLM insistence that the referendum be held on 9 January, an approach which was 'purely technical.' One official emphasized the efforts of the US and Israel to undermine Sudan and noted the historical record of Israeli support for Anyanya and the strong support of Jewish groups for the Enough Project and the Save Darfur campaign.

After his return to Sudan on 1 October, Salva repeated the message he delivered in the US: 'If I were to vote as a person and choose between the two options of unity and separation, I would vote for separation,' given the failure of Khartoum to make unity attractive (*Sudan Tribune*, 1 Oct 2010). Specifically it was claimed that during the almost six years of the interim period the NCP had failed to create a state with which southerners could identify, and the ruling party was faulted because it insisted on retaining sharia instead of adopting a secular form of government. The NCP jumped on Salva's statement of his personal preference for southern secession (Ali Osman said it was 'unacceptable,' while Bashir said he was 'reneging' on the agreement), the more so because a party leader and head of government cannot have private preferences separate from the party and government he leads.

The Machakos Protocol provided for NCP acceptance of self-determination for the south in return for the SPLM agreeing to sharia in the northern states. Since the SPLM had accepted this compromise, it was disingenuous for its leaders then to attribute the failure to make unity attractive to the NCP's adhering to sharia. The only qualification to accepting sharia in the north was that the rights of southern Christians in the north would be protected. Arguably those rights were not fully adhered to, as evidenced by continuing obstacles to church construction and problems related to restaurants opening during Ramadan. Beyond that, the social reality wase that northern Muslims, as much as the government, would simply not accept alcohol consumption or what could be considered immodest female dress. There was also a class element to the problem in that the chief victims of the alcohol prohibition were not middle-class or wealthy Christians, who were rarely interfered with, but southern women making alcohol for mostly Muslim customers. Meanwhile, the dress code was for the most part not applied to southern women, who did not dress much differently to their counterparts in Juba.[5] In any case, the SPLM Juba leadership never demonstrated much concern about the rights of southern Christians in Khartoum, so it was hard to take seriously claims that sharia was a major obstacle to unity when in any case it had no impact in autonomous southern Sudan. Indeed, the CPA provided for a commission to protect the rights of non-Muslims in Khartoum, which was duly formed, headed by a Christian nominated by the SPLM, and for the first five years of its existence never visited by a single southern official.[6]

Sharia in any case posed no obstacle to Christians running for office, including the presidency of Sudan. In fact many were disappointed that Salva Kiir, a Christian, did not run for the national presidency because he would have had a reasonable chance of winning, given a solid basis of support in the south, from southerners in the north, and among the marginalized peoples of Darfur, Nuba Mountains, southern Blue Nile, and the east. But he chose not to run, thereby sending a powerful message that he was not personally committed to the unity of the country. He gave further evidence of that by rarely going to Khartoum to assume his responsibilities as first vice president of the Republic. The SPLM also made little effort to ensure that the CPA quotas for southern-ers in the GNU were met, presumably because it wanted them to return to the south or out of concern that if they were given good jobs in Khartoum they might be reluctant to support secession.

As a result of these conditions the SPLM in the GNU was weak and easily manipulated by a more sophisticated and aggressive NCP. To be sure, assuming a governing role in the north would never have been easy given the SPLM's lack of experience and faced with a civil service that largely functioned as an extension of the NCP. But for the most part the SPLM never made a genuine effort, and this was particularly disconcerting in the minimal role it played in the Darfur peace process. Again, the NCP fought to retain a monopoly of this process, so it would have been difficult for Salva and his colleagues to make their mark, but the SPLM had the support of the Western countries and the Darfuri liberation movements, which were supporters of the SPLM and committed to its program of New Sudan.

Moreover, Salva and the SPLM leadership were not sincere when they implied that initially they were committed to unity and it was the experience of the six years of the CPA-stipulated transitional period that led them to conclude otherwise. Many of the leadership, including Salva, had been separatists for years. The author had the following exchange with Salva in 2001 in the SPLA headquarters of Yei:

> *General Salva, can you please explain your position on southern self-determination?*
>
> My position is that if we [the SPLA] capture Juba today we will declare the independence of southern Sudan tomorrow. Is that clear?
>
> *Yes general.* (interview, 24 March 2001)

Indeed, while Salva never had the popularity of Garang (nor his enemies) it was understood that he was closer in sentiment to his countrymen precisely because of his known sympathies for independence, unlike his predecessor who, appeared to support unity, but whose position was ultimately so complicated that no one could be entirely sure. Moreover, it is clear that the relative ease of negotiations between Salva and Paulino Matieb to integrate the SSDF into the SPLA followed in part from the SSDF leadership's understanding that Salva shared their beliefs on southern independence.

In an effort to avoid a crisis the SPLM leadership refused to take an official position endorsing either unity or separation and appeared to leave it up to individuals to make their own choice. In fact, while the party leadership officially sat on the sidelines, it instructed its various wings to campaign for secession. The Juba SPLM also repeatedly postponed a meeting of the ruling National Liberation Council, which would be expected to take a position on the issue of unity versus separation, on the unconvincing grounds that it did not fit into the busy schedule of the leaders. SPLM northern deputy secretary general Yassir Arman said that he saw no reason to hold such a meeting because the party position was clear. And by that he implied that the SPLM policy since its inception had favored a united Sudan and any NLC meeting would have to endorse that policy. Indeed, although the language of the 2008 SPLM Manifesto was not as strong in its commitment to Sudan's unity, it nonetheless affirmed the New Sudan vision.

Instead of the SPLM making a clear statement, its officials only added to the confusion. On 4 December *Al-Sudani* newspaper published excerpts from what it claimed was a SPLM document that made clear the party's support for secession. On 5 December SPLM secretary general Pagan Amum told the media that the document was forged with the intent of confusing the public, thus implying that the party did not support secession. On 11 December deputy secretary general of the southern sector of the SPLM, Anne Itto (Pagan's immediate subordinate), gave a press conference in which she said: 'Since unity has not been made attractive during the six-year interim period, we will not stop what our people want. We will promote what they want. If they need separation we will promote that because we are following

CONFIRMING THE INEVITABLE

the people.' She went on to say: 'This is not a general position of the SPLM; I'm talking on behalf of the SPLM Southern Sector.' Anne Itto may have thought she was bringing light to this murky area but she only made clear the web of contradictions the party leadership was caught up in.

The NCP was likewise caught up in its own contradictions. On 7 November President Omar al-Bashir announced the formation of a higher committee for the support of unity, headed by himself and including first vice president Salva Kiir and second vice president Ali Osman Taha. Bashir also appointed DUP leader Osman al-Mirghani, former president Abdul-Rahman Siwar al-Dahab, presidential adviser Bona Malwal, former minister Mohamed Yousif Abdallah, and Ibrahim Ghandour from the ruling NCP. Bashir also said that the committee would be composed of eleven subcommittees. But the announcement was little more than a weak attempt to con the northern public. It is highly unlikely that Salva was consulted about his membership of the committee in light of his repeated statements in favor of secession, and indeed nothing more was heard of this committee. What was intended was simply to give the appearance that the NCP was committing all its resources to the unity campaign, when it was doing nothing of the sort. Indeed, at the end of the peace process this was acknowledged by a senior NCP official, who told me that the party had largely given up on the unity campaign and that if it had been serious the party would have started to campaign very soon after the signing of the CPA. As a result, this official said, the scene was left to the SPLM.

For seventy years, until the 1990s, nationalism was the political ethos that united parties across a wide political spectrum in northern Sudan. But the rise to power of the NIF/NCP brought another ideology to prominence. 'Islam is the answer' is the slogan of all such parties and the NCP was no different. Political Islam as a movement has an international orientation, views the modern state as a construction of the colonial Christian powers, and aspires to re-create the Islamic Caliphate of the period immediately after the death of Prophet Muhammad. As early as 1976 one of its cadres reported that the NIF considered the separation of southern Sudan a necessary means to ensure the establishment of an Islamic order (El-Affendi, 1991: 149). And when in power the NCP quickly set about dismantling the service sector of the state while expanding its security wing. The result was a reduced role of the state in the lives of ordinary people, an enormous increase in inequality, declining faith in the state, and a retreat into the private sphere.

The NCP devoted considerable energy to weakening competing Islamic parties, notably the Umma and DUP, through bribery, encouraging schisms, and a range of restrictions and harassment. These actions proved remarkably effective, and the two parties at the center of Sudan since independence had their national bases seriously eroded and were almost completely shut out of the south, thus further undermining a national ethos. However, nationalism and democracy in Sudan never had their primary base in the ruling sectarian parties; instead their core was in one of the most active civil societies in Africa and the Middle East, and it was this that became the primary focus of most NCP repression. University faculties and their organizations were purged, trade unions were banished, liberal-minded army officers were killed, and ghost houses sapped the life from northern Sudan's democrats.

The decline of Sudanese nationalism cannot be attributed solely to the NCP, but is also due to the systematic failures in government of the mainstream political parties. In particular the Sadig al-Mahdi government between 1986 and 1989 paved the way for the NIF to come to power and went far in diminishing the hopes of Sudanese in democratic governance and undermining their faith in the country. But it was the rise to power of the NIF with its Islamist–Arabist ideology that served to shift the political center of gravity in the south from support for a restructured state within a united Sudan to growing support for self-determination. Very quickly after the NIF assumed power, the Frankfurt Statement of 1992, the Abuja I Communiqué of 26 May 1992, the Washington Declaration of 22 October 1993, and the IGADD DoP of 20 May 1994 all endorsed southern self-determination.

One of the anomalies of NCP rule was that while it appealed for support on the basis of Islam and not tribe, tribal identities grew exponentially in northern Sudan after it came to power in 1989. This is because even more than under the sectarian parties, government employment became increasingly conditional on tribal affiliations, to the extent that entire sectors, such as the security services, were dominated by particular tribes. Thus, while tribal and Islamic identities have grown, national identity declined.

Against that background launching a unity campaign based on nationalism was difficult, and made more so because the opposition parties were content to leave the ruling party alone to take responsibility for the impending dismemberment of the country. And that decision was made easier by the fact that the NCP was not prepared to pay a very high price to gain their support. This was because many in the ruling party saw southern secession as the best means to banish the SPLM's New Sudan ideology, with its dual threat of secularism and diversity. With the ideologies of the NUP and the DUP soft versions of the NCP's, and the Communist Party forced to the fringes after years of persecution, the only real threat the NCP still confronted was New Sudan.

Moreover, the attraction of the New Sudan ideology under the right leadership to large numbers of Sudanese living in the peripheries, secularists in the centre, and a range of people who supported progressive social, economic, and political programs was evident when millions of people in Khartoum went into the

streets to welcome John Garang on 8 July 2005. With Garang's
death and the coming to power of the uninspiring Salva Kiir,
the New Sudan ideology was seriously undermined. But even
then it was a sufficient threat in the election campaign of Yasir
Arman that the NCP colluded with the separatists in the SPLM to
have his candidacy withdrawn. His withdrawal further demoral-
ized northern believers in New Sudan. With the referendum
the NCP foresaw the possibility that it could end the threat of
New Sudan irrevocably. The cost was the secession of southern
Sudan, but for the Islamists that was not deemed too high a
price, particularly if they could gain desired concessions from the
SPLM and the international community. This position was most
actively campaigned for by one of Sudan's largest newspapers,
Al-Intibaha, published by Bashir's uncle, Tayyib Mustafa, and
associated with the ethnocentric party al-Salam al-'Adil (Just
Peace), both of which have long conducted racist campaigns to
rid the country of the south. As a result, according to the dean
of Sudanese journalism, Mahgoub Mohamed Salih, 'The Islamists
are split between those who welcome the departure of southern
Sudan and those who blame it on the international community'
(interview, 13 November 2010).

Meanwhile, Ali Osman stayed true to the agreement he signed
and mistakenly believed that Salva was a unionist, and was deeply
embarrassed by his espousal of secession. His confusion appeared
to derive from his reliance on Abel Alier and Joseph Okello, who
were supporters of unity. In spite of overwhelming support for
secession in the south, a senior NCP official close to Ali Osman
told the author in mid-October that only Equatorians were solidly
for secession, large sections of the Dinka and Nuer supporting
unity. Nonetheless, he said that as a result of SPLM machinations
the NCP expected a strong vote for secession. Another official
acknowledged that the NCP leadership had misunderstood the
southern public perception and was surprised at the level of

SPLM mobilization in the run-up to the referendum. A key shock, this informant told me, was the announcement by Turabi's deputy and former presidential candidate Abdullah Deng that he would be voting for secession. After the referendum another NCP official told the author, 'Ali was duped into believing the SPLM was unionist and therefore favoured a strategic partnership with it. But such an arrangement could never have existed given their polar opposite positions.'

Tensions between the Peace Partners

A week of interviews conducted by the author with senior NCP officials in mid-October 2010 made clear just how pessimistic they were about the peace process and the prospects for a successful outcome. Each of them said there was a strong possibility of war because of various efforts by the SPLM to foment divisions in the north, and that if this continued the NCP would not hesitate to unleash its own agents to cause disruption in the south. One of those interviewed, who had been a key negotiator in the Naivasha process, was so negative as to conclude that the CPA was 'a lousy agreement.' A commonly expressed fear at the time – and the NCP played to this sentiment – was of having the worst of both worlds: southern secession and war. From that it followed that unless the SPLM could convince the NCP that it would provide deliverable benefits for secession, or that the party had no choice but to accept the process, then it was better to skip secession and go straight to war. One NCP minister remarked to me that 'the party as a whole viewed it as an issue of survival.' But there was an option, and that was an all-encompassing agreement between the NCP and SPLM that recognized southern independence and thus dispensed with the referendum. That notion was considered in some NCP circles until mid-October, but it probably would never have gained the support of the SPLM.

The consistent SPLM discourse in both the north and the south right up to the eve of the referendum was simply that the vote would not be held, that the NCP would never permit the south to leave, and that a return to war was inevitable. One academic adviser to the southern party argued that, despite continuing support for New Sudan among some, if there was any attempt to remove Bashir before the south got independence, the SPLA would support him. At the same time he contended that the struggle for New Sudan would continue because the SPLM leadership understood that there could be no stable relations as long as the NCP remained in power. Meanwhile, the NCP viewed Salva as inexperienced, intellectually limited, inconsistent, and beholden to 'rabble rousers' like Pagan Amum and to an 'Abyei mafia' (Deng Alor, Luca Biong Edward Lino, etc.). The SPLM viewed the NCP as the worst in a long line of untrustworthy ruling parties, a party of Islamist terrorists which had no commitment to peace and would inevitably take the country back to war.

The SPLM tried to develop alliances with the northern opposition parties, but it got into the kind of contradictions noted above, while its performance in the April elections and the growing conviction that it had dispensed with its commitment to New Sudan led virtually all of the opposition parties, with the exception of the SCP, to be increasingly skeptical. More effective was the threat posed by thousands of SPLA soldiers from the Nuba Mountains and southern Blue Nile, which the SPLA refused to demobilize as required under the Security Arrangements Protocol. Some of these soldiers nominally left the army, but retained their weapons and possessed a level of organization that could be mobilized in the event of a return to war. And they in turn could be joined by larger numbers of Nuba and southern Blue Nile soldiers serving in the south if war broke out.

Darfur was another matter. The GoSS permitted Darfuri rebels to stay in the south, including Mini Minawi, who in 2010 had given up on the Darfur Peace Agreement. Abdel Wahid, leader of the rump Sudan Liberation Movement/Army, who had been a protégé of Garang and hence closer to the SPLM than other Darfuri leaders, also visited Juba. The NCP claimed that the SPLA was aiding Darfuri rebels who crossed from South Darfur into Northern Bahr el Ghazal. SAF responded with two Antonov bombing raids and numerous jet overflights in contested border areas of Northern Bahr el Ghazal, which led to a small number of civilian and SPLA injuries and deaths and some displacement. The NCP viewed SPLA support of the Darfuris as a 'very dangerous game' in the words of one minister to the author. The SPLM wanted to use the Darfuris and their compatriots in Blue Nile and Southern Kordofan as a means of bringing pressure on the NCP to ensure that the referendum would take place on time, as well as a means to advance its interests in the post-referendum negotiations. If the NCP concluded that the SPLM was in a strategic alliance with the Darfuri rebels it could have led to war, because encirclement was a perennial fear of the ruling party. That could also have been the result if the SPLA had responded militarily to the SAF attacks, but it did not do so either then or later in the face of further aerial bombings.

The NCP was not without its proxies in this game; indeed in late 2010 its ministers were bluntly saying that they could 'destabilize the south even more' than anything the SPLM was able to do in the north (and indeed a year later that would be borne out). Another said that while SAF was no longer in the south, the army could again play a 'double game' to protect itself. Among the forces that could be utilized were those of General Gordon Kong, who had become rump leader of the SSDF after most of the forces followed Paulino Matieb into the SPLA in January 2006. Many in the SAF JIU (Joint Integrated Unit) forces were made up of former SSDF members. Lt General George Athor (rtd), former SPLA deputy chief of staff, launched an insurgency after being defeated in his campaign for governor of Jonglei in the April election. He retreated to his home area of Khorflus in the northern part of the state, where successive attempts by the SPLA failed to dislodge him. Colonel Gatlauk Gai launched another insurgency in Unity state after Angelina Teny-Dhurgon – who had promised him a commissionership if she won – was denied her victory as governor by Taban Deng and the SPLA. And both were joined by other military officers, some from the south and some southerners from SAF. The specter of the Lord's Resistance Army being used to disrupt the referendum was regularly raised in the south, but there was no evidence that SAF still supplied or maintained relations with it. There was also little evidence that the SPLA was particularly concerned about it. Western Equatoria Governor Joseph Bakosoro pointedly said, 'The SPLA is not effective dealing with the LRA issue' (interview, 30 September 2010). In the northern states of Southern Kordofan and Blue Nile, and the territory of Abyei, where significant numbers of southerners lived who would be eligible to vote in the referendum, the SAF-armed PDF was active and could be used in a crisis. In the lead-up to the referendum there were a number of cases of buses carrying southerners and Ngok Dinka to Abyei being stopped by Misseirya and sometimes turned around, and in one incident being held for an extended period.

With an estimated 23,000 southerners serving in SAF and many thousands more in the police and other security services, there were potentially many recruits for such rebellions, in addition to tens of thousands of unemployed and disaffected southern youth. To what extent and to what ends the leadership in Khartoum intended to use these forces was not known and their objectives might in any case change, but clearly they posed a significant threat to the Juba regime.

Curiously, the NCP and SPLM jointly agreed to ask the UN to handle security for the referendum, but in the event their request came too late for the UN to be able to respond positively. The

NCP viewed UN involvement as the best protection against the kind of SPLA abuses that took place during the 2010 elections. Speaking on behalf of the party, Dirdiery Mohamed Ahmed pointedly said that if there was any evidence of such activity that the government would reject the outcome of the referendum (interview, 15 December 2010). The NCP was, however, completely opposed to the UN having a military presence along the border, as proposed by the SPLM, and this at a time when the NCP was already making clear that it wanted UNMIS to leave the north after 9 July 2011. Indeed, it wanted to see off a range of international, and particularly Western, agencies and for this to be understood by its constituency as one of the benefits resulting from the loss of the south. Meanwhile, in October and November the SPLA and SAF traded accusations of illegal troop movements in the border area. Minister of Foreign Affairs Ali Karti accused the SPLA of moving only a third of its forces from the north, while Salva said he was in danger of being assassinated, presumably by the NCP or its allies.

The failure to resolve the conflict over Abyei, inhabited by Ngok Dinka farmers and Misseirya nomads, was long recognized as having the potential to disrupt the north–south peace process, take the country back to war, or cause lingering conflict between the nomads and their settled neighbors to the south. The SPLM and its supporters claimed the problem stemmed from the failure of the NCP and Misseirya to accept the Abyei Protocol, the rulings of the Abyei Boundary Commission (ABC), and the Permanent Court of Arbitration at The Hague. They contended that these decisions made clear that only the Ngok Dinka had the right to vote in the CPA-stipulated referendum, whose outcome would without doubt lead to the territory joining southern Sudan. On weaker legal grounds the NCP and Misseirya – but with the agreement of most parties and people in the north – argued otherwise.

While only some sections of the Misseirya depended upon grazing and watering their cattle in Abyei and transiting the territory for suitable lands in southern Sudan, the rest of the tribe supported those affected. They were also skeptical of CPA promises that irrespective of the outcome of the referendum, the southern government would ensure them access to water and grazing lands for their cattle. In the 2010 migration the Misseirya nomads lost by some estimates as much as one-third of their stock because of SPLA opposition to their move into Unity state, and after some herders did enter the state they suffered further attacks by the SPLA. These attacks were later acknowledged by Unity governor Taban Deng and Southern Kordofan governor Ahmed Haroun, whereupon it was agreed that the SPLA would compensate the aggrieved nomads. Some of these negative attitudes stemmed from the legacy of the war, when many Misseirya received training and arms from SAF and used them to steal from their southern neighbors. The Misseirya claimed they had no interest in Abyei's oil and only wanted guaranteed access to land to graze and water their cattle, which they contended made them as much owners of the land as the settled farmers.

That, however, was not the case with the NCP. The ruling party wanted the oil even if the Abyei reserves were rapidly being depleted. As a result of an international arbitration decision the two largest oilfields in Heglig and Kharsana, which were estimated to produce less than 1 percent of total oil revenues, are now deemed to be in the north, outside the Abyei boundaries. The NCP was also anxious to keep the support of the Misseirya, not only as a force that could be used against the south but out of concern that this tribe could turn its weapons on the government if sufficiently aroused. As well as the weapons held by the Misseirya and the Ngok there was reason to believe that both the SPLA and SAF were operating in territory which they previously agreed should be army-free, apart from the JIUs.

But it was not just land and oil that fueled the conflict. The Misseirya claimed on sound historical grounds that they had moved to the area in the 1760s, more than a century before the arrival of the Dinka, with whom they shared their land. Moreover, the Misseirya were deeply aggrieved that a pact in blood between the ancestors of the Misseirya Babu Nimir and the Ngok Dinka Deng Majok in the early years of the twentieth century had been broken. A brotherhood pact was sealed in blood between the Misseirya chief Nazir Ali El Gulla and the Ngok Dinka chief Sultan Kuol Arab, but was based on the understanding that the land was part of the *dar* or homeland of the Misseirya and that it continued through to Deng Majok, leader of the Dinka and father to many of the prominent Ngok Dinkas today, including the SPLM's Luka Biong and Sudan's most famous son, Francis Deng,[7] and Babu Nimr, leader of the Misseirya and father to many of the current leaders of the tribe. According to Hurgas Merida, an elderly scholar of the tribe, 'Deng Majok and Babu Nimr were the needle and thread of north and south Sudan' (interview, 27 March 2011).

Deng Alor was the son of Deng Majok's half-brother Kuol. Many of Deng's sons moved to the Misseirya center of Muglad and then on to Khartoum to receive their education in the north at the expense of the Misseirya Council. That was the case with Deng Alor, who was raised as Ahmed and with Luka Biong. Hurgas Merida said that he had been one of Deng Alor's teachers in Muglad when relations were good between the tribes; but 'those with education don't come back to cattle and instead search for problems' (interview, 27 March 2011). Not only was the subsequent call of the Ngok for Abyei to join the south seen as a stab in the back to the Misseirya, but to make matters worse the next generation went on to acquire far higher educational attainments than the nomadic Misseirya.

In 1951 and 1952 Deng Majok rejected a British proposal for Abyei to join the south. It was only in 1964, as a result of Anyanya's efforts to highlight its claim that Abyei was part of the south, that conflict broke out and an estimated two hundred people were killed. This encouraged the young educated generation to call for Abyei to join the south, and the result was a round of conferences to consider the status of the area. This culminated in the oblique reference in the Addis Ababa Agreement that stated: 'Southern Provinces of Sudan means the Provinces of Bahr El Ghazal, Equatoria and Upper Nile in accordance with their boundaries as they stood on 1.1.1956, and any other areas as were culturally and geographically part of the Southern complex as may be decided by a referendum' (Article 3iii). Thus no mention was made of Abyei or a requirement for a referendum, and in the ensuing period successive national governments rejected the notion of a referendum for Abyei with the support of the traditional leaders of both the Misseirya and the Ngok Dinka. But the SPLM/A took up the cause of the Ngok intelligentsia, and the requirement for a referendum was stipulated in the Abyei Protocol, much to the anger of the Misseirya.

After not accepting the Abyei Boundary Commission and calling for more negotiations in the wake of the decision on the territory by the Arbitration Tribunal, the Misseirya and NCP also managed to ensure that no referendum was held simultaneously with that of southern Sudan. And beginning in late December 2010 Misseirya militia began obstructing the vehicle movement of Ngok Dinka to Abyei and southerners to the south, although some of the latter was a means of bringing pressure on Governor Taban Deng of neighboring Unity state to pay agreed compensation for Misseirya cattle stolen by the SPLA in the state. The USG's Scott Gration and Princeton Layman held negotiations in Addis Ababa in October 2010 with the NCP and SPLM, who brought along representatives of the Misseirya and the Ngok, and this time they proposed that those Misseirya who resided in Abyei for more than 185 days in a year could vote in the referendum. The NCP convinced a reluctant Misseirya to accept this compromise and then informed the mediators, but it was rejected by the SPLM.[8] The AU-sponsored Thabo Mbeki team, supported by the USG, made a number of proposals, one of which was to divide the territory into north and south sectors, which the NCP and Misseirya accepted, but the SPLM refused, after which the process was stymied. According to Dirdiery Mohamed Ahmed, the NCP's point man on Abyei, with the SPLM's rejection and NCP's acceptance on the division of Abyei, the 'negotiating process is now over' (interview, 2010). He was wrong, but it was true that without a compromise on these fundamental positions, there could be no permanent solution.

In the absence of movement at the negotiating table, the people on the ground began taking the initiative. The Ngok Dinka held a conference in Juba, where it was resolved that since they were not able to realize their rights to a referendum they would deny the Misseirya access to lands in Abyei. At the same conference they also threatened to organize their own referendum, but were prevailed upon not to do so. The delays made it impossible to hold the Abyei referendum simultaneously with the southern referendum, and with the impending departure of the south and assertions in Khartoum that Abyei was part of the north, the Ngok were becoming increasingly anxious as to their fate.

With no significant progress on the post-referendum issues, increasing tensions over Abyei, and large SAF and SPLA forces facing off along the north–south border, there was an ever-present danger of armed skirmishes (and, indeed, three minor incidents did take place in late 2010), but with the parties committed to negotiations and the SPLM firmly fixated on seeing through the referendum, the threat of full-scale war was unlikely, at least in the near future.

Confronting the Internal Opposition

Both the NCP and the SPLM appreciated the importance of reaching agreements with their respective opposition parties before the referendum, but in the end the former was not prepared to put enough on the table to win acceptance, while the latter put a lot on the table, won the necessary support, and then took it off the table after the referendum.

While the northern opposition parties strongly supported a united Sudan, they were marginal to the referendum process because they feared that any support for the unity campaign would be seen as giving support to the NCP and they wanted to have the ruling party alone assume responsibility for the impending loss of southern Sudan. It was also clear that after years of repression their capacity to conduct a campaign was limited. In keeping with their long-standing practice of focusing entirely on the NCP and SPLM, the international backers of the peace process never supported the demands of the northern opposition for the formation of a genuine national government to confront the impending break-up of the country. Moreover, since none of the opposition parties accepted the legitimacy of the April elections, a critical precondition for joining the government was agreement on holding genuinely democratic elections, which the NCP was not prepared to accept.

Although some NCP officials acknowledged that in the absence of any opposition parties in the government they felt exposed in leading the referendum process, others said there was no escaping responsibility for the crisis by the opposition parties. One official noted that the opposition parties supported the 1995 Asmara Declaration which recognized the right of the south to self-determination, and further stated that the decision of most of the opposition to drop out of the election meant that they could not participate in the process.

Against that background and with nowhere else to turn, opposition party leaders began holding out the threat of an intifada. Sudan saw popular uprisings in 1964 and 1985, but they were led largely by a powerful civil society and trade unions which no longer existed due to the efforts of the NCP. But the parties of the Juba Alliance or National Consensus Forces (NCF) were energized by the country's growing economic crisis and the impending loss of southern Sudan, and noted that economic problems and the war in the south had been precipitating factors in the uprisings of 1964 and 1985.

By July 2010 the Sudanese were suffering from rapidly rising prices and a depreciating currency, which in turn made imports more expensive. The crisis was in the first instance due to rapidly rising international prices for sugar, wheat, and corn, much of which was imported. Second, it was due to political instability, which led to a drying up of foreign investment and increasing demands for international hard currencies, notably the US dollar. As a result, by late 2010 the Sudanese pound had fallen from about 2.5 SDG to 3.5 to the USD. And, lastly, the crisis was due to the fact that a considerable portion of the national budget was devoted to the army and security services, funding that could not be cut in the midst of a political and security crisis. Instead of retaining some of the oil revenues for just such a crisis, the NCP had given priority to its needs, the consequences of which were now catching up with the country. The NCP had already largely gutted the provision of health, social, education and other public services and carried out privatization programs, so there was little it could draw on other than raising the prices of basic commodities. In the south the crisis was particularly severe in the urban centers and in the northern half of southern Sudan, which were almost entirely dependent on goods brought from the north. Moreover, the goods were transported in by northern merchants, many of whom felt increasingly insecure in the lead-up to the referendum. Some therefore left, either permanently or until the crisis was over, thus ensuring shortages and inflated prices. In other parts of the south the market was dominated by traders from East Africa; likewise, out of fear some of them also left the south as the elections loomed and, subsequently, when the referendum date approached.

In the midst of growing concern about the economy, on 18 December 2010, only three weeks before the referendum, Bashir told a rally in Gedarif: 'If south Sudan secedes, we will change the constitution and at that time there will be no time to speak of diversity of culture and ethnicity' (*New York Times*, 19 December 2010). Bashir was quoted as saying that 98 per cent of the people in the north were Muslims and as such were obligated to follow God's orders with regard to governing in accordance with sharia. He went on to say, 'Shariah and Islam will be the main source for the constitution, Islam the official religion and Arabic the official language.' Bashir's Gedarif statements came during a week in which Sudan was condemned for whipping a woman for wearing trousers, in a widely circulated video, and allegations by the ICC prosecutor that Bashir had deposited $9 billion in a personal account. For many in the NCP these unconnected events were evidence of an international conspiracy led by the West against the regime and heightened their sense of grievance and isolation. That was the immediate background of Bashir's statement, but the larger context was that the Islamist project had been seriously compromised by the high level of international engagement in the country due to the southern peace process, the war in Darfur, and the April elections. With the departure of the south, Bashir was telling his followers that the NCP could return to its core Islamist agenda. In addition, the speech could be interpreted as a threat to the West either to cooperate with his government or to face the prospect of a return to the early 1990s' militancy.

In the lead-up to the referendum Sadig al-Mahdi presented the NCP with a series of demands and said that if they were not met by 26 January 2011 he would either resign as leader of the Umma Party or join those calling for a struggle to overthrow the ruling party. As a result, the NCP responded positively on 22 January.[9] An Umma Party committee was appointed to consider this dialogue, although some of its members were very skeptical about the entire exercise. However, Sadig prevailed, the committee members relented, and negotiations dragged on for the remaining six months of the peace process without any conclusive results.

On 24 December 2010 Ansar followers of Sadig al-Mahdi left their party headquarters in Omdurman to attend Friday prayers at a nearby mosque of the Mahdi. They were attacked by the police and Sadig's daughter and party leader, Dr Maryom Sadig, suffered three breaks in her arm. An exasperated Sadig told the author: 'The police did not understand that Muslims typically demonstrate after they go to the mosque, not before, as was the case here' (interview, 4 January 2011, Khartoum). At almost the same time the Legitimate League of Muslim Preachers and Clerics (LLMPC), made up of clerics opposed to the official Association of Muslim Scholars, held a march in Khartoum to protest southern Sudan's upcoming referendum and to call for the government to fully implement sharia law, which they followed up with a press conference. LLMPC spokesperson Mohammed Abdel-Karim warned that southern secession would negatively affect the Islamic gains in the south and that it represented a secular drive to remove Islam from the region. This same Mohammed had issued a fatwa in August 2009 branding members of the Sudanese Communist Party infidels who should be divorced from their spouses and whose children should be deemed the products of adulterous relationships. The LLMPC included some Sudanese, but most members had been expelled from different countries in the Gulf for their views and political activities and were invited by the government to come to Sudan. Their demonstration was allowed by the police to proceed.

The LLMPC joined other Islamist groups, including the Sunna (no connection to the Ansar of the Umma Party), who came to international attention when on 8 December 2000 a dissident member of the sect, Abbas al-Baqir Abbas, shot dead twenty-two adherents at a mosque in Omdurman. There are also a number of Saudi Wahhabist groups in the country; they served as a conduit for funds that went to various social and education services. Yet another Islamist group was held responsible for the murder of the US diplomat John Granville and his driver on New Year's Eve 2007. In this case the perpetrators were captured and jailed in Kober Prison, but were later able to break out, almost certainly with the connivance of the authorities. In addition to these Islamist groups, the NCP has its own Islamic movement, headed by second vice president Ali Osman Taha.

While the police were beating up the NCP's political rivals, Salva was taking a different approach in the south, although ultimately there would be little difference between them. Despite the bitterness of the opposition parties toward the SPLM, virtually all were committed to the CPA-stipulated self-determination referendum. Even the few who preferred unity supported the right of the people of southern Sudan to determine freely whether they wanted to stay in Sudan or secede. And that shared commitment proved to be the basis for bringing the otherwise dissenting parties together.

Appreciating this, the veteran southern politician Bona Malwal convinced Salva to invite the twenty-four southern Sudanese party leaders to Juba on 13–17 October 2010 to discuss preparations for the referendum and the future governance of southern Sudan, the latter being the bait to bring the leaders on board. The conference agreed on preparations for a free and fair referendum, reconciliation among southerners, and a post-referendum roadmap for governance if southerners opted for secession. The parties also agreed to activate a leadership forum of all the political parties, which would meet regularly to ensure implementation of the resolutions of the conference. In addition, President Salva Kiir announced an amnesty for rebel groups. This was the high point of south–south reconciliation, and no doubt contributed to the peaceful conduct of the referendum, but after the referendum, when Salva no longer needed the opposition parties, the positive atmosphere rapidly deteriorated.

A Final Word from President Omar al-Bashir

Until the very eve of the referendum there were serious doubts about whether the process would go forward. The SPLM's insistence that it would not accept any delays imposed a crisis atmosphere. However, the technical support provided by the international community, together with the timely arrival of Senator John Kerry, who assured Bashir that the US would move quickly to remove Sudan from its sanctions list and establish normal bilateral relations if he accepted the process, further assuring him that the US stood behind the SPLM and that the referendum would take place on 9 January 2011, proved sufficient to ensure the process went ahead. In the US, however, the Obama policy on Sudan had its critics.[10] With all the parts in place and with no other cards to play Bashir made clear in his Independence Day speech that he would recognize the results of the referendum. On 4 January he flew to Juba, where he repeated the same sentiment:

> Whatever be the choice of the southerners, we will accept it and say welcome... But let us provide a good example for brothers in Africa, even if we separate and we will do it peacefully, we will cooperate and provide them with the example of how the United States of Africa could be ... We will not be sitting in a mourning

tent crying, if the southerners chose separation. We will not be happy either, but we will be the first to come and celebrate with southerners. (*PANA*, 4 January 2011)

With those words the referendum was on track and a lot of people heaved a sigh of relief.

Meanwhile, Bashir used the national media to argue that southern Sudan was never in practice part of Sudan and the expected referendum vote in favor of secession would largely be a confirmation of the existing position in the south. He also used the Islamic argument that in the interest of community stability, good Muslims were bound to support their leader, and he had resolved to permit the south to secede. He apparently used this argument in response to a handful of radical Muslim leaders who contended that under Islamic law the referendum was illegal and that the secession of part of an Islamic state was not permitted. Bashir held that the process by which the south was leaving was entirely legal and in accord with the CPA.

These statements again make clear that the NCP was more concerned about reassuring northerners about the impending secession than in convincing southerners that they should vote for unity. They also conveyed to the international community the efforts the NCP was making to ensure a peaceful and successful referendum process.

Referendum Mechanics

The Carter Center reported that the voter registration process for the southern Sudan referendum was 'generally credible,' but noted the failure of the peace partners to resolve 'the ambiguity surrounding the future of Abyei and the citizenship of nationals in both northern and southern Sudan before the registration ... [and] to bring all sections of the Sudanese political community into the process' (Carter Center, 15 December 2010). These sentiments were echoed in the EU Observation Mission statement. While there were problems with respect to administration, both the EU and the Carter Center were impressed with the performance of the SSRC and SSRB. As with the 2010 elections, the Carter Center concluded that the authorities and civil society failed when it came to education, which was dominated by southern groups that 'often mixed voter education activities with advocacy in favor of secession.' What passed for voter education in the south was dominated by groups that typically presented the issue in terms of a vote for unity being an endorsement of continued slavery, while a vote for secession represented support for freedom.

In turning to the campaign the EU Mission noted that

An almost complete absence of pro-unity campaigning created an environment where debate on the consequences of secession or the continued unity of Sudan was drowned out. The campaign climate focused on maximising voter turnout, in order to reach the 60 per cent threshold. Conversely, campaigning in the north, which focused on pro-unity messages, was much more subdued.

Unfortunately the SPLM and NCP campaigns rarely operated above the level of slogans, and the NCP campaign had all but petered out long before the vote. With the exception of the SPLM–DC and the UDF, southern political parties played only a minor role in the referendum campaign and the northern opposition parties even less (although the Communist Party was able to hold two pro-unity rallies in the south), thus furthering the sense that the campaign was an SPLM–NCP affair.

Voter turnout was extremely high in the south, with stories rife of SPLM cadres dragging the sick out of hospitals and the indigent off the streets to vote, but correspondingly low in the north. The Carter Center attributed this to the fact that transportation was not provided during voting, as it had been during voter registration; that many southerners went to the south to vote; and that those who remained were confused and anxious about the post-referendum period (Carter Center, 17 January 2011). The Center did not dig any deeper into why voter registration and turnout were low in the north, and the EU seemed unaware of it as an issue.

The major reason for the low registration and the subsequent low voter turnout in the north was the systematic campaign of the SPLM to deny southerners in the north their democratic right to vote, which followed directly from the party's earlier efforts in the National Assembly to disenfranchise them. The SPLM concern was that the NCP would encourage a high voter registration and then a low turnout in an effort to have the total vote less than the 60 per cent threshold necessary for recognition. There was also concern that southerners living in the north, and especially those employed with government agencies, would be coerced by the NCP to vote for unity. Indeed, there was evidence that government employees were encouraged by the NCP to vote in the expectation that it would be for unity, but in the event there was no evidence that they did so. There was evidence of southerners in the north being intimidated not to vote by the SPLM. The Carter Center noted threats against referendum officials in Uganda where some SPLM members pressed for a boycott of out-of-country registration and voting.

Parallel to this were efforts by the SPLM to move as many southerners to the south as possible so they would register and vote in the south, and indeed more than 180,000 southerners went to Southern Sudan in the ten weeks prior to the referendum.[11] By mid-May, the number of repatriated Sudanese refugees to Southern Sudan and Blue Nile state had reached a cumulative total of 331,785 since the signing of the CPA in 2005 (*CPA Monitor*, May 2011). A substantial number were supported in their move by GoSS-supplied transport, but soon the money ran out and many languished in northern camps or at the river transportation centre of Kosti long after the referendum was completed. I interviewed a number of these would-be returnees in Kosti and was impressed with both their patience and their positive views of the north they were leaving. The elderly Sultan James Kerdam insisted that 'no one chased us from Khartoum' and that 'there was no real border between the north and south, nothing called the 1956 border, and Sudan is still one' (interview, 10 February 2011). Figilio Waswas from Torit said that he had been in the north since 1967 and was going back 'because Garang made peace' and 'we are the sons of President Bashir, who gave us a peaceful referendum' (interview, 10 February 2011). He also stressed that 'there were no bad things in the north and I may go back for a visit' and that 'my neighbors in the north were crying' because of his departure. They also knew that they would be tarnished with the epithet *jallaba* in the south for their long years in the north, but were nonetheless convinced they would be welcome. These attitudes were common among southerners who developed roots in the north, but those steeped in poverty and living in the displaced camps on the outskirts of Omdurman and Khartoum North were not so sanguine.

This mass movement and the expectation that more southerners might be on the move led those not familiar with Sudanese realities to assume that a massacre along the lines of that which took place in Rwanda was possible, but that was far from the truth. While a handful of Islamist extremists wanted southerners to leave and the NCP government sent out mixed messages, most ordinary northern Sudanese responded to the impending break-up of their country with sadness and regret, but with the dignity that is so much a part of their character.

As well as these problems the observation missions reported a number of abuses by both the SPLM and NCP. One such case was that of the Jehovah's Witnesses in Western Equatoria state, whose beliefs did not allow them to register for the referendum.

The governor of the state and others publicly called them traitors, and a few days later their Kingdom Hall was burned down.[12] The EU Mission concluded that the governor's verbal abuse of the Jehovah's Witnesses 'represents an attack on the freedoms of expression, association, and religion' (EU Observation Mission, 17 January 2011). Also in the state, the 'Arrow Boys,' a local militia force close to the governor,[13] set up roadblocks to check for the ink on their hands that indicated they had voted, and those without ink were placed under temporary arrest. There were also reports of people being arrested for not closing down their shops during the referendum, of prisoners being forced to vote, and of sick people in hospitals being transported to polling stations. Representatives from the NISS[14] were present in most referendum centers in Jonglei and Upper Nile. At one polling station armed police were observed watching voters cast their ballots and unfolded them to check which way people had voted before placing them in the ballot box. Perhaps not surprisingly in that environment in seven counties in Central Equatoria, Jonglei, Upper Nile, and Western Equatoria states, the number of people who voted exceeded those registered, according to documents from the referendum organizing commission seen by Reuters (17 January 2011).

Another set of victims of the referendum were 260 Arab families from the Nazi, Sabaha and Kibeishab tribes, who traditionally lived in Fokhar in the Joda border area of Upper Nile, just north of Renk, and who as a result of harassment by the SPLA moved to a camp outside Rabak at Hadaib in White Nile state. These displaced farmers told the author that the 10,000 people who had lived in Fokhar had been forced to move to Hadaib because of SPLA harassment, even though they had good relations with the local Dinka population; indeed their paramount chief had urged them not to leave Upper Nile, as did the SPLM Commissioner of Renk. The Renk Commissioner confirmed his intervention, but insisted that the SPLA had not intimidated the Arabs. Displaced members of this community said they were harassed and encouraged to leave by the SPLA because it was suspected, correctly from what I could gather, that they would vote for unity. Later a GoSS minister told me, 'These people were not singled out; the SPLA mistreated all people, irrespective of their race or religion.'[15]

The observation missions did not seriously address the problem of the suitability of the political environment for conducting the referendum, and GoSS officials contended that there were no obstacles to those favoring unity expressing their views, holding rallies, and distributing propaganda. Indeed, there were no legal obstacles to such activities and the limited numbers of cases of security forces harassing unity supporters did not suggest a government-orchestrated campaign. It is hard to imagine why the GoSS would harass unity supporters when they represented a tiny minority that could not threaten the outcome of the referendum. But it is rare for political processes not to be infused with illogical or emotional sentiments, the more so when what is at stake is no less than the creation of a new country. The dominant feature of southern Sudanese political life at that stage was a strong sense of nationalism that for a short time transcended the many things that divided southerners and created an environment hostile to those who did not share those sentiments. Indeed, a NDI study of sixty-three focus groups found that unity for southern Sudanese was equated with domination by the north, war, and the end of the GoSS (National Democratic Institute, 25 October 2010). In other words, unity was equated with a centralized state, not the continuation of the decentralized model that then existed. Nothing was done during the campaign to correct this misconception and the observation missions failed to comment on it.

When a long-time loyal SPLM member and minister of petroleum in the GNU, Lual Deng, said in August 2010, 'I'm a unionist in the footsteps of a unitary leader John Garang de Mabior,' he was roundly condemned in the south as a sell-out, an agent of the NCP, someone who had been bribed, and there were appeals for his recall. But Lual was saying nothing that was not official SPLM policy. On three occasions the SPLM postponed scheduled meetings of the party's NLC to consider the party's position on unity versus southern secession, and there was little doubt that this was due to the fact that many, and possibly a majority, of its members still supported the commitment to a united, reformed Sudan.

The International Community
and the Referendum

At the height of the referendum in mid-January the author was party to a number of high-level meetings with a wide range of senior mediators, UN officials, and diplomats. One would have thought they would have been happy, given a technically sound referendum, a vote that could not be challenged, and Bashir's statements that he would accept the results. However, they were apprehensive. They worried about the lack of progress in resolving the post-referendum issues, radicals and spoilers in the north, the growing economic crisis and its potential for disrupting the peace process, and the need to convince the SPLM leadership not to press Bashir too hard as the fate of the peace process depended upon him and he was facing tough internal battles in the NCP. Indeed, in a short period of time Bashir had evolved from being a devil to being a 'moderate' whom the international community, and in particular the West, should protect. In this new discourse both the NCP and SPLM were committed to the CPA process from the beginning – as a UN official remarked, 'Bashir is the driving force behind the CPA.'

There were many words of praise for the NCP and nothing but condemnation for the northern opposition parties, which were seen as spoilers. And what was the opposition demanding? Basically, an all-party constitutional process and a national government, both of which would be recognized by most disinterested observers as critical elements in the country's democratic transformation. The international brigade could not oppose such demands directly, but instead condemned the parties for their weakness and lack of leadership. But the bottom line for the Western diplomats and the UN officials was stability, and in this light the opposition was viewed as a threat. This was the same position the diplomats took at the time the CPA process was unfolding and armed groups across the country were demanding to be part of the peace process.

While Sudan was breaking in two, the international diplomats from the UN, the AU, the US and Europe were also pulling their hair out at the prospect of further divisions in the north. They did not appreciate that their efforts at keeping non-SPLM groups out of the peace process and facilitating the secession of the south would naturally inspire separatists in other parts of Sudan. These same diplomats now emphasized the links between the different parts of the country, the need to address local concerns, and to focus on the big picture. Of course it would have been much easier to deal with Darfur in 2004–05 than in 2011, with its proliferation of armed groups. At the time the West supported the ultimately successful efforts of the NCP to keep other groups out of the negotiations with the promise of future peace processes, all of which came to nothing.

There was a dawning recognition that the economic crisis could cause instability and be used by the opposition to undermine the government. Hence, the representatives of the West wanted to support Bashir in the economic sphere. They were particularly anxious to overcome the obstacles to the north and the south receiving loans. Their interests seemed divided between ensuring the viability of the international economic system and the Western institutions that dominated it and going to bat for the governments in Khartoum and Juba. With the exception of the US and Austria, most of Sudan's debt was held by Gulf countries and private investors from the region, and the NCP had been paying the interest on those loans. Southern Sudan faced the problem of having so much money per capita as a result of oil revenues that it was not technically eligible to receive IMF loans. Curiously, nothing was said about the contradiction between southern Sudan awash in oil funds and desperately needing money from the international community.

There were fears that SPLM delays in the resolution of post-referendum issues, calculated to increase its bargaining position, were undermining Bashir. They positively gushed over Bashir's New Year's Eve and Juba speeches, although one European diplomat did note that he sometimes said different things away from the big cities. All the Western ambassadors called for increased development and relief assistance to the north and for deepening engagement with the regime. The problem with the latter objective was that none of them was permitted by their government to meet with Bashir because of the ICC warrants, a source of some embarrassment.

All of this was placed in the context of the need for stability, and this at a time when the Ben Ali government in Tunisia had just fallen and was soon to be followed by that of Mubarak in Egypt. The officials did not recognize that their concern with stability was what precipitated the Middle Eastern revolts. None of this would have surprised Umma Party leader Sadig al-Mahdi, who observed that 'The weakness of the US and Western diplomats in relation to Sudan is their narrow focus on security and little understanding of the country's politics and security' (interview, 27 December 2011). Also striking was the fact that the word 'democracy' never passed the lips of these leaders of the international community.

Forgotten by the Western diplomats was the long history of the NCP and Bashir as hard-core Islamists, the deeply flawed April elections, and the party's continuing, almost totalitarian, hold over northern society. Also not considered was the possibility that the NCP was tricking the West, or that while Bashir might presently be in the 'moderate' camp, he could soon shift to the 'radical Islamist' camp. In view of the international configuration of forces in support of the referendum process, evidence of the overwhelming support of southerners for secession, support from his core for southern secession, and doubts about the capacity of the national army, it would seem that Bashir took a prudent decision not to oppose the referendum overtly. Indeed, not to endorse the referendum would have meant a return to war with the south at a time when the war in Darfur was intensifying and when the West might support the SPLA, when Sudan had almost no friends internationally, even in the Arab and Muslim world, and when war would have meant the loss of all leverage with the US to get off the sanctions list and obtain debt relief. In other words, the NCP had no realistic choice but to endorse the referendum process, and that did not make Bashir either a statesman or a moderate.

Conclusion

After the early anxiety about the process and outcome of the referendum, the universal predictions that the vote would be overwhelmingly in favor of secession, the 60 per cent cut-off would be met, and the public assurances by President al-Bashir that he would endorse the results and that Sudan would be the first country to recognize the independence of the Republic of South Sudan (RoSS), the actual vote was anti-climatic. In the event, almost 4 million registered voters voted 98.3 percent for independence and only 1.7 percent for unity. The OCV vote was only slightly behind at 98.02 per cent for secession. South Darfur was the only area in which southerners voted for unity (59.43 percent of registered voters).

The vote, however, was not without its problems, particularly related to turn-outs of more than 100 percent in ten of the more than sixty counties where all of the ballots had been processed. The SSRC responded by quarantining results from polling stations where turn-out exceeded 105 percent of voters registered – rather than above 100 percent, as the international observers indicated was in keeping with international standards. The Commission said the problem resulted from the previous year's voter registration process. There were issues related to privacy of voting, assistance in voting, the presence of security officials in and around the polling stations, and other matters, but no one suggested that these failures seriously affected the outcome of the vote. The failure of the parties to create a conducive environment – which largely meant a democratic environment – was never really addressed by the observation missions, and the intimidation by the SPLM of voters in the north and at some OCV locations, and parallel examples of intimidation by the northern security services, were also not highlighted.

Bashir was magnanimous:

> We have received the result and we heartily accept it because it expresses the will of the South Sudan citizens. Today is one of the defining moments of the Sudan. While we congratulate our people in southern Sudan for their choice, we hope that today's event will be the departure point between war and peace in Sudan, not a departure point between unity and separation. (*Sudanwatch*, 8 February 2011)

He went on to issue a Republican Decree which accepted the results and committed both parties 'to work to resolve the remaining outstanding issues and build positive and constructive relationships between the two parts of the country.' This was followed by the approval of the Council of Ministers of the referendum results in an extraordinary session chaired by Bashir in the presence of his two vice presidents, Salva Kiir Mayardit and Ali Osman Mohamed Taha. The pieces were thus all in place to conclude that the referendum represented the democratic will of the people. With all this goodwill, the two presidents delivered speeches that focused on common objectives, a common determination, and the need to go forward quickly to create a soft border between the two states.

The leaders of the international community were also quick to make similar statements. Mbeki said the success of the referendum in Sudan would help promote democracy in Africa and that the outcome confirmed the commitment of the Sudanese people and leaders never to return to war.[16] President Barack Obama announced that the United States would recognize South Sudan as a 'sovereign, independent state' in July and went on to say: 'On behalf of the people of the United States, I congratulate the people of southern Sudan for a successful and inspiring referendum in which an overwhelmingly majority of voters chose independence' (White House Office of the Press Secretary, 7 February 2011).

Presumably such statements are expected in the circumstances, and indeed the people of southern Sudan deserved congratulations for their disciplined voting, but these speeches could not paper over the deceit and subterfuge that characterized the campaigns of the two ruling parties, or the fact that not for a moment did the leader of either party overcome his deep distrust of the other – and for good reason. Thus on Bashir's visit to Juba immediately prior to the referendum vote, Salva promised him that he would end support for Darfuri rebels and Bashir in turn assured him that he would stop supporting southern militias. But even before the referendum voting had been completed it became known that Darfuri rebel leaders had not been dismissed from Juba (indeed, many of them were staying in the GoSS-owned

Grand Hotel). Colonel Gatlauk Gai, who was angered by the
rigged election in Unity state which prevented Angelina Teny-
Dhurgon from assuming office as governor, and hence precluded
his appointment as commissioner, launched an insurgency with
the support of SAF.

As a result, party and military leaders on both sides of the
divide only set aside the referendum to consider how they could
use their respective proxies to advance their interests in the
post-referendum issues and Abyei. The NCP leadership continued
to consider whether it should use these proxies to weaken, undermine, or even overthrow the SPLM-led government, while in the
south their counterparts were debating whether the sovereignty
of their yet-to-be-born country and its stability necessitated the
overthrow of the NCP government. It never occurred to either
side to put down the gun, and indeed it would have been suicidal
to do so.

In the south the gloss had not yet been taken off the October
reconciliation between the opposition parties and the ruling
SPLM, but it soon would be. And what made that inevitable was
the mistaken view of the SPLM leadership that the overwhelming
vote for secession was an endorsement of their popularity. For
southerners only accepted SPLM domination as the best means
to ensure the secessionist project stayed on track. And with
that objective achieved, the gap between southerners and their
government steadily widened, and would soon produce increasing acrimony between the opposition parties and the southern
government.

While international spokespersons trotted out their well-worn
platitudes on the success of the referendum and hopes for a
glorious future for the two Sudans, behind closed doors they
were skeptical about the fulfillment of the peace process. There
was satisfaction that their main objective of achieving southern
independence had largely been accomplished, but they were

rightly concerned about the rocky road ahead. These closed-door meetings also revealed their continuing cynicism about democratic transformation, distrust of the opposition parties, and fawning admiration for President al-Bashir, whom their home governments did not permit them to meet and who officially viewed the NCP administration as a rogue government. Like the SPLM and NCP, their real assessment and objectives bore little relation to what they said publicly and completely sidestepped the CPA commitment to democratic transformation, which could now be ignored with the accepted separation of southern Sudan. Their conclusion that Bashir was a moderate and their dismissal of democratic transformation would soon return to haunt them, however.

FIVE

THE THREE AREAS: BLUE NILE, SOUTHERN KORDOFAN, AND ABYEI

With the completion of the national elections and referendum, the main requirements of the CPA outstanding were the elections in Southern Kordofan, the popular consultations of Blue Nile and Southern Kordofan, and resolution of the problem of Abyei. However, the Southern Kordofan elections were postponed from April 2010 to May 2011 because the SPLM did not accept the census on which the elections were to be based, and the popular consultations could only be started after elections had brought to power accountable state governments that could oversee the process and appoint commissions to conduct them. The consultations in Blue Nile were not successful and had not been completed when the peace process ended; consequently the national government passed legislation to extend the process by six months.

Meanwhile, the Southern Kordofan SPLM refused to accept the election result, which the sitting governor, Ahmed Haroun, won. Tensions increased further when SAF announced that all SPLA forces in the north must be disarmed. This led Southern Kordofan SPLM leader Abdel Aziz al-Hilu to launch an insurgency, which by the end of the peace process had SAF largely in control of the state's lowlands and the SPLA in control of most of the Nuba Mountains. The failure to hold the Abyei referendum and demands that the Misseirya be permitted to participate in any such exercise led to skirmishes between SAF and the SPLA and their allied armed groups in the first half of 2011, which ended with a full-scale invasion of the territory by SAF on 20 June. Although intimately linked to the northern insurgents, the southern SPLM/A formally stayed out of the conflict and continued negotiating with the NCP over the outstanding post-referendum issues. The resort to armed conflict to decide issues that should have been resolved in Naivasha pointed to the weakness of the CPA and raised the danger that the parties to the agreement would return to a full-fledged war.

Background to the Popular Consultations

Given his desire to give concrete expression to New Sudan, John Garang was anxious to carry the war to the north. His primary areas of interest were southern Blue Nile and the Nuba Mountains of Southern Kordofan. Both were adjacent to the south and populated by Africans and could be expected to be receptive to the SPLM/A's rhetoric of marginalization. Blue Nile state bordered Ethiopia, and the Derg twice assisted the SPLA to capture its southern region only to lose it again. But in 1997, with EPRDF assistance, the SPLA captured the area and held it until the end of the peace process. The SPLA never reached beyond the African and few Christianized tribes of the southern part of the state (notably the Uduk, Mabaan, and Jumjum) to win over the Arab and western tribes that inhabited the northern areas of the state, where the core of the economy was situated around the Rosseires Dam just outside the state capital of Damazine (Young 2004). Although Malik Agar Eyre from the local Ingessina tribe served as governor, the introduction of the largely Dinka and Nuer soldiers of the SPLA often caused tensions, and it would be some years before they could be replaced by fighters from local communities.

Southern Kordofan followed a different trajectory, with the SPLM/A emerging from the struggles of indigenous actors who came together under the leadership of Yusif Kuwa, a teacher and poet who launched an armed struggle in 1987 calling for respect for Nuba cultures and diversity, development, and against the loss of land to absentee riverain Arab owners of mechanized and commercial farms. Opposition to the central state increasingly took the form of an armed struggle, which was natural for a people with strong martial traditions. As well as fighting this solitary campaign, so many Nuba soldiers joined the southern SPLA that they probably constituted the largest component of the force in the 1980s and 1990s; a considerable number were still in the SPLA at the end of the peace process. Indeed, it was largely due to the loyalty of the Nuba soldiers that Garang was able to contain the Riek–Lam defection in 1991. SAF's efforts to defeat the Nuba SPLA involved the destruction of villages and the mass expulsion of civilians and their subsequent settlement in 'peace villages,' actions that equaled the crimes in Darfur, although they failed to gain a comparable level of international attention. The SPLA, however, was far from democratic; Africa Rights recorded a consistent pattern of human rights abuses, including forced conscription, killing of POWs, and theft of property (Justice Africa 1995).

Although the SPLA was never able to capture more than a small area in the Nuba Mountains, it posed a sufficient threat to Khartoum governments by the mid-1980s that SAF-established Misseirya militias became the principal means of confronting the insurgency, which brought a racial dimension to the conflict that had not previously existed. Until the outbreak of the war there was not a discernible Arab–African divide due both to the multiple ethnicities in the Nuba Mountains and to the tendency of tribal alliances to cut across racial divisions. The racial dimensions of the conflict were heightened with the rise to power of the NIF, which fought rising Nuba nationalism by arresting and subsequently killing hundreds of Nuba intellectuals in 1987 and in 1995 announcing a jihad against the SPLA fighters.

Meanwhile, the SPLA increasingly defined the enemy as Arabs and launched a full-scale war against them, although this caused divisions in the movement. In 1994 senior SPLM leaders in the Nuba Mountains, led by Awad al-Karim Kuku, wrote a letter to Yusif Kuwa explicitly complaining about the SPLA targeting of Arabs and the importing of Dinka commanders into the area. Yusif in turn raised the issue with Garang, who viewed the complaints as an act of rebellion and arranged for the twenty-five commanders to be taken to southern Sudan. Some died en route, some died in prison from torture, and those remaining were killed by placing them in sown bags weighed down with rocks and thrown into the Nile.[1] The racial dimension to the conflict in the Nuba Mountains contributed to the difficulties in the Naivasha negotiations, the disputed elections, and the resulting war.

Under the Southern Kordofan/Blue Nile Protocol, the NCP acquired 55 per cent of the seats and the SPLM 45 per cent; the leaders of the SPLM in the two states held the governorships for the first two years of the six-year CPA-stipulated interim period and the NCP held them for the next two years, after which elections were supposed to be held. Although these arrangements suggest a genuine sharing of power, the reality was very different. In Blue Nile and Southern Kordofan, as elsewhere in northern Sudan, the states had been completely reconstructed by the NCP – civil servants were screened to ensure their loyalty to the NCP, governors closely followed orders of NCP headquarters, and, crucially, the security services served as mere instruments of the ruling party. In the southern and underdeveloped part of Blue Nile the SPLA continued to maintain an unofficial presence, bolstered by a large SPLA contingent just inside the Upper Nile border. But the situation was far from ideal and many cadres in both states became disillusioned, particularly when they realized that the SPLM under Salva Kiir had turned away from the New Sudan vision and was dedicated to achieving southern independence. SPLA Brigadier General Isaac, the deputy commander of the JIU for Southern Kordofan, summed up the sentiments of many Nuba when he said 'The South took what they wanted from the CPA and left the Nuba Mountains ... The SPLA are part of the Nuba Mountains and everyone is disappointed in the CPA. The only thing we got from the CPA was the popular consultations' (interview, 28 October 2010).

In earlier years Malik Agar Eyre would muse about the various options for Blue Nile – unity with the south under the SPLM; unity with the north under a post-NCP government; the independence of Blue Nile or at least of its southern portion; or linking up with Ethiopia and the neighboring state of Benishangul, to which Blue Nile was culturally and economically closely tied. But neither independence nor joining Ethiopia was a serious option, and the CPA foreclosed the possibility of joining the south even if many in the SPLM in the state were in denial.

The April 2010 elections in Blue Nile were a bitterly fought affair, particularly for the governorship. We may never know the politicking behind the ultimate election of Malik, a contest where he was repeatedly reported as being behind his competitor, only to be declared victor. It seems likely that the SPLM leadership in Juba threatened to abort the entire election if Malik was denied the governorship, and the NCP felt compelled to bend. The NCP in turn picked up two-thirds of the legislative seats. Upon completion of the elections, attention increasingly turned to the popular consultations, with the SPLM attempting to push the envelope, arguing for self-determination, and the NCP leadership wanting to reduce the exercise to little more than a symbolic gesture.

Indeed, according to a NCP participant in the Naivasha negotiations, the commitment to popular consensus was only made to 'save the face of some members of the SPLM.' NCP ministers told the author that proposals for a wide-ranging popular consultation were being exploited by the SPLM and their American allies and if pressed would become 'a flash point.' They said the popular consultations were not meant to provide a blueprint for future constitutional arrangements in northern Sudan even though the protocol specifically said that they would serve as a 'model for solving the problems throughout the country.' For them, popular consultations were only designed to encourage dialogue and produce some 'minor reforms,' and certainly not any notion of confederalism as proposed by Malik Agar Eyre.

The Southern Kordofan/Nuba Mountains and Blue Nile Protocol defined popular consultation as 'a democratic right and mechanism to ascertain the views of the people of Southern Kordofan/Nuba Mountains and Blue Nile States on the Comprehensive Peace Agreement reached by the Government of Sudan and the Sudan People's Liberation Movement' (paragraph 3.1). The Protocol was followed by the 2010 People's Consultation Act for the states, which specified that the main area of focus for the popular consultation is

> the constitutional, political, administrative, and economic arrangements related to the structure, the type and the level of decentralised governance, institutions and authorities; the relationship between the state and the centre; the executive and legislative powers; and the share of each of the two states in wealth and national power as detailed in the Comprehensive Peace Agreement. (Article 3)

Blue Nile Popular Consultation

From the start of the process, senior SPLM Blue Nile legislators and others proclaimed their commitment to self-determination and said they intended to use the popular consultation to achieve this end, even if it involved a return to war, which many expected. Hashim Mohammed, a SPLM member of the state assembly, reflected that 'Conflict in Blue Nile has gone on since the inception of Sudan and conditions are regressing'; consequently he anticipated a 'genocide' of the African tribes (interview, 19 October 2010). Governor Malik meanwhile was widely quoted as saying he expected to put on his military uniform after the southern referendum, which meant that he expected a return to war. Malik Agar Eyre's problems included SPLM Juba's support for secession, which he opposed; the flawed elections, which left him as the only non-NCP governor in northern Sudan, and the leader of a minority party in the state assembly, which limited the realization of his agenda; a caucus divided over popular consultation; and his status as the leader of the SPLM in northern Sudan, the very existence of which was in doubt given repeated NCP threats to ban the party.

The NCP stressed that the protocol did not grant the state the right to self-determination, there was no provision for a referendum, and their intention was to work within the law and examine the topics listed in the Protocol. However, it soon became clear that not only was the state NCP divided internally on its approach to the popular consultations, but the state and central party were also divided, as was made evident when Afar Agar, the deputy governor, was appointed minister of parliamentary affairs in the GNU. The move, however, did not stop him from loudly proclaiming a commitment to a popular consultation that very closely resembled that proposed by Malik, whom he was known to meet regularly.[2] After Afar was removed, the NCP state assembly speaker, who had also been an exponent of a radical decentralization of power, suddenly became silent. There were stories of a stormy caucus meeting in which NCP legislators resorted to fisticuffs over how to handle the popular consultations.

One observer noted that, 'unlike Southern Kordofan where Haroun decides in Blue Nile all the NCP are puppets.' But as an official in the Peace Research Institute at the University of Khartoum, which was tasked with preparing background papers for the Commission, noted, 'no matter what party, all of them have gone local.'

General dissatisfaction with the implementation of the CPA was also expressed by other parties and civil society in the state. Most said they received no benefits from the rich resources of their state, which were controlled by riverain Arabs in the state and in Khartoum. They complained at the lack of development, the poor state of the roads, the failure of the government to provide services, and the influx of large numbers of SAF soldiers. And, cutting across party lines, almost everyone complained at the limited benefits they received from the Rosseires Dam, even though it provided electricity for a sizable portion of northern Sudan.

Nor was the security situation in the state conducive to a positive outcome from the popular consultations. The SAF contingent in the state probably numbered in the range of 15–20,000, considerably above the stipulations of the Security Arrangements Protocol, which reduced it to the pre-war level of two battalions or about 1,600 soldiers, and a further 3,000 in the JIUs. They were supported by an undetermined number of Popular Defense Force soldiers, who were used both as a fighting force and during the war as a means to press NCP religious practices on the people of the state, who frequently followed unorthodox approaches to Islam. The PDF was particularly active among the nomadic tribes – Rufa'a, Kennana, Falata, Omberaro, and so on – which crossed into Blue Nile state and southern Sudan on their yearly cycles, typically from mid-October to July. The SPLM commissioner of Kurmuk, Stephen Amot, complained that 'The basic problem in Kurmuk is the armed nomad militias … the SPLA militias turned over their weapons to the SPLA according to the CPA, but the NCP affiliated militias did not follow suit'; to make matters worse, he had no authority over the local police who could control these nomads (interview, 21 October 2010). Internally, security in the state was dominated by the Falata, originally part of the Fulani tribe of West Africa, with whom the NCP developed close relations.

Meanwhile, the SPLA initially moved most of its estimated 12–15,000 forces to the Upper Nile border centre of Guffa, but they regularly moved back and forth into southern Blue Nile, partly in the course of military maneuvers, partly to visit relatives and friends, and others who had retired or left the SPLA but still had links to it. In addition, the SPLA also had 3,000 soldiers in the JIUs.

Blue Nile was also affected by the ongoing conflict between Eritrea and neighboring Ethiopia. Eritrea supports Ethiopian dissidents, specifically Oromo and Benishangual rebels, who cross the Eritrean–Sudanese border to the north and then move south along the eastern frontier of Sudan to Blue Nile, after which they cross to Benishangual (Young 2007). Generally these fighters transit individually and there is nothing about their appearance that distinguishes them from Sudanese, but they are believed to be assisted by inhabitants of Blue Nile. Anxious to keep on the right side of the Ethiopian authorities, Sudanese security officials work closely with their Ethiopian counterparts on this problem.

Blue Nile Hearings

The two states were to appoint popular consultation commissions and assessment and evaluation commissions, both of which would present reports to their respective assemblies.[3] In the event the citizens of the two states were satisfied that with the implementation of the CPA the process would end, but if they were not satisfied then the state assemblies (which in practice meant the NCP and SPLM) would have to reach a common position and open negotiations with the GNU, even though the GNU passed out of existence before the popular consultations had been completed.

The Blue Nile Parliamentary Commission for Popular Consultation was established in October 2010, composed of 21 members, 13 from the NCP and 8 from the SPLM, all members of the state legislative assembly. The Blue Nile Commission specifically identified four broad themes to be considered in the public hearings: constitutional, administrative, political, and economic. Between 14 January and 2 February, 69,429 participants in 108 different locations made presentations at 116 public hearings covering six geographical areas around the state. One hearing, conducted by between two and four commissioners, was held in each area every day.

Despite these impressive numbers and the competence of the Commission the hearings did not live up to expectations. There were three principal and related problems. First, instead of reasoned discussion on the four designated themes of the popular consultations, the contributions were largely reduced to very brief statements in support of either 'autonomy' or 'federalism,' the respective positions of the SPLM and the NCP. Second, the mobilization by the dominant parties of their constituencies, which broadly followed tribal lines, threatened to exacerbate tribal tensions within the state. Third, the orchestration of the process by the SPLM and NCP undermined efforts to ascertain the views of the people of Blue Nile and also effectively marginalized the other political parties and civil society in the state and created an undemocratic environment.

The initial trial hearings in Damazine and Rosseires produced open and often emotional presentations, but the Popular

Consultation Commission made clear it would not accept such interventions or unruly behavior. The first five or six days of the hearings were orderly in character, but were still wide-ranging and gave no indication of being orchestrated. After that the SPLM began to instruct its followers to call for 'autonomy' or 'self-government' and development. A day or two later – and clearly in response to the SPLM's efforts – the NCP began directing its followers to call for 'federalism' or 'current government.' The NCP call for federalism or existing government was meant to indicate satisfaction with the existing state of affairs, but it quickly became apparent that was not the case. I attended a number of these hearings until forced to leave on account of the sheer boredom of listening to hundreds of people in succession parroting the slogans put in their mouths by the SPLM and NCP. But it quickly became apparent that virtually no one was happy with the implementation of the CPA and most supporters of both parties called for development. Sometimes the speakers said that by development they were calling for more water outlets, schools, clinics, and roads for the state. As a result, a day or two later NCP-coached followers added 'development' to their statements. According to Shukri, the SPLM chairman in Rosseires, 'The NCP in Blue Nile know that if they don't stand with the people they will commit suicide' (interview, 31 January 2011). Indeed, it was impossible to find anyone in the state irrespective of their party affiliation who did not complain at the state's lack of development, and in particular the fact that it produced a sizable portion of Sudan's electricity, but suffered from power shortages.

The NCP leadership could provide a definition of federalism, but SPLM leaders could not provide a consistent definition of autonomy. As a result, they pressed their supporters to call for a system of governance that they themselves had not agreed upon. The SPLM and NCP undermined the intent of the popular consultation hearings and effectively turned the hearings into a referendum, and as a result their monitors kept records of the statements at the hearings in favor of autonomy and federalism, and it would appear that those appearing at the hearings viewed them in the same way.

The Carter Center, which served as the only international observation mission, concluded that, 'To the extent that parties' actions curtail unfiltered expressions of citizens' views, such actions, while not contrary to law, undermine the overall goal and spirit of the popular consultations to gauge citizens' views' (Carter Center, 21 March 2011). As one member of an opposition party lamented, 'the official civic education was conducted by day, and by night the SPLM and NCP provided their own education.'

Another problem with the popular consultation hearings was that they pitted indigenous tribes – the largely SPLM-supporting Berta, Hamaj, Ingessina, Wataweet, Dawala, Gumuz, Barum, Uduk, and Jumjum, with the Upper Nile migrant tribes of the Mabaan, Dinka, and Shilluk against the NCP-supporting tribes that migrated to the area, the Arab Jallien, Shaggiya, Kamatir, Ashraf, Rufa'a, Kenana, Falata, and the Darfur tribes, Bagara, Zhagawa, Massalit, and Fur. As a result there was a clear correlation between a person's tribe and the support they gave to either federalism or autonomy, and this contributed to the tense environment of the hearings and in a few cases led to violence. But the crux of the tension was between the Arab tribes that began migrating to Blue Nile during the height of the Funj period in the eighteenth century and to some extent the Falata, who have been closely linked to successive Khartoum governments, and the various indigenous tribes. Alrah Younis, an SPLM official, explained this tension by observing, 'There was no tribal conflict in Blue Nile until 1990 when people first started understanding their rights because of SPLM mobilization. The struggle for rights was the cause of the tensions that can be seen in the hearings' (interview, 4 February 2011).

All the Blue Nile tribes, except the Uduk and Jumjum, are Muslim, so religion per se was not in dispute. However, all post-colonial governments in Khartoum attempted to implant riverain notions of Islam among the otherwise religiously diverse and flexible indigenous tribes. The NCP, however, went much further than other governments; through various Islamist NGOs operating in the state it imposed essentially Salafi notions of Islam on all the non-Arab tribes, but particularly the indigenous tribes. And among the indigenous tribes the Uduk and Jumjum were singled out because they were early supporters of the SPLM.

Although Arabs only constitute a small proportion of the population of Blue Nile state and the broad division in the hearings did not pit Arabs against Africans, nonetheless the state was in the front line in the battle over whether Sudan's identity was foremost Arab or African. And that in turn figured prominently in the ideological contest between Khartoum-based governments and the SPLM. This tension increased after the NCP came to power; hence, at the time of the signing of the CPA, virtually all leadership and administrative offices in Blue Nile were held by non-indigenous peoples, and even teachers above primary level were from the core areas in the north. Given its weak social base, particularly in the southern part of the state, the NCP encouraged the Falata to move to the state (although some had lived in the area since the time of the Mahdi), and as a consequence the local administration of Blue Nile was dominated by Arabs, Falata, and to a lesser extent tribes from western Sudan and nomads from the north. Meanwhile, Arabs dominated the formal economy: they purchased the gold; exported charcoal, fruit, and vegetables to the northern towns; imported consumer goods; and controlled most of the state's important mechanized agriculture industry.

Control of the state and economy by those considered outsiders was fiercely resented by the indigenous tribes, and the SPLM used this anger to win support. This in turn served to strengthen the links between the Arabs and non-indigenous tribes and the NCP. Only in recent years has the SPLM been able to move beyond its core support among the indigenous peoples and bring some Arabs, but very few Falata, into its ranks. The elderly Falata chief Arbab Mohamed Ismael noted that

> Inequality between the tribes only developed after Sudan's independence. The Falata historically were supporters of the Mahdi and the Umma Party, but in recent years almost all the tribe supported the NCP in the 2010 election [because] the black people think Falata and Arabs don't have rights to live here. (interview, 6 February 2011)

No doubt this support solidified with the election of Malik, who made a considerable effort to bring the indigenous tribes into the civil service. But changing the local dynamics did not change relations with Khartoum, where, as explained by SPLM minister of finance Mubarak, 'Ninety-five percent of Blue Nile's revenues come from the center, including salaries, and the result is that I spend all my time in Khartoum trying to get the money' (interview, 6 February 2011).

These tensions between the tribes were exacerbated by the popular consultation hearings. The SPLM and its supporters among the indigenous tribes viewed the consultations as a means to advance their interests in the state. The counterpoint to that was the fear it produced among the non-indigenous tribes. As a result, members of the non-indigenous tribes contended that if autonomy was accepted as the goal of the state they would be forced to leave, and the NCP played up this fear in its propaganda. This was denied by the SPLM, but it did not lack a basis in fact, as the following exchange between Governor Malik and the author suggests:

> *It appeared in the Popular Consultation hearings that the state's indigenous tribes supported autonomy while the other tribes*

supported federalism. Are you concerned about this process creating tribal tensions?

There are no tribal tensions. Yes, there was a very clear distribution between indigenous people for autonomy and settlers who wanted federalism.

Settlers?

You can call them migrants. They are from out of the area. If we had the ability we could have chased them away years ago. Look, we are not racist. We are not looking to chase anyone away. But we have a grievance and we want our case respected. We are underdeveloped. We are misgoverned … I mean the indigenous tribes. (interview, 6 February 2011)

As was the case elsewhere in Sudan, only the parties with money – and that was limited to the NCP and SPLM – could campaign, mobilize, and provide benefits for their supporters, while the other parties were largely left on the sidelines. As a result, in the April elections the NCP won 29 seats in the state legislature against the SPLM's 19 seats. Nonetheless, some effort was made to bring the other ten registered parties into the popular consultations, and a political council of the twelve parties was formed. The opposition parties were provided with some funding by the UN and the governor to participate in the civic education in the run-up to the popular consultation hearings. However, years of state repression and limited financial and human resources meant that, although the parties did provide observers for the hearings, their actual influence was negligible. Suliman Ali, chairman of the state branch of the Sudan Communist Party, complained that 'Other parties [than the NCP and SPLM] are not allowed to be part of the process [and with no resources] we are blocked from the rural areas' (interview, 19 October 2010).

One potentially positive contribution by the political council was an agreement on the eve of the hearings which bound all the parties to a popular consultation that would be transparent, free,

fair, and encourage the widest participation. In the event, most
of the opposition party representatives concluded that by using
the popular consultation hearings to press for their preferred
systems of governance, the SPLM and NCP undermined the
entire exercise.

While the civic education for the hearings was effective in
informing people about where the hearings were to be held,
who was eligible to participate, time limits, and other technical
concerns, it did not explain the objectives of the popular consultation and the broader issues of governance and security that
underpinned it. To ensure genuine and informed participation
in the hearings there would have had to be a sustained public
campaign to politically educate the people of the state on the CPA
and the Blue Nile/Southern Kordofan Protocol, but that was not
done. The Carter Center concluded there was a need for 'com-
municating the underlying purpose of the popular consultation
and creating an ongoing dialogue about the substantive topics at
issue' (Carter Center, 21 March 2011).

To the extent that the voice of the people of Blue Nile state was
heard, it spoke strongly of the need for development and improved
services such as schools, clinics, water, and – ironically given
the presence of the one of the biggest dams in the country just
outside Damazine and Rosseires – the need for a consistent supply
of electricity. Mention was also made that efforts under way to
extend the dam were causing dislocation. Possibly out of fear or
maybe ignorance of the scope of the hearings, very few people
raised the issue of security, even though there was no doubt that
was a primary concern for many people in the state, particularly
those living in the south and outside the major towns.

Immediately upon completion of the hearings controversy
developed over what to do with the results. Since the NCP and
SPLM treated the hearings like a referendum, with winners and
losers at each session, they now pressed for the results to be

translated into 'votes' for and against autonomy and federalism, but this raised the political temperature and brought the tabulation process to a virtual halt. Indeed, at the end of the peace process the parties were still locked in argument, and plans for thematic hearings of elite groups (defined as civil society groups and political parties) were in doubt. Moreover, the state SPLM began the popular consultation with a wide basis of support among the opposition parties, but as a result of its performance a coalition of these parties announced at a press conference its disagreement with the SPLM's 'abandonment of good relations with all involved stakeholders.'[4] The parties also concluded that the system of government was irrelevant as long as the popular consultations succeeded in achieving the true desires of the Blue Nile people, which they identified as development and restructuring the state's relationship to central government. They were highly skeptical of the proposed thematic hearings because they feared they would also be held captive by the preoccupation of the ruling parties with systems of governance.

Southern Kordofan Elections and Popular Consultations

Until 1994 Kordofan was administered as one territory, but in that year it was divided into three states – north, south (the tribes of the Nuba Mountains), and west (largely Misseirya). In August 2005, as a result of the CPA, the parties agreed to join Western Kordofan to Southern Kordofan. From the outset there were problems in the administration of Southern Kordofan, in part because of differences over land issues, management of the state legislature, and reaching agreement on the state constitution, and it was not until 7 March 2006 that a caretaker government was eventually established. The new state also brought together two deeply suspicious parties and and the Nuba, who were

thoroughly disenchanted with a CPA which ended their hope of
a New Sudan and also made it impossible to join the south, the
option most Nubans preferred. As a result there were periodic
clashes between NCP- and SPLM-aligned militias. Indeed, there
was already talk, and apparently some plans, to train Nuba forces
and stockpile arms in preparation for launching an insurgency at
the end of the peace process and with the separation of southern
Sudan (Mohamed 2008). Likewise, in 2008 the International
Crisis Group published a study, *Sudan's Southern Kordofan
Problem: The Next Darfur?*, which summed up a widely held
view.[5] According to the SPLM, the state's problems stemmed
from a lack of development, high levels of illiteracy, and the
absence of services, and thus it proposed democracy, dealing
constructively with the problem of traditional land alienation,
ending Arabization and Islamization of the educational system,
resolving a range of security issues, and taking up the concerns
of refugees and IDPs.

The attitudes of SPLM officials in Kadugli were similar to their
counterparts in Damazin in that many of them wanted to push
the popular consultation process beyond the Protocol-stipulated
limits. Some SPLM officials also indicated that if their demands
were not met they would return to war. Meanwhile, the NCP in
Southern Kordofan emphasized the actual law that determined
the process and stressed the fact that it did not grant the Nuba
Mountain people the right to self-determination, independence,
or autonomy. And, like their counterparts in Blue Nile, the state
NCP supported a considerable degree of decentralization and had
to respond to a community in the Nuba Mountains which was
bitterly aggrieved. The powerful NCP speaker of the State Assembly, Ibrahim Balandia, claimed that the parties were 'localists,'
and given that 'Southern Kordofan was 99 per cent dependent on
the center for its budget' there was thus a need 'to look deeply at
reforms' (interview, 14 March 2011).

Unlike Blue Nile, the elections to the state assembly of Southern Kordofan were not held in April 2010 because the SPLM
contended that the census undercounted the Nubas, and therefore
it was agreed that it would be redone. On 26 October 2010 it was
announced that the population of the state was 2.4 million, up a
million from the earlier census that the SPLM had rejected, but
far below the figure expected by most Nuba and SPLM leaders.
The details of the census were not released, but it was strongly
suspected that this new number was a 'political figure' cooked
up by the presidency. However, although suspect, it cleared the
way for holding the state elections.

Without the election of a state assembly the popular consultation could not be finalized, though a Technical Committee had
been established to do the preparatory work. In addition, to gain
a wider level of involvement, a Council of Elders was formed that
brought in a wide variety of distinguished people representing all
political persuasions in Southern Kordofan, and committees of
this body held meetings around the state.

Both parties suffered from divisions over their leadership, in
part because in neither case were they completely indigenous and
were imposed by the central party. Under the Protocol the SPLM
and NCP divided the governorship until the elections. Ismael
Khamis Gilab of the SPLM was appointed the first post-CPA
governor, but he accomplished little and tribal polarization grew.
He was followed by the NCP administration of Omar Suliman,
who also had little to show for his term of office. Furthermore,
his SPLM deputy, Daniel Kodie, was criticized for his heavy
drinking. As a result of continual infighting among the SPLM
leadership, Salva ordered the state leadership to Juba in February
2009, whereupon Abdel Aziz al-Hilu was selected as the overall
leader. However, dissatisfaction continued. The crisis deepened
with the boycott of the 2008 census. To save the situation Ahmed
Haroun, widely viewed in the NCP as one of its most talented

administrators – although his reputation was tarnished on account of his masterminding a terror campaign in Darfur, for which he was indicted by the ICC – became governor in May 2009. But his selection by the party leadership, specifically by Dr Nafie Ali Nafie, as a compromise between Nuba and Misseirya candidates also caused dissent.

Haroun immediately set about courting his deputy and state leader of the SPLM, Abdel Aziz Al-Hilu,[6] observing that 'It takes two to tango' and attributing the success of their relationship to the fact that 'both deal transparently with the other.' Haroun attempted to present himself as a pragmatist and contended that the CPA had diagnosed Sudan's problems and provided treatments; the popular consultation would assess both the peace and the treatments, and if they were not effective then other means would be proposed. For the first time in many years national resources were directed to the state: roads, hospitals, and a stadium in Kadugli were constructed, and security was improved. This was attributed to the political weight Haroun carried in Khartoum and his apparent threat that if he failed in Southern Kordofan and ended up before the ICC he would take others with him – the others including Bashir, who was also subject to ICC warrants.

This tough-guy approach earned Haroun enemies in the NCP, but most were prepared to bear with him if he could bring stability to the oil-producing border state of Southern Kordofan and undermine the threat posed by the SPLM with its large and militant constituency in the Nuba Mountains. Abdel Aziz, meanwhile, contended that much of the recent development in the state was due to Haroun, and together their relationship lowered the political temperature. However, within the SPLM there were many who thought otherwise and were opposed to his relationship with Haroun. 'I didn't fight for twenty years to get this kind of agreement,' a typical critic told me. The critics contended that cozying up to the governor compromised the SPLM's program. Abdel

Aziz struck back at the dissenters and carried out a purge of the party in January 2010 that saw the dismissal of sixty-two members of the party. One of those dismissed members, Sadig Monsour, the deputy speaker of the state assembly, complained that 'Abdel Aziz was imposed by the leadership and the SPLM operates in the shadow of dictatorship' (interview, 29 October 2010). At the same time Telefon Kuku, Abdel Aziz's most persistent critic, a veteran with a wide basis of support in the army and party, was arrested and held without charge in Juba. Telefon gained the ire of the Juba SPLM/A by contending that the Nuba soldiers in the SPLA should return to their homeland before the 2011 referendum. But the problem of the Nuba soldiers, who had joined the SPLA to fight for New Sudan and increasingly felt they were being sold out, did not go away, and in March 2010 Nuba Mountain soldiers held a conference in Yei, southern Sudan, to consider SPLM policies and the situation in Southern Kordofan in light of the impending secession of southern Sudan. The party's major leaders – Abdel Aziz, Khamis Gilab, Daniel Kodie, Telefon Kuku, and Abdel Aziz – were all invited, but Abdel Aziz failed to attend. This was unfortunate because the soldiers wanted assurances of unity. Despite these problems the international community strongly endorsed the partnership between Haroun and Abdel Aziz, seeing it as an isolated example of what it hoped would occur at all levels of government between the SPLM and NCP.

Throughout all of these internal struggles the role of Juba SPLM was unclear: was it simply supporting Abdel Aziz in his attempt to muzzle dissidents, or directing the affairs of the SPLM in Southern Kordofan? Was SPLM Juba protecting the rights of Nuba soldiers in the SPLA or anxious not to lose them because they were among its most politically reliable forces and had assumed key positions in the tank and artillery corps?

And where did the future of the Nuba Mountains lie? The protocol was clear that it was in the north, but it was not known if the Nuba people would accept that. On the eve of the state elections the Rashid County SPLM chairman, Younan Barout, asserted:

> one thing is clear – nobody is imagining the possibility of remaining in the North. We were marginalized for many decades under the authority of Khartoum.... That is why we joined the SPLM struggle. We fought these people, we killed them and they killed us. How will we join them? It is hard for you to join someone who was your enemy, is your enemy and will remain your enemy! (*News from Africa*, 10 March 2011)

Meanwhile, a NDI study found that of the major groups considered in the Three Areas, the Nuba were the least likely to accept the outcome of an election if someone from other than their ethnicity was elected governor (National Democratic Institute 2009).

Southern Kordofan Elections

The state SPLM wanted to win the election as a means of exerting its power in Southern Kordofan, 'win' the popular consultations that were to immediately follow the elections, and be best placed to confront Khartoum. The northern sector SPLM viewed Southern Kordofan as its heartland, a base for organizing resistance to the NCP, and for maintaining its existence in the face of demands that it be dissolved. The southern sector of the SPLM viewed the outcome as having important implications for security negotiations with the north and a basis on which to exert influence over the NCP. The NCP state party wanted to win the election so as to be able to dominate patronage and exert control over the popular consultations. And, to be better placed to negotiate with Khartoum, Haroun needed to demonstrate his utility to his NCP colleagues. The national NCP viewed the election as another opportunity to put more nails in the coffin of the New Sudan ideology, reduce the prospects for SPLM subversion in the state, and weaken the role of the SPLM in the popular consultations.

Many of the issues that came to the fore in the elections had important national implications. In the Misseirya-inhabited western part of the state, Abyei was the most important issue and there was virtual unanimity that whatever the final settlement the territory must remain in the north, a position completely opposed to that of the Ngok Dinka and the SPLM in both the south and the north, who viewed it as a southern territory. The Misseirya approached politics pragmatically: almost all their leaders were previously members of the Umma Party, but when its government was overthrown in 1989 tribal leaders fell in line with the NCP. However, the Misseirya held the NCP responsible for the Abyei Protocol, the Abyei Referendum Act, and the decisions of the Abyei Border Commission and the Arbitration Tribunal, and were angry at the government's decision to unite what had been their state of Western Kordofan with the Nuba Mountains to form Southern Kordofan. It spoke to the limited options of the Misseirya that they still grudgingly aligned with the NCP, but that loyalty to the party could not be taken for granted. Indeed, at the outset of the election the NCP promised to re-establish Western Kordofan as a means to win popularity among the Misseirya.[7] While the Nuba did not feel strongly about the loss of territory that would be dominated by the Misseirya, they would lose its valuable oil revenues. Not so the SPLM in Muglad in what would be the capital of Western Kordofan. According to Ibrahim Jabin, the deputy secretary of the local chapter of the SPLM, 'We don't want to be a party in a NCP-dominated state [and] such a state will suffer lack of development' (interview, 22 March 2011).

Environmental damage by petroleum companies was a concern in the far west, a number of protests were held, and in 2009 five Chinese oil workers were abducted to put pressure on the companies. Mohammed Yusif of the Babanusa Communist Party reflcted that 'The oil companies practice systematic segregation with most of the job holders coming from the north' (interview, 24 March 2011). There was an echo of this concern with damage done by mechanized farming in the Nuba Mountains. Land alienation, however, was a major issue in the Nuba Mountains, since a large amount of land had been transferred by the state to private interests – principally large Khartoum-based traders – and this caused much anger. The CPA called for land commissions to be formed to deal with such problems, but they never were.

Security was a major issue throughout the state given the fact that Southern Kordofan probably hosted more armed men than any other area in Sudan. This issue was of particular concern to the Nuba, as they felt the most vulnerable. Like Blue Nile, SAF almost certainly had a much larger presence in the state than was permitted under the Security Arrangements Protocol, and even more alarming was the large number of PDF groups that SAF and the government refused to acknowledge or to disarm. Meanwhile, the SPLA had an undetermined number of soldiers and retired soldiers in the state, together with thousands more at Jau, immediately across the border in Unity state, and they frequently visited the Nuba Mountains with their weapons.

There exists no state census for reference, but a very rough breakdown would suggest 40 per cent Arabs (most of whom were expected to vote NCP), 40 per cent Nuba (most of whom were expected to vote SPLM), and 15–20 per cent migrants from Darfur (whose vote was expected to split between the parties). Two factors stood out: first, as in other parts of Sudan, ethnicity figured strongly in party allegiance; second, all things being equal, a close election outcome was expected.

Surprisingly in view of the significance of the election and an increase of a million people as a result of the second census, according to the NEC 642,555 voters registered in the period 24 January to 12 February, some 100,000 fewer voters than during the April 2010 elections. According to the Carter Center, the only international organization observing the elections, this was due to the limited number of registration centres, insufficient voter education, poor preparations by the NEC, and limited participation and mobilization of civil society and other political parties other than the SPLM and NCP (Carter Center, 29 March 2011).

A jointly submitted complaint by the SPLM and seven other parties alleged that in Constituency number 30 in the west an additional voter registration team was added in the final days without the authority of the constituency officer. The same alliance of parties filed a petition on 28 February alleging that 38,374 voters were illicitly added to the electoral register in twenty geographical constituencies, and in twelve constituencies 20,044 voters were removed. The NEC sent an investigation team to the area and 16,000 names were removed from the voter list in Muglad. On 6 March the NEC dismissed the rest of the complaints. The SPLM accused the Sudanese police of bias and requested the JIUs assume responsibility for security, which, even though it was not legally permissible, they did during the election. SPLM leader in the north Malik Agar announced that demonstrations would be held on 10 May if there was rigging by the NCP and he left no one in doubt that was what he expected. Paradoxically, SPLM spokespersons also predicted great victories and thus created high expectations among the party's supporters.

On the eve of the election an estimated twenty-nine Nuba Tagoy civilians were killed by a PDF Salamat militia in the Rashad area of the Nuba Mountains, on the same day as a rally in the area was held for the SPLM gubernatorial candidate Abdel Aziz. The campaign was to witness a strong military presence of Sudan police, militias, SPLA and SAF JIUs, and other SPLA contingents (whose origin was never clear and probably illegal), and, while there were a couple of inter-clan Misseirya clashes in which dozens were killed, there were no other election-related violent incidents. The Carter Center concluded that the campaign environment in Southern Kordofan was undermined by the threat of violence from the large number of armed groups in the state. The Center also drew attention to the difference in the capacity to campaign between the state-linked parties of the NCP and SPLM and the opposition parties with their meager resources.

In the event, all of the opposition parties withdrew on the eve of the election, including Meki Belai of the Justice Party and Alzahir Khalil Hamouda of the Umma Party, who both stood down as candidates for the position of governor. Meki is a Nuba and close to Telefon Kuku, and thus it was expected his supporters would go to Telefon. The Umma Party candidate was a Misseirya from Lugawa: by stepping down he aided Haroun, and thus rumors quickly spread that he had been bribed, although officially he withdrew because the party lacked the finances to conduct a campaign. The Carter Center urged that Telefon Kuku either be freed from a SPLA prison immediately so that he could pursue his right to campaign or that charges be laid against him (Carter Center, 28 April 2011). In a number of cases high-profile SPLM members in the west tore up their party cards and publicly declared their allegiance to the NCP, the most notable being the SPLM candidate in the Misseirya heartland of Muglad, who switched parties on the eve of the official campaign. Bribes were strongly suspected in these cases.

Fourteen parties fielded candidates for the state legislature, together with eight independent candidates, but this obscured the reality that the election was dominated by the NCP and SPLM, which fielded candidates in thirty-two and thirty-one of the thirty-two constituencies respectively, followed by the Umma Party with candidates in fourteen constituencies. For the party lists, six parties each nominated the maximum eight candidates, including SPLM, NCP, DUP, Democratic Union Party, Muslim Brotherhood, and the Umma Party. With the exception of the

Muslim Brotherhood, they all fielded the full fourteen candidates for the women's list. The Popular Congress Party announced on 21 April that it would boycott the state assembly elections, but before that its chairman in Western Kordofan, Ishab al-Sadig, indicated that 'The Umma and other parties will join us in pulling out of these fraudulent elections and our focus is on working with youth groups to build momentum for a popular uprising after 9 July' (interview, 24 March 2011).

Various acts of intimidation against both leading parties were observed and also the use of inflammatory language, most notably by President al-Bashir at rallies for Ahmed Haroun in Muglad, Babanoosa, Fula, and Kadugli, on 26–28 April, which implied that the NCP would return to war if the SPLM did not accept the results of the election. Also found offensive by many NCP supporters was the SPLM slogan 'the star [i.e. the SPLM flag] or the gun.'

Prior to the election the SPLM led an alliance that included the SCP, DUP, NUP, National Party, Justice Party, PCP, and Ba'ath Party. But by the time the election started the only party aligned with the SPLM was the SCP, and that was a one-sided alliance whereby Communists stood down in every seat for the SPLM while the SPLM refused to stand down in one district, Babanousa (a railway town that elected a Communist in 1968, just months before Nimeiri's coup), for the SCP, as a result of which the two allies competed and the NCP took the seat.

Meanwhile, the NCP did not start with any alliance, but in the west of the state it organized Haroun for Governor committees in virtually every town, which were largely made up of NUP and DUP members, especially the former as this area had been one of its strongholds. In Khartoum the NUP and DUP officially took a neutral position, but that lead was not followed at the state level. In Fula, Western Kordofan, a local NUP official, Adam Kiir, became chairman of the 'Haroun for Governor' Committee; he

explained his support as being due to 'the similarity of mani-
festos of the NCP and NUP, similar positions on the return of
Western Kordofan, decentralization, and the creation of a national
government' (interview, 1 May 2011). Most opposition parties
supported the formation of a post-election 'national' government
in Kadugli in which they would all participate. Not coincidentally
the NUP and DUP were negotiating with the NCP in Khartoum
on the formation of a national government at the time. As a result,
Southern Kordofan served as a testing ground for the pursuit of
bigger political issues at the national level and for the reshaping
of Sudanese politics.

James Wani Igga, the speaker of the Southern Assembly, officially launched the SPLM campaign. The campaign committee
included many of the big names in the party, including Salva Kiir,
Pagan Amum, Rebecca Garang, and Malik Agar. The southern
SPLM also provided vehicles, resources, and personnel with election experience. Meanwhile, Bashir launched the NCP campaign
and was assisted in the state by Ali Osman, Dr Nafie Ali Nafie
and speaker of the National Assembly Ahmed Ibrahim al-Tahir.

In the west of the state many questioned the loyalty of the
SPLM given its support for southern secession, and raised the
specter that it would take Southern Kordofan into southern
Sudan; should it lose, it would foment violence. The party was
particularly weak in this region, due to the claim by its southern
sector that Abyei should be attached to the south. Rarely stated,
but believed to be of equal significance, was the view – perpetuated by the NCP – that the SPLM was soft on Islam. Indeed,
Ali-Mahdi Fadl al-Moula, an official of the Muglad-based Union
of Abyei Youth Locality, an NGO that advertised its support from
USAID, asserted that the SPLM is 'a party of disbelievers' and
that 'we can't accept the SPLM ruling over non-Muslims and the
CPA can go to hell' (interview, 3 May 2011). In the west the SPLM
also suffered from the perception that it was a party of the Nuba,

which was reinforced by the fact that Abdel Aziz rarely visited the area. In the east and the Nuba Mountains, the SPLM looked in complete control and spoke of the area as a 'closed district,' an unfortunate phrase since it implied that only the SPLM would be permitted to enter the area – a prohibition that was supported by a degree of anecdotal evidence.

Al-Ayam newspaper reported on 25 April that Khartoum state governor Abdurrahman Alkhidr had donated SDG1.3 million (approximately US$481,000) to development projects in Lagawa and Kufa areas of Southern Kordofan, in addition to SDG120,000 (approximately US$44,000) to the state. As was the case during the April 2010 the election, observers did nothing more than note such campaign financing; it was beyond their capacity to carry out any research in this critical area.

The SPLM raised many complaints during the course of the election, but the NEC, endorsed by the Carter Center, found them either unsubstantiated or impossible to investigate. The party then demanded that its complaints be addressed prior to the tabulation so that affected results could be annulled; this, together with SPLM walkouts, delayed the process by several days. While the SPLM refused to launch court cases because of a lack of trust in the judiciary, the NEC referred all complainants to the court, as required by the National Elections Act. The NEC decided to open another four stations to speed up the tabulation results, but, claiming it was not notified, the SPLM again walked out. On 13 May the SPLM accused the NEC of systematic 'rigging' of the election and announced it was considering

> Withdrawal and NOT TO PARTICIPATE at this stage of the process of matching and compilation of results; No RECOGNITION of the results proclaimed by the NEC whatsoever; No participation in the legislative and executive institutions resulting from these elections; [and to] Call upon the democratic forces and the masses of the state of South Kordofan, Sudan in general to work together in the

work of peaceful democratic [means] to correct this situation; We call on the guarantors of the CPA and the international community to re-evaluate the process and assistance in finding treatment for this anomaly. (Abdel Aziz al-Hilu/SPLM Press Conference, 15 May 2011)

The Carter Center's finding that 'South Kordofan's elections were generally peaceful and credible' was a pleasant surprise to the NCP, which generally expected a rough ride from the international community, while the SPLM was surprised and angry because it generally expected the international community, and particularly an organization that both parties (wrongly) assumed reflected the views of the US government, to side with it. In the absence of other international observers, most were prepared to accept the conclusion of the Carter Center, but some analysts were concerned about the process being described as 'credible,' which they found hard to accept given the performance of the NEC in the April 2010 elections. During those final tense days of voter tabulation it was noteworthy that, with the exception of the SCP, the opposition parties were highly critical of the SPLM's demands and urged it to redress its complaints through the courts.

In its final report on 18 May the Carter Center endorsed the NEC's election results, which concluded that in the race for governor Ahmed Haroun had received 201,455 votes against Abdul Aziz al-Hilu's 194,955 votes, with Telefon Kuku picking up 9,043 votes, while in the legislature the NCP won 33 seats against the SPLM's 22 seats. Both parties polled fairly evenly, with SPLM support being very strong in a small area (the Nuba Mountains), while the NCP won more constituency seats, but with a lower margin. In spite of the procedural lapses, the Carter Center did not observe systemic irregularities that would invalidate the results (Carter Center, 18 May 2011). Although it accepted the outcome, the Center found that election officials did not use the official database developed to handle the preliminary results, and which was programmed to reject results when the numbers did not reconcile and that could thus be quarantined and investigated before entered. The Center concluded: 'This process was bypassed by the SHEC, thus removing an important safeguard that can highlight anomalous results' (Carter Center, 18 May 2011). The Center also criticized the NEC for failing to establish adequate procedures for dealing with complaint forms.

It was an ignominious end to SPLM hopes after a predicted a landslide of 80 per cent, which had assumed that even core NCP supporters in the west would vote for the party. And to realize that objective it brought in thousands of observers and technical experts from southern Sudan, Blue Nile, and the northern sector of the party. And if in spite of this incredible effort the SPLM still lost, the leadership had an explanation: rigging by the NCP with the complicity of the NEC. It also led the public to believe that it had planned a response to the rigging, which would take the form of mass demonstrations in Southern Kordofan and Khartoum, and Malik Agar hinted at a military response based on the supposed 40,000 Nuba and southern Blue Nile soldiers under his command.

But all of this was fluff. The SPLM never had a hope of breaking into the NCP western stronghold, the less so because it ignored the interests of the people of the area. The primary concern of those in the area was Abyei and development, and the author never found anyone in Western Kordofan from any party that supported the SPLM premiss that Abyei was part of southern Sudan. Even SPLM officials in the west would preface their comments on Abyei with 'Well, my personal view is...' – and their personal view was invariably that Abyei was part of the north, which put them at odds with their own party. Typical was Salah Jula, the SPLM candidate for Babanusa and assistant secretary of the party, who reflected that 'The NCP created the Abyei problem by pushing tribal buttons and creating tensions,' adding that the resolution of the problem 'should be decided by the Ngok and Dinka' and that he 'personally' felt the Misseirya should get to vote in the referendum (interview, 2 May 2011). Thoughtful people understood that the Misseirya had been manipulated by successive governments in Khartoum and that there might well be ways to resolve the problem of Abyei outside the north–south box, but the NCP dominated the discourse and the SPLM never came close to presenting an alternative one, much less a program that met the interests of the people of Western Kordofan. The SPLM came out of the elections looking the same way as it did going into them: a Nuba Mountains-based party.

The surprise is not that the SPLM lost the governorship, but how well it performed in the elections, although that had nothing to do with its program because it never reached beyond its core constituency, instead being successful due to the low voter turnout in the west. The reason for this, according to the NCP, was that after Bashir had promised the Misseirya their own state they had no incentive to participate in the elections of a state they would soon be leaving. The SPLM, for its part, saw in the low voter turnout in the west evidence of Misseirya disenchantment with the ruling party, and that was more convincing. Many noted that had the SPLM reached a deal with Telefon, Abdel Aziz would probably have won, while others thought that if he had been released from prison Telefon would have seriously eroded the vote of both the SPLM, which intimidated citizens not to vote for him, and the NCP. One non-SPLM GoSS cabinet minister cynically concluded that 'the SPLM's collapse in Southern Kordofan was due to its failure to reach an agreement on the distribution of seats and governorship with the NCP as it had done in the April 2010 elections.'

John Garang's New Sudan ideology captured the essence of a Sudan dominated by a riverain core, but the SPLM failed to recognize that the marginalized periphery included far more people than its paltry supporters in the Nuba Mountains or the handful of tribes in southern Blue Nile. Indeed, the Misseirya had a good claim to being marginalized since they gained little from their alliance with the NCP, as their low level of development, poor services, and the appalling condition of their central town of Muglad revealed, and this in spite of the fact that the area was host to the oil industry. The SPLM did not lose the election in Southern Kordofan because of rigging or because of a lack of finances and personnel. It lost the election because it failed to move beyond its core constituency and embrace other marginalized groups, and because it was caught in a narrow Arab–African dichotomy. It also lost because it had a record of upsetting potential allies, and thus the completion of the elections in Southern Kordofan saw the party largely friendless, just as it found itself in Blue Nile.

Abyei

The Abyei Protocol had only been reached after arduous negotiations. It stipulated that a referendum be conducted simultaneously with that of southern Sudan to determine whether the inhabitants of the territory – defined as the Ngok Dinka and 'other residents'[8] – wished to remain in northern Sudan or be linked to northern BEG. Problems continued when the NCP objected to the report of the Abyei Boundaries Commission, and after more wrangling the SPLM agreed to have its report reconsidered before the Permanent Court of Arbitration at The Hague, which ruled that the ABC had overreached its authority and considerably decreased the size of the territory.[9] Dirdiery Mohamed Ahmed, who led the NCP legal team at The Hague, viewed the decision reached on 22 July 2009 as a vindication of the NCP's position and declared that the oil (essentially the Heglig and Kharsana fields) was now in the north. But the Misseirya made clear they did not view the tribunal ruling as a victory and wanted to continue the struggle.

With acceptance of The Hague decision the NCP changed tack and began advocating the right of the Misseirya to vote in the referendum.

The population of Abyei is a matter of dispute, as is the definition of the territory. The 2008 national census established that there were 197,000 Misseirya and 56,000 Ngok Dinka living in 'Abyei locality,' although in the court-awarded area the Misseirya were estimated by UN officials in Abyei town to be in the range of 5–10,000. These numbers (which should only be viewed as estimates) were based on settled residency, a major area of contention for the nomadic Misseirya.

Some Misseirya settled over the years, and there were reports that they were offered large amounts of money by the NCP to settle in Abyei, but UN officials I interviewed said there was no evidence of any significant pattern of the tribe settling down and its members were still largely devoted to a nomadic style of life. There are nine branches of the Misseirya, who come from the north-east, north, and north-west, and follow different migration routes and have different destinations, but Abyei provides the central corridor. As tensions developed and clashes broke out between Misseirya militia and Ngok farmers and southerners, the Ngok tried to block migration routes, and the Misseirya threw up blockades on trade from the north and on both Ngok returning from the north and southerners returning to the south after the referendum. Emir Hamdi acknowledged that '[we are] blocking roads as revenge to hurt them and restrict goods and people … [we have] no problem with any southern tribes, only the Ngok' (interview, 26 March 2011).

Under the CPA the only armed groups permitted in Abyei were the Joint Integrated Units and they were specifically tasked with ensuring that SAF and the SPLA did not enter Abyei, to support which effort they had bases in the north and south of the territory. But a visit to one of the northern bases along the main road revealed that the unit only searched vehicles for weapons and did not carry out any patrols. The central Abyei JIU did carry out patrols, but there were doubts as to their effectiveness. Contrary to an agreement that no people from local tribes serve in the JIU, Misseirya were represented in SAF. The 13th Brigade of the 3rd Division of the SPLA was suspected of operating north of Bahr el Ghazal in the Agok area, but the SPLA also had a presence through various tribal militias and, increasingly, through the police force. Meanwhile, SAF-supported Misseirya Popular Defence Force groups were found throughout the area.

Local Perspectives

The Misseirya felt they were denied their rights, but their understanding of the problem of Abyei varied considerably depending on where they lived, their livelihood, and whether they or their kin used or transited Abyei. Although some Misseirya are settled, some do not transit Abyei, others only spend a short portion of the year in the territory, and others spend many months there, virtually all Misseirya that I met in the period 2008–11 rejected the Abyei Protocol and the rulings of the ABC and Arbitration Tribunal. According to Emir Hamdi, 'The Protocol has destroyed the life of the Misseirya – it gave rights to cattle, but not to people,' by which he meant that the Misseirya were permitted to graze and water their cattle in Abyei, but not to own the land (interview, 26 March 2011).

In addition the Misseirya argued that they were not represented at the negotiating table, and gained nothing from the CPA and its provision that the region receive 2 per cent of the oil revenues; indeed, they typically said they had no interest in the oil, only in the land. Some of the tribe spent eight months of the year in Abyei and complained that even they did not have rights of citizenship or the right to live in the territory under the present arrangements. The Misseirya insisted that the NCP did not represent them. They also held that the Abyei referendum could not be held under existing conditions and some threatened to forcefully stop it. They further contended that the only thing they respected was the north–south boundary of 01–01–56 (the date of Sudan's independence). Emir[10] Sadig Harika of Lagawa probably spoke for many Misseirya when he said, 'while the lack of development of the tribe is a concern, the most pressing issue that needed addressing is our collective loss of rights' (interview, 23 November 2009). While their anger was widespread and deeply felt, there were differences between them. Emir Ismael in Lagawe insisted that the only basis for the referendum would be if all members of the Misseirya tribe participated, while Emir Sadig said that as a resident of Lagawe he should not have the right to vote in the referendum. However, he contended that anyone living in Abyei for at least three months of the year must have the right to vote.

Some Misseirya leaders insisted that the only acceptable basis for the referendum would be the participation of all members of the Misseirya tribe, while others said that only those who stayed in or transited Abyei should have the right to vote. Some spoke of a conflict between brother tribes based on the historical alliance between Deng Majok and Babu Nimr, and that although the problems between them had significantly worsened, they could still be resolved. Others were so angry as to say that the land was theirs alone, that after the Ngok Dinka became educated they turned against the Misseirya, and that they therefore no longer recognized the Ngok Dinka and would only negotiate with the Twic Dinka of Warrap state in southern Sudan. Curiously, however, the most senior Misseirya emir, Mochtar Babu Nimr, stated that 'Irrespective of whether Abyei joins the south we will still be brothers with the Dinka' (interview, 22 March 2011), and his brother and Umma Party official Sadig Babu Nimir said,

'As a tribe the Misseirya are much closer to the Dinka than to the Jalien or Shagiyya' (interview, 24 April 2011). Nonetheless, Mochtar's advice to the Ngok was that they should forget about the CPA and just deal with the problems on the ground with the Misseirya.

While the Misseirya were in the past largely linked to the Umma Party, most of their leaders shifted allegiance to the NCP, while the Ngok were under the sway of the SPLM/A. This occurred in tandem with the rise in status of the educated youth and the decline of the traditional leadership which had favored maintaining the old bond with the Misseirya. The SPLA was slow to defend the people of the territory and those in northern BEG against the Misseirya during the war, but there was little difference between the positions and attitudes of the SPLM/A and the Ngok people in Abyei. All were of the view that after being denied the promise of self-determination in the 1972 Addis Ababa Agreement and accepting both the ABC and the Arbitration Tribunal, they were not prepared to make any more 'concessions' to win the support of the NCP and the Misseirya.

Talk of the Deng Majok–Babu Nimr brotherhood of the tribes was greeted with derision, evidence of intermarriage between the tribes was denied ('no brown skin around here' was how one Ngok Dinka respondent put it, although many Misseirya are themselves very dark), and it was the conflict between them that was emphasized. The land was always owned by the Ngok, the cattle of the Misseirya were stolen from the Ngok, and the Misseirya were only permitted in the territory because of their willingness to share it. But that goodwill was now gone. While the Misseirya felt that the Ngok had gained the upper hand with their education and as a result of recent political developments, one Ngok elder remarked to me, 'We are poor and they [Misseirya] are rich and our survival depends on international contributions.'

With the determination of the boundaries, the common view was that there was now no reason to have any relations with the Misseirya. At the same time one respondent said that the problems of the local people will be solved elsewhere. Yet another Ngok interviewee said in words that could have just as easily come out of the mouth of a Misseirya, 'We are staying because it is our land and we have nowhere to go.'

Despite this negativism many people in the north continued to think that the resolution of the problem of Abyei should be left solely to the tribal elders of the Ngok and Misseirya, and in particular to ensure Dirdiery Mohamed Ahmed and Deng Alor, the most partisan representatives of the NCP and SPLM, be removed from the negotiations. Bona Malwal, who was raised near the borderlands of Abyei, was always convinced that Abyei was a 'tribal problem that could only be solved by mediation between the tribes because there was no fixed boundary between them' and that 'it was a mistake to implement any agreement without the Misseirya' (interview, 25 September 2010).

Rising Political Tensions

By April 2011, Ministry of Foreign Affairs official Dr Abdel-rahman, was expressing the fear that 'the various conflicts in the border territories could break out, undermine the CPA, and bring about conflict between the north and south [and that this in turn] could lead to international involvement, and we want these problems resolved internally' (interview, 5 April 2011). In Abyei tensions steadily grew between the SPLM and NCP and between the Ngok and the Misseirya in the period after the signing of the CPA. When it became clear that the Abyei referendum would not be held concurrently with that of the south as stipulated in the Protocol, plans were put in place for the Ngok to hold their own referendum. But when the Misseirya said they would obstruct any such efforts the proposal was set aside, although never rejected. Meanwhile, some Misseirya tried to gain their cause greater recognition by stopping, harassing, and sometimes robbing Ngok and southerners moving south in vehicles to Abyei and beyond, beginning in early January 2011. Roadblocks were also used in an effort to obtain the 2 million Sudanese pounds compensation promised to the tribe in negotiations between governors Taban Deng of Unity state and Ahmed Haroun of Southern Kordofan for cows stolen from the Misseirya by the SPLA in Unity state during the 2010 migration.

In response to the growing threat of outright war, the UN organized a conference of traditional leaders representing the Ngok Dinka and the Misseirya, the outcome of which was an agreement signed in Kadugli (and thereafter known as the Kadugli Agreement) followed by another in March. The key provisions of the two agreements were the deploying of JIUs to ensure the freedom of migration for Misseirya nomads to Abyei and further south, and security for the movement of internally displaced persons (IDPs) returning to Abyei or transiting the area en route to the south. The agreement also committed both SAF and the SPLA to withdraw all unauthorized forces from the Abyei area, leaving the maintenance of security to the JIUs and joint integrated police units.

But the agreement was never fully implemented and the Misseirya continued to block the roads. This led to prohibitive increases in food and fuel prices. The Misseirya alternately denied they were closing the roads and justified their action by accusing the Ngok of stopping them from moving their cattle. The political temperature further rose when it was revealed on 26 April 2011 that the southern Council of Ministers draft interim constitution included a geographical rendering of southern Sudan that included Abyei (Reuters, Juba, 26 April 2011). In response President al-Bashir made clear that he would not recognize the independence of South Sudan if the provision on Abyei was still in the interim constitution come 9 July.

These political gambits raised tensions between the armed groups in Abyei and on 1 May 2011 at Um Belai the UN reported in an internal memo that between 16.00 and 17.00 a firefight broke out between the South Sudan Police Service (the identity under which the SPLA masqueraded) and SAF in which seven SAF JIU soldiers were killed and two wounded, along with one SPLA soldier killed and an unknown number wounded.[11] The UN military monitors in Abyei were unclear as to who had started the fighting, while officials from north and south traded accusations. The most common view from SPLM and other sources in nearby Muglad, where I was at the time of the fighting, was that SAF was trying to advance its position by moving military supplies further south, but was ambushed by the SPLA, whereupon fourteen of its soldiers were killed, although the NCP insisted that the movement of these supplies was approved by the Joint Defense Board to balance the then better-equipped SPLA. The NCP responded to the attack by sending a delegation to Juba and demanding that the GoSS remove the references to Abyei in the proposed interim constitution and threatening to respond forcefully in the event of any more attacks.

On 5 May President Salva Kiir and Deng Alor, together with Vice President Ali Osman Taha, had a meeting with UN officials, US envoys, and a member of the AU panel on Sudan, all of whom pressed to have references to Abyei removed from the draft constitution and to restrain the SPLA. An agreement was reached which assured the various international interlocutors led by AUHIP that there would be no unilateral action taken by either party that might negatively affect the security or political situation in Abyei, and that neither government would include in the draft national constitutions an unconditional claim to Abyei, the status of which would remain unchanged until a political settlement was reached (*The Citizen*, 12 May 2011). However, the very next day Michael Makui Lueth, minister of parliamentary affairs, stated that his party maintained its position of including Abyei in the draft transitional constitution of South Sudan: 'The recommendation by the Constitutional Review Committee represents the position of the SPLM on Abyei. The inclusion of Abyei in the transitional constitution of South Sudan has permissible terms' (*Sudan Tribune*, 13 May 2011). The political temperature rose a few more degrees.

On 19 May an SAF convoy escorted by a UNMIS military detail was attacked. The UN internal report expressed no doubt that the SPLA was the perpetrator of the attack; this was confirmed by Deng Arop, the SPLM's chief administrator in Abyei, and indeed was acknowledged a few days later by the SPLA in Juba. SAF initially claimed that twenty-two of its soldiers were killed, but later revised this to 197 killed and missing, a figure that few accepted. The day after the attack, SAF entered Abyei, causing an enormous degree of dislocation among the citizenry, dissolution of the territory's administration, and the rapid retreat of the SPLA and its allies.

The SPLM explanation was that such attacks were accidents or the result of bad judgments by local-level SPLA officers. If these attacks had taken place in Upper Nile, Jonglei, or Unity state, that explanation would have been taken seriously given the wealth of examples in the first half of 2011 of the SPLA attacking forces being integrated into the SPLA and armed groups during agreed upon ceasefires (see Chapter 6). But it was harder to accept in the case of Abyei, probably the most politically sensitive territory in the country, and where it would be assumed that the top military and political leadership would be following and directing events closely. If the leadership was not in control of its army, and that possibility cannot be fully discounted, it could be accused of gross negligence.

Another interpretation was that the SPLA and the SPLM deliberately tried to provoke SAF into a major action that would cast the NCP's role in Abyei in a negative light and garner the attention of the international community, and specifically the Security Council, which was visiting Sudan at the time of the SPLA attack and the SAF invasion. The SPLM and SPLA had basically lost control of Abyei, and come 9 July the territory would effectively be considered part of the north, pending final resolution of the problem. This likelihood had already led the Council of Ministers to have Abyei declared part of the territory of an independent southern Sudan in the proposed interim constitution. But this was not going to save the situation and something more drastic had to be done.

The point was made that a SAF invasion on such a scale could not have been organized in a single day, between the SPLA attack on the SAF convoy on the 19th and the start of the SAF invasion on the 20th, but the NCP was probably preparing for any eventuality and after the first attack on its soldiers it might well have seen the thrust of SPLM policy and prepared a response. Or it could have been planning an attack on Abyei all along and was waiting for an excuse, which the SPLA readily supplied. The NCP view was that the attacks were orchestrated by Arop Deng, the SPLM Abyei administrator, even though constitutionally he had no authority over the army. But such anomalies were far from unusual, and in neighboring Unity state governor Taban Deng exerted considerable control over the SPLA. But something else was at issue: for a revolutionary army fighting the cause of the people, its attack on SAF and almost indecent retreat, leaving its own people defenseless, were hard to justify.

On 24 May Luka Biong, Ngok Dinka and minister of cabinet affairs in the GNU, resigned, saying: 'With war crimes being committed in Abyei at the hands of the National Congress Party, I could not in good faith continue to take part in such a government' (AFP, 24 May 2011). On 26 May Deng Alor, GoSS minister of regional cooperation and Ngok Dinka, declared that 'Without Abyei there will be no dialogue on pending issues (*Al- Sahafa*, 26 May 2011). The next day the more realistic Luka Biong said that the SPLM has no option but to negotiate with the NCP to resolve the Abyei problem (*Al-Akhbar*, 26 May 2011). In fact negotiations on post-referendum issues in Abyei between the NCP and SPLM continued, and apart from Luka no other SPLM member of the GNU resigned. The message from Juba could not have been more clear: although angry about SAF's takeover of Abyei the problem would not derail Salva's personal commitment to achieve south Sudan's independence on 9 July. At this point IGAD special envoy General Lazaro Sumbeiywo jumped into the fray. While his observation that the presidency had shown a 'lack of political will to resolve the Abyei issue' was no doubt correct, his proposal for an independent Abyei was not taken seriously (*Reuters*, 26 May 2011). A non-SPLM GoSS cabinet minister told me the crisis arose because the 'greedy boys of Abyei' did not accept the north–south division of the territory proposed by AUHIP and endorsed by the NCP.

There were indications that it was not only the SPLM that had problems with its military wing. Negotiations now invariably involved SAF officers, no doubt because of the known disenchantment among some sections of the army with the impending break-up of Sudan. A further indication of problems was that after the announcement of an NCP–SPLM agreement in Addis Ababa on demilitarizing the border zone in May, an SAF spokesperson went public to deny the report.

While the prevailing international view was that SAF's invasion was illegal, increasingly attention was directed at the ensuing humanitarian disaster as SAF soldiers and their Misseirya PDF allies burned down most of Abyei town and looted much of what was left. The displaced left for sanctuary in southern Sudan and arrived south of the Bahr al-Arab river in appalling conditions; some received a mixed reception from their fellow Dinkas, who were not always sympathetic to their cause. The estimated numbers of those displaced continued to grow in the two weeks after the attack and soon passed the 56,000 counted in the 2008 census. Government critics saw this as evidence of ethnic cleansing and war crimes, but SAF said its forces would not leave Abyei until the SPLA committed not to go north of 1-1-56 and to return to the Kadugli Agreement.

Although the SPLM government demonstrated restraint, two presidential advisers interviewed by the author at this time did not rule out war with the north after the south had achieved independence, when they were convinced they would be in a stronger position. But the SPLM went on negotiating with the NCP and on 20 June 2011 signed in Addis Ababa an 'Agreement between the Government of the Republic of Sudan and the Sudan People's Liberation Movement on Temporary Arrangements for the Administration and Security of the Abyei Area.'

Consistent with the CPA and the Abyei Protocol, the new agreement stipulated that the territory would remain part of the north until its future was decided and that the 1956 borders would continue to divide the north and south until and unless the parties decided otherwise or a referendum was held. Crucially the agreement did not tie Abyei's future solely to the referendum, but provided for the possibility for an agreement between the parties on the future of the territory. The agreement called for the redeployment of all SAF and SPLA forces, and for an Interim Security Force for Abyei composed of 4,200 Ethiopian troops under UN auspices to enforce security in a territory of 10,000 square kilometers that was to be demilitarized.

Without prejudging the final status of Abyei, an administration was to be established consisting of a chief administrator who was a nominee of the SPLM and agreed to by the GoS, a deputy chief administrator who was a nominee of the GoS and agreed to by the SPLM, and five heads of department, of whom three would be selected by the SPLM and two by the GoS. Decisions of the Executive Council would be made by consensus, and above it was the Abyei Joint Oversight Committee (AJOC) made up of two appointees from the SPLM and two from the GoS; this body reported directly to the presidents of Sudan and South Sudan on both administrative and security matters. An Abyei Police Service would be established, a component of which would deal with issues arising from nomadic migration and would accompany the nomads within the Abyei Area on their annual migrations. The parties committed to facilitating the rapid return of IDPs.

Article 40 stipulated that

> The Parties reiterate their commitment to resolve peacefully the final status of Abyei, and shall therefore consider, in good faith, proposals that the African Union High Level Implementation Panel shall make to resolve this matter. The Panel shall be advised by the President of Sudan and the President of the Government of Southern Sudan, on the time frame within which to present its proposals.

And, crucially, Article 42 stipulated that

> Any question regarding the interpretation of this Agreement shall be determined by the AJOC. In the event that the AJOC fails to agree on an interpretation, the Co-Chairs may refer the question to the Presidents for their joint resolution.

Immediately upon signing the agreement, Dirdiery Mohamed Ahmed, the NCP negotiator and Misseirya, set off a firestorm by claiming that the agreement would be permanent, there would be no referendum, and Abyei would remain in the north. He reached this conclusion based on the provision that the two presidents have the final say and their decision must be by consensus, thus ensuring maintenance of the status quo. Others, however, drew attention to the right of the AUHIP to make proposals to resolve the problems of the territory and the agreed-upon temporary nature of the agreement.[12] At least one critic, however, supported Dirdiery's view and held that the agreement would serve to make Abyei 'the new Halaib Triangle' (referring to the long-running dispute between Sudan and Egypt over a piece of territory in north-eastern Sudan) and that the dispute 'will continue forever without resolution.'[13] Although it might have been expected that the Misseirya emirs would happy with the results of the agreement, Emir Hamdi said that it 'did not resolve the problems and they would again come to the fore, that Abyei remained a "time bomb," and that nothing had changed in the attitudes of the Ngok, who still thought that they owned all the land' (interview, 6 July 2011). He spoke of the need for an agreement that acknowledged the right of the Misseirya to settle on the land. He also dismissed any notion that the Misseirya would give up or hand over their weapons to the Ethiopian army when 'grassing' their animals in Abyei or transiting the territory.

Meanwhile, the NCP government announced that as of 9 July UNMIS would have to leave Sudan. UN diplomats were taken aback by the decision, even though that had been the unofficial message from the government for months, and some mused that since the mission was a creation of the Security Council only it could terminate the mission. But Amin Hassan Omer, GNU minister of state at the Ministry of Foreign Affairs, said that foreign staff and soldiers would have to leave by 9 July, which was a 'sacred day' for the government (*Al-Rai Al-Aam*, 23 May 2011). Sacred day or not, the war in Abyei and the one that would soon break out in Southern Kordofan made this request highly problematic, but it was one the UN had to accept.

Crisis in Kordofan

A week after SAF's invasion of Abyei its spokesperson, al-Sawarmi Khalid Sa'ad, said that the SPLA must withdraw its forces from Blue Nile and Southern Kordofan states before 1 June 2011, and this was understood to include the SPLA components of the JIUs (*Voices for Sudan*, 29 May 2011). Meanwhile, chief of staff of the Fourteenth Infantry Division Corps, Major General Bashir Maki Albahy Almaki, confirmed this in a memo marked 'top secret' to the head of the State Security Committee – namely Governor Haroun – and the need to 'control the movements of the People's Liberation Army north of the 1956 boundaries' (1 June 2011), a more limited-sounding objective. But NCP officials reluctantly acknowledged that the Security Arrangements Agreement permitted the JIUs to remain in existence for some months after the end of the peace process. An NCP official said to me that this was 'a strategic mistake of the CPA'; that little attention had been paid in the CPA to the post-9 July 2011 period because an independent south was not seriously considered when John Garang and Ali Osman were leading the IGAD negotiations – the turn to southern secession only came with the rise to power of Salva Kiir. Indeed, it is hard to understand the rationale for maintaining the JIUs after the referendum (when SAF forces had left the south) and even more after the end of the peace process when it would involve two independent countries having the right to maintain armies in one another's countries.

Given the confusion over provisions of the Security Arrangements, it is worth quoting at length the 'Special Report of the Secretary General on the Sudan' of 17 May 2011, which found that

> The SPLA redeployment from sectors IV, V and VI [i.e. Blue Nile and Southern Kordofan] had gradually reached 37.7 percent (20,622 troops out of 59,168) by … December 2010. The redeployment of

SPLA elements in Blue Nile State to the assembly point at Quffa (just outside Blue Nile State in Upper Nile State) was to have been completed in 2009. However, during a monitoring and verification mission in 2010, the majority of 4,003 SPLA elements were found just inside Blue Nile State, at Yafta. In regard to the redeployment of SPLA from Southern Kordofan, a monitoring and verification mission in April 2011 found 3,071 of 5,147 SPLA elements at the SPLA assembly point at White Lake [i.e. Jau].

Thus, apart from the SPLA forces that were part of the JIUs, the rest of its soldiers, and they were a considerable number, should not have been north of the 1–1–56 border at the end of the peace agreement. So, legally, the SPLA was also in the wrong.

The SPLM argued that the SPLA soldiers in Blue Nile and Southern Kordofan were from the two states and could not be disarmed by the mother army. Nor was it realistic to assume these soldiers could readily be integrated into SAF in an environment of mutual distrust and hostility and without the resolution through popular consultation of outstanding political grievances. Against that background the SPLM argued for an agreement on security arrangements in the two states to parallel that under the CPA. That is, until the changes agreed to under the popular consultations were fully implemented, the SPLA could keep a standing force in the two states. With implementation a more positive political climate would presumably have developed that would permit integration into SAF or a non-threatening disarmament as part of an agreed-upon DDR program.

Reasonable though that sounded, it was at the time a non-starter with the NCP, which would not accept what amounted to an extension of the CPA and give the SPLM/A the opportunity for further meddling in the north, spreading its New Sudan virus both in these states and beyond, and possibly accomplishing what the southern SPLM/A had failed to do, namely toppling the NCP government. Negotiations should still have been the route to a compromise, but, given the attitude of the leadership of the SPLM north and its Southern Kordofan and Blue Nile components towards the NCP and vice versa, that was probably not realistic, and became distinctly unrealistic after its failed bid to win the governorship. This failure, the party had assured its supporters, was inconceivable unless the NCP had rigged the election. Thus, with the SPLM's Nuba supporters convinced that they were destined to be attacked by Khartoum, there was no apparent recourse but to fight.

The NCP's defense of their military moves on Southern Kordofan did not follow from provisions of the Security Arrangements Protocol, but from the claim of an impending insurgency in the state. The government contended that Abdel Aziz al-Hilu, in cooperation with Yasir Arman and other elements in the SPLM northern sector, had planned to use the occasion of the Southern Kordofan elections to launch an insurgency that they hoped could be linked to the campaigns of the Darfuri rebels, the SPLA in Blue Nile, and possibly civilian actions in Khartoum and the northern towns. There was an upsurge in JEM activity in the area, including its brief capture of a landing strip at Heglig, and claims were made by both parties of cooperation, but Malik's earlier announcement of a demonstration in Khartoum for 10 May in the event of election rigging came to nothing. Indeed, the link to Darfur was obvious given adjacent territory, similar armed struggles against marginalization, and the large presence of people from the area in Southern Kordofan, including Abdel Aziz. Hence the popularization of the term 'New South' to suggest the commonalities between conditions in Blue Nile, Southern Kordofan, and Southern Darfur. Professor Abdel Ghaffar preferred 'Third Sudan,' which he argued 'could become a focus of struggle or a valuable link between north and south and eventually lead to the reintegration of the country' (6 July 2011). Meanwhile, Yasir Arman raised the specter of a war stretching from 'Blue

Nile to Darfur' if the government did not make the necessary concessions on Southern Kordofan. Thus the attempt by the SPLM/A to control the Nuba Mountains would, in the words of a NCP presidential adviser, become 'a foothold in the north and another Benghazi that could attract supplies from the south and Uganda.'

The SPLM had long taken the view that either the NCP would win the elections as a result of rigging or the SPLM would win and be denied the opportunity to take power. Thus a political campaign to denounce the outcome of the elections would prepare the ground for what was to appear as a spontaneous revolt of the SPLA and its supporters in the eastern Southern Kordofan. The SPLA integrated police and wildlife forces were mobilized, while SPLA soldiers in Jau moved across the border, and more soldiers were brought in under the cover of being bodyguards to protect SPLM leaders during the election campaign. All international observers in the eastern parts of Southern Kordofan noted a large increase in the number of SPLA soldiers during the elections. It would appear these forces had the objective of capturing Kadugli and Dilling and establishing defensive positions in smaller centers and the mountains around them. That said, local residents had been reporting an even larger movement of SAF soldiers and allied militias into Southern Kordofan since the referendum in January 2011, and that build-up would be seen as a threat to both the SPLA and the SPLM and in breach of the Security Arrangements Protocol.

As was the case in Abyei, SAF's invasion appeared well planned and took advantage of a series of attacks attributed to the SPLA. These began with the takeover by the SPLA on 4 June of a police station in Kadugli, which was held for the next three days, apparently to collect arms and munitions. A clash took place between SAF and the SPLA in the early morning of 5 June at Um Durmain. On the same day, SAF offered to negotiate a solution before things got out of control, but the SPLM claimed this was part of a plan to assassinate Abdel Aziz.[14]

The problem with this trajectory was that it did not follow the script preferred by most of the Juba SPLM leadership to use Southern Kordofan to apply pressure on the NCP in the post-referendum negotiations, but not have the peace process derailed on the route to 9 July. There were thus multilayered concerns when on 9 June in a speech from an unknown location Abdel Aziz called for the 'toppling' of the NCP government by both military and political means. He said that the problems of Sudan were not confined to the Nuba Mountains, that everyone suffered from the NCP, and that everyone should be actively engaged in replacing the present regime with a democratic government that recognized the rights of the regions and accepted diversity. Regrettable as the timing of the announcement was for the southern SPLM, it could not let its ally flounder and thereby lose its biggest bargaining chip when negotiating the post-referendum issues. The SPLM was also anxious to keep the NCP on the defensive, particularly when its army was in striking distance of the southern oil fields.

It seems almost certain that Abdel Aziz had not only consulted Yasir and Malik, but also won approval of Garangists such as Pagan and the 'Abyei boys' – Deng Alor, Major-General Piang Deng, Luka Biong, and Edward Lino, if not other members of the leadership. By this time their homeland had been occupied by SAF and many concluded that of the options their best prospect lay in entering into an all-out confrontation with Khartoum. It can also be assumed that during the lengthy visit of Yasir, Abdel Aziz, and Malik to the US in March (which was extended at the personal request of Susan Rice) that the upcoming Southern Kordofan election and various options would have been discussed at length and indications of US support may well have been made, though that cannot be confirmed. The SPLM and SPLA could not, however, acknowledge that those forces fighting in Southern

Kordofan were theirs, and Salva used the occasion of the 5th Speaker's Forum on the Constitution to uphold that deception (11 June 2011).

For the southern opposition it looked like the SPLM had either conveyed a mistaken message of support to Abdel Aziz or that the Nuba were following the lead of the Ngok Dinka and trying to drag the south into a war it did not want. A GoSS presidential adviser said that the leaders of Abyei and Southern Kordofan should not subject southerners to their conflicts, with the danger that if the south was sacrificed their territories would also be overcome (interview with Alfred Gore, 17 June 2011). And for those in the Southern Kordofan SPLM who had been dismissed and marginalized by Abdel Aziz for their criticism of his relationship with Haroun, the events justified their conviction that his leadership was disastrous for the party and the Nuba people. Meanwhile, the other northerners, both in Southern Kordofan and beyond, whom the SPLM had done so much to alienate since the signing of the CPA, could only throw up their hands in despair at Abdel Aziz's appeal for support.

Meanwhile, Governor Malik Agar made clear there would be no violence in Blue Nile: 'I will not allow any insecurity in the state as long as I remain at the head of the government here and I would be against anyone, even be it the SPLA, who starts shooting in the area' (*Al-Sahafa*, 8 June 2011). He went on to say that Blue Nile state would never become a launch pad for military activities in northern Sudan. This represented a marked climbdown from his earlier implicit threats to use 40,000 SPLA soldiers under his command to challenge the NCP, although he did warn the NCP not to attempt to disarm the SPLA in Blue Nile.

Another problem with the SPLM insurgency was the favorable assessment of the election given by the Carter Center and other independent observers, although few of the sensationalist reports that subsequently appeared in the Western media noted the report and instead simply declared that the elections were in dispute and focused on the abuses of the incoming army and the historical grievances of the Nuba people. Abdel Aziz could not have mobilized the Nuba without their deep distrust of the Khartoum government, which had done little during six and a half years to overcome the past abuses by the army and their bitterness at being used to advance the interests of the southern SPLA, only to be discarded when the Salva leadership opted for secession.[15]

On an even larger scale than the humanitarian disaster in Abyei, the Southern Kordofan SPLM left its people exposed to the brutality of SAF and its PDF militias, which descended on Kadugli and other towns killing, looting, in some cases singling out Christians, and opening the door to communal murders on both sides, for which neither the SPLA nor UNMIS could offer any protection. Very quickly after the outbreak of fighting more than 7,000 people sought sanctuary outside the UNMIS Kadugli base, but even there they were not safe from the PDF, which arrested suspected SPLM supporters. When on 20 June SAF informed UNMIS that the displaced people had forty-eight hours to leave, UNMIS could not provide a response and in the event SAF duly arrived and took the people away in buses. By the end of June UNMIS bases throughout northern Sudan were busy preparing for their closure at midnight on 8 July.

Meanwhile, any Nuba who could do so fled either to El Obeid in neighboring Northern Kordofan state, to Khartoum, or to their mountain refuge, which began to replicate the conditions and dynamics of the war that the CPA supposedly ended. SAF permitted the establishment of IDP camps for fleeing non-Nuba in El Obeid, but refused the provision of services for Nuba. Such actions were designed to intimidate the Nuba, and in less than a week most of the population of Kadugli had left.

Responsibility for the humanitarian disaster must in the first instance lie with the NCP, but a liberation movement worthy of the name would consider the consequences of its actions and either not subject its people to such dangers or ensure that it had the capacity to protect them once the onslaught began. The state SPLM/A leadership repeatedly said that it expected to go back to war with the NCP, and there were indications that it made preparations for such a prospect by moving supplies and personnel to the Nuba Mountains before the outbreak of the fighting, but its political strategy was weak. The party lost most of its northern allies, with the exception of the Communists, before the election began and northern Sudanese generally had lost faith in the SPLM when it revealed its true colours as a separatist party. Moreover, the divisions in the state SPLM that the leadership of Abdel Aziz had done so much to create became even more apparent during the elections when a former SPLM governor, Khamis Gilab, and a deputy governor, Daniel Kodie, were sent on missions to Europe instead of actively campaigning. When Kodie returned he was relieved of his position as a presidential adviser to Salva. More defections took place after Abdel Aziz launched the insurgency.

While Blue Nile governor Malik Agar had previously directed the most aggressive language of any of the SPLM leaders at Khartoum, his approach quickly changed after SAF's invasion of Southern Kordofan, and there is little doubt that was because he feared a replay of these events in his state, which had also been threatened by the army. Blue Nile was more vulnerable than the Nuba Mountains because it could not draw on the same number of soldiers, those that could be called upon were not as skilled as the Nuba Mountains soldiers, the people did not have the same martial values, and the generally flat terrain of the state was far more difficult to defend, particularly given SAF's advantages in tanks and artillery.

When the other elements in the SPLM 'plan' failed to materialize – taking over key Southern Kordofan towns, mobilization of northern Sudanese, making common cause with Darfuri rebels, and drawing the south more deeply into the conflict – the northern sector entered the AUHIP-sponsored negotiations in Addis Ababa. As was the case before the outbreak of hostilities, the focus was on reaching a political settlement with the NCP that it was hoped would result in an agreement on a process of political reform, a phased draw-down of the SPLA in conjunction with implementation of the political reforms, and acceptance of the SPLM (albeit under a different name) in post-9 July northern Sudan. That the leadership of the northern sector of the SPLM was not arrested after Abdel Aziz launched his rebellion was due to two factors: first, Salva had made clear to Bashir that he could only negotiate with the northern sector of the SPLM on northern issues, and second, the NCP needed a peace partner given its failure to overcome the rebellion.

The desired political reform was part of a process that began with the popular consultations, but that had not produced the desired outcomes and that stood to end with the completion of the CPA on 9 July. Moreover, the original provisions of the popular consultations assumed a strong SPLM presence in the National Assembly, a presidency in which Salva was first vice president, and SPLM membership of the Council of Regions, which was to receive any final appeals in the event of a failure to reach agreement with the Government of Sudan, and all of those institutions would be thoroughly weakened – in the eyes of the northern sector of the SPLM – after 9 July. The SPLM wanted to carry the reform process forward, use the leverage of the northern SPLA soldiers to press forward its demands, and come to an agreement on the fate of the northern soldiers in the SPLA. That included those soldiers still fighting in the Nuba Mountains, Blue Nile, and an undetermined number of other SPLA soldiers from these areas still in the south. A northern-sector SPLM spokesperson repeatedly made clear that the organization did not want to go into the post-9 July period with a 'militia' and instead saw its future as a civilian party dedicated to realizing the New Sudan vision and operating within the rule of law.[16]

It was never entirely clear, however, who controlled these northern forces in the SPLA – Juba, which paid their salaries and to which they legally belonged; Malik, as leader of the northern branch of the party; Abdel Aziz, as leader in Southern Kordofan – or whether they were effectively on their own. Also problematic was the NCP commitment to its supporters that with the end of the Naivasha peace process, the northern sector of the SPLM would be either banished or tamed. The NCP was concerned with the link of the party to what would soon be a foreign country and its pursuit of the 'alien' New Sudan philosophy. The Abdel Aziz-launched insurgency provided grounds for an outright ban on the party, but unless SAF could militarily defeat the rebels the NCP needed a negotiated settlement and that meant dealing with the SPLM.

Apart from this process, the Southern Kordofan state SPLM leadership was left with the hope that the southern SPLM and the international community would come to its aid, but it should have realized what unreliable partners they were. Juba was preoccupied with reaching 9 July and declaring southern independence, and only after that might it be prepared to offer more substantive support to the rebels. Meanwhile, the international community had ignored the plight of the Nuba when they suffered far more at the hands of the same NCP in the 1990s than in 2011, and it then teamed up with the southern SPLM to end the struggle for the New Sudan to which they had been committed and to impose a CPA which left the Nuba people facing the Khartoum Islamists virtually on their own. That said, there was a strong lobby in Washington in support of the Nuba Mountains rebels and who, like Juba, could not envisage their military defeat.

Trying to understand the situation was made more difficult by the singular focus of the international media on horror stories, and even newspapers like the *New York Times* lost all sense of objectivity, so keen were they on sensationalizing and simplifying the problem (Gettlleman and Kron 2011). In an article datelined Juba *NYT* authors wrote that SAF was 'threatening to seize two more areas' (i.e. Southern Kordofan and Blue Nile), although how it could 'seize' areas that were recognized as part of north Sudan was not explained, and it was only later in the article that it was acknowledged that Southern Kordofan was 'technically' part of the north. The article then explained that the territory was defended by 'southern allied fighters' – this would have been the SPLA, which paid and equipped these forces, although that too would not be understood by most readers. Moreover and contrary to the accepted view of the Western media, southern SPLA soldiers were involved in the fighting.

But things did not go completely in the favor of the NCP. Apart from the cascade of media reports and statements by Western leaders, including Barack Obama, condemning the NCP's intervention in Southern Kordofan and its abuses against the civilian population, under the pressures of the invasion the army demonstrated some of the same tribal divisions evident in the SPLA. Thus on 5 June two largely Nuba-staffed SAF brigades stationed in Southern Kordofan rebelled when ordered to disarm fellow Nuba SPLA soldiers. Just as the SPLA had depended to a considerable extent on Nuba soldiers up until the Juba Declaration, which brought large numbers of Nuer and others into its ranks, so SAF also had large numbers of Nuba soldiers as well as soldiers from other areas in revolt against Khartoum. While the presence of soldiers and officers from Darfur caused problems in its operations in that rebellious state and led to major purges, so in Southern Kordofan SAF faced similar problems. Moreover, the SPLA defeated SAF at Umdurmain and took over the garrison, while SAF did not even make a serious attempt to fight in the mountains and instead concentrated on aerial bombardments and laying a siege. Within the NCP complaints were laid against Haroun, who it was held had shown too much flexibility toward the SPLM, ignoring SPLA weapons going into the state, and permitting the SPLM to control parts of the Nuba Mountains.

But when events seemed the darkest, the AUHIP team in Addis Ababa came up with a peace agreement, or appeared to do so. On 28 June 2011 the GoS and 'SPLM (North)' reached a 'framework agreement' on 'Political Partnership between NCP and SPLM, and Political and Security Arrangements in Blue Nile and Southern Kordofan States.' The key elements of the agreement included the formation of a joint committee to address all relevant issues related to Southern Kordofan and Blue Nile, and 'SPLMN to continue as a legal political party.' It also affirmed that 'The popular consultation process is a democratic right and mechanism to ascertain the views of the people of Southern Kordofan and Blue Nile and shall be completed and its outcome fully implemented and fed into the constitutional reform,' and implementation of remaining provisions of the Southern Kordofan and Blue Nile Protocol, Popular Consultation to extend beyond 9 July 2011. The parties also agreed that 'the issue of governance in South Kordofan shall be discussed and resolved amicably … within thirty days' and that they should begin working on a ceasefire and allow humanitarian access in the state. With respect to security arrangements, the agreement stipulated that Sudan would have one national army and that SPLA forces from Southern Kordofan and Blue Nile would be integrated into SAF 'over a period of time' (widely reported as nine months) and 'any disarmament should be done in accordance with agreed upon plans and without resorting to force' and that a joint committee be formed to enact these provisions. The agreement was signed by Dr Nafie Ali Nafie, 'Government of Sudan National Congress

Party,' and by Malik Agar Eyre, 'Sudan People's Liberation Movement (North).'

The next day – 29 June – the SPLM and NCP signed an agreement that had been in the works for months to establish a 10-kilometer-wide demilitarized zone on each side of the border. Billed as a means to build trust, encourage stability, and economic development, it was to be policed by a team of unarmed military observers from the UN in the north and the south, who would come from Ethiopia (*Sudan Tribune*, 29 June 2011).

The agreement on a demilitarized border zone did not raise any eyebrows, but many were surprised at the unqualified recognition of the SPLM North and provisions that suggested a 'Naivasha II' type arrangement in which the SPLA forces would be integrated over time while negotiations to reach a political settlement proceeded, something the SPLM had been advocating for months and which had been repeatedly and firmly rejected by the NCP. The fact that the agreement was signed by the hardliner Dr Nafie led many to think the agreement would stick. But Nafie returned to Khartoum and immediately placed the emphasis on the fact that the framework agreement did not include a ceasefire, and shortly thereafter Bashir announced that he had instructed the army to continue its fight and that it should carry out 'purges' in the area and 'arrest and bring to trial the rebel' Abdel Aziz al-Hilu.[17] With the SPLA operating largely from mountainous areas and with the advent of the rainy season it was hard to imagine that SAF could defeat the SPLA, and as a result most of its efforts were directed to carrying out highly inaccurate aerial attacks that probably killed more civilians than SPLA fighters.

It quickly became apparent that both Nafie and Bashir had been bushwhacked by the SAF leadership, which refused to accept 'Naivasha II.' In the 30 June 2011 editorial of *Alqwat Almoslha*, the official organ of SAF, titled 'NCP Plays with Fire,' Brigadier General Mohammed Ajeeb wrote that the

NCP is negotiating with the SPLM in Addis Ababa to sign an agreement that can lead to an amendment of the Political Parties Act and allow the SPLM to form its political party in North Sudan, exercise all its legal and constitutional rights such as the other parties while it owes allegiance to another country which can be described as an enemy state. (Ajeeb 2011)

Couched in references to the Quran and the Hadiths, the article described the agreement in Addis Ababa as a 'betrayal of religion and the homeland.'

The next day, 1 July, the NCP Politburo held a seven-hour meeting, in which Nafie and his negotiating team were roundly condemned and accused of not having the authority of either the party or the government to sign the agreement and of doing 'a strange thing' (interview with Ismail el Hag Musa, 7 July 2011). Parroting the army officers, the NCP concluded that the provisions of the Addis Ababa agreement on the SPLM North were unacceptable and that the party had to meet the requirements of the Political Parties Act before it could be accepted in the north. Although NCP party spokesperson Ibrahim Ghandour went on insisting that the Addis Ababa agreement was still intact and the party united (*Sudan Tribune*, 6 July 2011), within a week a campaign was under way to tarnish the agreement and besmirch Dr Nafie, led by among others the Just Peace Forum of al-Tayyib Mustafa, editor of the racist *al-Intibaha* newspaper.

The question immediately arose as to how far the army would go in pressing its agenda. Only weeks before, a senior NCP official had warned the author of extremists in the security services and the fragile nature of the alliance between the politicians and the generals. The official also said that relations had deteriorated between the NCP and SPLM to such an extent that government ministers just wanted to be rid of the south and of southerners in the north, and some even talked about building an Israel-style wall between north and south Sudan. The official claimed that any concessions to the south at this point would have led northerners to revolt, although there was little evidence of such resentment and no popular calls for the expulsion of southerners, other than from the *Intibaha* crowd. Instead, it seemed that SAF's invasions of Abyei and Southern Kordofan were at least in part due to a desire to win popular approval at a time when many in the north had great misgivings about the dismemberment of their country and would derive some satisfaction from knowing that Abyei and Southern Korodfan would remain in the north. On the Islamist street, sentiments supported the army in rejecting the Addis Ababa agreement, in large part because of anger at how the NCP had signed an agreement that it had insisted for months was unacceptable.

Meanwhile two investigations, one published by the UN Office of the High Commissioner for Human Rights and the other leaked by UNMIS, concluded that serious violations of human rights and humanitarian law were committed after the conflict erupted in Southern Kordofan on 5 June.

At the end of the peace process, leading Nuba figures within and outside the SPLM/A were meeting in Khartoum to endeavor to find a way out of the impasse, all with the conviction that Abdel Aziz had made a mistake in launching his insurgency.[18] They also wanted the 'sons of Nuba' to resolve the problems, and accused the SPLM leadership of not representing their interests in the Addis Ababa negotiations. Late in the day, the NCP passed legislation extending the popular consultations, but Malik objected because, according to the Popular Consultation Act, the Council of States was to be the formal mediation forum. However, with the secession of the ten southern states, the composition of the Council became distinctly less favorable to the SPLM.

Conclusion

The peace process came close to breaking down entirely over conflicts in the Three Areas on the eve of the end of the process, and may yet take the parties back to war. Years of state neglect, alienation of Nuba land, and the practice of successive governments in pursuing counter-insurgency on the cheap by using local allies to fight the SPLA went hand in hand with the gut response of the movement to reduce Sudan's manifold conflicts to Arabs versus Africans, or, in the case of Blue Nile, to settler versus indigenous tribes. Together the intellectuals on both sides of the divide effectively continued the efforts of Nimeiri to break down local traditional administrations and relations, but without managing to establish viable alternatives. And this is hardly surprising because both Political Islam and New Sudan had little meaning when carried to the area by armies which had no idea how to meet the material and political needs of the people. The result in Abyei, Southern Kordofan, and Blue Nile was that racial and tribal tensions, which had been minimal or at least manageable and never systemic before the SPLA–SAF conflict, had by the end of the peace process become both endemic and explosive, with little prospect of being resolved. And to make matters worse there was good reason to be skeptical about the viability of the AU-facilitated security agreements on Abyei, Southern Kordofan, and the establishment of a demilitarized zone.

In neighboring Ethiopia, the Tigrayan leaders of the revolution established complementary ethnic-based parties and linked them all under the rubric of the EPRDF. But Garang rejected this approach and had one army and one party for the entire country, although, as a result of the failure of the SPLM/A to develop a wide basis of support in the east and west, he had to cooperate with existing parties. But the presence of the SPLA and SPLM in northern Sudan were – as Garang undoubtedly understood – time bombs that would challenge the stability in the north. What he could not have imagined was that he would die and a leadership would emerge that did not appreciate that the self-determination and security of southern Sudan depended on maintaining the alliance. Garang was a dictator, but not without a vision and some notion of how it could be realized; he was followed by those whose notion of liberation went no further than being free of the *jallaba*. Meanwhile, the international backers of the peace process increasingly viewed the CPA as a road map for the secession of southern Sudan, and in that light the Three Areas were mere security issues that needed resolution or containment so that the peace process could be fulfilled. That got the international community through to 9 July, but the conflict in Abyei remained unresolved and could erupt again at any time, the armed struggle in Southern Kordofan continued, and in early September 2011 the stand-off in Blue Nile broke down and war broke out.

SIX

A CHANGING LANDSCAPE: POLITICAL TRANSITIONS IN SOUTH AND NORTH SUDAN

With the completion of the elections and referendum the soon-to-be-rump northern Sudan and the Republic of South Sudan entered a period of transition. But the legacy of the past and the need to implement key provisions of the CPA, including the popular consultations in Southern Kordofan and Blue Nile, permanent settlement of Abyei, and agreement on a range of outstanding post-referendum issues, weighed heavily on the parties and threatened to take them back to war. Indeed, after the self-congratulatory speeches in the wake of the referendum the SPLM and NCP resumed their normal antagonistic relationship. Of immediate concern for both parties were constitutions to meet the new conditions.

The October conference of the southern political parties went far to overcome the bitterness created by the election, but it became clear that the SPLM's intent was only to achieve unity in the lead-up to the referendum; after the referendum was successfully accomplished it approached the opposition parties in the same arrogant and dismissive manner as it had done before. As a result, the post-referendum priorities of the SPLM involved constructing a constitution based on a rejection of holding early elections and a broad-based government, and support for a strong, if not a potentially dictatorial, presidency. As a result, the authoritarianism that had been a central feature of the SPLM from its inception increasingly came to the fore as it strove to achieve a hegemonic position. This approach also made it difficult to deal with the mounting internal security problems the SPLM faced, which also became increasingly apparent in the wake of the vote for independence. Like that of the politicians, the discontent of the soldiers was kept in check by the concern not to take any action that could undermine the march to independence, but with it completed, an armed response was almost inevitable, and the surprise was merely that an insurrection began earlier – after the conduct of the referendum but before actual independence on 9 July.

The NCP also needed a new constitution, and this was closely linked with its efforts to form a broad-based government. Both of these objectives were meant to strengthen its position in the wake of the loss of the south, a deepening economic crisis, wars in Darfur and Southern Kordofan, and the regional context of the Arab uprisings. After spending decades trying to weaken and divide the Umma Party and the DUP, the NCP now looked to these moderate Islamist parties to give legitimacy to the constitutional review, participate in the government, and divide the opposition. Meanwhile, the 'hard' opposition, as represented by the National Consensus Forces and some elements of civil society, attempted to use the constitutional review to mobilize in opposition to NCP hegemony, obstruct the alliance of Islamist parties, and prepare the grounds for a popular uprising. The northern sector of the SPLM was primarily focused on the war in Southern Kordofan, the popular consultations, and its own legality as a party in the face of NCP threats to banish it, but it was sympathetic to the broad opposition goal of either weakening or overthrowing the NCP. The peace process formally ended with almost nothing resolved except the secession of South Sudan.

End of Internal Unity in the South

With the referendum successfully completed and independence effectively in the bag, the remarkable display of unity by southern Sudanese of all tribes and political persuasions ended and the SPLM government began facing attacks on multiple fronts. The discontent with the government had been steadily building and the causes were well known – abuse of power by the government and the security services, systemic corruption, limited services, failure to provide security in large sections of rural southern Sudan, cronyism and nepotism, and the widespread fear that the SPLM would take the south into another war with the north. Beyond these concerns there was a division in attitudes between rural and urban southerners, between the educated and the traditional, and among the various political parties. Nor was it easy to draw conclusions about southern Sudanese collectively when the national ethos was so little developed and the large majority derived their primary identity and loyalty from an estimated 150 tribes. Crucially, however, views and approaches could be examined through the lenses of three broad geographical–ethnic blocs of Greater Equatoria, Greater Bahr el Ghazal, and Greater Upper Nile, although only rarely do these blocs operate as politically coherent units. Although resentment with the SPLM-led government had many causes, the political battle lines after the referendum increasingly developed over the party-proposed interim constitution.

The problem came to the fore with the breakdown of the Political Parties Leadership Forum, which had shown much promise when twenty-four southern political parties were brought together at the invitation of President Salva Kiir, in Juba on 13–17 October 2010. According to the conference's final communiqué, after the announcement of the results of the referendum a National Constitutional Review Commission would be convened which would review the 2005 Interim Constitution for Southern Sudan (ICSS) for adoption as a transitional constitution. This was to be followed by an all-party constitutional conference that would consider a permanent constitution and form a broad-based transitional government led by Salva that would govern from 9 July for the duration of the transitional period. This transitional government would oversee the holding of a census and elections for a constituent assembly, which would then promulgate a permanent constitution. It was also agreed at the October meeting that one week after the official announcement of the results of the referendum the parties would reconvene in Juba and begin planning for the transition.

But the goodwill achieved in October quickly dissipated when Salva issued a presidential decree on 21 January (No. 2/2011) authorizing the establishment of the Technical Committee to Review the ICSS. According to Article 208 (5) of the ICSS, in the event of a vote for secession all components of the constitution that provide for national institutions, rights, duties, and obligations shall be duly repealed and replaced with provisions appropriate to the status of southern Sudan as an independent state. But the Technical Committee developed a virtually new constitution, and it was this that caused the problems. The article also stipulated that the final draft of the interim constitution be presented to the president by 25 April 2011 for submission to the South Sudan Legislative Assembly (SSLA). The ICSS further required that amendments to the constitution be submitted to the SSLA two months before being voted on, for the interim constitution to be operational by 9 July, and thus they had to be submitted by early May. The SPLM leadership knew from the signing of the CPA that in the event of a vote for secession – and, as noted above, with the passing of Garang on 30 July 2006, almost all of the leadership favored such an outcome – that it had to put in place an interim constitution by 9 July. However, the entire process was compressed into a final hectic few months.

Not surprisingly many thought this mad rush was due either to incompetence or to a concerted effort by the SPLM leadership to push their desired interim constitution through the Assembly. Also worrying was the fact that the proposed interim constitution would provide the basis for a permanent constitution, and there was no indication as to when this would be agreed upon, other than Salva's commitment that the process would be completed before the holding of another election four years from July 2011.

Salva's decree appointed twenty members to the Committee, as well as four legal advisers, led by the minister of legal and constitutional affairs John Luk Jok, and parliamentary affairs minister Michael Micquai. It was widely speculated that the right of the president to dismiss governors was to have John Luk's enemy, Jonglei governor Kuol Manyang, removed, but other governors soon felt threatened and joined the campaign against this provision. All of those appointed to the Committee were SPLM members and supporters, with the exception of the minister of culture and youth and leader of the UDSF, Gabriel Changeson, who stepped down on the grounds that he could not participate in a process that contravened the October agreement. But it quickly became apparent that having gained the necessary unity to conduct the referendum successfully the SPLM leadership saw little use for the Political Parties Leadership Forum (PPLF) and argued that it had no legal basis. John Luk Jok further contended that there was no need for political representation on the Committee because its tasks were purely technical, a misrepresentation that would quickly be exposed.

After Bona Malwal, the elder statesman, met with Salva Kiir there was an agreement to hold a meeting of the PPLF, which was eventually held in Juba on 16–17 February. The main concerns of the opposition parties were to reaffirm the process agreed to in October and reach agreement on the length of an interim period (the opposition favored 18–24 months) and power-sharing (the opposition proposed a 50–50 split). In the event, both of these measures were rejected by the SPLM. The meeting was thus reduced to giving approval to the GoSS referendum task force, the name of the country, its coat of arms, and its flag, which would be that of the SPLA (leaving the army to come up with a replacement.) And these measures would in any case have to be voted on by the SSLA. The meeting did agree that membership of the Technical Committee would be expanded to include opposition, civil society, and faith-based groups and that approval of the Technical Committee's draft constitution would be submitted to the PPLF for 'review' before it was presented to the SSLA. But almost immediately there were differences of opinion as to what 'review' entailed, with the SPLM arguing that the PPLF could only examine the document before passing it over to the SSLA, while the opposition parties argued more convincingly that 'review' meant having the right to change the document. Salva then issued Presidential Decree No. 08/2011 on 17 February, appointing twelve more members to the Committee – eleven representatives from the opposition and a final person to represent civil society, Angelo Beda, although that appointment was later contested and he was removed.

What limited goodwill that gesture created was immediately discounted by Salva's further decision to appoint another seventeen SPLM supporters to the Technical Committee. As a result, representatives of five opposition parties led by Lam Akol's SPLM–DC withdrew from the Committee, citing the appointment of the additional SPLM members, attempts to undermine the ruling of the PPLF that Committee decisions were to be reached by consensus, and refusal of the SPLM to discuss the length of the interim period and power-sharing in the transitional government.

After deliberations, the Technical Committee submitted the draft transitional constitution to President Salva, on 20 April 2011. On 28 April he convened a meeting of the PPLF to present the draft transitional constitution to the parties ahead of its sub-mission to the SSLA. When it was made clear that the Forum would not be given authority to amend the draft constitution or consider power-sharing and the length of the transition, the same five parties that walked out of the Technical Committee left the PPLF.

The remaining eighteen opposition parties together with the SPLM continued their deliberations and submitted a list of recommendations, the key measures being that Abyei, which under the proposed constitution was included in the definition of southern Sudan – and which so angered Khartoum – be dropped, and provisions that permitted the president of the GoSS to dis-solve state legislatures and remove elected governors and the vice president be removed. Meanwhile, the parties accepted Salva's four-year term and in a climbdown requested only 35 per cent of the ministries instead of the previous 50 per cent. They also requested that their list of proposals be forwarded to the Council of Ministers and on to the SSLA for consideration. All of the re-quests of the opposition parties were rejected and their proposals were not submitted to the Council of Ministers or to the SSLA. The Political Parties Leadership Forum had effectively come to an inglorious end. Likewise, the efforts at reconciliation with the armed groups faded; as Gordon Kong said, 'When the SPLM got power they didn't want to see us again' (interview, 5 July 2011).

Revolt of the Regions

Equatorian unhappiness during the first autonomous government derived not simply from domination of the political organs by Dinkas, but by unqualified Dinkas. Land alienation in the Juba area by the incoming politically powerful Dinkas was also a source of grievance, as was the perennial conflict between Dinka cattle herders and Equatorian farmers. All of these problems again came to the fore after the SPLM-led government was established in 2005. Knowing how unwelcome and even unsafe it would be for his fellow tribesmen to reside in Juba when many of the local Equatorians would not readily accept them, Garang originally wanted the Dinka-inhabited area near Rumbek made the national capital. But Clement Wani, leader of the powerful Mundari militia, veteran of Anyanya, and former senior figure in the SSDF, jumped ship and reached an agreement with Garang that saw him appointed governor of Central Equatoria, and that made it possible for Juba to serve as the capital.

With their easier access to the urban centers of power, Equatorians are typically more effective at political mobilization, but, with the exception of tribes such as the Taposa and Mundari, they do not have the martial traditions of their Nilotic cousins. Only some 10 percent of SPLA soldiers were Equatorians and they rarely figured in the army's top leadership. And the gun, and the ability to mobilize large numbers of gun-carriers, is what has underpinned most southern Sudanese politics. As a result, Equatorians began expressing their disenchantment with the government through political mobilization, and in mid-April 2011 representatives from the three states that constitute Greater Equatoria held a large and well-organized conference that went far toward spelling out their grievances.

Central Equatoria governor Clement Wani blasted the recently trained police in his own state and accused them of being directly responsible for the increasing number of reported robberies. Delegates complained about the forced demolitions Juba was experiencing and the potential dislocation if a new capital were built. Western Equatoria governor Colonel Bangasi Bokosoro complained about the lack of security and development in his state, where his Zande are among the most disaffected in southern Sudan.

Clement Wani almost certainly lost his April 2010 election bid for governor to Lt General Alfred Ladu Gore (rtd), but was kept in office by the SPLM and the SPLA because his Mundari militia ensured security in Central Equatoria. To alienate Wani ran the risk of him making common cause with the political opposition or even those involved in armed struggle. Bangasi Bokosoro, meanwhile, ran as an independent in the April 2010 election, defeating the SPLM candidate in a campaign that witnessed some of the worst government rigging in southern Sudan. Pushed too hard, he also might have jumped ship, particularly after 9 July. In the end the conference endorsed a call for South Sudan to be a federal state with considerable decentralization of power. This was an astute demand because, as well as summing up Equatorian complaints and being code for opposition to Dinka domination, it followed from the demands of southerners from the pre-independence conference of 1947, through to the commitment of the SPLM in its 1983 manifesto, down to the present, for federalism. It also dovetailed with growing frustration over the SPLM's efforts to force a highly centralized interim constitution on the opposition parties, the regional assembly, the states, and even over the heads of many of their own MPs.

The SPLM leadership attempted to use party loyalty and the contention that the interim constitution would soon be overtaken by a permanent constitution to force its members to accept without amendment the draft constitution of the Technical Committee. As one Equatorian SPLM MP charged, 'one ethnic group was trying to control everything.' With their traditional fear of Dinka domination, Equatorian MPs were soon trying to stop the steamrolling ruling party. In a series of meetings in May and June, MPs, members of the opposition parties, and civil society activists began articulating their grievances.

Under the proposed draft, state powers were delegated by the president and local powers virtually ignored. The critical notion under federalism that the three levels of government would operate independently was put to rest, with the presidency granted the right to dismiss elected governors and overrule state legislatures, while security was centralized and there were no provisions for state police or independent revenues for local governments. Some found it amusing that the draft constitution gave the president the right to dismiss his vice president, which in the present circumstances would mean a Dinka president firing his Nuer vice, and possibly igniting a tribal war. Likewise the lines between the executive, legislature, and judiciary at the center were blurred and made increasingly subject to the purview of the presidency.

Not only were Equatorians keen proponents of federalism, but they were strongly opposed to measures in the draft constitution to grant 'seasonal rights' to pastoralists for grazing and water. This concern left little doubt that what was at issue was the perennial problem of Dinka herders running afoul of Equatorian farmers. Likewise Equatorians were anxious to ensure state and local control over land out of the same fear that it could fall prey to outsiders.

Equatorians objected to the Abyei Ngok Dinka being identified in the constitution (see above) and suspected this was due to the desire of John Luk Jok to win the support of the Ngok Dinka. Equatorians were particularly upset that some twenty SPLA soldiers from Equatoria died in SAF's 20 May 2011 attack on Abyei.

Joseph Lagu, former Anyanya leader and president of the Southern High Executive Council and then GoSS presidential adviser, said there was greater delegation of powers under Nimeiri than under the SPLM's constitution. Lagu said that the southern executive was more accessible in the first period of autonomy than under the SPLM and, while he had easy access to Salva, many presidential advisers had not met him since their appointment in April 2010.[1] Lagu advised of the dangers of a dictatorship, said that term limits were essential for leaders, and thought the intent of the constitution was to permit Dinka revenge against the

Equatorians. He also said that in the event of a failure to modify significantly the centralizing measures proposed in the constitution, struggle for Equatorian independence should not be ruled out, and this was greeted with a round of applause. Indeed, that was precisely the concern of other MPs who were anxious that the system of government implemented was not based on regions which had opened the door to Equatorian secessionist tendencies in the 1972–83 period.

Dissenting Equatorian MPs and others were angry at a process which tied up consideration of the draft interim constitution in four SSLA clusters that would permit only two days of open debate, and consideration of proposed amendments in the plenary, before the final reading on 8 July, in time for it to be implemented at midnight. There were complaints that the draft constitution did not include a time frame for the development and adoption of a permanent constitution and the holding of elections at the end of the transitional period. Equatorians also complained at the provision that would take southern MPs in the National Assembly and Council of States into the SSLA, contending that it was undemocratic, undermined the powers of duly elected MPs in the current Assembly, and would prove very expensive. Many were unhappy at the intention to eliminate Arabic as an official language. As Onyeti, parliamentary leader of the SPLM–DC and leader of the Opposition in the Assembly noted, 'Salva has to use Arabic to speak to his own army officers at Bilfam' (i.e. SPLA headquarters) (interview, 9 June 2011) In a meeting of dissenting SPLM Equatorian MPs, one declared that 'People wouldn't have voted for secession if this [the proposed constitution] was the result ... [we] are replicating what we rejected.' Although the emphasis varied, the concerns of the Equatorians echoed those of the opposition parties of the PPLF, but what had changed was that, except for the SPLM–DC, which had four representatives in the SSLA, the other parties had been marginalized and opposition to the 'SPLM constitution' – and that is what it was widely being called – depended largely on dissenting SPLM MPs. Because the proposed interim constitution did not address the form of governance, it was left up to Dr Lam Akol, who concluded that

> Presidential systems are, therefore, associated with the concentration of power in the hands of one person (the President) which is in line with totalitarianism. It is, therefore, not surprising, the critics of presidential system argue, that the system was born out of military coups. During the negotiations that culminated in the signing of the Comprehensive Peace Agreement, the presidential system was not challenged by the SPLM side and was therefore adopted, as it was in the 1998 Constitution with minor changes.[2]

In opposition to the party leadership the dissenting MPs organized half-day public hearings for each of the four clusters that were to review the interim constitution. The hearings were largely dominated by interest groups, the key ones being churches, the disabled, journalists, and women. The churches argued forcefully against the separation of state and religion, against secularism, and for these spheres to be 'interrelated,' that they should have the right to run profit-making organizations, have their status recognized at official functions, and for prayers to be brought back to the SSLA. It was a curious argument to be made in light of southern demands for religion to be separated from the state when Islam dominated. Journalists argued that their rights needed to be strengthened under the proposed constitution, given the constant harassment they faced at the hands of security agencies and the obstacles thrown up by government officials to the provision of information. Since the formation of the GoSS, southern journalists had demanded a media law. Women's organizations appreciated the 25 percent representation in the SSLA, but argued that it should be increased to a 30 percent floor. Otherwise the contributions of the elite participants at the hearings stressed the same issues heard at the meeting of the Equatorians: concern with the centralization of power under the president, opposition to the recognition of Abyei, and concern as to when the process to start consideration of a permanent constitution would begin. The public hearing for the security, judiciary, and states cluster went badly when the chairman, Leu Ayen Leu, repeatedly admonished those attending for not proposing changes to the articles of concern to the cluster, ordered journalists to 'shut up,' and then abruptly walked out, ending the hearings.

One ally of those discontented with the proposed constitutional changes was vice president Riek Machar, who shared many of the concerns of the Equatorians. Indeed, he submitted to the SSLA his 'Additional Suggested Amendments.'[3] Riek opposed granting the president power to remove sitting governors, dissolve state legislatures, and appoint caretaker governors. He proposed that after the transitional period the president and vice president be elected on a joint 'ticket,' that the vice president serve out the term of office of the president if it fell vacant, that the assembly not have the power to impeach the vice president, and that the president not have the authority to remove the vice president. He also favored strengthening the powers of the Council of States, recognizing Arabic as a national language, eliminating the power of the president to dissolve or suspend any institution of the National Executive in the event of a declaration of a state of emergency, raising the women's quota to 30 percent, and recognizing a state police force. Antipas Nyok, the SPLM secretary for political affairs, was outraged that Riek would challenge the government, linked him with the opposition, who were 'enemies of South Sudan,' and said his proposals constituted 'an illegal document' (interview, 10 June 2011).

It was, however, the leader of the Opposition in the SSLA, Onyoti Adigo, a Shilluk whose tribe had recently been on the receiving end of SPLA abuses, who drew attention to the failure of the draft constitution to end the link between the army and the SPLM and to call for the SPLA to be 'called the South Sudan National Armed Forces on July 9, 2011.'⁴ There were reports that Salva was concerned about the SPLA, but feared that any changes could unleash a storm, and indeed coup rumors were widespread in the days leading up to independence.

Such was the state of affairs when President Salva Kiir delivered a three-hour speech in Juba on 8 June.⁵ He warned members of the SSLA not to change the draft transitional constitution and said that changes could be considered at length in debate over the permanent constitution. Salva noted that since Riek was at the Council of Ministers meeting when the draft constitution was accepted; he thus had no right to put forward alternative proposals and they would not be considered. He criticized demands that Arabic be given recognition as a second official language, calling it the language of the colonizers (forgetting apparently that English was also the language of the colonizers). He also criticized those who called for a 24-month interim period before having an election and threatened to call an election after six months if that provision was approved. Salva said that it was not appropriate to demand federalism at this time and that the priority was development. He accused the opposition of supporting militias in Upper Nile and Southern Kordofan. He said that there were major security problems in the states, which they could not control, and their governments were asking for his support (he singled out Lakes, Warrap, and Western Equatoria); hence his need for more powers. He said that he had no intention of being president for life. Salva told the MPs that if they did not pass the draft constitution there would not be a vacuum because the Interim Constitution of Southern Sudan 2005 would still be valid for the rest of the four-year period and he would simply rule by presidential decree. He blamed the SSLA speaker, deputy speaker, and chief whip for causing confusion and creating problems in the constitutional process by allowing public hearings to be held. In a concession on Abyei he directed the MPs to include the following sentence: 'Abyei will become part of South Sudan in case the people of Abyei vote in a referendum and choose their suitable destination.'

Meanwhile, Salva's attack on Riek brought many to the latter's defense, including an Equatorian presidential adviser who spoke of the 'tremendous role of Riek in the government' and how 'the most difficult tasks were carried out by Riek,' and accused Salva of being 'obsessed' with his vice president and wanting to 'vilify' him. Kiir had repeatedly and publicly berated Riek since he indicated at the 2008 SPLM Convention his desire to run against him for the presidency of the party. But his attack on James Wani Igga, the speaker of the SSLA and an Equatorian, was a surprise since he was considered Salva's chief sycophant in the government. Nonetheless, Igga went on to make a clear statement in favor of federalism, thus ensuring his credibility among his fellow Equatorians (*Sudan Tribune*, 25 June 2011).

What became clear in this drama was that the meek-mannered Salva Kiir, who had spent most of his life in the shadow of John Garang, wished to possess his former master's authority. But he did not have Garang's intelligence or vision, or indeed the respect of the SPLM/A and southerners generally. He was merely the instrument for realizing southern self-determination. His ambitions were widely seen as overreaching his capacities, and he in turn was being used by powerful people around him.

Despite all the MPs' talk of resistance to Salva, after a marathon session on 6 July 2011 the SSLA passed the proposed transitional constitution on its fourth reading by a vote of 140 to 5 (4 SPLM–DC and one independent voting against it). The controversial provisions empowering Kiir to sack governors and dissolve state assemblies were passed as presented by the Technical Committee, although 42 MPs voted against this provision. Curiously, the dissenters did not include members of the subcommittee, who drafted alternative language that would have added oversight to the Council of States. The dispute over whether the system of government was to be described as federalism or decentralization was resolved in favor of the latter by a vote of 113 to 42. The government also got its way on the appointment of sixty-six members to what would become the National Assembly of South Sudan. Likewise the vote favored the government on the appointment to the Council of States of thirty members by Salva, and a further twenty by the Khartoum Council, but by a much smaller majority, the vote being 79 to 57 with 15 abstentions.

The minor defeats of the government included the decision that the permanent constitution would have a timeline added to the final document, that the Anti-Corruption Commission be given the power to prosecute as well as investigate, and that arrested suspects would not be held for more than twenty-four hours before being brought to court, as opposed to the seven days that the former judge John Luk Jok had wanted.

Despite much tough talk by MPs in the weeks before the final vote, they succumbed to pressure in the final days, including Salva Kiir's threat to institute a military government if the constitution was not passed. MPs were asked, 'Are you with the president, or against, because this is the president's constitution?' In the wake of the approval of the constitution, the leader of the Opposition in the SSLA, Onyoti Andigo, was badly beaten up by members of the military intelligence.

RoSS had a constitution to start its existence as an independent state. Now it needed a set of economic policies.

Revolt in the Periphery

The relative quiescence of the Nuer during the first six years of the peace agreement was a surprise to the government and to themselves. But such was their desire to achieve southern independence and not be held responsible for problems along the way that they bore many insults, including the humiliation of their leaders, such as Paulino Matieb and Riek Machar. But with the referendum successfully completed and impatience being the typical characteristic of the Nuer, many could not wait for 9 July and wanted to express their anger. And instead of holding meetings Equatorian-style, their youth began going to the bush with Maj. General Peter Gadet and Lt General George Athor.

Gadet is a career military officer who was trained as a paratrooper in SAF and fought in the First Gulf War. After returning to Sudan, he joined the SPLA, but defected when Riek Machar broke with John Garang. When Riek returned to the SPLA, Gadet stayed in the north and became a senior officer under SSDF leader Paulino Matieb. Both are Bul Nuers from Mayom county in Unity state. Gadet repeatedly changed alliance between the Khartoum government and the SPLA during the course of the war before finally rejoining the SPLA as a result of the Juba Declaration. He then became head of the air defense directorate in SPLA headquarters Bilfam, the most senior position held by a former SSDF officer apart from Paulino. He served in Abyei in 2008 when fighting broke out and later was deputy commander of SPLA Division 4 in Warrap state on the Abyei border. Short for a Nuer, wiry, and reserved, Gadet is said to wash only one side of his face at a time so that he can always keep an eye open.

Gadet's complaints mirrored those of other dissidents, but he gave particular attention to military issues. He noted there were two officers' lists in the SPLA: one denoting the original SPLA officers, who received regular promotions, had priority for training courses, had the confidence of the army leadership, and were assigned positions of responsibility; and a second list of suspect officers that included those who at one time had defected. He said that with the approach of the referendum large numbers of former SSDF officers were declared 'inactive' or placed on reserve. Gadet drew on the anger of former SSDF officers and soldiers at what they felt was a flawed integration process that followed the Juba Declaration of January 2006 and claimed that it was modeled on that carried out on Anyanya after the Addis Ababa Agreement (interview, 13 May 2011, Khartoum).[6]

Another rebelling officer, Colonel Gatlauk Gai, went to the bush before Gadet because of resentment over the election rigging that prevented Angelina Teny-Dhurgon winning the governorship in Unity state and appointing him commissioner. Colonel Mathew Puol Jang, another SSDF veteran and an aide to Paulino (who was at his house in Bentiu when it was attacked and burned down with the loss of sixteen bodyguards by forces under Taban Deng), also joined Gadet. Jang had attempted to integrate his forces into the SPLA, but this ended after they were reportedly attacked by the SPLA. Another defecting officer was SAF Major General Babiny Monytuil, brother of the former state governor, health minister, and presidential adviser Dr Joseph Monytuil, who had been selected by the Unity state SPLM to run for governor instead of Taban Deng, but was overruled by Salva's Electoral College.

Underlying all of these complaints was the rallying cry of Dinka domination. Although the chief of defense staff at the time, Lt General James Hoth, was a Nuer, the former SSDF rebels attributed the failings of the SPLA to Dinka domination, which went up the chain to Salva as a Dinka and commander in chief. The same logic was applied to Taban Deng, who was a Nuer, but was held to be an agent of the Dinkas who directed the SPLA.

Gadet launched his insurgency among the Bul clan in his home county of Mayom in Unity state. It was expected that people in the state who abhorred the governor and disapproved of his rigging of the April elections would be sympathetic. On 11 April 2011 the rebels, who took the historical name of Anyanya's South Sudan Liberation Army, issued the 'Mayom Declaration.' The Declaration listed the usual grievances: corruption, bad and

undemocratic leadership, insecurity, politicized judiciary, flawed
elections, pursuit of 'exclusion politics,' and the failure to create
a 'truly professional national army.' As if speaking directly to
the Juba politicians, it called for a transitional government that
'shall carry out a general election in the Republic of South Sudan
within two years to elect the Constituent Assembly that shall
promulgate the permanent constitution of the Republic of South
Sudan. Priority to be given to services delivery to our people.'[7]
It was clear who Gadet looked to for support: 'I appeal to the
officers, NCOs, men and women of the SPLA to abandon the
clique in Juba and join us in the struggle to set South Sudan on
a correct path as the difficult task of joining the club of nations
of the world.'

By late May, Mayom county was the focus of an SPLA siege,
which the commissioner, Charles Machieng Kuol, said led to
almost 8,000 tukuls (grass huts) being burnt and the killing and
displacement of civilians, as Taban Deng attempted to turn the
state's other Nuer clans against the Bul. For these public comments the commissioner was sent into exile in Juba; after refusing
to apologize he was dismissed on 30 June 2011 (*Sudan Tribune*,
4 July 2011). A GoSS presidential adviser informed me that the
SPLA actions amounted to 'a failed government resorting to a
dirty strategy.' Nuer organizations in the US and Canada appealed
to the international community based on the public statement
by the Mayom county commissioner, and on allegations that the
SPLA had assisted Warrap cattle raiders steal 23,000 cattle from
the besieged people of the area.[8] Salva denounced his accusers in
the international community and their demand that he be taken
to The Hague for violating human rights in Mayom county.[9]

Soon after had Gadet launched his insurgency the state capital,
Bentiu, was cut off, with all roads subject to mining by his forces,
while political leaders in Lakes and Warrap expressed growing
fears about the conflict spreading to their areas. Critics of the

SPLM suggested that Dinka concerns stemmed from fears that Gadet would seek revenge for the attacks on the Bul. But Governor Taban Deng had a different explanation; he stated in a telephone interview from Bentiu that the NCP had never accepted the results of the referendum and were using the SSLA and other armed groups to bring the south back to Sudan. Moreover, he claimed that 'Gadet, the Misseirya, and SAF are fighting together in Abyei, outside Kadugli, and Unity and have lots of armaments and mines' (telephone interview, 17 May 2011).

As well as the discontented former SSDF officers and men who were integrated into the SPLA, there were also an unknown number who refused to accept the Juba Declaration and remained aligned with SAF under Major General Gordon Kong, who became the leader of the rump SSDF in Khartoum. Some of these soldiers, particularly those under Gabriel Tangyangi and Thomas Maboir, served as members of SAF in the JIUs and were a continuing source of instability, and on two occasions the civilians of Malakal were caught in the middle of fighting between the largely SSDF-manned SAF JIU and the SPLA JIU.

On 17 January 2011 Gabriel, Thomas, and Gatwe began moving a heavily armed force from the north (and hence clearly supplied by SAF) into Upper Nile along the west bank of the river. The fact that they were heavily armed suggested that SAF expected them to fight the SPLA, but in view of the events that unfolded it appears that they tricked their northern benefactors and intended on integrating these forces into the SPLA. On 7 April Gabriel's estimated 7,000 soldiers (which included many youth and women who had only recently joined Gabriel as a means to gain positions in the SPLA) began being integrated into the SPLA at their base in Kaldak, just south-west of Malakal. During this period Gabriel was reportedly regularly in phone conversation with Salva Kiir, who apparently supported the integration efforts. But on 18 April, it is reliably reported, Peter Gatwich, the JIU SPLA commander, known to oppose the integration, fired three shots in the air in the vicinity of the integration (possibly as a signal), after which the largely Dinka SPLA soldiers began firing wildly and scattered Gabriel's forces. As a result, an estimated 400–500 soldiers and civilians were killed by the rampaging SPLA soldiers. About 2,000 of those not killed or lost were rounded up by Gabriel, who asked that the integration continue. However, Gabriel and his two fellow officers were arrested and taken to Juba. About 300 of Gabriel's soldiers were taken to Ramshel near Juba for integration, and an estimated 2,000 soldiers, most of whom still possessed their weapons, were placed at Papeei near Dolip Hill, south of Malakal on the Sobat river, where they waited until the SPLA high command decided their fate.

As dangerous as these dissident SPLA generals were to the government, there were more Nuer leaders capable of mobilizing an almost unlimited number of discontented youth from the cattle camps standing in the wings, and beyond them were the equally discontented youth in the Western diaspora. These youth, sometimes directed by frustrated politicians and military officers, but just as often under local leadership, repeatedly demonstrated their capacity to challenge and defeat local contingents of the SPLA. In the aftermath of the signing of the CPA, an irregular or 'White Army' of the Lou Nuer youth of Jongeli refused to give up their weapons when taking their cattle into a Dinka area, the upshot of which was a series of confrontations with the SPLA, which ultimately led to the defeat of the White Army and its retreat to an area south of Malakal, but not before hundreds of SPLA soldiers had been killed.[10] In eastern Upper Nile the Jikany Nuer of Nasir have long had a conflictual relationship with the Lou Nuer of Akobo to the south. In the interest of protecting their stock they established a militia linked to the local commissioner, Major General and former SSDF leader, Garouth Gatkouth. After this organization concluded that a SPLA-guarded UN convoy moving along the

Sobat river from Malakal to Nasir and on to Akobo carried arms to
their enemies, they killed dozens in the army and forced it to retreat
and bring back all its detachments in the county to Nasir. The
cattle camp youth subsequently agreed to disarm and Gatkouth
was removed from his commissionership, but it demonstrated the
potential of the disaffected youth of the cattle camps.

The South Sudan Liberation Army posed the most serious
military threat to the southern government, but it was by no
means the only one. Lt General George Athor (rtd) launched
a rebellion in the wake of his failed attempt to remove SPLM
strongman Kuol Manyang from the governorship of Jonglei in
the April 2010 elections. Athor demanded a ceasefire followed
by supervised elections, the integration of his forces into the
SPLA, and compensation for those abused by the government. He
said that 'after coming to power the SPLM/A lost its values and
became a police state' (telephone interview, 3 July 2011). Athor's
rebellion was also seen as a challenge to Gier Chaung Aluong,
SPLM minister of the interior and a Dinka section leader. Like
Gadet, Athor was able to mobilize some discontented military
officers, but his primary basis of support was among the Lou
Nuer, who had been forcibly disarmed by the SPLA and were
in search of weapons to protect themselves and their cattle from
the neighboring Murle tribe. Athor reputedly issued his soldiers
with two guns apiece, one for personal use and one to be sent
to their family, because he knew that protection of the family
and cattle was the primary reason they had joined his army. A
number of SPLA expeditions sent to defeat Athor were either
defeated or could not find him. In October 2010 President Salva
Kiir announced a pardon for all rebels; Athor entered talks with
various intermediaries, but the process broke down after the
SPLA attacked his forces.

In late February 2010 Athor's forces attacked and captured
from the SPLA Pom El Zeraf (sometimes called New Fanjak) in

north-east Jonglei state; a large number of civilians were killed. More were killed the next day when the SPLA retook the town. Local anger was directed at both Athor for the attack and at the SPLA for not providing adequate protection. Despite this attack Salva renewed his offer of a pardon. However, only a few days later, while moving through a designated ceasefire corridor and in the company of church mediators, George Athor's forces were again attacked by the SPLA. His problems were compounded when at the end of the dry season in May many of his Lou Nuer forces deserted him to participate in raids against the Murle, but with the onset of rains an undetermined number returned. And with their return, fighting became intense in the Ayod area of central Jonglei, where the SPLA carried out a campaign similar to that in Mayom, involving human rights abuses, polluting of wells, burning of villages, and rape.

Meanwhile, Murle fighters of another aggrieved candidate from the April elections, David Yau Yau, launched a rebellion from the south-east corner of Jonglei. Again there were reports of attacks on SPLA installations and broken ceasefires. Crucial to this conflict was Sultan Ismael Konyi, paramount chief of the Murle, former major general in the SSDF, and a presidential adviser in the GoSS. The Murle were never successfully integrated into the SPLA or completely disarmed, and there were suspicions that Ismael was not committed to these projects and might still have links with Khartoum, which he frequently visited. The Murle numbered only 150,000 in the last census, but their proclivity for raiding and child abductions terrified a wide area of Jonglei, Upper Nile, and beyond. However, on the eve of independence David Yau Yau signed an agreement with the GoSS that called for an immediate ceasefire, the reintegration of his forces into the SPLA, and the establishment of a joint committee to consider power-sharing issues – although that committee never material-ized (*Alahdath*, 15 June 2011). The fact that Sultan Ismael Konyi signed the agreement on behalf of the GoSS gave reason to believe it might stick.

The SPLA also faced challenges in Upper Nile from Shilluk militias that formed to defend their land from Dinka interlopers who had launched a campaign to remove the tribe from the east bank of the Nile and even from Malakal in 2009, areas which had long been seen as part of the Shilluk homeland. Fighting had waxed and waned for two years, with the Shilluk being the principal victims as the Dinkas were supported by elements in the SPLA. This led to Shilluk defections from the SPLA and other security agencies, including that of Robert Gwang, but on 27 August 2010 he signed the Fashoda Agreement, which called for a ceasefire, reintegration into the SPLA, and a commitment to reach agreement on internal tribal borders. In the event, a ceasefire held, but it took five months to carry out the reintegration, as a result of which his deputy, Johnson Olony, and his followers left. Nor was the commitment to internal border demarcation carried out – a responsibility of Riek Machar and a source of contention and potential violence in many parts of south Sudan.

Olony had been a fighter in Lam Akol's SPLM–United, but left years previously and became a trader in Canal on the banks of the Sobat south of Malakal. When the Dinka–Shilluk war broke out he was displaced from Canal and lost all his property; thus the events that followed may have been due to a desire for revenge. Olony returned to the integration process at Dur, a village 8 kilometers south-west of Malakal, but a conflict broke out in which the largely Dinka-manned SPLA attacked Olony's forces; sixty people were estimated to have been killed and 7,000 civilians were dislocated. Olony's forces then went on to attack Malakal in the early morning of 12 March, reaching the center of the town before being forced to retreat. According to Human Rights Watch, a further forty-five soldiers and rebels were killed in that fighting. Olony's ability to attack Malakal successfully was attributed to the fact that most SPLA forces at the time had been sent to the Pom El Zeraf and Khor-Fulus to fight George Athor. After the attack many Shilluk were arrested, beaten, and accused of being members of SPLM–DC.

Pagan Amum, secretary general of the SPLM, minister of peace, and a Shilluk, stated categorically that Olony was an agent of SPLM–DC, a claim that led Lam Akol to demand that Pagan give up his parliamentary immunity so he could be sued. In a meeting with the author in Khartoum, Olony denied any linkages with Lam and instead said that he held the position of chief of staff under Athor.[11] Pagan and the other senior SPLM Shilluk are isolated in the state, where despite rigging all of the Shilluk seats in the April elections were won by SPLM–DC candidates. It is also clear that the Shilluk voted massively against the official SPLM candidate for governor of Upper Nile, Simon Kunn, who it was widely believed only acquired his position due to the personal intervention of Salva and considerable rigging. The real winner was considered to be Gatlauk Deng, who had twice before served as the NCP governor of the state and who in April 2010 ran as an independent.

The Dinka are of a different order to the Equatorians and Nuer of Greater Upper Nile and might be expected to follow a government led by one of their own and which included many from their tribe. But reports from Greater Bahr el Ghazal and the Dinka-inhabited south-west Jonglei suggest a more complex picture. The failure of the SPLA to maintain security, the lack of jobs and development, and a host of local-level grievances, such as the jailing of young men for impregnating young women in Lakes state, all contributed to Dinka anger. The Dinka are prone to sectional fighting, and May and June 2011 witnessed another such round that even reached into the town of Rumbek and involved the killing of women and children in revenge. By 2010 cattle raiding throughout Dinkaland became endemic. Although long at the center of SPLM/A politics under Garang, the Bor Dinka contended they were passed over by Salva's Warrap countrymen, particularly in the distribution of cabinet seats in the post-9 July government. Despite this contention, few Dinka in Warrap and the other states in Greater Bahr el Ghazal were motivated by the armed struggle of fellow tribesman George Athor in Jonglei.

Nor were they moved by the announced rebellion of the aging Dinka Sultan Abdu al-Baqi Akol from his home in Merim in Southern Kordofan, supposedly because of anger over the mistreatment of Muslims by the SPLM in southern Sudan. Abdu al-Baqi had fought Anyanya in the 1960s, the SPLA in the 1980s and 1990s, was a member of the SSDF after its formation in 1997, became a deputy to Paulino Matieb, and joined the GoSS as a presidential adviser on 17 May 2007 to resolve conflicts between tribes living in the border areas of Darfur and Southern Kordofan (a curious assignment since neither territory was in southern Sudan). He was subsequently dismissed because – he claimed – he criticized the binge drinking in the SPLM/A and for saying that 'a country where bars are everywhere is a cursed one.' As a result he was accused of wanting to introduce sharia in the south (*Sudan Vision*, 3 July 2011). Abdu al-Baqi had sixty-seven wives (all Dinkas); so his sons virtually constituted an army on their own, although they appeared evenly split between the SPLA and SAF. His forces were led by his son Hassan, a devotee of Turabi. In any case his supposed rebellion did not get far and he soon made his peace with the SPLM.

The migration routes of pastoralists in Greater Upper Nile and Greater Bahr el Ghazal normally see an increase in violence during the grazing season and particularly at its end, when pastoralists no longer need to get along with their typically suspicious hosts. But the increased conflict in Jonglei and Greater Bahr el Ghazal in the final weeks of the peace process appeared to be influenced by a different set of factors. Insecurity in the north–south border areas and the resulting movement of large numbers of SPLA soldiers to areas of potential conflict with SAF would upset local communities. The NCP blockade on fuel and food to the south created artificial shortages and soaring prices, and this too would be destabilizing. There were also local conditions that fostered violence.

But also significant was the impact the insurgencies had on neighboring areas. In particular, Athor's arming of the Lou Nuer had the entirely predictable result that they turned their weapons on the Murle; but what was not expected was the scale of the cattle raiding, in which tens of thousands of cattle were stolen and hundreds of Nuer and Murle were killed in fighting. These rebellions had a number of first-order causes: the illegitimate, weak, and ineffectual governance of the SPLM, particularly at the state level; the corruption and mismanagement of the SPLA; the inability of the SPLA to provide security for the civilian population once armed groups were demobilized or disarmed; and the reality that ambitious soldiers and frustrated politicians found it all too easy to go to the bush and raise armies among the large pool of unemployed and disaffected young men whose options were so limited that recruitment into armies or receiving benefits from being demobilized was the best option in the circumstances.

The majority of soldiers in the rebellions at the end of the peace process were Nuer of Greater Upper Nile. This reflected a greater sense of grievance, which gave their struggle a level of unity. However, the Nuer culture is fractious, and typically if they are able to come together to pursue a particular objective it will only be for short periods before they start to feud among themselves. But the biggest danger posed by the Nuer struggle was that, since 'Dinka domination' was their key rallying cry, they could well find themselves in a war with the Dinka. This occurred in the 1990s and the results were horrifying; probably more people were killed in that conflict than in the north–south war, and that prospect was again on the horizon.

Without any consultation with his colleagues Gadet entered into talks with the government in Nairobi on 3 August, which continued in Juba; an agreement on a ceasefire was reached in principle, after which his forces began assembling in Kaikang, Mayom county. It was further agreed that the forces would be moved to Mapel, an SPLA training base in Western Bahr el Ghazal, where they would be integrated. According to estimates made available to the author, these forces numbered between 500 and 600, including non-combatants who accompanied them. At the beginning of 2012 Gadet was still a guest of the government at the Regency Hotel in Juba, while his forces were still awaiting integration in Mapel and refused to be disarmed until ranks and assignments had been allocated. In September forces of Gatluak Gai and Gabriel Tangyangi joined those of Gadet in Mapel. There was little doubt that the delay in integration was due to the opposition of SPLA chief of staff James Hoth Mai and other senior officers, who feared that integration of unreliable soldiers undermined the capacity of the army. The same people obstructed the integration of the SSDF after the Juba Declaration in 2006 for the same reasons.

As well as the integration, Gadet said that Salva agreed to the establishment of a joint political committee that would address national ills, including corruption.[12] However, there was no written agreement and no political committee was ever established, none of Gadet's allies have been appointed to the government, he has not returned to the army, and there was an ongoing threat that the approximately 1,700 soldiers waiting to be integrated at Mapel would sooner or later end up in a fight with the SPLA.

The biggest flaw of the process is that it did not end the insurgency in Unity state since most of the SSLA forces remained intact and Lt General James Gai Yeach assumed command with

Babiny Monytuil as his deputy. In early November 1,000 soldiers from this force briefly captured Mayom and in the following weeks moved widely in the northern half of Unity state, home to most of South Sudan's oilfields. Despite their limited numbers they were able to operate because of the cooperation of local chiefs and cattle herders and dissent in SPLA forces unwilling to risk their lives to defend the widely hated regime of Taban Deng. Although at the end of 2011 the SSLA had not captured its principal target of Bentiu, the SPLA had proved incapable of overcoming them and the contest was far from settled. While the rebels denied it, there were reliable reports that the SSLA was forcibly conscripting South Sudanese youth, and not just Nuer, in Khartoum and other centers for the next round of attacks in Unity state.

After Gadet's submission to the GoSS the remaining SSLA leadership appeared committed to achieving substantial military victories before considering negotiations with Juba. Not so Athor, who with the intervention of Meridith Preston from the Geneva-based INGO Humanitarian Dialogue convinced him to come to Nairobi in mid-November for two days of meetings with security officials from President Salva Kiir's office. However, Athor's demands for senior positions in the GoSS, compensation for those who had suffered as a result of war in Jonglei, dismissal of the Jonglei state government, and agreement on early national elections were rejected. Despite this, Athor declared 'I am prepared to resume negotiations at any time' and did not rule out the possibility of them again being held in Nairobi (telephone interview, 20 November 2011). Three weeks later Athor told me that 'Kenyans cannot be trusted as they can always be bought' and said he was looking for a suitable third-party mediator (interview, 10 December 2011).

The failure of the negotiations was held up by the GoSS as a political victory in so far as the rebels demonstrated their internal divisions and the SSLA leadership was furious with Athor, whose actions had also set back their efforts to form one united rebel organization under a single leadership. And given the fact that Athor was a Dinka and the large majority of his forces were Nuers he was not deemed a suitable overall leader. Indeed, one SSLA leader told the author, 'If the NCP tries to impose Athor on us as leader, we would prefer Salva,' while another Nuer rebel said that having a Dinka leading a Nuer army 'would leave Salva laughing.'

It became clear that the preferred candidate of the SSLA for leader of the proposed united organization of rebels was Gordon Buay. a bright young law student in Ottawa who served as the spokesperson for the organization. Buay's rise in stature was related to a number of factors: he is a Nuer from Nasser in eastern Upper Nile, which some held had not received its due among the leadership, is educated, fluent in English, did not come from the military, and crucially was from the Nuer diaspora which was exerting increasing influence on political developments in South Sudan. Moreover, by late 2011 this largely North American-based Nuer diaspora (and the Nuer form the largest group of South Sudan's diaspora) was becoming increasingly radicalized. The majority of the Nuer diaspora supported the Lou 'White Army' because of resentment at the government's disarmament policies, which they contended left them vulnerable to their neighbors, the Murle, particularly after the attack on their community in August 2011 – itself in retaliation for a Lou attack in June – in which an estimated 700 people were killed, dozens abducted, and tens of thousands of cattle stolen. Meanwhile, a minority concluded that the SPLM could not be reformed and that the interests of the Nuer could only be realized by overthrowing the government and thus – like Gordon Buay – joining the rebels.

James Nuot Puot, spokesperson for the SSDA and another member of the diaspora based in Khartoum, reported that on 12

December the organization's security officials had uncovered an SPLA plot to assassinate Athor in Khartoum and those involved were being held by the Government of Sudan (telephone interview, 17 December 2011). However, to hide the fact that Athor was in Khartoum it was announced in a subsequent press release that the plot took place in his home area of Khorflus in Jonglei state. Although some doubted that there was any plot, on 21 December Athor was killed, along with Thomas Duoth, a US citizen and member of the SSLA. My investigations revealed that Ugandan officials first approached Athor during his negotiations with the SPLM in Nairobi and told him that Museveni wanted to meet him one-on-one in Kampala (they had met on two occasions before in Athor's capacity as SPLA deputy chief of staff), an invitation that was repeated in the following weeks. James Puot said that both he and the Sudanese security forces urged Athor not to go, but he insisted. Under the arrangements proposed by the Ugandans he flew to Kigali to hide his ultimate destination and from there took a car to Kampala (telephone interview, 21 December 2011). Almost certainly he and Duoth were shot dead by the security forces of Uganda's President Museveni while sleeping in a Kampala hotel and their bodies turned over to the SPLA, although there is a remote possibility that they were taken to the Ugandan–South Sudan border and handed over to the SPLA, which made the unlikely claim that they were killed while trying to launch a two-person rebellion on 19 December in Morobo county of Central Equatoria.

According to James Puot, 'Killing Athor will not bring peace because the SPLA has only managed to cut off a top branch and hasn't touched the roots of the problem' (telephone interview, 21 December 2011). While there was considerable public rejoicing in GoSS circles, the rebels said that without Athor their objective of achieving unity would be easier and that there was now no possibility of any negotiations in East Africa or without a strong mediator. The immediate impact of Athor's death was to increase insecurity in Juba, already suffering from a crime wave – which Governor Clement Wani attributed to the police – and where it was feared that Athor's relatives and friends might launch revenge attacks. In any case the rejoicing did not last long: on 23 December 2011 the Lou Nuer 'White Army' launched a massive attack on the Murle. Following the Murle attack on the Lou in August a revenge attack was in the offing and in response the government, UN, and churches conducted a wide-ranging reconciliation process. In addition, both the GoSS and the UN sent forces to Pibor to protect civilians. But the peace process broke down and the armed presence in the Murle land did not dissuade the Lou, and by early December an attack was expected.

Not expected was the scale of the attack, which involved 6,000 well-armed Lou youth (largely armed by Athor, although the SSDA wanted the Lou to fight the government, not the Murle) together with smaller numbers of Jikany Nuer, Gawaar Nuer, and Twic Dinka from Bor. In the following two weeks the Murle commissioner of Pibor claimed the attack had displaced 100,000 and killed more than 3,000 Murle, burned down most of the settled areas in the district, and captured 80,000 cattle, although many thought these figures were too high since most of the Murle youth were able to flee to the bush with their cattle.[13] The rationale for the attack was clearly spelled out in a blood-curdling press release that was datelined Akobo, Jonglei, but almost certainly was prepared by the Nuer diaspora in the US. It said:

> Since the very government which disarmed the civilians in 2006 failed to protect the Nuer from from Murle, the Nuer Youth have decided to protect their livelihood from Murle. To do so, we have decided to invade Murleland and wipe out the entire Murle tribe on the face of the earth as the only solution to guarantee long-term security of Nuer's cattle. There is no other way to resolve Murle

problem other than wiping them out through the barrel of the gun.[14]

To his credit Vice President Riek Machar rushed to the scene and at considerable risk tried to convince the Lou youth to desist, but he was ignored, just as he was by his fellow Nuer rebels. Salva Kiir, meanwhile, spent most of this period visiting his home area in Warrap, only later returning. In a statement on South Sudan Television he claimed there were high rates of venereal disease among the Murle which led to low birth rates, causing the tribe to abduct children from their neighbors.[15] The SPLA made a token effort at confronting the White Army, but it was clear that most of its soldiers did not want to fight the Lou, probably many of them agreed with their objectives, and significant numbers assisted or joined the White Army. Meanwhile in Pibor the SPLA and UN forces stood aside and did not interfere while the White Army burned down the town and killed any youth and others they could find. The Nuer youth also claimed to have freed some captured children. The statements issued later by the GoSS and UN congratulating themselves for their efforts, attributing their failures to a lack of resources, and claiming they forced the White Army to leave were self-serving and unconvincing. At the height of the White Army attack all the UN could do was to advise the Murle to 'Run for your lives!' In the event, the White Army was not chased away by either the SPLA or the UN, but left to its own devices, after its leaders concluded that its objectives had been realized. *The Times* placed little responsibility on the GoSS, which it dismissed as a 'failed state,' and instead concluded that 'The UN has failed in its most elemental task: preventing war, saving lives and halting violence. It is a disgrace and worse, a familiar one' (Editorial, 16 January 2012).

The response of the government was to call for another round of disarmament, a policy which had repeatedly been attempted and failed, and in fact had led directly to the most recent disaster. With UN support the SPLA conducted a massive disarmament campaign in Jonglei in 2006, which again led to the rise of the White Army and clashes between it and the SPLA. In the end the SPLA stopped its campaign before disarming the Murle, with the inevitable result that the Murle used their advantage in arms to attack their neighbors. I traveled widely in Jonglei in 2006 and everywhere people told me they would willingly hand over their weapons to the SPLA if it could guarantee their security and assure them that all the tribes were similarily disarmed.[16] But the SPLA could not provide security and the other tribes had little option but to sell some of their cattle and acquire weapons to defend themselves, thus setting off another round of tribal fighting. And I was in Jonglei again in 2009 to witness another SPLA disarmament campaign, which had the same disastrous oucome. Indeed, the failure of that campaign provided the opening for Athor to develop relations with the Lou by providing them with weapons. Despite this record of failure and of the White Army onslaught on the Murle, the SPLM government again recommended a policy of disarmament.

The southern rebels who had not been able to mobilize the independent-minded Lou cattle herders and their allies and had never mobilized such an effective force on their own were nonetheless delighted at both the achievements of the White Army and the prospect of the SPLA trying to disarm them. SSLA deputy leader Major General Babiny Monytuil said: 'Salva declared war on the Lou and if the SPLA fights the Lou they will come to the SSLA' (telephone interview, 5 January 2012), while another rebel leader observed that if the SPLA tries to disarm the Lou, 'the rebels will be dancing.' Gai Bol, the North American representative of the White Army, noted that 'The White Army has no links or relations with the rebels and is not involved in a rebellion against the government,' although he also acknowledged that 'the fight of the White Army was benefiting the rebels' (telephone interview, 5 January 2012). There was also no evidence of Khartoum support for the White Army. Despite its gruesome threat to wipe out the entire Murle tribe, the White Army was not the same force that had fought with Riek Machar in his horrific attack on Bor in 1991, and perhaps not even the same as the White Army that fought an ultimately losing battle against the SPLA in 2006. According to Gordon Buay,

> the White Army is linked to a global environment where they have cellphones and want to acquire Western goods and are increasingly no longer satisfied with life as cattle herders ... the rebels can convince them that the only way their cattle can be protected, their areas experience development, and they acquire desired posses-sions is to direct their military skills to political ends and the overthrow of the government. (telephone interview, 5 January 2012)

Even while the White Army fighters were taking their ac-cumulated loot and cattle home, Murle in the SPLA and South Sudan Police Force began defecting and launching revenge attacks on Lou civilians, in which dozens were killed. David Yau Yau, a Murle and former teacher, who had launched a rebellion and later reached an agreement with the government, also defected and with his followers headed to Boma in south-east Jonglei. There were also reports of Taposa and members of other tribes that usually aligned with the Murle leaving the SPLA and heading to their home areas. The SPLA had never succeeded in overcom-ing the tribal identities of its soldiers and developing a national ethos, and as a result the army often operated as a collection of militias and warring factions whose members were more loyal to their tribe or individual leaders than to the SPLA hierarchy. As a result, the SPLA was more likely to exacerbate local conflicts than bring them to a satisfactory end.

While the disorder in Greater Upper Nile stood out, law-lessness, cattle rustling, and revenge killings were common in

Greater Bahr el Ghazal. There were also indications that dissent was rising in hitherto secure areas. Thus Peter Sule, a veteran Bari politician from Central Equatoria, attempted – and failed disastrously – to launch an armed struggle in Western Equatoria, and Major-General Tong Lual Ayat, a Dinka from Northern Bahr el Ghazal and leader of the tiny United Democratic Party, launched what he called the South Sudan People's Liberation Movement with – he claimed – 5,000 soldiers (telephone interview, 29 December 2011), although few took him seriously. Nonetheless, only half a year after gaining independence the SPLM-led South Sudan looked distinctly fragile and the threat of internal disorder looked even more daunting than that posed by Khartoum, although the two were clearly linked. Still, the GoSS gained a measure of confidence from the curiously timed announcement by President Obama that he had approved the sale of weapons to South Sudan.[17] This decision was followed up by another Obama decree to send five senior US soldiers to South Sudan to help the UN, which Freeman said involved 'militarizing US relations with South Sudan' and also drew attention to US hypocrisy in that the justification for sending these soldiers was that they could not be prosecuted by the ICC since South Sudan was not a member – this of course at a time when the US was pressing the GoS to reach an agreement with the same ICC over charges against President al-Bashir.[18]

The objectives of the NCP were never clear: whether it wanted to increase its bargaining position with respect to the post-referendum issues and ensure a continuing weak GoSS, or endeavor to overthrow the SPLM government. The conclusive referendum vote and the NCP's acceptance of it meant that the independence of southern Sudan could not be denied, so the only reason to support the overthrow of the SPLM government was to have it replaced by others whom the NCP would find easier to deal with. That was certainly a possibility, and objectives can sometimes change with bewildering speed in Sudan, but on balance at the end of the peace process it seemed most likely that the NCP wanted to use its proxies as counterweights to those of the SPLM, keep the southern government preoccupied with security concerns for probably the indefinite future, and press for agreement on a range of outstanding post-referendum issues. But the NCP is both pragmatic and opportunist, and if it appeared that it could assist in bringing about the collapse of the SPLM government without too much financial or political cost to itself, then it would probably not face much internal opposition to going all the way.

Building an Economy of Dependency

South Sudan became independent with 98 percent of its government income of $1 billion a year coming from oil revenues. It had done nothing during twenty-two years of armed struggle and six and a half years in government to develop alternative revenue sources or restructure the economy. The problem was particularly severe in the Nilotic-inhabited communities. These suffered from almost total reliance on traditional forms of cattle-raising that were not only unproductive but directly responsible for the steady growth of cattle theft and violent conflict between the pastoralists, which the SPLA had been completely unsuccessful in containing since the peace agreement. The oil industry encouraged an already deeply entrenched corruption, furthered income inequalities in a society that had until very recently been highly egalitarian, produced growing environmental problems, and made the government dependent on rents instead of taxes. Moreover, if foreign experience is a guide, oil-dependent states have inflated currencies, which undermine local industry and agriculture, and spend vastly more on their military than non-oil-producing states. Indeed, more than 40 percent of government expenditures were directed to the security services.

Faced with these conditions, government economic policies were directed at buying support through the provision of jobs (i.e. assuming the role of 'jobbists' that the 1983 SPLM Manifesto had criticized Anyanya for), to the extent that it was estimated that 77 percent of revenues went to paying salaries, which left little for actual development programming. The RoSS National Assembly had set the course by absorbing southern members from the Khartoum Assembly and Council of Ministers, thus making the southern government one of the largest in the world for its population. Patrimonialism had replaced New Sudan as the ruling ideology of the SPLM.

The government looked to foreign investment to meet its infrastructural needs, for service delivery, and to assume the leading role in development. According to Vice President Riek Machar, the facilities paid for and built by investors would be handed over to the government within an agreed period of time. Riek declared, 'We will raise 500 billion dollars from private investments in the next five years to build this nation to catch up with the rest of the world in infrastructure development' (*Sudan Tribune*, 2 July 2011). In this light the Council of Ministers meeting passed the Investment Promotion Act Bill 2011 and the Taxation Act Bill 2011 to make the environment 'conducive for potential investors.'

Evidence of the government's economic philosophy could also be seen in its approval of the selling or leasing of state resources, principally land. According to a study by the Norwegian People's Aid, the international NGO closest to the SPLA during the war, the government had sold 9 percent of its land to foreign investors by the time of independence. Some 2.6 million hectares were supposed to be used for establishing agricultural projects, the generation of biofuels, and the establishment of forests. The study found that the land was sold at nominal prices, sometimes as low as four pennies a hectare.

It was not surprising that a party–army which had spent its entire existence in dependent political relationships and never demonstrated concern for southern autonomy apart from being rid of the *jallaba* would look to complementary dependent economic policies to build the new country of South Sudan.

Regime Change in the North?

On 30 January 2011 demonstrations organized by various youth organizations swept the three towns of Khartoum, various universities, and other northern towns to correspond with the release of the preliminary results of the southern referendum. Demonstrators who had organized online social networking sites modeled on the Tunisian protests the month before called on Bashir to resign and for regime change. They also chanted, 'No to high prices, no to corruption' and 'Tunisia, Egypt, Sudan together as one.' Dozens of students were arrested, including a number of children of Sudan's political elite; one later died; and there were reports of torture and sexual abuse of those arrested on a scale never heard of before in northern Sudan. Periodic youth-organized demonstrations continued into May in northern Sudan and Darfur, but the northern opposition parties largely stayed aloof and only helped with communications and the provision of legal assistance for those arrested and medical help for those injured.

The Facebook core of the demonstrations involved a fringe of radical university students, many whom had not previously taken an active role in politics, as well as other 'youth,' an elastic term in Sudan which can encompass people aged from 15 to 40. In the past Sudanese universities were often centers of rebellion, but under the NCP, which considerably expanded their numbers, they were Islamized and become instruments of government control. As a result most university student unions are led by the NCP, sometimes as a result of generally free elections. Thus the universities were not a natural base for revolt as was the case in Tunisia and Egypt. Some students from areas of political discontent – southern Blue Nile, Nuba Mountains, eastern Sudan, and Darfur – were potentially receptive to radically challenging the government and had a greater proclivity for violence. That was evident in the wake of the riots after John Garang died, which were dominated by youth from Darfur and the Nuba Mountains. There were also a minority of students and youth from the riverine core who were inspired by the unfolding events in Tunisia and particularly Egypt. Like their northern counterparts Sudanese youth had to overcome their natural fears in the face of a government that would not limit its use of violence against unarmed protestors, and unlike the Egyptians they are not imbued with the same deep hatred of the government and the security forces. Beyond these privileged youth were the lumpen youth of Khartoum and other towns – poor, unemployed, and with few prospects – who may have little political understanding, but who also have little to lose and could be drawn into popular struggles, although by the beginning of 2012 they had not been.

While the political parties did not initiate, much less lead, the demonstrations, to some extent they used them as a cat's paw to test the attitudes of Sudanese and their willingness to challenge the regime. Among the parties only two could be considered fully committed to a popular uprising – the PCP and the SCP, both of which had small memberships and limited appeal among the general population. Communism is equated with atheism for most Sudanese and thus abhorred, while the PCP is equated with Turabi, who remained the most hated person in the country. Nonetheless, the two parties have organizational capacity and clearer ideological visions than the other opposition parties. As a result, both were the focus of government harassment and arrests, especially the PCP. Indeed, there was an abiding fear in NCP

circles that since Turabi and some of his colleagues had selected
and led many among the current leadership in the security and
intelligence services, they could have 'sleepers' who could be
called upon to oppose the regime if the time was deemed right.
Few forgot that the NCP was unable to use its army to confront
the JEM attack on Omdurman in 2008 and instead relied on the
NISS forces of Salah Gosh. There were many explanations for
the absence of the army, but the most widely held was that the
NCP feared some of its key officers were under the influence of
Turabi. Ibrahim Sanousi, Turabi's first lieutenant, was correct
to conclude 'The opposition is weak because the government
divided the parties and their leaders were not prepared to go
to jail' (interview, 15 March 2011). The one exception was the
elderly SCP leader Ibrahim Nugud, who alone among the party
leaders went to the streets. He attend a demonstration in central
Khartoum for about one minute – long enough to have his picture
taken – before being arrested.

The capacity of the security forces to arrest protestors quickly,
use extreme brutality, and successfully infiltrate social network
sites, and the fact that participation on these sites was much
smaller than similar sites in Tunisia and Egypt, all partly explain
the failure of the demonstrations to mobilize more people. The
lack of commitment to them by the opposition parties, some of
whom still hoped to head off a popular uprising through negotiations with the NCP, is another. Even for those who favored an
intifada, there were doubts about the timing. Some feared that
the NCP wanted to precipitate an early uprising that could be put
down before it gathered steam. Others wanted the government
thoroughly discredited by the departure of the south and did not
want to be seen as interfering with the peace process.

During the years of Islamist rule many northern Sudanese
became disillusioned and lost their faith in politics, their country,
and most of all their leaders, while the youth have known nothing

but the NCP, have little knowledge of the combative traditions of the generation that preceded them, and are struggling to come to grips with the turmoil in their midst and in the Greater Middle East and chart their own course. The leaders of the Umma and Democratic Unionist Parties have had their day and failed, Turabi's Popular Congress Party is rightly held by most northern Sudanese as the ultimate cause of Sudan's disintegration, while the Communist Party is reduced to making alliances with a largely discredited SPLM.

Confusion in the northern sector of the SPLM was another reason for the weak response to the appeals for a popular uprising in 2011. While elements in the party led by Yasir Arman wanted to make common cause with other opposition forces, he was stymied by the southern sector of the SPLM, which wanted stability to ensure the realization of the peace process and by his immediate leader, Malik Agar Eyre, who distrusted the northern parties and was focused on the popular consultations. On 6 February 2011 Malik told the author that

> The wind of change is blowing. But I don't think it is right for us to engage in this [intifada] now. The northern parties are not confrontational. They've historically relied on SPLM to confront the NCP for them. They've wanted to ride on our backs to the palace. But we realized that if we can carry someone to the palace, why don't we just carry ourselves? But we will go for it if they take the initiative. There is a need for leadership and only the SPLM has the leadership. I don't think we should confront the NCP. The other parties are so weak that they could turn away at any moment.[19]

The SPLM–N had made no plans for the possibility that tensions would arise that would lead to the party's assets being confiscated by the Sudanese security services, or that Yasir Arman would be forced to flee the country, something which the Communist Party had warned about.

Moreover, the party was divided by its loyalties to the south and – like its southern counterpart – had a propensity to look to military solutions to political problems that was not in keeping with the mood of the Sudanese public in the wake of the Arab Spring. This also included the repeated appeals for US military intervention in Sudan by Yasir Arman. Meanwhile, the SPLM–North's call for regime change were made by Malik and Abdel Aziz, who were protected by their armies and by Yasir outside Sudan, while party members in the country were never consulted. One NCP official told me, 'Yasir wanted to have a foothold in the north, another Benghazi, and get supplies from the south and perhaps Uganda.'

A further asset of the regime was that, although relations still remained tense with the US and most of Europe, unlike in the 1990s Sudan was no longer isolated in the region. At the end of the peace process the NCP had cooperative relations with Ethiopia, had reached a breakthrough with Chad's Idris Deby on ending support for one another's proxies that to the surprise of many endured, and still had cordial relations with the mercurial Isias Aferworki of Eritrea. Relations with Egypt were far from clear given its unsettled status, but the NCP welcomed the departure of the Mubarak regime and had high hopes in the growing influence of the Muslim Brothers, with whom it had close relations. Likewise, the NCP gave material support to the opposition in Libya,[20] again because of its hopes that the country's Islamists would do well in a post-Gaddafi government and because Gaddafi had become the foremost supporter of JEM. While the popular uprisings that spread across the Middle East in 2011 caused more than a shiver down the spines of NCP leaders, they felt – as they often did – that if they could just weather the present political storms the broader regional currents were with them and the regime would come out of its crises stronger than ever. But probably most significant, according to the SPLM's

Monsour Khalid, 'was the weakness of the regime's opponents,' which he said were the most ineffective he had seen in his lifetime (interview, 22 October 2011).

The NCP insisted that conditions in Sudan could not be compared to Tunisia and Egypt, although the leading intellectual and reformist in the party, Dr Ghazi Salhudin, found in these developments 'an impetus to the cause of democracy' and wrote,

> In the past it was generally held that the so called ideological parties [presumably including the NIF/NCP] have conspired against democratic regimes, in favour of their own parochial views on government and society. This may be changing – there are no unequivocal statements of adherence to democracy by all, including the rising Islamist parties which will go a big way towards stabilizing and entrenching democracy in the region and in Sudan.[21]

In particular, Dr Ghazi contended that the fact that Islamists were coming to power through democratic elections in the Arab world will reassure Sudan's Islamists. Against a background of continuing arrests of politicians and human rights activists, and the closure of newspapers, progress toward achieving democracy was not in evidence.

Meanwhile, efforts were made to render the regime immune to the changes sweeping the region. In September 2011 the 67-year-old Bashir announced he would not run for president again and appeared to endorse calls for a cut-off age of 60 for presidential candidates. The party reinvigorated its work with youth groups, who were supplied with material and human resources, and took up the cause of the government by finding them employment and even providing jobs, organizing social activities, and developing a focus for their interests, all so that reforms could be made to the system without the convulsions that were under way in the Middle East.[22] As evidenced by the attitudes of many Western diplomats, the NCP was also successful in presenting itself as a party of moderation. Sadig al-Mahdi commented: 'The NCP uses Mubarak's tactic of saying that if you reject us you will get the extremists and as a result the only organized political party in Egypt is the Muslim Brothers' (interview, 27 December 2010). Another approach of the regime was for younger people to be appointed to ministerial and other positions. One such appointment that received a lot of attention in the Khartoum media was that of Sane Hamid as the state minister of information. At 31, with an academic background, and a self-described 'liberal Islamist' she represented the new image the NCP was trying to present to the world. While often critical of decision-making in the NCP she made clear that there were red lines that she could not cross with respect to party policies, and the political positions and the values she espoused were not much different to those of the mainstream party. As a result, the NCP not only faced the challenge of the opposition; it also had to decide to what extent it would respond to the growing pressure from its own members demanding reforms.

The NCP, a Broad-based Government, and Constitution-making

NCP efforts at constitution construction and the formation of a broad-based government were designed to reconnect with a constituency disenchanted with the CPA and international intervention in the country, and to share some of the responsibility for the disaster of southern secession and thus protect itself from the radical national and regional currents. But getting the balance right would not be easy. Pleasing supporters who wanted a clearly Islamist constitution and policies did not mesh with efforts to lure into government the soft Islamists of the Umma Party and DUP, who needed a range of concessions to appease their supporters. Barring these concessions, the more radical elements in these parties favored working with the National Consensus Forces to press for an intifada.

The negotiations became a higher priority for the ruling party in the wake of the southern vote for secession and Sadig al-Mahdi's threat to join those calling for regime change if he could not reach agreement with the NCP. From the outset the secretary general of the NUP, Siddeeg Mohammed Ismail, led the negotiations and was its most avid supporter. Ismail viewed the negotiations as the last opportunity for the ruling party to have a soft landing, after which the NUP would have no option but to support removing the government through an intifada.[23] What was desired was a democratic constitution that would permit all the parties to participate, achieve good relations with South Sudan, support human rights, create a workable federation, resolve the conflict in Darfur, and agree on a process leading to national elections within three years on the basis of a reconstructed NEC. In mid-March Siddeeg Ismail said that he was 'optimistic' of a successful outcome within a week and expected the process to be finalized with a meeting between Bashir and Sadig. By the end of the peace process there were no agreements between the NCP and the lead opposition parties.

Although both party leaders held out the option of an intifada, in fact the prospect probably gave them more sleepless nights than Bashir and his colleagues, who contended that the NCP was immune to the rebellions sweeping the Arab world because of a supposed liberalization and a decentralization of powers to the states. Sadig and Mirghani desperately wanted to go into the government, but they needed assurances they were not bolstering a dictatorship and thus ensure the support of party members. There was also no doubting the genuine fears of at least Sadig al-Mahdi that the country could go the way of Libya, given the large number of armed groups, including more than a few affiliated with the NCP and possibly some from Islamist groups abroad.

Sadig acknowledged that he might be 'utopian,' but nonetheless hoped for 'an Arab Spring without the violence' (interview, 26 June 2011). But the NCP was not without cards to play. Bashir might prefer to bring the NUP and DUP into the government, but if the price was deemed too high then the NCP could turn the other way and align with – the albeit smaller – Islamist factions such as the Just Peace Forum (JPF) headed by President al-Bashir's uncle and the chief of *al-Intibaha*, al-Tayyib Mustafa, the Wahhabi Ansar al-Sunna, and the Muslim Brothers.

On 2 June Bashir announced that, following the separation of South Sudan, a new constitution for Sudan would be formulated, as part of the 'Second Republic,' that it would be presented in a popular referendum for approval, and that the NCP would work to involve all the Sudanese political forces to formulate it. He linked this to the formation of a 'broad-based government' on the basis of an agenda agreed with other parties. By the end of the peace process the NCP had carried out the necessary technical changes to the constitution; in the post-9 July period the concern would be to reach an agreement on a permanent constitution, which officials claimed would be achieved by November 2011.[24] Lest these proposed changes should suggest weakness, Bashir ruled out early elections, saying that the next one would be held in 2015 as planned. He told the Shura Council that it was the opposition parties that were weak and that the ruling party did not face any real competition.

Interest in the constitution grew steadily in the wake of the referendum and as the end of the peace process approached. This was evidenced by the increasing number of political party and civil-society-led meetings held to consider the best process to examine and debate the constitution and prepare drafts for consideration. Although not as not as clearly formulated as in the south, the more developed civil society in the north quickly and more effectively took up these tasks. As in the south, however, a battle began around the desire of the government to control the process, minimize participation, and achieve particular ends; the opposition parties and civil society, for their part, wanted a lengthy and broad-based process in order to debate the issues thoroughly, educate the public, and make use of the public space provided to press for democratic transformation. But Ghazi Salhudin, the reform-minded NCP leader, was surely correct to write,

> The adage 'There is no democracy without democrats' is true and the parties need to reevaluate their democratic mettle. In the majority of the political parties democratic traditions are fickle. Institutionalization is lacking and the parties rely for their existence, almost exclusively, on the genius and personal talents of their almost immortal leaders.[25]

Since 1956 the typical means by which governments wrote constitutions in Sudan was to form committees and then present their reports to parliament for final resolution, and this includes NCP's 1998 constitution. This constitution was replaced by that of the CPA, which remained in effect until 9 July 2011. The secular CPA-based constitution was hard to stomach for the NCP, even though the agreement on which it was based was a lifeline for the ruling party. With the end of the peace process the old issue of an Islamic-based constitution came to the fore. The NCP used this debate to reconnect with its base and make the case that one of the benefits of the departure of the south was that the north could return to its 'true' Islamic character and be rid of secular ideas popularized by the SPLM and its notions of New Sudan.

The NIF/NCP had long used the constitution as a means to divide and weaken the sectarian parties, knowing how difficult it was for them to be seen to oppose the role of Islam. The Umma Party and DUP wanted to avoid this cul-de-sac by contending that there were other more important issues to address, but it was doubtful that argument would avoid the trap the NCP set for them, in particular their Islamist orientations, which would make unity with the secular opposition virtually impossible. What was different from earlier debates that went nowhere was that they took place in the context of the disastrous loss of the south and amidst wars in Darfur and Southern Kordofan in which the rebelling parties demanded recognition of diversity, and in the case of Abdel Wahid, Abdel Aziz, and Malik specifically advocated secularism. An unrefined secular constitution was politically unrealistic in the circumstances, but the debate did provide an opportunity to educate and mobilize people around different positions.

While the reformist civil society endeavored to use the need for a new constitution to press for a thoroughgoing democracy, the opposition parties were divided, with some following the civil society activists and others using the process to advance their bargaining position for a place in the government. The starting point was to oppose the tried and failed traditional process of constitution construction, and by the end of the peace process many across the political spectrum were calling for a society-wide debate. The primary issues of concern were whether the system should be parliamentary or presidential, the role – if any – of Islam in the constitution, federalism, the powers of the president, and whether the federal units should follow the existing pattern of fifteen states or revert back to the six units originally established by the British colonial authorities. Such a far-reaching debate, it was argued, was consistent with recent international experience.

Civil society and the political parties approached the constitution in much the same spirit as they approached the April 2010 elections, which is to say with marked skepticism, but not wanting to pass up on the opportunity to connect with their memberships and either to push the government to make the desired compromises or – having given the NCP the way out – to direct their energies to organizing a popular uprising. Some in the opposition clearly had their heart set on an uprising, while others saw constitution construction as an instrument not only for mobilization, but also for the society as a whole to develop coherent ideas of what it wanted, including its views on the economy. As one academic put it, this was the best means to ensure the revolution was not hijacked by other groups, as appeared to be the case in Egypt and Tunisia.[26] The unstated fear of the opposition, however, was not only that the NCP government would not budge – indeed, it might not be able to budge given the sentiments of its constituency – but that no one would support the uprising were it called. Indeed, given the disorganization and divisions within the opposition, if an intifada were to take place it would be in spite of the political parties and not because of them.

Although the three opposition Islamic parties – Umma, DUP, and PCP – were still debating their positions at the end of the peace process, there was little doubt they would ultimately support an Islamic-based constitution, either out of conviction or from fear of being labeled anti-Islam by the NCP. Meanwhile, militant Islamists were playing a leading role through the Islamic Constitution Front to the President, the positions they held in the government, and through their use of fatwas to intimidate.

The NCP had created a climate in which even the Sudan Communist Party did not take a clear position in support of secularism and instead called for a hybrid constitution. In any case, the CPA-based constitution in the north identified Islamic sharia and the consensus of the people as the sources of legislation. Only the Republican Brothers endorsed a completely secular constitution, contending that Islam discriminated against Christians and women. Since April 2011 the group had been holding twice-weekly meetings at their headquarters in Omdurman and getting favorable turnouts. (They even held Saturday morning sessions for children.) The Republican Brothers worried that, should the NCP insist on an Islamic-based constitution, secularists like themselves would become victims. Not surprisingly they still had vivid memories of the execution of their founder, Mahmoud Taha, by Turabi and Nimeiri for apostasy and feared that experience could be repeated.[27]

The National Consensus Forces also called for a secular constitution, but in practice this was the position of a number of small leftist parties and independents and would have to be considerably watered down if it was to win the support of the large sectarian parties, whose leaders could not accept a formal commitment to secularism. Meanwhile, the NCF was angered by a group of intellectuals organized by the Friedrich-Ebert-Stiftung, which called for a hybrid constitution. They in turn explained that their desire was for the middle ground: to modify the Islamic nature of the state, and to strengthen the Bill of Rights as a means to emphasize the rights of citizens in the constitution.[28] While the NCP was pressing for Islam to be the sole or major source of legislation, the Umma Party and DUP favored other sources and also wanted a strong Bill of Rights. It was also not lost on anyone that the NCP's version of political Islam had not proved an attractive model for any country anywhere. As a result, groups like the Muslim Brothers modified their position, given the appeal of the Turkish model, which combined notions of Islam with a commitment to democracy.

One area of controversy was the domination of Sudanese banking by the Islamic sector, to which the NCP had long had close links. Some thought this was not a problem because the prohibition of interest payments simply encouraged accountants to find creative ways to make loans without involving interest. The refusal of the south to accept northern Islamic banking led to a wholesale departure of banks, a virtual collapse in the banking sphere, and the subsequent dominance of Kenyan banks.

The issue of banking in turn raised the question of the type of economy desired and the need for both business and union participation in the constitutional debate.

Another area of controversy was over the system of governance, with the NCP preferring a presidential model, while most of the opposition parties favored a parliamentary model, or a hybrid parliamentary-presidential system like that of France. Related to this was the issue of whether the president should be directly or indirectly elected. The opposition parties also opposed the application of *hudud* punishments, which were already in the penal code but rarely practiced. Most of the opposition wanted to have these measures removed and were worried that the NCP wanted to expand their use and to start carrying them out. The specter of Bashir's Gederif speech on the eve of the southern referendum, in which he denied the reality of northern Sudan's diversity and called for a full-fledged Islamization, weighed heavily on the opposition. As a result, some called for a specific acknowledgement of Sudan's diversity.

A major debate was expected over federalism. No one actually opposed federalism, but people contended that it must be another instrument to realize the hopes for democratization, and in particular that it should divide the country's wealth more equitably. Under present arrangements the national government provided subsidies to the states, but without any clear formulas they were based on political criteria and served as a means to reward friends and punish enemies. A decision also had to be made on whether to endorse a parliamentary, a presidential, or a mixed system like the French. Parallel to experience in the south many in the NCP were not happy with the limits placed on the powers of the president and in particular the fact that he had no means to remove governors. It was ironic that on the eve of independence the SSLA endorsed just such powers for President Salva Kiir. Many more felt the need to review center–state fiscal relations thoroughly in light of the experience of the past six and a half years. A decision also had to be made on whether to adopt a winner-takes-all Westminster-type parliamentary system, which – with the exception of periods of military rule – Sudan had used until the CPA, a proportional-based system, or a mixed model based on the CPA, which also reserved 25 percent of seats for women. Unlike in the West, where the dominant discourse delinks democracy from economics, the recent experience in the Middle East and in Sudan was to recognize their intimate connection. Indeed, the NCF specifically requested that the constitution oppose the free market, although that would be a non-starter with the right-wing NCP.

Just as the Juba government was officially committed to federalism but attempted, against considerable opposition, to centralize powers, so in Khartoum the NCP was committed to federalism, but feared that real devolution of powers would undermine its hegemonic control over the country. The armed struggles in Darfur, Southern Kordofan, and Blue Nile, as well as the simmering resentment in eastern Sudan and other parts of the country, were all part of an age-old struggle for power between the center and the peripheries and were linked to acceptance of diversity.

By the end of 2011 little progress had been made on constructing a post-secession constitution, although to the surprise of many Osman al-Mirghani's DUP was lured into the government with the offer of cabinet positions and other inducements. This in turn led to some key party members who vocally opposed going into the government being dismissed. Although Sadig al-Mahdi had to bend to the will of his party and not enter the NCP-led coalition, he also distanced himself from the National Consensus Forces and their appeal for a popular uprising. The NCP did not get the kind of broad-based government they wanted, but they had succeeded in dividing the opposition, and with the DUP onside they could hope for progress in formulating a constitution that

would have a measure of legitimacy. But all of these efforts were
something of a sideshow to the fundamental – and unaddressed
– need to lay the grounds for democratic transformation.

Divisions in the NCP

Divisions between the cerebral vice president Ali Osman Taha
and the pit bull deputy head of the NCP and presidential assistant
Dr Nafie Ali Nafie were evident since at least the signing of the
CPA in 2005, when Nafie criticized Ali Osman for his belief that
the US would improve relations with Sudan for signing the peace
agreement, a critical element in his selling of the agreement to
his colleagues. Since then, with a certain amount of regularity,
tensions between the two officials came to light, but were always
kept in check. However, Bashir's announcement that he would not
run in the next election set the stage for competition as to who
would replace him, the two leading candidates being Ali Osman
and Nafie. In that light the refutation by elements in the army
and party of the agreement Nafie signed with the SPLM–North
in Addis Ababa on Southern Kordofan and the status of the
SPLM–North (see previous chapter) were held by some in the
party to put paid to his leadership ambitions.

The third person in the NCP hierarchy who has made little
secret of his leadership ambitions is Salah Gosh, the long-time
head of NISS who acquired a name in the West after he oversaw an
intelligence-sharing relationship with the CIA and other Western
intelligence agencies as part of the so-called war on terror in the
wake of 9/11. Sudanese intelligence provided information and
analysis on a range of Islamists, many of whom the NCP hosted,
served as a center in the US rendition program, and is known to
have held and tortured suspects from a number of countries. After
the US invasion of Iraq, NISS was there again to give a helping
hand. Sudanese intelligence provided information and analysis

on a range of Islamists as well as serving in the US rendition program, and is known to have held and tortured suspects from a number of Western countries.

One of the victims of this relationship was Sudanese-Canadian Abousfain Abdelrazik, who on returning to Sudan in August 2003 to visit his sick mother was thrown in jail at the request of the Canadian Security Intelligence Service, who suspected him of terrorism. After investigating the case the Government of Sudan informed the Canadian government that this treatment constituted a human rights violation and released him.[29] But Prime Minister Harper refused to arrange for Abdelrazik to return to Canada, so he languished for months at the Canadian embassy in Khartoum. He was only permitted to return after the Canadian Supreme Court intervened. No charges were ever laid against him.

Gosh claimed this intelligence cooperation with the West protected the NCP, but some party supporters were outraged. In August 2009 Gosh was abruptly sacked by Bashir for reasons that were never made clear, although his dismissal was somewhat compensated for by his appointment as presidential adviser on security; he was later assigned to lead the post-referendum negotiations with the SPLM.

On 25 April 2011 Gosh was again sacked by Bashir and relieved of all his titles and government and party tasks, with the exception of his position as an MP. Ostensibly his dismissal was the result of a public spat with Nafie over who was to lead negotiations with the opposition parties over the formation of a new government. Gosh claimed he had the authority of Bashir, but the president and the Political Bureau of the NCP came down firmly on the side of Nafie. Then head of party organization Gutbi Mahdi indicated that the dialogue with opposition parties 'represents only a small part' of the problem, and that Gosh's activities had raised many questions, which had led the party to re-evaluate his position. He further added that Gosh was 'grooming himself'

to take over Sudan's presidency (*Sudan Tribune*, 5 May 2011).
Suspicions within the party leadership had been growing for some
time regarding Gosh's ambitions and his attempt to give greater
authority to NISS, which had led to fears of an overreaching
security agency, like those in Latin America that had carried
out a number of coups.[30] Even politicians outside the NCP were
made aware of Gosh's desire to replace Bashir either before or
after his anticipated retirement in 2015. However, many ordinary
supporters of the NCP viewed Gosh as a hero who came to
the rescue of the regime in 2008 with his security forces when
JEM forces attacked Omdurman and SAF was nowhere to be
seen. But when he developed close relations with the opposition,
particularly Sadig al-Mahdi, and with a handful of SAF officers,
alarm bells rang.

Tribal affiliations also figured in the leadership dispute as
Gosh is Shaggiya and had long been linked to fellow tribesmen
Ali Osman Taha, Awad al-Jaz (minister of industry at the time),
and Kamal Obeid (minister of information), and they were pitted
against Bashir and Nafie, both Jalien. Parallel to this division the
NCP security agencies were dominated by Shaggiya while the army
leadership is predominantly Jalien. Tribal identity in northern
Sudan was strengthened under the NCP because of the continuing
domination of the state by the riverain tribes and the further division of the government ministries and agencies between them, and
the governing elite's major engagement in the economy.

Given the devious way in which the NCP came to power, many
people in Sudan never believed the ruling party had really broken
with Turabi and insisted this was just another trick to delude the
international community and reduce the pressures on the government. Indeed, there were numerous attempts by NCP leaders in
the early years after the split to reunite the two Islamist factions,
but they all came to naught. There were also various attempts
by individual Islamists and Islamist parties to reunite the PCP

and NCP. Tunisian Islamist leader Rashid al-Ghanmushi visited Khartoum in May 2011 and attempted reconciliation; a month later the Egyptian Muslim Brothers announced a similar objective in Khartoum. But while reconciliation of the two Islamist parties had a measure of support in their bases, the leaders had largely lost interest in it. An NCP official told the author, 'Turabi is out to get the NCP, which is now the main mission in his life.'

Northern Economy

The peace process came to an end without an agreement over revenue sharing and with the north in a decidedly insecure position. Ali Mahmood Hassanein, the minister of finance and national economy, told the National Assembly that 73 percent of the country's oil lay in the south, 26 percent in the north and 1 percent in the contested region of Abyei, and that the north stood to lose 36.5 percent of its revenues as a result of southern secession (Reuters, 14 June 2011). While most of Sudan's proven daily output of 500,000 barrels was extracted from oilfields in the south, the pipeline infrastructure, refineries, and port were based in the north, requiring the south to pay a fee to transport its oil and ship it abroad from Port Sudan. The GoSS negotiators preferred the principle of paying increased rates for these services rather than agreeing to the north retaining a share of the oil, which is what the NCP wanted, although in the end it backed down. Exacerbating the problem was that the NCP had failed to build up any financial reserves and thus austerity measures had to be taken. Some of the subsidies on sugar, wheat, and petroleum products were removed, and some imports were banned to preserve foreign exchange reserves. But more cutbacks were on the horizon, even if the ruling party put a brave face on the situation and Bashir announced that no new taxes would be imposed. 'With oil revenue constituting more than half of government revenue and 90 percent of exports, the economy will need to adjust to a permanent shock, particularly at a time when the country has little access to external financing,' observed an IMF report (*Sudan Tribune*, 19 April 2011). In addition, the NCP government faced a national debt of $39 billion at the end of the peace process. How this was to be tackled depended on the outcome of negotiations with the SPLM and the sympathy of the international community, particularly the US – and that had markedly declined after the invasions of Abyei and Southern Kordofan. And, to make things worse, after secession Juba launched a new currency, despite having earlier agreed to accept the Sudanese pound for six months. In response the Central Bank of Sudan also issued a new currency.

The IMF proposed that the government reduce spending, lift fuel subsidies, reduce tax exemptions and enhance revenue administration. Bashir responded positively to all these proposals. In addition, the number of ministers was reduced and Nafie Ali Nafie was appointed to head a committee charged with drawing up a new taxation policy. Bashir also promised to enhance transparency and accountability in a government considered to be one of the most corrupt in the world. Significantly, given how the NCP had repeatedly purged the civil service and stacked it with party loyalists, Bashir now announced: 'We will start the process of reform first by excluding the civil service and public service of politicization and political appointments' (*Sudan Tribune*, 2 June 2011). Earlier in 2011 Bashir established an anti-corruption commission. Almost as important, the media censors permitted a degree of discussion of corruption by the political elite, including members of the president's own family, that heretofore would have sent journalists promptly to jail. Government officials also suggested that a virtual gold rush had begun in 2009, which the minister of finance estimated would garner $1.2 billion in the next two years. The problem was that most of this revenue went directly to the prospectors and the government had yet to find ways to tax it efficiently.

The regime, however, did itself no favors when it gave southerners mixed messages about their welcome in the north and thus effectively encouraged them to leave. This not only served to break Bashir's promise that he would personally assume responsibility for protecting them, but it also disrupted key sectors of the economy like construction and agriculture, which depended on southern laborers.

From the time of the referendum relations with the US appeared to be improving. The NCP leadership was particularly impressed with Senator John Kerry and held there to be a growing, albeit small, constituency in the US that wanted to turn the page in relations. But the avalanche of negative media coverage in the final two months of the peace process and a stream of statements by Susan Rice, Hillary Clinton, and Barack Obama condemning the regime for its activities in Abyei and Southern Kordofan appeared to kill whatever opening the NCP optimists had perceived. The response of the NCP leadership was a blunt, 'We never trusted you!' and the assertion that they never had any expectations of being taken off the sanctions list and achieving normal relations.[31] The emphasis on Southern Kordofan was just 'a useful weapon' for 'those people who love to hate us' and it would pass, one presidential adviser told me. The NCP claimed that US rhetoric was empty, designed to 'score points,' and that the US 'has too much on its plate and is less inclined to take practical steps' than was the case in the 1990s. They also noted that, unlike in the 1990s, the NCP had generally positive relations with its neighbors and was far less vulnerable. Ruling party officials also claimed they could live without improved US relations. Indeed, the ineffectiveness of diplomacy in the circumstances was also becoming increasingly acknowledged by the diplomats. 'We can issue statements, but where's the leverage?' reflected a despondent Western diplomat.

Conclusion

The peace process ran its course with most of the post-referendum issues – borders, citizenship, oil revenue-sharing, national debt, treaties, currencies, and so on – still unresolved, but the ruling parties in Juba and Khartoum had transitional constitutions that permitted them to operate as successor states to the old Sudan, which died at midnight 8 July 2011. While the prevailing view in the north was one of restrained regret at the loss of the south, the old state had not met the needs of many in the country, not just in the south, and its passing was not lamented. Because of war a generation of northern Sudanese had never known southern Sudan, and Islamist propaganda constantly drove home the message that the non-Muslim south had never been fully linked to the Muslim north. Southerners celebrated the birth of their new country and tried to forget for a short while all the problems the RoSS faced. Those problems would return soon enough, beginning with a constitution that Salva and his ministers would intimidate his own party members into passing, and which represented the kind of government southerners had fought against their entire political lives.

Since its inception in 1983 the Garang- and now Salva-led SPLM had resisted democratic transformation, even while calling for it in Khartoum, had appealed for a united reformed Sudan while it struggled to achieve southern secession, had used the rhetoric of New Sudan to win allies in the north to fight its battles with Khartoum, and then, having won those battles, cast the northern allies aside. The legacy of the armed struggle and of the CPA years of autonomy bore heavily on the SPLM, and with southern independence it had to deliver on its promises of development and the provision of services even while it found ways to confront armed insurgencies and a government in Khartoum that would continue to exploit every sign of weakness. As was the case throughout its history, the SPLM looked to its friends in the international community to provide the development and services that it was incapable of achieving itself.

In light of the commentary above, the Republic of South Sudan does not meet Weber's basic tenet of statehood that a national government must have a monopoly of force in the territory under its jurisdiction. Instead – and only unlike other African states in the extent to which the SPLA has failed either to control wide swathes of territory or eliminate competing armed groups – South Sudan can only claim statehood through recognition by the international state system. In 1982 Jackson and Rosberg published a path-breaking article in which they argued that in the case of some countries in Africa – Zaire was their preferred example – Weber's empirical definition of statehood had been replaced by a juridical definition, and the result was that the international community often sustained and perpetuated incompetent and corrupt governments.[32] The only qualification to this conception is that, unlike Eritrea or Somaliland, which could claim colonial status, South Sudan was entirely a creation of the international community.

Faced with a daunting range of problems, the SPLM-led RoSS will look to the international community for assistance, and this will reinforce the dependency that has characterized the party since its inception. In the first instance, the SPLM will endeavor to strengthen its economic and political ties with the Western-aligned East African countries. Over the six and a half years of the interim period, the South Sudan economy became closely integrated with that of Uganda and Kenya, with most banking controlled by the latter, retailing and services by the former; much of the hospitality and hotels sector is run by Ethiopians and Eritreans; while the Somalis run the petrol stations and the foreign exchange outlets. Some of the traditional *jallaba* remain in the south, although they are outnumbered by the ambitious, but capital-limited, Darfuris. Even with its instability and weak governance, southern Sudan became a magnet for construction companies from Nairobi and Kampala. International agencies, meanwhile, largely relied on Baganda and Kikuyu drivers and transport companies. Even Juba's growing number of sex workers – estimated in a recent study to number perhaps 10,000 – came from East Africa and were attracted by the easy money and corruption. One Kenyan sex worker was quoted as saying, 'I target tall Dinka men who drive cars with number plates written GOSS.'[33]

While the NCP was anxious to rid the north of UNMIS, the SPLM was keen to strengthen its role in the independent south. Established as the UN Mission in South Sudan (UNMISS) under Chapter VII of the UN Charter, it began after 9 July with a mandate for one year, which will almost certainly be renewed for many years to come. The mission consists of 7,000 military personnel, including military liaison officers and staff officers, 900 civilian police personnel supported by technical, human rights, and investigation expertise. It is led by Hilde Johnson, a former Norwegian cabinet minister and a big supporter of the SPLM (and which in turn actively campaigned for her to get the position), who played a role in the Naivasha Peace Process, although nowhere near as significant as she contends in her self-serving book.[34] The veteran southern politician Jimmy Wongo prophetically predicted that to protect civilians 'the UN would establish a protectorate to divide savage tribal armies of southern Sudan' (interview, 30 March 2011). Early indications, however, were that UNMISS under Johnson would misconstrue protection of southern civilians with protection of the regime, and not even manage to do that competently.

Israel was quick to see advantages in developing relations with an anti-Arab state on the periphery of the Arab world which has a key position on Egypt's lifeline the Nile and supports a number of anti-NCP armed groups in the north. An early indication of the desire of the SPLM to win Washington's favor and participate in its regional security nexus was Salva's announcement that his government would establish an embassy in occupied Jerusalem. Israel was one of the first countries to recognize the independence of South Sudan; their officials were quick to visit Juba; and in mid-December 2011 President Salva made a state visit to Tel Aviv and thus provoked the ire of Khartoum. In a further attempt to ingratiate itself with the US the government announced its intention to send peacekeepers to Somalia.[35] US agro-industrial corporations are taking positions in South Sudan (see Jarch Capital and Nile Trading and Development) and will no doubt be followed by energy and mining companies. DynCorp, McDonnell Douglas, Lockheed Martin, and other US security companies were active in South Sudan at the end of the peace process and the US was providing $100 million for training the SPLA.[36] With American special forces operating in Chad, Uganda, Ethiopia, Kenya, and the Combined Joint Task Force for the Horn of Africa at Camp Lemonier in Djibouti, it cannot be long before the US military assumes a direct role in South Sudan. Having expended countless lives in a struggle ultimately devoted to achieving independence, at the end of the peace process South Sudan's sovereignty was being undermined by SPLM relations with the US, its allies, and client states in East Africa.

CONCLUSION

THE LEGACY
OF A FLAWED PEACE PROCESS

The Horn has suffered from intra and inter-state conflict more than any other region in Africa. This has led to the emergence of two new internationally recognized states, Eritrea and South Sudan, as well as the de facto existence of Somaliland, and arguably that of Puntland. Moreover, unlike the rest of Africa, where the OAU/AU principle of accepting colonial boundaries has held, in the Horn it has been subject to continuous challenge. Long before the secession of South Sudan it was clear from the experience of Ethiopia, Eritrea, and Somalia that separation did not yield peace and stability, much less democracy, and instead produced a new set of conditions that led to inter-state wars and a proliferation of internal conflicts. But, despite the overwhelming evidence of the failure of this approach, local actors in south and north Sudan worked with the US-led international community to facilitate the secession of South Sudan and thus prepare the context and stimulus for another set of conflicts.

After Eritrea's peaceful referendum on its secession, war broke out between Addis Ababa and Asmara in 1988. This was accompanied by a number of insurgencies in both countries that were aided and abetted by the other. Not stopping there, the conflict also involved each attempting to inflict economic hardship on the other and the support of proxy armed groups in Somalia. A not dissimilar pattern is emerging in the two Sudans. The referendum and actual secession of South Sudan proceeded peacefully, but even before the south formally achieved independence both governments were actively supporting one another's dissidents, and these conflicts intensified in the post-9 July period. Both countries have also attempted to inflict economic harm on the other, such as encouraging southerners to leave the north and pursuing an economic blockade of the south,[1] failing to reach agreement on free trade and open borders, and deadlock over oil revenues and the national debt. Oil revenues have proved to be the most explosive issue, and with the failure to reach an agreement Sudan began confiscating a portion of South Sudan's oil as a means of payment, which led Juba to threaten to launch a lawsuit, build another pipeline, and cut off the oil entirely until an agreement was reached.

The common pattern in the Horn is of ethnic-based elites using the state to advance their material interests and create a false homogeneity by pressing their culture and ideology on the disparate peoples that make up these countries. In the absence of democratic alternatives this has produced resistance in the form of armed movements struggling for self-determination. As Markakis points out, the typical response to the state-building projects of the Horn's elites is state destruction by the victims of the process.[2] The leaders of the new states that emerged from this process – Eritrea and South Sudan – quickly assumed the same pattern of hegemonic rule over their ethnically and religiously diverse peoples, and this in turn is producing resistance, and thus the cycle continues. This is the context in which the various armed struggles in north and south Sudan are taking place. The South Sudan-government-supported armed struggles in the Three Areas and Darfur are devoted to regime change – as was the earlier struggle of the SPLM against Khartoum – but should this objective prove impossible, then it can be surmised that they will focus on self-determination, leading to either secession or the union of parts of Darfur, the Ngok-inhabited southern Abyei, the Nuba Mountains, and southern Blue Nile with South Sudan. Such a development would encourage further internal struggles, which would take the form of African–Arab conflicts.

South Sudan is itself by no means immune to such struggles. The southern SPLM/A always suffered from elite and tribal domination, which produced factional and tribal-based armed struggles. With independence and the failure of the SPLM to reform the institutions of governance and the military, and to provide services and balanced development, the present armed struggles may well advance to the level of posing a strategic threat or lead to demands for ethnic or regional self-determination. And in the shadows lies the experience of complete state breakdown in Somalia, which is frequently posed as yet another possibility of what might be in store for the people of north and south Sudan. None of this is entirely surprising given the weak basis of state-hood – particularly in South Sudan – but what is surprising is that while the mediators concerned with post-referendum issues did highlight the need to ensure that the two successor states were viable, it was never a concern during the peacemaking stage.

Peacemaking Gone Wrong

The failure of southern Sudan's rebels and different Khartoum governments to resolve the country's conflicts militarily or politically opened the door to outside intervention, and that experience – as this study has illustrated – has not been positive. The resort to IGAD to take the lead in peacemaking did not, as its supporters claimed, amount to African solutions to African problems, but instead was an example of a weak Third World agency used to pursue the interests of the US and its allies. The impetus for the formation of IGAD and its engagement in peacemaking came from international donors, and the same donors pressed it to take an active role in mediation and peace-building efforts in Somalia and Sudan. But at all times the process was dominated by the US and its close allies, operating through Kenya, a state which has a history of subservience to Western interests. IGAD had no capacity to structure the peace process or influence its course or objectives; it was not even permitted under the CPA to play a role in the so-called post-conflict era.[3]

US engagement was in the first instance based on security concerns – overcoming the threats posed by a failed state, fear that the Sudan conflict would spill over borders, and with NCP attempts to export its Islamist ideology. The US also wanted to build the capacity of the AU and its subregional components like IGAD so they could assume increasing responsibility for its so-called war on terror in Africa. Additionally, President Bush wanted a successful peace process as a means to respond to the concerns of American black and advocacy activists and to be seen internationally as assuming a leading role in the peace process at a time when the US was widely criticized for its policies in the Muslim world. In the event, by the time the agreement was reached in January 2005, US television screens were filled with images of the tragedy in Darfur, and celebrating peace in the south would have appeared cavalier and not provide the desired political pay-off. The Obama administration played a less overt role in Sudan, in part because by 9 July 2011 it was involved in military campaigns in three Muslim countries – Afghanistan, Iraq, and Libya – and other uprisings in the Middle East were a growing concern. Meanwhile, the battles in Abyei and Southern Kordofan in the final days of the peace process and the failure to resolve the post-referendum issues limited the international community to cheering the secession of the south.

The approach employed in the Sudan mediation was consistent with liberal peacemaking theory, which places peace above structural and democratic transformation of the state. The danger is that the resulting agreement may not prove sustainable and comprehensive, and will not conclusively address the underlying causes of the conflict, and that indeed was the case in Sudan. Moreover, the fact that the conflict in Sudan could not be reduced to a north–south problem, but involved much of the country, and had been under way since independence, made clear that it was a product of major structural faults that were not amenable to the limited approach employed.

The major impact of the peace process was to reinforce the power of elites in the state by guaranteeing their existence for the six and a half years of the peace agreement. The mediation endeavored to find space in the central state for the SPLM/A during the interim period and create a state in the south dominated by the SPLM/A for the long term. However, by reinforcing the power of the state and its exploitive relationship with the peripheries – now in the north and the south – the mediation undermined its other stated objectives of making unity attractive, achieving a sustainable peace, and democratic transformation.

The marked scepticism about the peace process on the part of both the NCP and SPLM/A is not surprising in the Horn of Africa, where war is the more likely road to peace than negotiated settlements. Thus the conflicts between the EPLF and the Derg, and between the EPRDF and the Derg, were resolved with only minimal resort to negotiations. Likewise, Yoweri Museveni's NRM/A war against successive Ugandan governments ended with the overthrow of Tito Okello without third-party mediation. IGAD's efforts to achieve a negotiated end to the conflict in Somalia have not to date succeeded, and with their failure the Ethiopian, Kenyan, and US governments have taken unilateral military action. The international community placed great hopes in the CPA to serve as a door-opener to end the conflict in Darfur, but the Darfur Peace Agreement collapsed within days of its signing. Only the Eastern Sudan Peace Agreement held, but it was largely an agreement between the governments of Eritrea and Sudan that undermined the interests of the people of the region. This less than positive experience with peacemaking in the Horn should caution against undue faith in the arts of diplomacy and mediation informed by liberal models of peacemaking and -building.

There were many technical and substantive failings in the mediation and the resulting peace process, but they flowed from the failure to commit to democratic transformation and question a project whose end would be the birth of a SPLM-led state that could not provide the most elementary functions of governance. Nathan identifies the main structural conditions producing conflict in Africa that need to be addressed in any mediation as being authoritarian rule, marginalization of ethnic minorities, socio-economic deprivation and weak states that lack the institutional capacity to manage political and social conflict effectively (Nathan 2001). Added to this in the Sudanese context is the importance of overcoming cultural oppression. Rarely considered during the course of the peace process was whether the SPLM had the capacity to administer South Sudan. By excluding the SSDF, political parties, and civil society from the peace process, the peacemakers reduced the prospect of an all-party national government taking form whose prospects of governing would at least have been greater than leaving government solely to the SPLM with its many limitations. But even to list these areas of concern suggests a transformative project far beyond the imagination or interests of those involved in the peacemaking and -building process in Sudan.

The legacy of Sudan, and which South Sudan is following, is one in which periphery-inhabiting peoples are denigrated and marginalized, traditional authorities often have more legitimacy than urban elites, communal and usufruct land-holding practices still hold sway in many areas, and the input of capitalist forms of agriculture are producing alienation of land, rural poverty, environmental collapse, and growing disparities in wealth. This legacy is also one in which rule is based on the gun and increasingly financed by oil rents. Under such conditions popular empowerment must be the objective, but this is not to be equated with a circulation of urban elites through periodic flawed elections and devotion to market-based models of economic organization favored by international financial institutions and would-be liberal peacemakers.

An alternative process would proceed from a very different set of assumptions than that of the Naivasha peacemakers. First, the objective of democratic transformation would not be – as liberal peace-building would have it – an add-on to facilitate the realization of peace or provide legitimacy and then to be dispensed with when it faces challenges, but is inseparable from sustainable peace; indeed, it is integral to the very definition of peace and must inform every stage of the peace process. Second, peace-building must be genuinely comprehensive in both the level of participation in the exercise and in terms of its scope. Third, for citizens to feel they own the peace process they must be duly and effectively informed as to its progress and be able through democratic institutions to respond to developments. Fourth, priority must always be given to local actors leading efforts at peacemaking and peace-building, and when that is not possible for the region to assume a dominant role. For reasons considered above, the failure of the Sudanese and the region to resolve the wars led directly to the US and its allies dominating the process, with a resulting loss of sovereignty. Fifth, while a peripheral state like Sudan cannot on its own overcome the structural inequities inherent in the global economy and international state system, the root causes of conflict within its powers must be responded to. Lastly, if the combatants will not accept a commitment to democratic transformation, then the mediators should withdraw.

This is precisely what occurred when the GoS refused to accept IGAD's first DoP, authored by Ethiopian foreign minister Seyoum Mesfin, and the mediators had the courage and principles to walk away.

This will not satisfy the devotees of liberal models of peacemaking, who will contend that even a flawed peace is better than no peace because it saves lives, and that the problems that beset the Sudan peace process were caused by technical failures and difficulties of implementation. But after a decade of liberal peacemaking large swathes of Sudan and South Sudan suffer from rebellions and lawlessness, almost as many people are displaced or living as refugees as when the CPA was signed in January 2005, and none of the outstanding post-referendum issues has been resolved. The repeatedly stated objective of mediators to oversee the creation of two viable states should southerners opt for secession has not been realized, and nor have the mediators been successful in encouraging workable relations between the successor states. As a result, a return to full-fledged north–south war or deepening civil wars is the most likely prospect for both Sudan and South Sudan. Such is the legacy of enormous expenditures in financial and political capital. Unfortunately, rather than recognize the failures of the internationally driven peace process, the conflicts and problems that continue to afflict Sudan and South Sudan will predictably lead to appeals for more international interventions.

POSTSCRIPT

On 20 January 2012 the GoSS stopped all oil production in South Sudan in response to the GoS confiscating oil at what it considered unreasonably high rates, in the absence of an agreement on fees for carrying its oil to Port Sudan. Thus at a stroke the government cut off 98 per cent of its own revenues. With Khartoum already suffering from a deepening economic crisis after the loss of oil fields to South Sudan with the end of the peace process and its inability to overcome the SPLA-supported revolts in the Nuba Mountains and Darfur (it had more success in Blue Nile), the loss of an important revenue stream was understood to be part of a greater effort to bring about its collapse. Meanwhile, the GoSS signed MOUs with Kenya and Ethiopia to build pipelines and sought international funding to build them and to finance the state when its financial reserves ran out, but little came of these efforts.

According to a World Bank briefing for President Salva Kiir and several ministers, GoSS leaders had little appreciation of the consequences of their decision to stop oil production. They included a collapse of the country's gross domestic product, massive depreciation of the South Sudan pound, an exponential rise in inflation, depletion of financial reserves, a rise from 51 per cent to 83 per cent in those living in poverty, doubling of child mortality from 10 per cent to 20 per cent, and a drop in school enrolment from 50 per cent to 20 per cent by 2013. The briefing concluded that the international community did not understand nor support the way the government was behaving. *Foreign Policy* magazine summed up the situation as 'World Bank to South Sudan: Are you out of your freaking mind?!'

Oil continued to be the focus of the Khartoum–Juba conflict when after a skirmish on the Unity state–Southern Kordofan border on 26 March 2012, SPLA and Darfuri rebels followed the retreating SAF and ended up occupying Heglig in Southern Kordofan, which produced half of Sudan's 120,000 bpd of oil. Salva ordered his forces to return to South Sudan, but in response to Khartoum's aerial bombardments in the border states, which terrorized civilians, the SPLA and JEM again occupied Heglig on 11 April. This time Salva announced his refusal to leave an area which he said belonged to South Sudan, a claim, however, which had not previously been identified as one of the five contested border areas under the AUHIP mediation. To the shock of Juba the SPLA's occupation of Heglig was roundly condemned by the UN, AU, Arab League, EU, and even the US government, and as a result on 20 April Salva announced a three-day withdrawal of his forces and those of JEM. Instead of an orderly withdrawal the retreating forces suffered grievous losses at the hands of the SSLA and Misseirya irregulars supported by SAF. Before they left, the oil installations were severely damaged, apparently on the orders of Governor Taban Deng. While the SPLA claimed a great victory in capturing Heglig and SAF claimed an equally impressive victory in forcing the invaders to leave, in fact both armies suffered major defeats.

The GoSS said the incursion brought its claim to Heglig to international attention, but the cost was high because the NCP rewarded the SSLA and the other southern rebel groups with increased support in their war against the SPLA. Moreover, the decisions to shut down the oil production and occupy Heglig shocked the US, which no longer viewed the SPLM government as simply a victim of the NCP, but as part of the problem. Despite this changing perception, both the SPLM and the NCP still assumed that Washington would not permit a complete collapse of the South Sudanese state. Meanwhile, sentiments among the people in both countries had been raised to fever pitch; although this – at least temporarily – reinforced the increasingly discredited governments in Khartoum and Juba, it also brought the possibility of full-fledged war to the fore.

To save the situation the Security Council on 2 May 2012 unanimously accepted Resolution 2046 under Chapter VII, which called for a cessation of hostilities within 48 hours, a resumption of negotiations led by AUHIP within two weeks (they resumed on 29 May), the GoS to negotiate with the SPLM–N on the basis of the agreement of 28 June 2011, the Council to regularly review progress, and in the event that either or both parties failed to comply with the resolution to apply sanctions. As well as the continuing central role for the AU, Ethiopia's Meles Zenawi was formally recognized in his capacity as chairman of IGAD as joint chair with Thabo Mbeki of the peace process. Khartoum was outraged at the demand that it negotiate with SPLM–N on the basis of a party-to-party agreement that it had rejected (see above), the formal imposition of IGAD (which the GoSS had called for to replace the AU mediators, but the GoS viewed as biased), and by the equation of its aerial bombing with the occupation and destruction of its oil installations. Hoping to regain international favor after the diplomatic disaster of Heglig, the GoSS accepted without qualification Resolution 2046 and withdrew its police from Abyei. This increased the pressure on the Sudanese army, which announced its withdrawal on 28

May. Khartoum reluctantly endorsed the UN resolution, but was divided on the way forward, and unhappy that China and Russia had voted for the resolution, even though they indicated their reluctance to support sanctions.

Resolution 2046 represented another phase of the peace process, but the model was the same as that which had failed over the previous decade: a top-down foreign-directed approach that disregarded the interests of the non-gun-carrying majorities in the north and south, ignored the link between sustainable peace and democratic transformation, and overlooked the need for structural change in both Sudan and South Sudan. Bendana noted that failures of liberal peacemaking invariably lead to more such interventions, but never in the history of peacemaking in Sudan has that approach looked so problematic. Indeed, in the wake of increased distrust between the parties, the growing dependence of the two governments on their rebel allies, and the significance attached to the economic pain each was causing the other, Juba and Khartoum looked more to overthrowing the other than to a negotiated end to their conflict.

29 May 2012, Khartoum

NOTES

PREFACE

1. Practice in the Islamic world is to use an individual's first name, as the second name refers to the father, and the third to the grandfather. Sudanese Muslims are flexible with some names, but the principle still applies; South Sudan, although somewhat different, generally follows this pattern. As a central theme of my book is criticism of Western domination of the peace process, Muslim names are here employed in their usual forms.

INTRODUCTION

1. In 2000 confirmation of state dominance by the riverine core was exposed by dissidents within the ruling regime. In that year the 'Black Book' began to be handed out in Khartoum at mosques after Friday prayers and soon became widely circulated underground; its thesis, based on a wealth of statistics, that people from the north held a disproportionate number of positions in the various organs of the state became a national scandal. In its first table the Black Book reported that people from the northern region, with only 5.4 percent of the population, had 79.5 percent of central government positions, and as such the south was only one of a number of disadvantaged regions and by no means suffered the most (See Black Book, JEM website).

CHAPTER 1

1. Making clear Israel's opportunist involvement in Sudan, in 1983 Sudanese diplomats reached an agreement with Israeli officials not to aid southern dissidents in return for Sudan's cooperation in facilitating the transit of Falasha Jews from Ethiopia. Interview with Lt General Joseph Lagu, 8 June 2011, Khartoum.
2. Interview with Ibrahim Nugud, chairman of the Sudan Commnist Party, Khartoum, 17 May 2011.
3. Interview with Lt General Joseph Lagu, Juba, 8 June 2011.

4. Interview with Ibrahim Sanoussi, deputy leader, Popular Congress Party, Khartoum, 28 May 2011.
5. Interview with Ibrahim Sanoussi, 28 May 2011.
6. Quoted in *The Citizen*, 7 July 2011.
7. Interview with Ibrahim Sanoussi, 28 May 2011.
8. Joseph Oduhu history blog, oduhu-history-online.blogspot.com 12 March 2009. Joseph was a founding member of the SPLM.
9. Originally the NDA meeting was planned to be held in Egypt and its government assumed all the costs, but because of sensitive Egyptian–Sudanese relations and fear of open support for the rebels it was decided at the last moment to hold it in Asmara, a major error in the later view of the Egyptians, who would never have permitted an endorsement of southern self-determination.
10. Information acquired over numerous meetings with General Tsadkan in Addis Ababa, Khartoum, and Juba. See also Young 2004.
11. John Young, Interview with Salva Kiir, Yei, Southern Sudan, 16 March 2001.
12. Young 2002. This point is also made in Akol 2009.
13. Interview with Ibrahim Sanoussi, Khartoum, 28 May 2011.
14. Interview with Salva Kiir, Yei, 24 March 2001.
15. *Sudan Tribune*, www.sudantribune.com/spip.php?page=imprimanle&id_article=26320

CHAPTER 2

1. Interview with Sadig al-Mahdi, Khartoum, 15 January 2003.
2. One critic of the Machakos notion of self-determination noted that the conceptions developed in the DoP and found in the Asmara Declaration were constructed by Africans and neighbors who understood the Sudan, while that found in the Machakos Protocol was the product of Western lawyers and diplomats who did not understand the country. See Dr Abdul Hassan Farah, DUP official in attendance at the Asmara conference, Khartoum, 23 June 2011.
3. Malwal 2005.
4. Interview with Malik Agar Eyre, Khartoum, 7 April 2001.
5. Security Council Press Release no. 8306, New York, 8 February 2005.
6. Interview, IRIN, www.irinnews.org/fr/Report/56592/SUDAN-Interview-with-Al-Sadiq-Al-Mahdi-Ummah-party-president.

CHAPTER 3

1. On 21 May 2009, the Central Bureau of Statistics (CBS) officially released the 'Sudan Census Priority Results' at a press conference in Khartoum. The total enumerated population from the 2008 census was 39,154,490 persons, of which 20,073,977 were males and 19,080,513 were females. The sex ratio is 105 males per 100 females. 30,894, 000 (78.9 percent) were enumerated in North Sudan and 8,260,490 (21.1 percent) enumerated in South Sudan. Khartoum state has the largest number of persons (5,274,321), followed by Southern Darfur (4,093,594), Gezira (3,575,280), Northern Kordofan (2,920,992), and Northern Darfur (2,113,626). The state with the smallest number of persons is Western Bahr el Ghazal (333,341), followed by Unity (585,801), Western Equatoria (619,029), and Lakes (695,730). The age distribution continues to show a youthful population typical of developing countries, with 14.9 percent aged 0–4 years, 42.6 percent aged under 15 years,

54.0 percent aged 15–64 years, and 3.38 percent aged 65 years and over. See CPA 2011.

2. During the armed struggle Nhial held the position of foreign minister, although in practice Garang handled the important elements of this portfolio and it was widely anticipated that Salva Kiir would appoint him as minister of foreign affairs in the GNU, but instead he was appointed cabinet secretary. Whether for that reason or others he left the government and the country and resided in the UK until the SPLM convention; consequently his decision to challenge Kiir for the leadership was a surprise.

3. www.girifna.com/blog-girifna/?page_id=2520.

4. Dr Gutbi said that the NCP found it difficult to reconcile the interests of competing tribes in the selection of candidates and that those rejected could either run under a different party or as an independent. Most of the independents in the north were from the NCP and were expected to withdraw in the coming weeks, although with the date of withdrawal passed this will be informal. Those withdrawing would expect benefits from the party.

5. In December 2009 the author met a number of Unity State SPLM officials effectively living in exile in Juba after being chased out of the state by Governor Taban.

6. Taban's attack on the house of Paulino (while he was in Juba) could also be considered revenge, because when both of them were aligned with the Khartoum government Dr Riek Machar was appointed Taban governor of Unity state, but he was rejected by Paulino, who had two of his ministers killed and forced Taban to run back to Khartoum for safety. Dr Joseph Manytuel, then Paulino's personal physician, was appointed state governor, and again Paulino objected, but did not attempt to remove him. After the signing of the CPA and the Juba Declaration, when all of these men were affiliated with the GoSS, it was Salva's decision to select the governor and he initially refused to accept Taban's candidacy; but after Taban won the approval of Paulino, Salva relented.

7. The NCP also repeatedly brought up the unfounded claim during the campaign that Yasir Arman had killed a fellow student while active in university politics.

8. Dr Lam Akol, chairman, SPLM–DC, Khartoum, 22 June 2011.

9. 'US Official Says Abdel Wahid Forfeited Peace Opportunity,' *Sudan Tribune*, 1 March 2010.

10. White House, Office of the Press Secretary, Washington DC, 20 April 2010.

CHAPTER 4

1. Interview with Dr Ghazi Salahdien, presidential adviser, Khartoum, 23 June 2011.

2. SSRA, Art. 2; 27(2). The eight out-of-country locations were Ethiopia, Kenya, Uganda, Australia, Britain, the United States, Canada, and Egypt.

3. Interview with Farok Abu Issa, Independent MP and secretary of the National Consensus Forces, Khartoum, 24 May 2011.

4. 'Gen. Salva Kiir Mayardit, First Vice President of the Republic of the Sudan and President of the Government of Southern Sudan, Keynote Address on the Occasion of the Congressional Black Caucus Foundation 40th Annual Conference,' Washington DC, 17 September 2010.

5. There have been numerous incidents of women in Juba being harassed by the police because of their attire. After completing a much-lauded program in mid-

December 2010 to train 6,000 to serve in a new multi-ethnic police force made up of members who had never fought in the war and were untainted by guerrilla warfare experience, the new recruits were involved in serious abuses, according to Human Rights Watch. In particular they were linked to a series of incidents in Juba and other southern towns in which they harassed and assaulted civilians on account of their clothing or hair style, especially women wearing tight clothes or trousers, of which they disapproved. See Human Rights Watch, 'South Sudan: Improve Accountability for Security Forces Abuses,' 8 February 2011.

6. Interviews with Professor Al-Tayib Zain al-Abdin, Khartoum, 2011.

7. While Francis Deng generally followed the political leadership of Garang and later endorsed the call for Abyei to join the south, he was far more reluctant to speak negatively of the Misseirya than Deng Alor and Edward Lino out of respect for the positions of his late father and his own scholarly studies, in which he repeatedly described Abyei as a microcosm of Sudan and of Africa.

8. Interview with Dirdiery Mohamed Ahmed, NCP official and lead legal adviser for the GoS at The Hague Arbitration Tribunal, Khartoum, 28 October 2010.

9. Interview with Nasir al-Dien al-Hadi, member of the committee in question, Khartoum, 31 May 2011.

10. However, on 11 November 2010, President Bush's special envoy on Sudan, Richard Williamson contended in the US establishment *Foreign Policy* magazine that because of 'northern belligerence and the naiveté of US President Barack Obama and his advisors, we are once again staring into the abyss – as the administration's desperate appeal to Khartoum for forbearance in exchange for its removal from the state sponsors of terrorism list makes clear' (Williamson 2010). This clear attack on Senator John Kerry, representing President Obama, and the stipulation that the government of Sudan must cooperate with respect to the southern referendum if it was to be removed from the terrorism list, would ring alarm bells in NCP circles, where US promises are not held in high regard. While Gration made clear his desire to reward Bashir and the NCP for their cooperation in the implementation of the referendum, other US voices were not always saying the same thing. Thus US chargé to Sudan, Robert Whitehead, said that the performance of the NCP in the peace negotiations with respect to southern Sudan and Darfur were prerequisites to Sudan having improved relations with the US (*Al-Ahdath*, 20 January 2011, Khartoum). This statement was followed two days later by one by Senator John Kerry, who reminded Sudanese officials that prospects of improved relations with the US hinge on progress in Darfur (AP, 22 January 2011). It would appear that Whitehead and Kerry were distancing themselves from Gration's commitments. It would also be very difficult for Susan Rice – with her well-known antipathy to the NCP – to stomach the kind of concessions to the NCP favored by Gration. And it would be even more difficult for the Sudan advocacy community and the American public to accept rewarding a regime that has been demonized in the media for the past twenty-two years.

11. *Humanitarian Update: Returns to Southern Sudan, Office for the Coordination of Humanitarian Affairs*, 13 January 2011. This number reflects the number of returns from northern to southern Sudan tracked by the International Organization for Migration between 1 November 2010 and 11 January 2011.

12. This serious incident was dealt with in a brief footnote (Carter Center, 17 January 2011).

13. The Arrow Boys started as a village self-defense group against the LRA because of

the failure of the SPLA to provide adequate protection for the local people, but the group also became involved in harassing the Omberaro, a West African nomadic tribe that sometimes passed through Western Equatoria and was hated by the local inhabitants. By the time of the April 2010 elections there were indications that the Arrow Boys had come under the influence of the elected governor.

14. The NISS was a national security agency, but with a separate southern component under the direction of SPLA General Majak D'Agoot.

15. Although they moved north to White Nile and had renamed their village 'New Joda,' they were still eligible to vote in the referendum because of their historic residence in the area, but regrettably none had.

16. Remarks by Thabo Mbeki, Auhip chairperson, at the ceremony to announce the final results of the South Sudan Referendum, Khartoum, 7 February 2011.

CHAPTER 5

1. Interview with Dr Siddig Tower, professor of physics at El Nilein University, Ba'athist official, and writer in Sudanese newspapers on Nuba issues, Khartoum, 6 July 2011. That twenty-five and perhaps more Nuba officers either died or were killed for 'contact with the enemy' was also confirmed by Daniel Kodie, Khartoum, 10 July 2011.

2. Interviews with Afar Agar, Khartoum, 6 March 2011 and 26 May 2011.

3. See Sections 3.3 and 3.4 of the Protocol Between the Government of Sudan and the Sudan People's Liberation Movement on the Resolution of the Conflict in Southern Kordofan/Nuba Mountains and Blue Nile States, Naivasha Kenya, 26 May 2004.

4. Blue Nile State Political Parties Press Conference, Damazine, 30 March 2011.

5. International Crisis Group, 21 October 2008.

6. Haroun said that he first met Abdel Aziz in 2002 in Switzerland, again during the Naivasha negotiations, and through these meetings they established a relationship of trust. Interview with Governor Ahmed Haroun, Kadugli, 27 February 2011.

7. The proposed establishment of Western Kordofan state was not without its problems, particularly with respect to its border, because the Misseirya contended that the new state would include the area of Lagawa, while the Nuba were equally vehement that Lagawa was historically part of the Nuba Mountains – and they appeared to have the stronger case.

8. This term was the subject of considerable debate. Misseirya and the NCP focused on the 'other' and said that included them, while the Ngok and the SPLM focused on the word 'resident' to say that it only included the small number of non-Ngok who lived year round in the territory and could not include Misseirya, who only transited the territory.

9. On 22 July 2009, the Abyei Arbitral Tribunal at the Permanent Court of Arbitration found that the Abyei Boundaries Commission (ABC) had exceeded its mandate in some locations, but it upheld ABC recommendations in others. The Tribunal determined that the Abyei Area's northern boundary lies along latitude 10°10′ North, its western boundary along longitude 27°50′ East, and its eastern boundary along longitude 29°00′ East.

10. As a result of reforms to the local administration the traditional leaders of the Misseirya – the emirs – are appointed by the government and as such they are in effect, although not always in practice, agents of the NCP.

11. The UN report recorded 'a SAF JIU with about 7 vehicles mounted with machines guns clashed with SSPS [South Sudan Police Service] or SPLA at TODACH (about 17 km N of ABYEI). Reportedly, 7 SAF JIU soldiers were killed and 2 SAF officers were wounded. One SSPS/SPLA was killed and unknown numbers were wounded.'

12. See in particular, Mahgoub Mohamed Salih, 'Abyei Future Still Undecided!', and Faisal Mohammed Salih, 'Wishful Thinking,' both articles in *The Citizen*, Khartoum, 27 June 2011.

13. Interview with Dr Abdul Hassan Farah, member of DUP Exective Committee, Khartoum, 25 June 2011.

14. Interview with Ali Al-Nour, SPLM member of the Southern Kordofan Elections Committee, Juba, 11 June 2011.

15. Nuba nationalists note that their right to self-determination was denied at the SPLM National Conference at Chukudum in 1994, the IGAD Declaration of Principles of 1994, the Asmara Declaration of 1995, and the Machakos Protocol of 2002.

16. Interview with Ali Abdul Latif, spokesperson for the SPLM Northern Sector, Khartoum, 25 June 2011.

17. A witness to the negotiations reported that Dr Nafie kept in constant touch with Bashir by phone about the state of the negotiations, so there could be no claim that he was not informed.

18. Interview with Daniel Kodie, Khartoum, 10 July 2011.

CHAPTER 6

1. Joseph Lagu, speaking at a meeting of Equatorian MPs, opposition, and civil society members, Juba, 5 June 2011.

2. SPLM–DC, 'System of Government in South Sudan,' paper presented to the South–South Dialogue Conference, Juba, Southern Sudan, October 2010.

3. Office of the Vice President, Draft Amended Interim Constitution of Southern Sudan, 2005/Transitional Constitution of South Sudan, 2011, 'Additional Suggested Amendments,' 23 May 2011.

4. Office of the Leader of the Opposition, SSLA, 'Position of the Opposition on the Transitional Constitution of the Republic of South Sudan, 2011,' 23 May 2011.

5. The author did not attend President Kiir's speech; the material drawn from it comes from people who did attend and his speech notes.

6. However, Lt General Joseph Lagu, whose Anyanya army was integrated into the national forces, discounted this contention and said that his forces were treated fairly and that were was no denial of ranks, promotions, responsibilities, or access to education. Indeed, one of the beneficiaries of the scholarships made available during this period was John Garang, who took extended leave from the army to study in the US. Instead, Lagu said, a handful of young officers led by John Garang, and some politicians led by Gordon Motot, tried to disrupt the integration. Interview with Joseph Lagu, Juba, 6 June 2011.

7. South Sudan Liberation Army, 'The Mayom Declaration,' signed by Major General Peter Gadet Yak; former commander air defence and deputy commander of division three SPLA; Brigadier General Carlo Kol, Deputy Commander of joint integrated units Juba SPLA; and Hon. Col. Bol Gatkouth Kol, former Member of Parliament (SSLA 2011).

8. Chairman, Peter Gatkuoth Wadar Kuel and secretary general, Gatluke Chuol Reat, Nuer Association of the US and Canada, 'The SPLA Committed War Crimes and Crimes Against Humanity in Unity State of South Sudan,' 30 May 2011, Washington State and Ontario.

9. President Salva Kiir, speech delivered to the 5th Speakers Forum, Juba, 8 June 2011.

10. Those youth not killed, however, were still around years later to be used in anti-SPLA actions or just as likely to join the SPLA as a means to escape unemployment. See John Young, 'The White Army: An Introduction and Overview,' Small Arms Survey, Graduate Institute of International Studies, Geneva, June 2007.

11. Interview with Johnson Olony, Khartoum, 9 October 2011.

12. Interviews with Major General Peter Gadet in Juba, 29 October and 7 November 2011.

13. 'South Sudan Massacre Leaves as Many as 3000 Dead,' AFP, Juba, 6 January 2012.

14. Information Office, Lou and Jikany White Army, Akobo, Jonglei, South Sudan, 25 December 2011.

15. It is widely believed in South Sudan that the reason the Murle abduct children is because they suffer from venereal diseases and also have sexual practices that cause pregnancy disorders. While these beliefs may be true, they are not backed up with any scientific research. What is known is that from at least the early nineteenth century the Murle bought children from the neighboring Bor Dinka and that in more recent times some Murle youth have made a virtual business of forcefully abducting children and selling them to members of their tribe in exchange for cattle, which they then use for dowries. The abducted children are raised as Murle.

16. Young 2007c.

17. 'SPLA Hailes Obama Decision Allowing South Sudan to Buy US Weapons,' *The Citizen*, Juba, 8 January 2012.

18. Lawrence Freeman, 'Obama's Hypocricy Skirting ICC to Send Troops to South Sudan,' EIRNS, 11 January 2012.

19. Interview with Malik Agar in Damazine, Blue Nile, 6 February 2011.

20. 'Sudan says it supports the Libyan Opposition,' *Sudan Tribune*, Khartoum, 6 July 2011. Sudanese officials expressed support for the No Fly Zone, and in an interview with the London-based *Al-Sharq Al-Awsat* newspaper, presidential assistant Nafie Ali Nafie said that Sudan backs the Libyan people's desire for change recognizes the Transitional National Counci as a leader of this movement. Later it was revealed that the GoS provided direct support to the Libyan rebels.

21. Salahdien 2011: 7.

22. Interview with the president of the National Federation of Sudanese Youth, 10 July 2011 in Khartoum.

23. Interview with Siddeeg Mohammed Ismaiel, general secretary of the National Umma Party, in Khartoum 12 March 2011

24. Interview with Professor Ismail El Hag Musa, NCP deputy speaker, Council of States in Khartoum, 7 July 2011.

25. Salahdien 2011: 6.

26. Interview with Professor Balghis Badri, director of the Regional Institute of Gender, Diversity, Peace and Rights, Ahfad University for Women, Omdurman, 9 July 2011.

27. Interview with Alustadh Mahmoud, M. Taha Cultural Center, Omdurman, 2 July 2011.
28. Interview with Professor Al-Tayib Zain Al-Abdin, adviser to the vice chancellor, University of Khartoum and member of the Shura Council, Khartoum, 3 July 2011.
29. Reuel Amdur, 'War on Civil Liberties: Canadian Citizen Abandoned by His Government,' *Towards Freedom*, 14 May 2008.
30. This explanation was provided by a NCP official and government office holder.
31. The presence on the US state sponsors of terrorism list bars a country from receiving US arms exports, controls sales of items with military and civilian applications, limits US aid and requires Washington to vote against loans to the country from international financial institutions.
32. Jackson and Rosberg 1982.
33. 'Kenyan Trafficked to South Sudan for Sex Work – Report,' TrustLaw, Nairobi, 10 January 2012.
34. Johnson 2011.
35. BBC, 'Focus on Africa,' www.bbc.co./uk/news/world-africa-14534875.
36. Maggie Fick, 'US Millions Fund South Sudan Army; Worries over Abuses,' AP, Juba, 2 July 2011.

CONCLUSION

1. A senior NCP official said that the Sudan's economic blockade 'was hard to justify, but necessary ... and there were indications that Salva was feeling the pinch of the blockade,' interview, Khartoum, 10 October 2011.
2. John Markakis, letter to author, 4 September 2011.
3. An illustration of the weakness of IGAD is that the organization was not even given an official copy of the CPA. As a result the best it could do was convince General Sumbeiywo to share his copy for an hour so that pictures could be taken of it surrounded by its officials, after which he took it away with him.

REFERENCES

Accord and Concordis International (2006) *Peace by Piece: Addressing Sudan's Conflicts*, www.c-r.org/our- work/accord/sudan/index.php.

Adwok, Peter (2000) *The Politics of Liberation in South Sudan: An Insider's View*, Kampala: Fountain Publishers.

African Centre for Justice and Peace Studies (2010) 'Building on a Cracked Foundation: An Analysis of the Election Registration Process in Sudan and its Impact on the Potential for Free and Fair Elections,' 9 February.

African Centre for Justice and Peace Studies (2010) 'Sifting through Shattered Hopes: Assessing the Electoral Process in Sudan,' May.

African Centre for Justice and Peace Studies (2011) 'Perceived SPLM–Northern Sector Supporters Arrested throughout Northern Sudan,' press release, 6 September.

African Rights (1997) *Food and Power in Sudan: A Critique of Humanitarianism*, London: African Rights.

Ahmad Elbadawi, Ibrahim (2011) and Atta El-Battahin, 'Sudan Multiple Transitions 2005–2011: Analyzing the Dynamics of Post-Conflict Impasse,' unpublished paper, April.

Ahmed, Abdel Ghaffer (2008) *One Against All: The National Islamic Front (NIF) and Sudanese Sectarian and Secular Parties*, Bergen: Chr. Michelsen Institute.

Ajeeb, Mohammed (2011) 'NCP Plays with Fire,' *Alqwat Almoslha*, Khartoum, 30 June.

Akol, Lam (2009) *SPLM/SPLA: Inside An African Revolution*, Khartoum: Khartoum University Press.

Anglin, D. (1998) 'International Election Monitoring: The African Experience,' *African Affairs*, vol. 97, no. 389.

Arendt, Hannah (1979) *The Origins of Totalitarianism*, San Diego, New York, London: Harcourt Brace Jovanovich.

Bendana, Alejandro (2002) 'What Kind of Peace is Being Built? Critical Assessments from the South,' IDRC, Ottawa, January.

Bjornlund, E., M. Bratton, and C. Gibson (1992) 'Observing Multiparty Elections in Africa: Lessons from Zambia,' *African Affairs*, vol. 91, no. 364.

Boutros-Ghali, Boutros (1992) *An Agenda for Peace*, New York: United Nations.

Branch, Adam, and Zachariah Cherian Mampilly (2005) 'Winning the War but Losing the Peace? The Dilemma of SPLM/A Civil Administration and the Tasks Ahead,' *Journal of Modern African Studies*, vol. 43, no. 1.

Call, C., and E. Cousens (2007) 'Ending Wars and Building Peace: International Responses to War-Torn Societies,' *International Studies Perspectives* 9.

Carter Center (2010) 'Preliminary Statement on the Final Stages of Sudan's Electoral Process,' 17 March.

Carter Center (2010) 'Preliminary Statement of the Election Observation Mission in Sudan Presidential, Gubernatorial, and Legislative Elections,' 17 April.

Carter Center (2010) 'Carter Center Reports Widespread Irregularities in Sudan's Vote Tabulation and Strongly Urges Steps to Increase Transparency,' 10 May.

Carter Center (2010) 'Preliminary Statement on the Voter Registration Process for the Southern Sudan Referendum,' 15 December.

Carter Center (2011) Preliminary Statement: Carter Center Finds Sudanese Referendum Peaceful and Credible,' 17 January.

Carter Center (2011) 'Carter Center Urges Political Parties and Blue Nile Popular Consultation Commission to Ensure Genuine Dialogue on Key Issues in Blue Nile State,' Khartoum, 21 March.

Carter Center (2011) 'The Carter Center Notes Concerns with Security In Southern Kordofan, Progress in Polling Representations,' 28 April.

Carter Center (2011) 'Southern Kordofan Gubernatorial and State Legislative Elections, Preliminary Statement,' 18 May.

Cliffe, Lionel (1999) 'Regional Dimensions of conflict in the Horn of Africa,' *Third World Quarterly*, vol. 20, no. 1.

Cliffe, Lionel, and Philip White (2002) 'Conflict Management and Resolution in the Horn of Africa,' in Ciru Muamu and Suzanne Schmeidi (eds), *Early Warning and Conflict Management in the Horn of Africa*, Lawrenceville NJ: Red Sea Press.

Collier, Paul (2009) *Wars, Guns, and Votes: Democracy in Dangerous Places*, London: Bodley Head.

Collins, Robert (2008) *Modern Sudan*, Cambridge: Cambridge University Press.

CPA Monitor (2011) 'Monthly Report on the Implementation of the CPA,' vol. 7, no. 66, May.

Danforth, John (Special Envoy for Peace) (2002) 'Report to the President of the United States on the Outlook for Peace in Sudan,' 26 April.

de Waal, Alex (1997) *Famine Crimes: Politics and the Disaster Relief Industry in Africa*, Oxford: James Currey.

Duffield, M. (2002) 'Social Reconstruction and Radicalization of Development Aid as a Relation of Global Liberal Governance,' *Development and Change*, vol. 33, no. 5.

El-Affendi, Abdelwahab (1991) *Turabi's Revolution: Islam and Power in Sudan*, London: Grey Seal, 1991.

El-Affendi, Abdelwahab (2001) 'The Impasse in the IGAD Peace Process for Sudan: The Limits of Regional Peacemaking?' *African Affairs*, vol. 100, no. 401.

El-Affendi, Abdelwahab (2010) 'Peace-Making and State-Building in Africa: Lessons from Sudan's "Hybrid" Case,' Nordiska Afrikainstitutet Forum, 15 October.

El-Amin, Khalid Ali (2003) 'The Economics and Politics of Poverty Reduction in Sudan 1990–2000,' Institute of Development Studies and Research, University of Khartoum, unpublished manuscript.

Elbadawi, Ibrahim Ahmed, and Atta El-Battahini (2011) Unpublished manuscript, April.

374 THE FATE OF SUDAN

El-Battahini, Atta (2011) Unpublished manuscript, April.

EU Election Observation Mission (2011) 'Preliminary Statement: Peaceful, Credible Voting Process, with Overwhelming Turnout Marks Southern Sudan Referendum,' 17 January.

Fegley, Randall (2009) 'Local Needs and Agency Conflict: A Case Study of Kajo Kiji County,' *African Studies Quarterly*, vol. 2, no. 1, Fall.

Flueh-Lobban, Carolyn (1991) 'Islamization in Sudan: A Critical Assessment,' in John Voll (ed.), *State and Society in Crisis Sudan*, Bloomington: Indiana University Press.

Foreign Policy magazine (2010) www.foreignpolicy.com/articles/2010/11/11/how_obama_betrayed_sudan.

Fukuyama, Francis (1992). *The End of History and the Last Man*. New York: Free Press.

Gallab, Abdullahi (2008) *The First Islamist Republic: Development and Disintegration of Islamism in the Sudan*, Aldershot: Ashgate.

Gettleman, J., and J. Kron (2011) 'Sudan Threatens to Occupy 2 More Disputed Areas,' *New York Times*, 29 May.

Gibson, Richard (1972) *African Liberation Movements*, Oxford: Oxford University Press.

Glickman, Harvey, and Emma Rodman (2008) 'Islamism in Sudan,' *Middle East Review of International Affairs*, vol. 12, no. 3, September.

Government of Sudan (2009) South Sudan Referendum Act, Khartoum.

Hafiz, Mohammed (2008) 'The Risk of Rebellion in Kordofan,' *Justice Africa*, London, 12 August.

Haugerudbraaten, Henning (1998) 'Peacebuilding: Six Dimensions and Two Concepts,' *African Security Review*, vol. 7, no. 6.

Human Rights Watch (2011) 'South Sudan: Improve Accountability for Security Forces Abuses,' 8 February.

Hyden, Gordon (1980) *Capturing the Peasantry*, Berkeley: University of California Press.

ICG (2008) 'Sudan's Southern Kordofan Problem: The Next Darfur?' International Crisis Group, *Africa Report* 145, 21 October.

IGADD Peace Initiative (1994) 'Declaration of Principles,' Nairobi, 20 July.

Jackson, R.H., and C.G Rosberg (1982) 'Why Africa's Weak States Persist: The Empirical and the Juridical in Statehood, *World Politics* 27.

Johns Hopkins University (2006) 'Peacemaking–Overview, Conflict Management Toolkit,' School of Advanced International Studies, Conflict Management Program, 15 February.

Johnson, Douglas (1998) 'The Sudan People's Liberation Army and the Problem of Factionalism,' in C. Clapham (ed.), *African Guerrillas*, Oxford: James Currey.

Johnson, Hilde (2011) *Waging Peace in Sudan*, Brighton: Academic Press.

'Juba Declaration On Unity and Integration Between The Sudan Peoples' Liberation Army and the South Sudan Defence Forces' 2006, Juba, 8 January.

Justice Africa (1995) *Facing Genocide: The Nuba of Sudan*, London.

Kiir Mayardit, Salva (2010) Election Manifesto.

Lesch, Ann (1998) *The Sudan: Contested National Identities*, Bloomington: Indiana University Press.

Los Angeles Times (2005) 'Official Pariah Sudan Valuable to America's War on Terrorism,' 29 April.

Luttwak, Edward N. (1999) 'Give War a Chance,' *Foreign Affairs*, vol. 78, no. 4, July–August.

Machakos Protocol (2002) 'Machakos Protocol Between the Government of Sudan and the Sudan People's Liberation Movement/Army,' IGAD Secretariat on Peace in the Sudan, Machakos, 20 July.

Madut-Arop, Arop (2006) *Sudan's Painful Road to Peace,* Nairobi: Booksurge LLC.

Malwal, Bona (2005) *Sudan's Latest Peace Agreement: An Accord that is Neither Fair Nor Comprehensive,* Omdurman: Abdel Karim Mirghani Cultural Centre.

Martin, Hariot (2006) *Kings of Peace Pawns of War: The Untold Story of Peace-making,* London: Continuum.

Mbeki, Thabo (AUHIP chairperson) (2011) 'Remarks,' at the Ceremony to Announce the Final Results of the South Sudan Referendum, Khartoum, 7 February.

Mkandawire, Thandika (2002) 'The Terrible Post-colonial 'Rebel Movements' in Africa: Towards an Explanation of the Violence against the Peasantry,' *Journal of Modern African Studies,* vol. 40, no. 2.

Nathan, Laurie (2001) 'The Four Horsemen of the Apocalypse: The Structural Cause of Violence in Africa,' *Track Two,* vol. 10, no. 2 (Cape Town), August.

National Democratic Institute (2009) 'Losing Hope: Citizen Perceptions of Peace and Reconciliation in the Three Areas,' findings from focus groups conducted 1 April–7 August 2008, Washington DC, 31 March.

National Democratic Institute (2010) 'Southern Sudan at the Crossroads,' 25 October.

Netherlands Ministry of Foreign Affairs (2010) *Aiding the Peace: A Multi-donor Evaluation of Support to Conflict Prevention and Peacebuilding Activities in Southern Sudan 2005–2010,* The Hague: Netherlands Ministry of Foreign Affairs.

New York Times (1999) 'Misguided Relief to Sudan,' Editorial, 6 December.

Nyaba, Peter Adwok (1997) *The Politics of Liberation in Southern Sudan: An Insider's View,* Kampala: Fountain Publishers.

O'Ballance, Edgar (1977) *The Secret War in Sudan: 1955–1972,* London: Faber.

Odukoya, Adelaja (2007) 'Democracy, Elections, Election Monitoring and Peace-Building in West Africa,' *African Journal of International Affairs,* vol. 10, nos 1 and 2.

Office of the Leader of the Opposition, SSLA (2011) 'Position of the Opposition on the Transitional Constitution of the Republic of South Sudan, 2011,' 23 May.

Office of the Vice President (2011) Draft Amended Interim Constitution of Southern Sudan, 2005/Transitional Constitution of South Sudan, 2011, 'Additional Suggested Amendments,' 23 May.

PANA (2010) 'Sudan Referendum: Al-Bashir Visits Southern Sudan, to "Celebrate" Referendum Outcome,' Pan African News Agency, 4 January.

Paris, Roland (1997) 'Peacebuilding and the Limits of Liberal Internationalism,' *International Security,* vol. 22, no. 2 (Autumn).

Paris, Roland (2002) 'International Peace-building and the Mission Civilisatrice,' *Review of International Studies* 28.

Paris, Roland (2010) 'Saving Liberal Peacemaking,' *Review of International Studies* 36.

Potter, Antonio (2006) 'In Search of the Textbook Mediator,' in H. Martin (ed.), *Kings of Peace, Pawns of War: The Untold Story of Peace-making,* London Continuum.

Protocol between the Government of Sudan and the Sudan People's Liberation Movement on the Resolution of the Conflict in Southern Kordofan/Nuba Mountains and Blue Nile States (2004) Naivasha, Kenya, 26 May.

Rolandsen, Oystein (2005) *Guerrilla Government: Political Changes in the Southern Sudan During the 1990s,* Nordiskainstitutet, Oslo.

Rostow, W.W. (1960) *The Stages of Economic Growth: A Non-communist Manifesto,* Cambridge: Cambridge University Press.

Rotberg, Robert (2005) *Battling Terrorism in the Horn of Africa*, Washington DC: Brookings Institution Press.

Ryle, John (2004) 'Disaster in Darfur,' *New York Review of Books*, 12 August.

Salahdien, Ghazi (2011) 'Post-Secession Sudan: Challenges and Opportunities,' School of Oriental and African Studies, London, 17 December.

Shinn, David (2004) 'Addis Ababa Agreement: Was It Destined to Fail and Are There Lessons for the Current Peace Process?' *Annales d'Ethiopie*, vol. 20, no. 20.

Sikainga, Ahmad Alawad (1993) 'Some Comments on Militias in the Contemporary Sudan,' in M.W. Daly and Ahmad Alawad Sikainga (eds), *Civil War in the Sudan*, London: British Academic Press.

Soremekun, Kayode (1999) 'Disguised Tourism and the Electoral Process in Africa: A Study of International Observers and the 1998 Local Government Elections in Nigeria,' *Issue*, vol. 27, no. 1.

SSLA (2011) 'The Mayom Declaration,' South Sudan Liberation Army 4 April.

SPLM (1983) 'The Manifesto of the SPLM,' 31 July.

SPLM/A (2002) 'SPLM/SPLA Update,' pamphlet.

SPLM–DC (2010) 'The Party's Election Manifesto,' Khartoum, February.

SPLM–DC (2010) 'System of Government in South Sudan,' paper presented to the South–South Dialogue Conference, Juba, October.

al-Turabi, Hassan (1992) *Islam as a Pan-National Movement and Nation States: An Islamic Doctrine of Human Association*, London: Sudan Foundation.

al-Turabi, Hassan (2008) *The Islamic Movement in Sudan: Its Development, Approach, and Achievements*, Beirut: Alam Alalanya, .

UN (2001) *Security Council Addresses Comprehensive Approach to Peace-Building in Presidential Statement*, UN 4278th Meeting, New York, 20 February.

Vambheim, Marit Magelssen (2007) 'Making Peace While Waging War: A Peacemaking Effort in the Sudanese Civil War 1965–1966,' M.A. thesis, University of Bergen,

Villalón, L. (1998) 'The African State at the End of the Twentieth Century: Parameters of Critical Juncture,' in L. Villalón and P. Huxtable (eds), *The African State at a Critical Juncture: Between disintegration and re-configuration*, Boulder CO and London: Lynne Rienner.

Waihenya, Waithaka (2006) *The Mediator: Gen. Lazaro Sumbeiywo and the Southern Sudan Peace Process*, Nairobi: Kenway Publications.

Warburg, Gabriel, *Historical Discord in the Nile Valley*, London: Hurst, 1992.

Weinstein, Jeremy (2005) 'Autonomous Recovery and International Intervention in Comparative Perspective,' Working Paper No. 57, Washington DC: Center for Global Development.

White House (2010) Office of the Press Secretary, Statement by the Press Secretary on Elections in Sudan, 20 April.

White House (2011), Office of the Press Secretary, 7 February.

Wikileaks (2007) Confidential Section 01 of 02. 000470, Khartoum, 25 March.

Williamson, Richard (2010) 'How Obama Betrayed Sudan,' *Foreign Policy* , 11 November, www.foreignpolicy.com/articles/2010/11/11/how_obama_betrayed_sudan.

Willis, Justin, Atta el-Battahani, and Peter Woodward (2009) *Elections in Sudan: Learning from Experience*, Nairobi: Rift Valley Institute.

Young, John (2002) 'Le SPLM/SPLA et le government du Sud-Soudan,' *Politique Africain* 88, December.

Young, John (2004) 'South Sudan's Blue Nile Territory and the Struggle against Marginalisation,' in Paul Kingston and Ian Spears (eds), *States Within States: Incipient Political Entities in the Post-War Era*, New York: Palgrave Macmillan.

Young, John (2005a) 'Sudan: A Flawed Peace Process Leading to a Flawed Peace,' *Review of African Political Economy*, vol. 32, no. 103.

Young, John (2005b) 'John Garang's Legacy to the Peace Process, the SPLM/A & the South,' *Review of African Political Economy*, vol. 32, no. 106.

Young, John (2006a) 'Eastern Sudan: Caught in a Web of External Interests,' *Review of African Political Economy*, vol. 33, no. 109.

Young, John (2006b) 'The South Sudan Defence Forces,' Small Arms Survey, Graduate Institute of International Studies, Geneva, November.

Young, John (2007a) 'Armed Groups Along Sudan's Eastern Frontier: An Overview and Analysis,' Small Arms Survey, Graduate Institute of International Studies, Geneva, November.

Young, John (2007b) 'The White Army: An Introduction and Overview,' Small Arms Survey, Graduate Institute of International Studies, Geneva, June.

John Young (2007c) 'Sudan People's Liberation Army: Disarmament in Jonglei and Its Implications,' Occasional Paper 137, Institute of Security Studies, Pretoria, April.

INDEX

Murle tribe, 311, 315, 320–23
Museveni, Yoweri, 55, 83, 161, 319
Muslim Brothers, 29
Mustafa, Tayyib, 155, 196, 285, 335
Musyoka, Kalonzo, 84, 103, 104

Nafi, Nafie Ali: and Gosh, 343;
leadership ambition, 342; NCP
candidate selection, 150, 245; peace
negotiations, 108, 284–5; taxation
policy, 346
Naivasha peace process, 13–14
Nakuru Framework, 102
National Alliance for Salvation of the
Country (NASC), 29, 51
National Elections Commission (NEC):
2010 election, 139, 140, 144, 159, 166,
167; Kordofan, 250, 254–5
nationalism: decline, 193–5
Natsios, Andrew, 125–6
NCP (National Congress Party): and
2010 elections, 136, 141–4, 149–52;
and 2011 popular uprising, 327–33;
al-Hilu's call for overthrow of NCP
government, 276–7; and Blue
Nile, 232, 235–6, 273–4; coalition
government with DUP, 341;
cooperative regional relations, 331;
distrust of SPLM/A, 117; and GoSS,
324–5; and Islamism, 193–4; lack
of commitment to democracy, 10;
leadership disputes, 342–5; objectives,
44; party of moderation, 332–3;
peace negotiations, 14, 83–4, 89–90,
98, 102–8, 132; reforms, 332–3; and
Southern Kordofan, 243, 244–5, 247,
251–2, 253, 255, 273–4; Southern
Kordofan peace agreement, 284–5;
Torit capture, 101, 117; and traditional
authorities, 74; unity vs secession, 177,
186, 193; see also al-Bashir, Omar
NDA (National Democratic Alliance),
13, 57–8, 85, 94; excluded from IGAD
peace talks, 109
New South, 274
New Sudan Council of Churches, 74, 116
New Sudan ideology: components, 42;
Garang's support for, 68; NCP view
of, 151; northern view of, 195–6; Nuba
support for, 242–3; southern view of,
65–6, 98, 153–4; SPLM break with,

156, 186
Ngok Dinka tribe: conflict with
Misseirya, 200, 204, 259, 262–4;
historical alliance with Misseirya, 203,
261–2; in interim constitution, 298;
population census, 259; see also Abyei
NIF (National Islamic Front): 1976
attempted coup, 26; 1986 election
success, 29–30; 1989 coup, 31–2, 81;
economic reforms, 34–5; Islamist
program, 32–6; and Khartoum Peace
Agreement, 56–7; name change, 44;
opposes peacemaking efforts, 90;
resistance to, 35; and southern
self-determination, 194–5; SPLA war
'a jihad', 79, 81; student support, 30;
support for Ethiopian rebels, 53
Nigeria: peace initiatives, 81–2, 88
Nile, control of, 184–5
Nimeiri, Jafaar: 1976 attempted coup
against, 26; and Addis Ababa
Agreement, 80; and communists,
24–5; and constitution, 26;
implementation of sharia law, 27–9;
national debt, 12; seizes power, 24;
and the south, 27; and the West, 26
Nimr, Babu, 203, 261
Nimr, Mochtar Babu, 261
Nimr, Sadig Babu, 261–2
NISS (National Intelligence and
Security Service), 43, 180, 216, 342–3,
344
Northern Bahr el Ghazal, 162, 199
northern opposition parties: and 2010
elections, 141–2, 157–9, 166–7; and
popular uprising, 328–9, 330–31; and
referendum, 206, 209–10, 219
Norway: 2010 elections, 168; and peace
process, 121–2, 127
Nuba Mountains: Asmara Declaration,
58; disenchantment with CPA, 242–3;
land alienation, 249; and the North,
246–7; and SPLM/A, 228–9, 228–30,
246
Nuba National Party, 20
Nuer tribes: Bul Nuer, 304–7; diaspora,
318; and Dinka conflict, 116, 315–16;
Jikany Nuer, 309–10; Lou Nuer, 55,
309, 310–11, 315; and Murle, 311, 315,
320–23; White Army, 309, 318, 321–3
Nugud, Ibrahim, 24, 158, 166, 327, 329

language, 27, 299, 302; Assembly election results, 173; British colonial policy, 3, 19; capital city, 118; corruption, 71-2, 76-7; decentralized nature, 64; dependence on international aid, 71; dependence on oil, 11-12; discontent, 291; interim constitution, 291-5, 297-304; Juba Declaration (2006), 14; Nimeiri's 1983 division, 27, 51; Political Parties Leadership Forum (PPLF), 291, 294, 295; post-colonial divisions, 22; state governorship election results, 173-4; Sudanese army presence, 105-6, 107; and Sudanese unity, 97-9, 217-18; *see also* secession; self-determination; South Sudan (2011-)
Southern Sudanese: in the north, 183, 215-16
SPDF (Sudan People's Democratic Front), 57
SPLA-Nasir, 55
SPLM Bahr el Ghazal Group, 56
SPLM Juba, 153, 192, 246
SPLM-DC (Democratic Change): 2010 elections, 151, 159-60, 162
SPLM-North, 155, 283-5, 331, 342
SPLM/A (Sudan Peoples Liberation Movement/Army): 1983-91 armed struggle, 50-54; 1994 Convention, 69-70; 2010 elections, 136-7, 141-3, 144, 148-9, 150-52, 159; 2010 presidency election boycott, 153-6; 2011 popular uprising, 330-31; and Abuja talks, 81-2; in Abyei, 265-71; and African liberation movements, 62, 63, 66; background, 44-50; and Blue Nile hearings, 235-6, 239; Civil Administration of New Sudan (CANS), 70-71; civilian abuse, 73; corruption, 72, 76-7; and Ethiopia, 52, 53-4; factionalism, 48-9, 54-5, 56, 63-5, 118, 142-3, 354; foreign relations, 42, 68; IGAD peace process, 102-8, 118; Kurmuk and Blue Nile capture, 58-9; local governance failures, 69-71, 73; Manifesto, 46-8; military doctrine, 49, 66-7; northern forces, 153-4, 178, 247, 274, 280-81, 284; and Nuba Mountains, 228-30, 246; and oil, 41, 183-4; and PCP, 75-6;

Political Military High command, 45, 54; referendum, 218; refusal to demobilize, 198; relations with countries of the region, 59-60, 61, 85-6; and Southern Kordofan, 244-6; and Southern Kordofan election, 247, 250, 252-8; Southern Kordofan peace agreement, 284; SSDF integration process, 14, 120-21, 305-6, 308-9, 316; terrorist body, 52; Torit capture, 101, 117; and traditional authorities, 74; tribal identities, 323; Ugandan support, 55, 83, 100; weaknesses, 15-16, 66-8, 70, 78
SPLM/A-United, 55, 56
SSCC (South Sudan Coordinating Council), 56, 57
SSDF (South Sudan Defense Force): exclusion from peace talks, 13-14, 109, 120; Juba Declaration and integration into SPLA, 14, 120-21, 305-6, 308-9, 316; and Khartoum Agreement, 56-7; NCP proxy, 199; oil industry security, 40
SSIM (South Sudanese Independence Movement), 56, 86
SSLA (South Sudan Liberation Army), 316-20
SSRB (Southern Sudan Referendum Bureau), 181
SSRC (South Sudan Rehabilitation Commission), 72
SSRC (Southern Sudan Referendum Commission), 180-81, 222
Sule, Peter, 160
Sumbeiywo, Lazaro: and Abyei, 268; and civil society, 109; and elections, 136; IGAD peace negotiations, 91, 92-3, 101, 113, 128-31; reduced role, 108

Taban Deng, *see* Deng, Taban
Taha, Ali Osman: and Abyei, 265; and CPA, 132-3; leadership ambition, 342; peace negotiations, 103-8, 118-19; referendums, 179; and unity, 196; Yasir Arman as presidential candidate, 151-2
Taha, Mahmoud, 28-9
TAMAM al-Khatim Adlan Center, 163
Tangyangi, Gabriel, 308-9, 316